D1564950

New Essays on Phillis Wheatley

New Essays on *Phillis Wheatley*

Edited by John C. Shields and Eric D. Lamore

The University of Tennessee Press • Knoxville

Copyright © 2011 by The University of Tennessee Press / Knoxville.
All Rights Reserved. Manufactured in the United States of America.
First Edition.

The paper in this book meets the requirements of American National Standards
Institute / National Information Standards Organization specification Z39.48-1992
(Permanence of Paper). It contains 30 percent post-consumer waste and is certified
by the Forest Stewardship Council.

Library of Congress Cataloging-in-Publication Data

New essays on Phillis Wheatley / edited by John C. Shields and Eric D. Lamore. —
1st ed.
    p. cm.
Includes bibliographical references and index.
ISBN-13: 978-1-57233-726-8 (hardcover: alk. paper)
ISBN-10: 1-57233-726-5 (hardcover: alk. paper)
  1. Wheatley, Phillis, 1753–1784—Criticism and interpretation.
  2. American literature—African American authors—History and criticism.
  I. Shields, John C., 1944–
  II. Lamore, Eric D.

PS866.W5Z67 2011
811'.1—dc22   2011001958

To JAMES A. LEVERNIER
For his irreplaceable support and encouragement

Contents

PART II

Placing Phillis Wheatley in Newly Applied Historical Contexts

Acknowledgments

It is a considerable pleasure to offer gratitude to those individuals who have encouraged this project. The Illinois State University Libraries, as always, have given us unusual and generous guidance, especially Cheryl A. Elzy, University Librarian, Professor Vanetta Mae Schwartz of Milner Library, and Gary R. Thiel, Library Assistant. Irene Taylor, Angela Scott, Diane Smith, and Jan R. Ballowe, each and all certainly make life easier for us at Illinois State.

We received much encouragement and valuable counsel from our two readers, Cedric May, Professor of English at the University of Texas, Arlington, and Raymond Craig, Professor of English at the Kent State University.

Members of the University of Tennessee Press who have given us constant support over the course of this evolving project are Robert Land, freelance copyeditor (a sharp and always constructive reader); Stan Ivester, Managing Editor (always conscientious); and Thomas Wells, Editorial Assistant (just an all around nice guy). But the person who liked the idea of doing a collection of all new, never before published essays on Wheatley, when we were in the initial planning stages for this volume, was Scot Danforth, Director of the Press.

As well we would like to express appreciation to the Houghton Library (of rare materials) of the Harvard College Library (the Widener) for their Xerox copy of a letter by Hannah More to Frances Reynolds (sister to Joshua Reynolds). The date of the letter is 10 September 1774; its identification code is MS Hyde 25(3). This letter was secured by Zach Petrea and used in his essay "Her Untangled Web: Mapping Phillis Wheatley's Network of Support in America and Great Britain." Zach Petrea has also been good enough to prepare our volume's index.

As senior editor of this collection, I take great pleasure in dedicating this volume to James A. Levernier, Professor of English at the University of

Arkansas at Little Rock. This exemplary scholar and excellent human being has generosity beyond description. Through the years, for example, he has steadily supported me, intellectually and spiritually. Were it not for this man and his positive reinforcement, I think I would have given up long ago.

Introduction

John C. Shields

Recently, scholarly studies of Phillis Wheatley, the first African American to publish a book on any subject, have astonishingly begun to burgeon, as the present collection attests. These critical essays comprising *New Essays*, fourteen in number, have the remarkable distinction of having never before appeared in print. The publication of so many new essays strongly affirms the rise of this accomplished poet into the first rank of American authors. As we will soon learn, this collection also ascertains that Wheatley's texts evidence meaning on multiple levels, thereby leading her readers to recognize her genius.

Perhaps the most substantial measure of Wheatley's multilayered texts resides in her deft handling of classical materials. Not surprisingly, the first section of this project, "Examining New Manifestations of Classicism in the Poetics of Phillis Wheatley," deals exclusively with our writer's extensive investment in classicism.

Maureen Anderson, in her "Phillis Wheatley's Dido: An Analysis of 'An Hymn to Humanity. To S.P.G. Esq.,'" rejects the notion that Wheatley deliberately looks to the Judeo-Christian religious tradition for instruction on hymn writing. Rather, as Anderson holds, the poet appropriates, in her "Hymn to Humanity," salient parts from Vergil's *Aeneid*, and in particular the poet's interest in the feminine figure, Dido, to advance her own critiques of a racist and patriarchal Early American culture.

Devona Mallory contributes another layer to our understanding of Wheatley's use of ancient classicism in her "I Remember Mama: Honoring the Goddess-Mother While Denouncing the Slaveowner-God in Phillis Wheatley's Poetry." Mallory begins her examination with the important observation that Wheatley composed verse in a time "well before aggressive antislavery activism." Contextualizing the historical period in which Wheatley wrote, however, denies that this poet was muted because of the institution of slavery. As this critic submits, Wheatley settles on classical representations of mother-goddesses to celebrate her mother's memory while adapting the classical idiom familiar to her white readers and at the same time subversively critiquing these white readers.

Throughout the essay Mallory points out that the goddesses in "On Recollection," "An Hymn to the Morning," and "An Hymn to the Evening" all may be identified as strong mother figures. "Mneme," or Mnemosyne, for example, was Mother to all the nine Muses (upon which Wheatley was so fond of calling), while the hymns to the morning and evening cite the goddess of the dawn, Aurora, often appearing to represent the young Wheatley's recollection of her mother pouring out water toward the rising sun, and invoke Calliope, Muse of epic poetry, hence directing her readers' attention to her experiments with the epic. Noting that "Losing a child or a parent to slavery is akin to losing one to death," Mallory concludes that "placing her long-lost mother on a divine pedestal helped Wheatley to endure her kidnapping, enslavement, and short life of hardship."

In "The Interaction of the Classical Traditions of Literature and Politics in the Work of Phillis Wheatley," Karen Dovell adds a formidable layer to our understanding of Wheatley's use of the classics as political tools. Dovell, first, provides a succinct discussion on how Early Americans utilized the ancient classical tradition, and then moves to analyze the texts of Wheatley. By paying particular attention to such concepts as virtue, liberty, and natural law, this African American poet, Dovell argues, draws upon both the literary and political dimensions of ancient classical thought to reject her status as a slave in colonial Boston, and to fight for the rights of other individuals of color.

Eric Ashley Hairston, with considerable ingenuity, capitalizes upon Wheatley's obvious classicism by applying to her work the trope of the Trojan horse. In "The Trojan Horse: Classics, Memory, Transformation, and Afric Ambition in *Poems on Various Subjects, Religious and Moral*," Hairston instructs us that we as readers of this fine poet should incorporate into our thought the knowledge that, while the Wheatleys may have indeed named Wheatley for the slaver, the *Phillis*, the name Phillis, in a classical context, bore certainly more positive associations for the maturing poet.

While closely arguing that Wheatley's use in her poems of classical materials indicates much more than the typically held notion that they serve as mere window dressing, Hairston submits that "Wheatley masks her desires and her ambitions for freedom, abolition, or Christian equality in a Homeric

John C. Shields

Trojan horse of classicism and eighteenth-century verse." In addition to focusing on classical materials, Hairston helpfully emphasizes Wheatley's marketing skills, her appreciation of Christian homiletics, and her extensive circle of contemporary intellectuals willing to provide her with encouragement and inspiration.

Patrick Moseley establishes still another approach assessing Wheatley's classicism. In "Empowerment through Classicism in Phillis Wheatley's 'Ode to Neptune,'" Moseley, unlike some of our authors who take into consideration the interplay of classical discourse throughout her oeuvre, focuses his attention on a single poem. While assuredly concerned with Wheatley's evidentiary classicism, Moseley cautions against reading Wheatley within an exclusively Judeo-Christian, neoclassical context, for such a reading can prescribe, according to Moseley, that Wheatley only provokes interest because her poems have "been composed by a little black slave girl."

Holding that Wheatley may indeed have more in common "with Wordsworth and Keats than she does with Pope or Dryden," Moseley investigates the proposition that Wheatley makes traceable use of Vergil's *Aeneid* in her "Ode to Neptune." Arguing Wheatley's *Poems* "is a tightly woven tapestry" wherein no one poem "can be fully appreciated without reference to the others," the author shows how Wheatley "tweaks the form of the Horatian Ode" while subtly incorporating portions of the *Aeneid* in her "Ode." Calling "Ode to Neptune" "a practical application of the theoretics of the imagination," Moseley judiciously concludes that this poem builds herein a characterization of herself both as Aeneas and his mother, Venus. These uses of classical materials in "Ode to Neptune," Moseley affirms, serve Wheatley to "express authorial as well as personal empowerment."

In "Phillis Wheatley's Use of the Georgic," Eric D. Lamore focuses attention on Wheatley's debt to Vergil's *Georgics*. While close readers of our poet are probably all well aware of connections traceable between Wheatley's texts and those of Ovid's *Metamorphoses*, Vergil's *Eclogues* and *Aeneid*, Homer's *Iliad*, and Terence's comedies, no one, before Lamore, has ascertained that Wheatley had, and profited from, extensive knowledge of Vergil's *Georgics*. Lamore is careful to point out that Wheatley's incorporation of the georgic mode resonates in fruitful ways with her African heritage. This clear presence of georgic materials enables Lamore to argue that this genre makes significant and observable contributions to the development of her individual poetics.

As readers of Phillis Wheatley continue to engage her multilayered texts, they inevitably apply innovative approaches. These new approaches, as seen in our second section of this collection, titled "Placing Phillis Wheatley in Newly Applied Historical Contexts," serve at least two functions: they recontextualize her rich texts, and they demonstrate that her late-eighteenth-century works remain current, affecting a strain of timelessness.

In "Works of Wonder, Wondering Eyes, and the Wondrous Poet: The Use of Wonder in Phillis Wheatley's Marvelous Poetics," Jennifer Billingsley takes an approach unique among critics of this poet. After describing how Hannah Arendt's identification of the wonderful and/or the marvelous amounts to a touchstone one may use to discover affirmation of an accurate perception of genius, Billingsley argues that Phillis Wheatley's poetics and how she applies that poetics affirm Wheatley's genius. Billingsley holds that it is Wheatley's application of classicism that so tellingly displays her particular sense of the marvelous and the wonderful.

Effectively contextualizing the sense of wonder as having origins as early as Plato's *Theaetetus*, Billingsley then submits that Wheatley's extensive knowledge of the classical world very likely directed her toward an appreciation of the sense of wonder. While noting Stephen Greenblatt's *Marvelous Possessions: The Wonder of the New World*, Billingsley next traces example after example of how Wheatley's use of the wonderful comes to characterize her poetic oeuvre.

Tom O. McCulley becomes the first reader in Wheatley Studies to apply queer theoretics to the texts of our poet. In his provocative title, "Queering Phillis Wheatley," McCulley maintains that Wheatley's penchant for subversion invites his remarkable reading. The author then proceeds to call our attention to the fact that, like gay men and women of today, Wheatley surely had a "keen awareness of herself as a body outside of the normative expectations of her society."

Claiming that his expansive grasp of Queer Theory is not limited "to gay studies or to the idea of sexuality itself," McCulley then suggests how Eve Kosofsky Sedgwick's now well-known emphasis on "performativity" as a possible indication of instances of silences may be effectively applied to Wheatley. Such an understanding leads McCulley to posit that Wheatley's self-consciousness, thought by white folks to be an "other," resulted in her offering to her white audience "closeted," subversive poetic performances. A Queer Theory reading of her oeuvre permits Wheatley's readers to recognize that the poet reinvents what otherwise may remain a "fractured identity"; this reinvention empowers Wheatley to cope with an oppressive society dominated by white folks.

John C. Shields

Focusing largely on archival research, Jennifer R. Young, in her "Marketing a Sable Muse: Phillis Wheatley and the Antebellum Press," concentrates on the cultural reception of Wheatley's *Poems* in and outside of eighteenth-century America. While Young submits that the African American artist worked to fashion her own identity, this critic investigates how, following the 1773 publication of *Poems*, both pro-slavery and abolitionist causes relied on the figure of Wheatley and her texts to promote their own political agendas, and how Wheatley and her texts were appropriated to advance arguments on "the nature of the African."

In "Phillis Wheatley: The Consensual Blackness of Early African American Writing," Phillip M. Richards traces how eighteenth-century black writers utilized the language of sentiment as an important rhetorical vehicle for arguing, to a white audience, for a more inclusive and harmonized society. Richards locates the roots of this sentimental rhetoric in seventeenth- and eighteenth-century New England execution sermons and criminal narratives wherein Puritan ministers appropriated the predicament of the black criminal or black individual tempted by sin in order to push their New England readers to examine their religious commitments.

The presence of this sentimental language describing blacks in the Puritan execution sermon and criminal narrative, Richards holds, granted the possibility of interracial harmony, and established the potential for further developing this rhetorical terrain as eighteenth-century black writers, including Lucy Terry, Olaudah Equiano, Jupiter Hammon, Lemuel Haynes, and Phillis Wheatley, constructed their own texts. The texts of Wheatley, argues Richards, most emphatically capture the dynamic of the black sentimental voice as this poet attempts to establish the parameters of a more inclusive social environment via her poetry.

Moving from an emphasis on Wheatley's concern for the Atlantic slave trade to a perception of our poet as a pioneer in Pan-Africanism, Babacar M'Baye leads Wheatley's readers to reconsider allegations that her work displays an "occasional ambivalence" toward her African homeland. In "The Pan-African and Puritan Dimensions of Phillis Wheatley's Poems and Letters," M'Baye points to the several prompts regarding Wheatley's origins in Africa which may be traced in her writings. M'Baye speaks of her somewhat syncretized Methodist Calvinism joined with elements of African religious influence, such as reflect a "Senegambian-Islamic worldview." It should be observed that M'Baye had no opportunity to view J. Shields's chapter, "African Origins," in his just published *Phillis Wheatley's Poetics of Liberation: Backgrounds and Contexts*.

M'Baye is careful not to ignore Wheatley's letters. At one place in the author's investigation, for example, M'Baye relates how closely the Wolof tale, "Kumba the Orphan Girl," parallels elements Wheatley brings up in a letter to Obour Tanner, Wheatley's most frequent correspondent among her extant letters and a black woman older than Wheatley who may have been brought to America along with Wheatley.

This author reminds us that, "despite her disruptive relations with Africa" (for example, ostensibly in "On Being Brought from Africa to America"), in "To Maecenas" she praises Terence, the Roman playwright, because of his African descent. So Wheatley obviously takes pride in her origins in Africa. M'Baye concludes with much force that Wheatley's often positive emphasis in her writings on her African origins ascertains that "she used literature as a strategic means of resistance."

In his meticulously researched essay, "An Untangled Web: Mapping Phillis Wheatley's Network of Support in America and Great Britain," Zachary Petrea first outlines the dynamics and function(s) of the eighteenth-century salon culture. Observing that the salon culture promoted female education by encouraging the establishment of women's seminaries, Petrea makes ample use of the recently published writings of Milcah Moore and Annis Boudinot Stockton in order to argue that the American salon culture provided a ready venue in which to advance the work of Phillis Wheatley. While recounting the journal writings of such figures as Esther Burr, daughter of Jonathan Edwards, and Sarah Prince, Petrea takes us across the Atlantic to Ann Letitia Barbauld and Selina Hastings, Countess of Huntingdon, Wheatley's correspondent and patron for the publication of the 1773 *Poems*.

This type of literary and cultural work, analogous to that of a literary detective, "reveals [Wheatley's] extensive influence on the intellectual climate of the late eighteenth-century." Another dynamic component of this essay, however, lies in the author's poignant observation that this work productively "exposes a number of potentially fruitful comparative treatments" for future contributions to Wheatley Studies.

In "Phillis Wheatley's Theoretics of the Imagination: An Untold Chapter in the History of Early American Literary Aesthetics," John C. Shields analyzes discussions of the imaginative faculty in several seventeenth- and eighteenth-century literary circles in both Great Britain and Early America in order to argue that, not only was Wheatley familiar with these discussions of

John C. Shields

the imagination, but that they prepared her for constructing her own original and revolutionary interpretation of the imagination.

While framing her essay within the era of such Enlightenment thinkers as Descartes, Locke, and Berkeley, Mary McAleer Balkun argues that the "body" of work by Phillis Wheatley opens to an oppressed member of an oppressed race a means "to manage the material fact of race . . . not only hers but that of all 'Africans.'" In "To 'pursue th' unbodied mind': Phillis Wheatley and the Body in Early America," Balkun shows how Wheatley moves "beyond the body" in her work to focus attention on the operations of her mental capacities.

In such poems as "On Recollection" and "On Imagination," for example, Wheatley demonstrates to a largely white audience that her "veneration of the mind," which her poetic accomplishment attests in the writing of this poem, diverts her white readers' attention away from the black body which houses her accomplishment. Balkun effectively convinces us that Wheatley's efforts to produce texts represent an admirably successful quest to overcome racist oppression of her black body.

We offer these fourteen essays as concrete evidence that the extant oeuvre of Phillis Wheatley merits still further scrutiny. Obviously, now, if not demonstrated earlier, her texts, both poems and letters, sustain intense analysis. Just as each contribution emphasizes the depth of Wheatley's literary achievement, all these readings, we expect, will stimulate a substantial amount of additional work and will encourage established critics, along with new ones, to draw on and to depart from the essays in this volume.

I should like to take this opportunity to describe the series of monographs and essay collections that I serve as general editor to be published by the University of Tennessee Press; this series publishes studies which explicate the impact of classicism on American culture, extending from the time of Peter Martyr's *Decades* (first three of eight published by 1516; Arber, 61) to the present moment. As *New Essays on Phillis Wheatley,* with its strong concentration on Wheatley as a consummate classicist resulting in acute analysis of her sophisticated interpretation of culture, and of American culture in particular, this volume effectively establishes the emphasis and direction of the entire series, and therefore serves as its harbinger.

New Essays, along with forthcoming contributions to the series, receives remarkable urgency when evaluated alongside the recent publication of *The Oxford Handbook of Early American Literature* (2008), edited by Kevin J.

Hayes. The Hayes collection has much to recommend it. Hayes, in his "Introduction," for example, is studious to point out the importance to Early American literature that the newfound land (new at least to white folks and Africans) exercised on Early American literary productions; I assuredly agree with Hayes's judgment here. As well, I warmly endorse his determination to bring the parameters of Early American literature to encompass that writing produced within the boundaries of the "British colonies [from 1607] on the American mainland and, after 1776, in the United States." These parameters, according to Hayes, include the period "to the mid-1790s" (Hayes 16). To cast about for new texts among writings produced in parts of New France, New Spain, and the Caribbean dilutes a more certain and more teachable focus on those literary works composed within the colonial and incipient United States of America.

Hayes and his contributors miss the mark, however, first, when they promote prose over poetry; second, when they all but ignore the major role classicism contributes to the shaping of our Early American (and general American) cultural consciousness; and third, when they determine that Early American letters woefully lacks a close participation in the field of literary aesthetics. Prose, for example, comprises the subject of some 530 pages out of a total of 611, leaving a mere 81 or so pages for poetry. As for the pantheon he proposes for literary productions before the mid-1790s, Hayes names St. Jean de Crèvecoeur, Jonathan Edwards, Benjamin Franklin, Alexander Hamilton (1712–1756), and Captain John Smith.

Note that not a single poet numbers among the figures on this list. While I, for one, might immediately question the inclusion of Edwards, who was assuredly one of our first and most original philosophers (vide his *Freedom of the Will*) and must be considered a master of homiletics—but hardly a master of creative letters—and John Smith, a champion of promotional narrative, a genre not heretofore raised to such a high status, where are some of America's best poets? Why are Anne Bradstreet, Edward Taylor, Mather Byles, Phillis Wheatley, and Philip Freneau not celebrated as major authors? This obvious bias toward prose is clearly predicted by Carla Mulford, one of Hayes's contributors, in her recently published *Early American Writings;* in her anthology of 1,124 pages, 152 are given to poetry, but 972 to prose, roughly mirroring the proportion of prose to poetry we observed in the Hayes collection.

Hayes claims, in his "Introduction," to be inclusive. In Hayes's words, "There has never been a comprehensive, collaborative literary history of early

American literature—until now" (13). I for one am certainly not convinced that Hayes and his contributors have produced a text which comes even close to his overweening assertion. The genres he identifies, which he and his contributors would have us believe cover the literary output of Early Americans, comprise autobiographies, captivity narratives, diaries, novels, plays, political writings, promotional tracts, slave narratives, travel writings, natural history and history discourses, "Native American voices" (one chapter), "and poetry," which, out of twenty-six chapters, "receives three" (17). While the chapter on "Revolutionary Verse" does briefly, but wholly inadequately, treat epic, where are to be found considerations of the other classical genres of the ode (lyric), pastoral, pastoral elegy, epyllion, verse epistle, georgic, and meditatio, much less such additional genres of poetry as elegies (ultimately also a classical genre, though adapted by the Puritans), philosophical poems, biblical paraphrases, literary independence poems, nature poems, ekphrastic poems (arguably originating also as a classical genre), translations, poems about literary aesthetics, narrative poems, and occasional verse?

Surely, then, we can readily grasp that the most glaring weakness of Hayes's *Oxford Handbook* is its failure to give poetry something resembling just attention and/or space. In my forthcoming *An Anthology of Eighteenth-Century American Poetry: Based on Classical Principles* (projected to have 1,200 pages), I herald classicism, which dominates poems composed by Early Americans from about 1720, the approximate cut-off date for Meserole's *Seventeenth-Century American Poetry,* through the mid-1790s. This volume, which will serve as contribution to the series on classicism in American culture, will be dedicated to Harrison T. Meserole. Although all poems of *Eighteenth-Century American Poetry* have not been composed within strict definitions of classical genres, the influence of classical genres and the poems' frequency of classical elements overwhelm the poetry composed during this period, so much so that we may begin to speak of this era as that of American classicism, not that of an "Augustan Age," echoing a British designation.

The ascription to the eighteenth century by Hayes of the identifier, "The Augustan Age in America," immediately and, I suppose, purposefully brings to mind the Augustan Age in Britain. Yet I have demonstrated in *The American Aeneas: Classical Origins of the American Self* that a surprising quantity of prose and poetry was produced in Early America which can be (and has been) proven not to be derivative of British letters. Rather this body of literature attempts self-consciously to address the cultural imperatives encountered by persons geographically relocated on the North American strand as they begin to understand themselves first as Pennsylvanians, Virginians, New Yorkers, Carolinians, Marylanders, or New Englanders (etc.), but later who gradually view themselves as Americans, and certainly not ever as displaced Brits.

I should add that such poems as American pastoral elegies and literary independence poems, which I identified in *Aeneas* as examples of poems crafted to serve American cultural imperatives, do not include a few or even several but substantial numbers. When I wrote *The American Aeneas*, for example, I had found only seventeen pastoral elegies and about ten literary independence poems. Now I have more than doubled the examples for both these genres. The literary independence poem I discovered owed a great debt to classicism; indeed, each example claims that the culture, literary and/or political, which Early Americans are engaged in constructing promises to rival that of Greece and/or Rome.

When we observe that Vergil's eclogues deal extensively with the subject of beauty and as well that students attending the Latin grammar schools of Colonial America were instructed to compose Latin imitations of the eclogues, we have actually hit upon the source for construction of a uniquely Early American literary aesthetics. That is, we can now identify classicism as the origin of American aesthetics.

Pastoral elegies, derived from Vergil's eclogue on Daphnis (the fifth of ten), display in Early America a remarkable pattern of self-referentiality (see *Aeneas*, 145–63), a pattern which Hayes finds in Jefferson's and Adams's correspondence as each former president mentions Thomas Morton (4–5). A clear relationship of referentiality, for example, obtains among pastoral elegies by Joseph Seccombe (not mentioned in the Hayes Handbook), Jeremy Belknap (whose poetry the *Handbook* ignores), and Joseph Green (not identified by the *Handbook* as a classicist). But note that the self-referentiality of which I speak in *Aeneas* occurs within a wholly classical poetic genre, not in prose tracts.

Hayes says he believes his *Handbook* to be "a celebration of American culture" (17), yet he advances no attempt to delineate of what an "American culture" consists. As the period which preceded the establishment of the United States of America has been shown to owe a now undeniable and substantial debt to classicism (vide *Aeneas*, which demonstrates that the myths of Adam and Aeneas constitute two halves of the American self), should not the Hayes *Handbook* describe American culture in terms of the mythoi of Adam and Aeneas? Yet the Hayes *Handbook* appears to be aware only of the Adamic

John C. Shields

myth. Having acknowledged the preponderance of both would assuredly have led to a just incorporation of how formative to American culture have been the cultures of ancient Greece and Rome.

The publication of *New Essays on Phillis Wheatley*, with its consistent treatment by fourteen contributors of Wheatley's sophisticated classicism, will certainly expose the *Handbook's* failure to capture an accurate description of "American culture." Indeed, if classicism serves Wheatley so demonstrably well, could it possibly be that classicism impacted only her work and her idea of culture? As she puts it so well in her "Liberty and Peace," mentioned in the *Handbook* (513), "And new-born Rome shall give Britannia Law," though the *Handbook* quotes not a single line from this important poem of 1784 which attempts to define American culture following the Treaty of Paris in September 1783. To be sure, the suggestion that classicism could have impacted only Wheatley points directly to its absurdity and further exposes the *Handbook's* inadequacy.

This sort of denial of the importance of classicism bespeaks a pattern that I identify in *Aeneas* as one of "acceptance and denial," describing an acceptance of things classical but then promptly denying their origins (*Aeneas* passim). A particularly onerous illustration of this pattern of acceptance and denial occurs in Carla Mulford's *Early American Writings*, named above. In the biographical material introducing selections from Wheatley's oeuvre, Mulford claims that Wheatley "read classical writers in translation (including Ovid, Horace, and Vergil)," ignoring completely the testimony given by John Wheatley (the poet's master) in Boston on November 14, 1772, and published in Wheatley's 1773 *Poems* that "She has a great Inclination to learn the Latin Tongue, and has made some Progress in it" (*Collected Works*, vi).

By the time she published her 1773 *Poems* the following August, she was able to adorn her volume with as fine a translation of Ovid's *Metamorphoses*, book 6 (the Niobe episode) as I have seen. As well, I and others have through the years in several venues extolled her thoroughly intelligent use of classicism. And now we have assembled fourteen essays by scholars from around the country, and even outside the country, that still more extensively ascertain her classical achievement. There cannot now be any doubt that Wheatley did not require translations of Ovid, Horace, or Vergil; she would indeed have read these authors in their original Latin. Such an implacable position as that assumed by Mulford, which has no serious intellectual base, approaches the irrational. This implacable position in fact symptomatically bespeaks a contemporary attitude in American literary studies that classical elements, when they appear in texts by American authors, bespeak, as I have observed, nothing more than window dressing. Given the appearance of *The American Aeneas,* preceding publication of the *Handbook* by seven years, this "window dressing" notion has quite simply been rendered obsolete.

In his "Introduction," Hayes allots a page and a half to "How Edgar Allan Poe Read Early American Literature." When we acknowledge that Hayes has written one single-author volume on Poe and edited another, the space he gives to Poe comes as no surprise. Hayes notes in the "Introduction" that Poe finds fault with the selections of poems from Samuel Kettell's 1829 *Specimens of American Poetry* (three volumes). In Poe's words, quoted by Hayes:

> The "specimens" of Kettell were specimens of nothing but the ignorance and ill taste of the compiler. A large proportion of what he gave to the world as American poetry, to the exclusion of *much* that was really so, was the doggerel composition of individuals unheard of and undreamed of, except by Mr. Kettell himself. (7)

What particularly and immediately arrests my attention in this quote is the phrase "to the exclusion of *much* [my emphasis] that was really so." Poe suggests here that his selection would have moved far beyond Kettell's ignorance, suggesting Poe had some intimacy with American literature from the era Kettell emphasizes (that of eighteenth-century America). Hayes does not explore this possibility. Given Poe's known achievement as a substantial classicist, I am tempted to suppose that Poe may well have read extensively in American poetry of the eighteenth century, perhaps even discovering the excellent and thoroughly classical poetry of Phillis Wheatley, or the poems of such additional authors as John Parke, Philip Freneau, Timothy Dwight, and Thomas Odiorne. Odiorne's *The Progress of Refinement* (1792), for example, besides displaying numerous classical elements, treats all five of the aesthetic categories (the sublime, the beautiful, the imagination, the picturesque, and taste) and would doubtlessly have appealed to Poe's aesthetic nature. And had Poe come across the poetry of Richard Lewis, I think it would have delighted him. Hayes insists, nevertheless, that Poe "simply cared little for early American literature" (7); this generalization has yet to be proven.

Claiming that Moses Coit Tyler, in his four-volume history of *Early American Literature (1878–97),* "brought to the field a seriousness and dedication the finest literary scholars have since emulated," Hayes lends remarkable credence to Tyler's observation that "Undoubtedly literature for its own sake was not much thought of or lived for, in those days'" (9–10). For, with little variance, Hayes and his contributors subscribe to this same jaundiced view of Early American literature, especially regarding the possibility of an aesthetic preoccupation among Early American authors before the mid-1790s. Regrettably Hayes fails to caution readers of Tyler to take into account his implacable bias against neoclassicism, especially its fondness for the heroic couplet. Tyler consistently promotes the more varied forms (ode/lyric, e.g.) of Romanticism. Perhaps it was this neoclassical bias that caused Tyler not to recognize the aesthetic concerns of such authors as Wheatley, Mather Byles, and Odiorne.

Chris Beyers, one of Hayes's contributors, does recognize at least the possibility of aesthetic interests in the poems of Byles and Nathaniel Evans. In an essay on poetry of the eighteenth century, composed before the Revolutionary era, for example, Beyers notes that in Byles's poem on Milton, the Early American poet soon to become Congregational minister of Old South Church, Boston, "stresses the aesthetic and affective." Then he points out Evans's definition of poetry in aesthetic terms in Evans's long essay which precedes his 1772 collection of poems.

Had Beyers chosen to go into more detail about Byles and aesthetics, perhaps he would have come across Byles's prose essay, "Bombastic and Grubstreet Style," in which Byles examines issues of taste and the literary imagination. As well, the remainder of Evans's prefatory essay displays no little aesthetic sophistication.

As Beyers's essay marks one of the few places in the *Handbook* wherein the word "aesthetic" even appears, the *Handbook's* failure to pursue the topic of aesthetics in more detail outlines the third serious problem for this collection. My contribution to *New Essays,* "Phillis Wheatley's Theoretics of the Imagination: An Untold Chapter in the History of Early American Literary Aesthetics," takes a concentrated look at the extensive conditions of aesthetics that did in fact embrace the oeuvre of Phillis Wheatley; what I conclude is that Wheatley articulated a sophisticated aesthetics that closely predicts the several European romanticisms. I should emphasize that this aesthetics was innovative and original. For that matter, Wheatley's traceable and substantial theoretics of imagination has moved me to complete a single-author monograph, *Phillis Wheatley and the Romantics,* recently published by the University of Tennessee Press. This new volume complements my recently published *Phillis Wheatley's Poetics of Liberation.* If nothing else, all this attention paid to Wheatley argues that she should be accorded the status of, not just major Early American author, but major American author. The treatment she receives at the hands of Hayes and company quite simply bespeaks mere tokenism.

New Essays, nevertheless, by itself, exposes the *Handbook's* significant shortcomings: promotion of prose over, or at the expense of, poetry; devaluation of the obvious classicism that prevails among practically all Early American authors and which contributed so much to defining the American self; and the remarkable failure to recognize an Early American preoccupation with literary aesthetics. Indeed, considering Wheatley's accomplishment in aesthetics, which cannot have been unique, how much more work is to be done toward assessing the literary aesthetics of numerous other Early American authors? On the inside flap of the *Handbook's* dust jacket, the editors of Oxford University Press grandly proclaim that all volumes in the series "offer a state-of-the-art survey of current thinking and research." Yet as we have learned, this particular volume in the series provides neither an acceptable "survey" nor a defensible description of "state-of-the-art . . . thinking."

If, as has been declared by a renowned classical scholar, "Fundamental knowledge is essential" and "emphasis is historically circumstantial" (Lempriére, vii), *The Oxford Handbook of Early American Literature* perhaps meets the sense of one of these axioms. Surely, the *Handbook* may not be consulted as an accurate tool for "comprehensive" knowledge, albeit the historical circumstances of the present would seem to militate against a just treatment of poetry and of our national origins in ancient classicism. I am prompted to exclaim, nevertheless, what culture can call itself sophisticated if it lacks a proper appreciation of poetry, does not accurately celebrate its national origins, and refuses to discover that its early authors were steeped in an originating aesthetic appreciation and praxis which preceded and helped to shape that culture's determination to be a free and independent people?

Already I can say that at least three scholars among the contributors to *New Essays* have proposed volumes for the Series on Classicism in American Culture. So I am pleased to challenge all other scholars who share a commitment to exploration of the importance of classicism to American culture at large *vadere nobiscum,* to walk with us.

John C. Shields

WORKS CITED

Arber, Edward, ed. *The First Three English Books on America*. (1885) New York: Kraus Reprint Co., 1971—includes the first three decades (of ten) by Peter Martyr in Richard Eden's English translation.

Hayes, Kevin J., ed. *The Oxford Handbook of Early American Literature*. New York: Oxford UP, 2008.

Lemprière, John. *Lemprière's Classical Dictionary*. 3rd ed. New York: Routledge and Kegan Paul, 1984.

Mulford, Carla, gen. ed. *Early American Writings*. New York: Oxford UP, 2002.

Shields, John C. *The American Aeneas: Classical Origins of the American Self*. Knoxville: U of Tennessee P, 2001.

——. *The Collected Works of Phillis Wheatley*. New York: Oxford UP, 1988.

PART I

Examining New Manifestations of Classicism in the Poetics of Phillis Wheatley

Phillis Wheatley's Dido: An Analysis of "An Hymn to Humanity. To S.P.G. Esq."

Maureen Anderson

A profound misconception about the construction and use of hymn in Early American literature is that it is exclusively modeled after earlier Christian hymn forms. Previous to the eighteenth-century American writers, the hymn was adopted and celebrated as a Christian form.[1] William Harmon and C. Hugh Holman, however, explain in *A Handbook to Literature*, that a hymn, now used to express "religious emotion and generally intended to be sung by a chorus," is originally, especially in classical discourse, "referred to almost any song of praise, whether of gods or famous people" (257). In his *The American Aeneas: Classical Origins of the American Self*, John C. Shields investigates the hymns of Phillis Wheatley as "epic hymns, a form strictly classical in origins but widely adapted by Renaissance poets from Spenser to Milton" (236). Citing Francis C. Blessington's "'The Undisturbed Song of Pure Conceit': *Paradise Lost* and the Epic Hymn," Shields explains,

> epic hymns may be defined as lyrics of praise that celebrate "a moment of solemn relief from the inexorable action related in the narrative, and dramatic structures [of epic], a moment without [outside] the movement of narrative time, an escape into an ideal world." These epic hymns, Blessington continues, provide "a pause in the action in order to acknowledge the ideal toward which the epic struggles." [472–73] (236)

In Shields's investigation of Wheatley's use of the epic hymn, he shows how her use of the classical form expresses "her portrayal of the feminine principle" (236). Wheatley employs the epic hymn form, therefore, to celebrate and champion the feminine within a subversive, though powerful, expression of poetry.[2] Shields explains Wheatley's use of the epic hymn not as a tool through which she expresses a subjective role to a Christian god, but rather as a vehicle through which she explores and defends the feminine:

> Wheatley construes these epic hymns as powerful represen-
> tations of: woman in nature, in "An Hymn to the Morning";
> woman in art, in "On Imagination" and "On Recollection";
> woman in society, in "On Virtue"; and woman in politics, in
> "Niobe in Distress," and "To . . . General Washington." (237)

Though William Scheick and other scholars, nonetheless, attest that "Scripture, in fact, profoundly influenced [Phillis Wheatley's] writings" (122), alongside an in-depth analysis of biblical verse and Wheatley's well-placed words, many scholars still refuse to acknowledge, or rather sidestep, her use of classicism when evaluating her work. Scheick asserts that "the King James version of the Bible was among a handful of [Wheatley's] favorite books" without a mention of Wheatley's classical learning and numerous classical allusions (122). Consequently, many of her more seemingly religious poems are undervalued for her trademark subversive messages and are given a mere nod as being a good Christian poem or, worse, considered ambiguous or imitative of Alexander Pope. Phillis Wheatley, however, is not a simple poet and her classical devices are more often than not dismissed or unnoticed. A significant part of Wheatley's message within her poetry, consequently, is also lost or remains undiscovered. In fact, to suggest any of her poetry is merely Christian is not only to insult her skill in weaving the English language to her advantage but also to underestimate the brilliance of her rebellion through words.

"An Hymn to Humanity. To S.P.G. Esq." certainly seems, upon an initial cursory reading, to be a poem that celebrates Jesus and biblical myth; however, considering Wheatley was certainly no stranger to Virgil and his *Aeneid* and/or Dryden's translation, the hymn may be interpreted as more than Christian. Wheatley's knowledge of classicism is tightly interwoven into the language of the poem, so much so that most scholars judge the work to be a Christian hymn. By analyzing the poem through a classical lens and particularly alongside Dryden's translation of the *Aeneid* (a work that was readily accessible and popular in Early America), however, the allusions within the poem take an alternative shape than that suggested by reading this poem as Christian inspired. In light of Vergil's *Aeneid* as translated by Dryden (though Wheatley could certainly read the original Latin, though many of her contemporaries could not),

Maureen Anderson

the "prince of heav'nly birth" and his "empire" within the poem suggest not Jesus or a Christian God figure, but rather and more appropriately Aeneas, the hero of Virgil's epic. The voice of the speaker in the poem is, furthermore, one who is subject to his "desire" and is forsaken by the "prince"; hence, the speaker in the poem may be seen as none other than Dido, the *"Afric"* queen of Carthage.[3] "An Hymn to Humanity," therefore, is not a Christian poem or even a hymn in the Christian sense, but rather an epic hymn drawing on the classical tradition, one that celebrates a hero and the gods as sung by Dido. By utilizing the voice of Dido, moreover, the hymn also charges her contemporary Early American audience with the travesty of their dismissal, cruelty, and crimes against humanity.

The hegemony of the Adamic myth, according to Shields, "has concealed the Aeneas myth" (x) and yet the myth of Aeneas is an integral part of American selfhood, particularly during the formation of Early America. Hence, discovering allusions to the myth of Aeneas and the use of classicism in Early American poetry becomes a significant and necessary part in identifying the whole of the Early American sense of self and purpose. When Mary Balkun asserts, *"Wheatley* casts the audience as critical of the prevailing ideology, expecting its members 'to perform increasingly more challenging [rhetorical] tasks' [Mailloux 115]" (121), she conveys Wheatley's deep knowledge of her audience. Wheatley was certainly aware of the development of the American selfhood as attested by her observation in "Liberty and Peace" that "new-born *Rome* [the United States] shall give *Britannia* law" (154), and successfully addresses in "An Hymn to Humanity" the image her countrymen held as a prime example of an American: Aeneas. Wheatley knew her audience well; often consisting of slaveholders, she knew not merely how the populace identified with the myth of Aeneas, but also how to manipulate the myth of Aeneas to deliver a subversive message that would address the subservient roles of women as well as slaves in the early American colonies.[4]

In Wheatley's "An Hymn to Humanity," she composes the hymn we can hold, from the perspective of Dido, a feminine position of suppression and disadvantage. By using the voice of Dido, moreover, Wheatley points directly to her own position as a female slave. As seen in book 4 of Vergil's *Aeneid*, Dido is both a powerful feminine figure and yet is also brought to a low position through her encounter with Aeneas. Dido is both the founder of Carthage as well as a powerful queen. While numerous sources relate the tragedy of Dido—her love and suicide after the arrival of Aeneas on her shores—few, if any, perceive her role to be a heroic one. In the *Aeneid*, Vergil portrays Dido, the legendary founder of Carthage, as the love-stricken, fallen woman of Carthage who, after being poisoned by Cupid's[5] saliva, falls to her fate in love with the son of Venus,[6] Aeneas. When Aeneas is urged to continue on his journey and therefore departs Carthage, however, Dido is torn between Cupid's curse of love for Aeneas and her duty as a queen, and throws herself on a pyre.

Dido, however, is hardly the fallen femme fatale, as many continue to portray her. Wheatley, furthermore, would have been well aware of Dido's significance. By assuming the voice of Dido within the poem, Wheatley creates a platform from which she may address her Early American contemporaries who identify with the Aeneas myth. Wheatley also creates a place where she, via the position of Dido, is justified to offer a rebuke and to comment on the injustices of slavery to which she and others have been subjected. By delivering her message by means of the Aeneas myth, Wheatley also includes herself, as a slave and poet, within the mythical Aeneas ideology inherent in the formation of an Early American identity.

Dido, like Aeneas, may be considered a heroic figure, one who parallels and distinguishes the story of Aeneas. Like Aeneas and his exiled Trojans founding a new Troy (Rome) in the west, Dido precedes him in her founding of Carthage, not merely as one who follows destiny in light of tragedy, but one who uses her virtues of wisdom and *pietas,* the classical virtue endorsing devotion to the gods, motherland, and family. When Dido does die, moreover, she does so by her own choice, taking her fate into her own hands: "For since she dy'd, not doom'd by Heav'ns Decree, / Or her own Crime; but Human Casualty" (4.997–98). By employing the voice of Dido within her own poem, Wheatley draws both on a figure of feminine strength and wisdom as well as upon one who has been disadvantaged, betrayed, and prevented from acquiring her freedom in life.

Dido's voice in the poem, however, is not immediately perceptible to Wheatley's immediate audience. Instead, Wheatley lures her audience into the fold of her poem by bringing Aeneas to the forefront. As the poem opens, she exclaims, "Lo! for this dark terrestrial ball / Forsakes his azure-paved hall" (95). While her audience may or may not perceive the voice as being Dido's, the line parallels Dryden's translation of book 4 of the *Aeneid.* According to Dryden's translation, Dido is left in "endless Night" (4.992) and speaks from a position of one who has been deceived: "All only to deceive unhappy me?" (4.973). Dido prophesies after Aeneas asserts, "Forc'd by my Fate, I leave your happy Land," that

Maureen Anderson

Dido shall come, in a black Sulph'ry flame
When Death has once dissolv'd her Mortal frame.
Shall smile to see the Traitor [Aeneas]vainly weep,
Her angry Ghost arising from the Deep,
Shall haunt thee waking, and disturb thy Sleep. (555–59)

Here, Dido also "turns away" from Aeneas, "shun[ning] the sight of Day" (Wheatley 103), emphasizing her choice to die by fire, a death that symbolizes her passion, the curse of Cupid, as well as what Aeneas has done to her. In her shunning "the sight of Day," Dido also refuses both to acknowledge Aeneas, the son of Venus, and to continue her own life. Hence, "his azure-paved hall" of the next line in Wheatley's poem refers directly to the ocean and Aeneas' journey and Aeneas' abandonment and destruction of Dido. Dido, therefore, recalls Aeneas' arrival to her shores and addresses him directly.

Wheatley's contemporaries, however, were unlikely to make the connection to Dido's position early on in the poem. Instead, Wheatley swiftly calls attention to her focus, Aeneas himself, as "A prince of heav'nly birth! / Divine Humanity behold" (95). Wheatley distinguishes Aeneas as a hero, one of divine lineage through Venus and yet one who is human: "Divine Humanity" (95). And while Wheatley may, at this stage, seem to shape a Jesus figure, the next two lines imply otherwise. From the stance of Dido, the words are angry, yet they give the illusion that she is lauding her subject by suggesting that she will list his wonderful feats. Wheatley's verse, however, is as complex as it is poignant, and her list is one comprising rage and rebuttal: "What wonders rise, what charms unfold / At his descent to earth!" (95). According to the Oxford English Dictionary, a "wonder" is "A marvellous [sic] object; a marvel," yet primarily an object to an eighteenth-century audience. Furthermore, "charms" to the eighteenth-century audience are certainly not miracles in a Christian sense, but rather instruments of magic: "The chanting or recitation of a verse supposed to possess magic power or occult influence; incantation, enchantment; hence, any action, process, verse, sentence, word, or material thing, credited with such properties; a magic spell; a talisman" (OED). By placing the two items together within the one line, therefore, the reader may infer what sorts of "charms" were used to "rise" what "wonders" (Wheatley 95) between Dido and Aeneas.

The implication of Aeneas' taking advantage of Dido is further asserted when, in the next lines, Wheatley, in the voice of Dido, parallels Aeneas' founding of a nation with his sexual mistreatment of her:

The bosoms of the great and good
With wonder and delight he view'd,
And fix's his empire there. (95)

The implication is twofold. Not only does Wheatley's Aeneas found an empire, but he subjugates others, particularly Dido and Carthage, in order to do so. The "great and good" who are perceived with "wonder and delight" convey an Aeneas who is attracted to and manipulates the "great and good" "bosoms" of Dido and her people. Furthermore, considering Wheatley possessed knowledge of both the *Aeneid* and of the American identity with the Aeneas myth, her message is not one about one man's desire and dismissal of a woman, but rather about those who subjugate others through slavery, particularly her African brothers and sisters, in order to maintain and establish the new country. Dido, Queen of Carthage, adopts Africa as her home, and is brought down from her powerful position as a queen to be a tool in Aeneas' founding of Rome.

As the poem progresses, moreover, Venus and Aeneas' fate of founding a nation are not in any way exempt from the wrath of Wheatley's Dido. When "The fire of gods and men" addresses the "prince" Aeneas in the next stanza, Wheatley does not allude to a Christian deity (particularly when referring to "gods" or a pantheon-like array of gods) in her poem. Indeed, considering the construction of the lines, the "fire of gods and men," the poem does not refer to Christ or a Christian god figure, but rather addresses the male figure in the poem, Aeneas.

Wheatley's lines are, of course, intentionally subversive and grammatically sly. The message she conveys is not an easy one for her audience mostly comprising white, often slaveholding men. Wheatley establishes within the first two lines of the second stanza that the "he" of the poem "view[s]" "The bosoms of the great and good" "with wonder and delight," then, following a colon, not a period, she begins the next line with "Him," a pronoun that refers back to the "he" of the previous line. The "he," in turn, refers back to the antecedent in the first stanza, "prince of heav'nly birth" (95). Following the colon, moreover, it is "Him" who "The fire of gods and men addres[s]" and not a "Him" to another additional "Him" and certainly not a singular God addressing a "he." Indeed, considering the allusions to Vergil's *Aeneid* within the poem, the "fire of gods and men," "fire" conveying love and passion is anything but a "he" or a "Him;" we have a she: Venus addressing her son.

Maureen Anderson

Within the second stanza, moreover, the reader again hears the words from book 4 of Vergil's *Aeneid*. In Dryden's translation, Dido is "consum[ed]" and "Love is fir'd" (4.142). Indeed, throughout book 4 of the *Aeneid*, Vergil describes Dido as being on fire with the flames of passion after she is kissed by Cupid and placed under the spell or "charms" of Venus. Dido is, in a very real way, subjugated to a form of slavery to Venus' will, to be used as nothing much more than entertainment for Aeneas. Venus, embodying the element of fire in Wheatley's poem as well as in the *Aeneid*, becomes a deity that Wheatley, from Dido's perspective and the perspective of a slave in early America, can explore and challenge as both a negative as well as a positive attribute. Venus, as "The fire of gods and men," addresses Aeneas, her "son" or "sun":

> "My son, my heav'nly fair!
> "Descend to earth, there place thy throne;
> "To succor man's afflicted son
> "Each human heart inspire:
> "To act in bounties unconfin'd
> "Enlarge the close contracted mind,
> "And fill it with thy fire." (96)

The stanza is latent with subversive commentary on American slavery. Unlike Wheatley's immediate audience of white male slaveholders, Aeneas "act[s] in bounties unconfin'd," exemplified in book 5 of the *Aeneid* where Aeneas is exceedingly generous during the funeral games. Aeneas' generosity marks a striking contrast between his embodiment of *pietas* and the lack of either in the white slave-holders.

By this stage of the poem, moreover, fire is also an attribute of Venus and Aeneas as both positive and negative passions. While Venus commands her son, Aeneas, to establish a "throne" on earth, she also urges him to treat and teach others with love, to "fill" "close[d] contracted mind[s]" with "fire" (96). However, unlike the passionate fire Dido suffers earlier in the poem, Wheatley alludes to another sort of fire, a passionate fire for justice and inspiration, which is also conveyed by Venus and a fire that Aeneas, himself, possesses: "fill it with thy fire" (96).

Also within this stanza, Wheatley describes the "fire" of Aeneas as acts that he is charged with doing as he founds his new nation, acts that convey the freedom to convince others to expand their minds: "To act in bounties unconfin'd / Enlarge the close constricted mind" (96). As Wheatley utilizes the myth of

Aeneas for the purpose of constructing her version of American identity, she charges those who identify and use the myth of Aeneas in their construction of an American identity with the same: to "act in bounties unconfin'd" or to reap the benefits of the new nation and the founding of a new nationhood without confining others in slavery. Wheatley then commands, through the voice of Venus, that her readers should "Enlarge the close contracted mind," to resist and remain passionate against the injustices of slavery.

Soon after Aeneas receives a message from Mercury to leave Dido's land in Dryden's translation, Aeneas "longs to fly" and "loathes the charming land" (99). The events in Wheatley's poem parallel the action and the language in book 4 of the *Aeneid*. In Wheatley's poem, soon after his mother, a fiery Venus, commands him to "place" his "throne" and "To act in bounties unconfin'd," the speaker states that "Quick as the word, with swift career / He wings his course from star to star" (96), alluding to both Aeneas' successful founding of Rome as well as to his apotheosis. While Vergil's *Aeneid* describes in book 4 that Aeneas "longs to fly," in Wheatley's poem, the voice of Dido conveys that he does indeed fly "from star to star / And leaves the bright abode" (96), or, more specifically (and as Wheatley's contemporaries would be well aware of), from eastern to western stars: Aeneas flies west to found Rome. More pertinent to Wheatley's poem, however, is that Aeneas flies from the "star" of Dido's "bright abode" to the star of the west, a Rome/America.

Wheatley, however, is not yet done with charging Aeneas with the crimes he commits against Dido or Western man with the crimes he commits against those held in slavery. Indeed, Wheatley strikes her audience by invoking the Roman concept of *pietas*. Like Samuel Cooper before her who praises King George for attributes he should exhibit rather than for those he did, by calling attention to the English monarch's glaring faults, Wheatley follows this same line of critique. By calling attention to the virtue of *pietas* in her poem (Aeneas is the embodiment of Roman *pietas*), Wheatley consequently calls attention to the terrible crimes of slavery committed by her countrymen, slaveholders who, in their founding of a new Western nation, identify with Aeneas.

Wheatley continues her poem by explaining, "The *Virtue* did his charms impart" (italics Wheatley's) (96). Within this line, Wheatley delivers a three-fold condemnation to her contemporaries. Wheatley not only places "*Virtue*" in italics, but also capitalizes the word, presenting the word as a proper noun, directly alluding to the embodiment of "*Virtue*" in the Vergilian character of Aeneas. Furthermore, because she alludes to Aeneas, she does not suggest a sense of mere Christian virtue, but rather alludes to the Latin *virtus*. The Latin *virtus* is a civic virtue or as it pertains to Aeneas, *pietas:* devotion to gods, country, and family. Furthermore, within the same line, she explains that it is "*Virtue*" that "[Aeneas'] charms impart" (96).

Considering the earlier implication of the word "charms" in the first stanza of the poem, the meaning of this line is as bold as it is subversive. In one sense, she celebrates the embodied "*Virtue*" of Aeneas, yet in another, she conveys that Aeneas, from Dido's perspective, uses "charms" or unjust means to "impart" a false "*Virtue*" (96). As the voice of the poem may be read as Dido's, the implication that Aeneas may have used "charms" or Venus' assistance to appear to be the embodiment of *pietas* is understandable. Dido, within Wheatley's poem, as well as in Vergil's, is scorned and angry. Vergil's Dido is "Bereft of Honour, and expos'd to Shame" (4.466) and directly accuses Aeneas of being false:

> False as thou art, and more than false, forsworn;
> Not sprung from Noble Blood, nor Goddess-born,
> But hewn from hardned [*sic*] entrails of a Rock
> (4.522–24)

Wheatley, however, also directly makes a comment on her contemporaries who would claim that the founding of a new nation was built on the idea of *pietas*, but who, as slaveholders, merely wear a façade of real *pietas*. In other words, Wheatley boldly exposes those slaveholders who use their own "charms" to "impart" a false "*Virtue*" (96).

Wheatley's linguistic sting, however, hardly ends with an allusion to Roman *pietas*. Considering the added Christian implication of "virtue," of innocence and purity, Wheatley also conveys to her audience that they are not pure or innocent in any sense of the Christian concept. Even Wheatley's reference to a Christianized "virtue," likewise, refers back to Vergil's *Aeneid* when Dido scorns him and announces that even Aeneas "makes Heav'n accessory to his Deeds" (4.543), or rather, he would use his beliefs to give the false appearance of "*Virtue*."

As the poem continues, Wheatley deliberately makes the presence of Dido and her own position as a poet more apparent. Within the fifth stanza, Wheatley delicately intertwines her position as a poet and a slave with the position of Dido. Wheatley conveys that when Aeneas' "pitying eye did see" her as a "languid muse in low degree," she was under the impression that she would receive succor by "the celestial nine" or the Muses. Like Dido, as a slave, Wheatley is also "Bereft of Honour, and expos'd to Shame" (4.466) by the unjust actions of others. Yet, like Dido, she is deceived. Wheatley does not state that she is blessed by the Muses, but rather she states, "methought they deign'd to shine, / And deign'd to string my lyre" (96). Indeed, just as Dido's pleas for position did not help her, Wheatley's Muses do not seem to assist in her predicament as a slave.

As Wheatley concludes her poem, her lines echo the words of Dido. Wheatley draws on similar emotions, of being discarded and used by Aeneas or her contemporaries. As the stanza begins, Wheatley's Dido asks:

> Can Afric's muse forgetful prove?
> Or can such friendship fail to move
> A tender human heart? (97)

The opening lines to the last stanza are powerful as well as expressive of both Dido and Wheatley's pain. Wheatley alludes directly to Dido's position in Africa, as an African or Carthaginian queen by naming her and herself the "*Afric* muse" (97). The line also directly points to Wheatley herself, as in the volume of *Poems* she occasionally refers to herself as "*Afric*" in third person and in italics. The line itself alludes to Vergil's *Aeneid* wherein Dido explains, "Nor cou'd my Kindness and Compassion move, / Nor plighted Vows, nor dearer bands of Love!" (4.443–44). Both poems in this instance, in response to Aeneas, imply the voice of the disenfranchised feminine figure, a woman who remarks that neither emotional bonds of love or compassion seem to assist them in their individual plights.

The last three lines of the poem, perhaps the most subversive and striking, seem to suggest an upward swing or a calm resolution. Wheatley, however, again insinuates final judgment on her audience. Wheatley concludes,

> Immortal *Friendship* laurel-crown'd
> The smiling *Graces* all surround
> With ev'ry heav'nly *Art*. (97)

Wheatley communicates that real friendship, "Immortal *Friendship*," is indeed "laurel-crown'd" or blessed by the Muses. Within this line, the poet emphasizes "*Friendship*" with italics, conveying the word's importance within the poem. Within the next line, however, she alludes again to Venus, since she is often accompanied by the Graces. In classical myth, the Graces are minor goddesses and are the embodiment of beauty, enhancing all aspects of life. The Graces, furthermore, often accompany the Muses as well as Venus and are often given credit for contributing to the most perfect forms of art. By alluding to the Graces, Wheatley intertwines her role as a poet with the role of the Dido/Aeneas myth. On the one hand, the Graces accompany the charms of love or Venus while, on the other hand, they also purvey the Muses and the finest of art.

Wheatley and Dido's commentary seems, at this point in the poem, to be resolved, without anger and even with a slight tone of resignation. However, Wheatley and Dido are not yet finished. Within the last line, Wheatley states that the "*Graces* all surround / With ev'ry heav'nly *Art*" (97). By italicizing "*Graces*" and "*Art*," Wheatley alludes again to the *Aeneid* and makes a statement about the deception of Dido as well as herself. While the Graces do, indeed, attend art in a classical sense by accompanying the Muses, the "*Art*" Wheatley alludes to is not merely one of poetry. The lines directly allude to book 4 of the *Aeneid* wherein Dido discovers her betrayal as well as the deception:

> But soon the Queen perceives the thin Disguise;
> (What Arts can blind a jealous Woman's Eyes!)
> (4.425–26)

The concluding lines of Wheatley's poem, therefore, recall not merely Dido's state, but also refer back to the "charms" in the first and fourth stanzas of her poem as instruments of deception and dishonor. Wheatley's italicized and capitalized "*Art*" (97) corresponds to Dryden's translation and to his capitalized "Arts" that "blind" (4.426); both, consequently, refer to devices of deception or, as Wheatley designates them, "charms."

Also parallel to Vergil's *Aeneid* is Wheatley's mention of the Muses. Vergil waits strategically until book 7 of the *Aeneid* before he calls on the Muses for assistance. Vergil's call to the Muses, moreover, immediately precedes graphic scenes of war and difficulty. In other words, Vergil's call to the Muses is a cry for help in order to convey the violence and ugliness of war. Like Vergil, Wheatley waits until the last two stanzas to mention the Muses. Unlike Vergil, however, Wheatley does not invoke the Muses. Indeed, "the celestial nine" are at the command of another: "Then, then thy desire / Descended the celestial nine" (96). The "thy" within the line refers back to the figure of Aeneas within the poem. Furthermore, her repetition of "Then, then" creates a break within the rhythm of the poem, one that emphasizes that not only are the Muses at the command of another, but they also indicate a stop-start motion of the muse for her as a poet and a slave.

Wheatley's repetition brilliantly illustrates her frustration as a poet who does not appear to have access to the freedom of her own Muse. Though Wheatley refers to the Muses, she does not invoke the Muses, because, as the poem conveys, she does not have the freedom to do so. And, like Vergil calling on the Muses immediately before scenes of war and violence, Wheatley waits until the conclusion of the poem to mention the Muses, allowing her anger and the anger of Dido to end the poem. By concluding the poem with the Muses and Graces in place of opening the poem with either, Wheatley invites the reader to see that all is not well and there may be more to follow than words of poetry can capture.

Regardless of how many allusions, direct and otherwise, to Vergil's *Aeneid* Wheatley makes, the African American artist does not directly name Dido or Virgil within the lines of her poem. Instead, Wheatley relies on the classical knowledge of her readers to tease apart the lines in order to discover the true meaning and message behind her words. By making allusions to the words of Virgil without directly stating the names of Aeneas or Dido, Wheatley successfully pulls her readers into the poem far enough and deep enough that the message may be imparted. As an epic hymn, "An Hymn to Humanity," in Shields's definition, "provide[s] "a pause in the action in order to acknowledge the ideal toward which the epic struggles" (236). In the case of Dido, therefore, Wheatley successfully pauses the action in the *Aeneid*, focuses on the role of Dido, and explores the ideal of *pietas* in the context of an emerging American identity.

As a slave, Wheatley's subversive strategies would not have been well received by her audience. For her own safety, the message was disguised. Finally, had Wheatley named any of the characters within Vergil's epic, the message would no longer have been subversive and the real angst, rage, and betrayal of Dido would have been too apparent. Considering the surface Christian message of the poem, a message that often prevents readers from delving further into the poem, the poem was also seemingly docile enough for publication, tucked within the pages of her book; therefore, she was able to continue to deliver her charge against humanity.

As a prime example of Phillis Wheatley's subversive voice in her poetry, "An Hymn to Humanity" appears in her 1773 version of *Poems*. In 1772,

Wheatley was judged before a roomful of white, prominent men who would attest whether the young African woman was capable of producing such remarkable poetry. In "An Hymn to Humanity," however, Wheatley turns the respective tables against these same "evaluators" of her work. The tone of anger is subversive, but also powerful. Wheatley does not condemn the abilities of her contemporaries; rather, she charges them with crimes against "humanity" manifested in the falsehoods they perpetuate as slave-holders. By taking on the voice of Dido, and particularly of Dido addressing Aeneas, she challenges not only the motives behind her contemporaries' treatment of her as an African and a slave, but their own sense of self and their sense of nationhood; thereby she challenges her countrymen's idea of an American Aeneas and their concept of a true American *pietas*.

NOTES

1. The Christian hymn experienced popularity in the Middle Ages with monastic choirs, such as the Gregorian Chant. The Protestant Reformation also fueled an upsurge of Christian hymns with the rise of congregational singing and hymn writing. While Christianity was certainly instrumental in the preservation of the hymn form, the tradition dates as far back as ancient Greece (the word "hymn" derives from the Greek [ὕμνος] *hymnos* or "song of praise") as a prize-song in adoration of a god, goddess, or other significant figure.

2. Coinciding with Wheatley's use of the epic hymn form to examine the feminine principle, in his "Re-membering America: Phillis Wheatley's Intertextual Epic," Robert Kendrick suggests that Wheatley's use of the epic device of beginning *in medias res* directs the reader's attention to her position as an African American in early America:

> Once the reader enters Wheatley's text(s), points of beginning
> and ending cannot be identified (and without these points, there
> is no proper middle either), leaving the reader in the "middle" of
> repeating and re-membering the traces of "past," "present," and
> "future" moments in the narrative(s). As a result, Wheatley's
> "epic" signifies on the temporal order that beginning *in medias
> res* would establish. Signifyin(g) on her "past" critiques the no-
> tion that she, or anyone else, does not belong in American culture

by virtue of their "alien" past, because once one has entered into the process of "becoming" American, one's "origin" no longer serves as a teleological mark. Wheatley's African-ness is important as a mark of her "Otherness," and her exploitation of this mark for strategic and rhetorical purposes has been noted, but this mark becomes of strategic and rhetorical importance only as it is re-marked/repeated by Wheatley as she "becomes" an African American. (84)

In "An Hymn to Humanity," Wheatley begins *in medias res* with the lines, "Lo! For this dark terrestrial ball / Forsakes his azure-paved hall / A prince of heav'nly birth!" (97), emphasizing both the anger of Dido in book 4 of the *Aeneid* as well as positioning her audience within the "temporal order" that signifies the past.

3. Dido (Gr.: Elissa) was the founder and first queen of Carthage (modern Tunisia). There are various early representations of Dido in addition to Vergil's treatment. One full account is that of Vergil's contemporary, Gnaeus Pompeius Trogus, in his *Philippic Histories*, where he refers to earlier depictions of Dido. According to Trogus, Dido originates from Tyre and is sister to King Pygmalion. After her husband (her wealthy uncle and second in the line to the throne) dies, she escapes from Tyre to found Carthage. In versions that contrast to Vergil's account of her death in the *Aeneid*, she commits suicide via a Greek soldier's death by impaling herself on her sword. According to the alternate account, the neighboring king from Larbas demands Dido to be his wife or he will make war on the newborn Carthage. In response, Dido constructs a funeral pyre, claiming she wishes to make a final offering to her departed husband in preparation for the marriage to the king of Larbas. Dido, however, ascends the pyre, asserting that she will remain faithful to her first husband, then falls on her sword. The alternative depiction of Dido/Elissa explains her deification and celebration as a heroine/goddess in Carthage.

4. In *The American Aeneas*, Shields explains how and why early Americans identified with the myth of Aeneas:

The simple fact is that, years before the Puritan settlers identified their own errand in the American wilderness, Englishmen (not to mention Italians, Portuguese, Frenchmen, and Spaniards, among other Europeans) were disposed to see the New World in terms

Maureen Anderson

of Aeneas's perilous sea voyage to discover the land to the west. . . . From the earliest days when an "America" emerged as an idea, that entity, rather than being alienated from classicism, was conceived in terms classical as well as biblical. (xxv)

5. Cupid (Gr.: Eros) is the Roman god of love. Son to Venus and Vulcan, Cupid appears in book 1 of the *Aeneid* when Venus sends him to take the place of Ascanius to incite love between Dido and Aeneas. Cupid also appears in Apuleius's *Golden Ass* in the story of Cupid and Psyche and, though not considered a significant god, his image often appeared on coffins as a symbol of life after death.

6. Originally an Italian goddess, Venus is identified with the Greek Aphrodite, goddess of love, charm, beauty, and passion. Significant to the Julian line, which included Julius Caesar and Nero, is the fact that Aeneas was the son of Venus. The Julian line claimed to be the descendants of Aeneas's son, Iulus (Ascanius), and, hence, to Venus. Politically, the Julian line's connection to Venus signified their link to divinity, vital to their position as the ruling family of Rome.

WORKS CITED

Balkun, Mary McAleer. "Phillis Wheatley's Construction of Otherness and the Rhetoric of Performed Ideology." *African American Review* 36.1 (Spring 2002): 121–36.

Harmon, William, and C. Hugh Holman. *A Handbook to Literature.* 7th ed. Upper Saddle River: Prentice Hall, 1996.

Kendrick, Robert. "Re-membering America: Phillis Wheatley's Intertextual Epic." *African American Review* 30.1 (Spring 1996): 71–91.

Scheick, William. "Subjection and Prophecy in Phillis Wheatley's Verse: Paraphrases of Scripture." *College Literature* 22.3 (October 1995): 122–31.

Shields, John C. *The American Aeneas: Classical Origins of the American Self.* Knoxville: U of Tennessee P, 2001.

Virgil. *Aeneid.* Trans. John Dryden. New York: Penguin Books, 1997.

Wheatley, Phillis. *The Collected Works of Phillis Wheatley.* Ed. John C. Shields. New York: Oxford UP, 1988.

I Remember Mama: Honoring the Goddess-Mother While Denouncing the Slaveowner-God in Phillis Wheatley's Poetry

Devona Mallory

Still contrary to popular belief, Phillis Wheatley consistently honors her African homeland while critiquing the very institution of slavery that inspired her poetic gifts. Potentially in an awkward situation of ambiguity, she fights against the system that has taken her away from her family and now enslaves her, but at the same time she reaps what little benefits that system providing for her. In her work, Wheatley, in this act of writing, fights back by wielding her pen in remembrance of her mother and birthplace. Indeed Wheatley has to be careful. If she explicitly honors Africa, the white society in which she lives may think she is ungrateful, and she may not be able to publish her work. Therefore, she cloaks her remembrance in a form recognizable to whites: classicism. This way, she may not be readily considered a threat. Moreover, I will demonstrate that in at least three of Wheatley's poems, "An Hymn to the Morning," "On Recollection," and "An Hymn to the Evening," Wheatley honors her mother as a classical goddess-mother, thereby maintaining her memories yet fooling the slaveowners. Not only that, she denounces the enslavement that separates her from her mother. Furthermore, by honoring her mother, Wheatley covertly and subversively dedicates these poems to her.

Wheatley's kidnapping and enslavement as a young child simultaneously traumatized and opened her to new opportunities for growth. Her owners, John and Susannah Wheatley, treated her better than most slaveholders and even allowed her to publish poetry. Of course, writing poetry was a creative outlet for Wheatley; however, because she was a black female slave, she knew that she had to be careful about what she had said and how she said it. Therefore, Wheatley's poetry, composed in the late eighteenth century, a time before aggressive antislavery activism, does not allow her blatant freedom of expression.

However, this limitation enhances the meaning of her poetry because it forces her to cloak her biting and forceful remarks in such a clever way that many still cannot comprehend what she is really saying. Two such critics, Michele McKay and William J. Scheick, completely misunderstand her:

> By her own account, she seems to have been robbed of her memories of Africa, with one important exception: a recollection of her mother offering libations to the rising sun. . . . Bereft of her African heritage, she turned to neoclassical English as a prominent literary discourse available to her as an aspiring poet. (71)

In this quotation, McKay and Scheick get part of it right. Wheatley's mother pouring out water for an offering to the rising sun and then prostrating herself in front of it is the only memory that Wheatley provided to her slaveowners (Shields 241–42). That does not mean, however, that that is the only memory she had; it is the only one she shared with white people. She states in "Phillis's Reply to the Answer" that she comes from Gambia, West Africa (line 22). Secondly, the notion that she turned to neoclassicism because her African heritage was taken from her is misleading. As a slave, Wheatley had no easy power or control over her life. To be sure, Wheatley was bereft because she was kidnapped and enslaved at the age of seven. So, taken from her home and forced into slavery, the only real control she could exercise was through her poetry. In fact, Wheatley discusses her enslavement in her poem "To the Right Honourable William, Earl of Dartmouth, His Majesty's Principal Secretary of State for North America, &c":

> I, young in life, by seeming cruel fate
> Was snatch'd from *Afric's* fancy'd happy seat:
> What pangs excruciating must molest,
> What sorrows labour'd in my parent's breast?
> Steel'd was that soul and by no misery mov'd,
> That from a father seiz'd his babe belov'd:
> Such, such my case. And can I then but pray
> Others may never feel tyrannic sway? (74–75)

Here she claims she was taken from her father. This event may or may not be true. Still, it is a very significant line because she is writing to a male. This event sounds more traumatic to a male because a mother would be presumed too weak to stop violence, but if a child is taken from her or his father, it shows that the institution of slavery was too powerful even for her father to overcome. As

Devona Mallory

head of the household, he has been particularly shamed by the practice. As well, she wants to drive home how slavery destroys families as well as civilization, especially the lines, "And I can then but Pray / Others may never feel tyrannic sway" (lines 30–31). Wheatley utilizes the classical mode as a readily available outlet for her to relate her other memories of Africa; she does so, nevertheless, in a way that it is difficult to detect. What better way to avenge her plight than to turn the weapons used to keep her in her place against her oppressors?

In one combative vein of this poetics, goddess-mothers hold an important place.[1] Goddesses, of course, are female deities with special powers that reign over humankind. According to Tikva Frymer-Kensky, the goddess-mother and her daughter in many aspects have a realistically typical mother-daughter relationship, which includes a uniquely "direct and complex" bond of mutual love, loyalty, and respect. Furthermore:

> The mother's devotion and loyalty to her children is her domi-
> nant, perhaps even her defining, characteristic. This attachment
> does not stop even with the death of the child, for it is, above all,
> the mother who mourns the death of her child. The very act of
> lamenting was particularly associated with children. (17)

Also, with regards to mythology, the child becomes aware of the mother's "power and anger" when the mother is crossed (19). Unfortunately, we do not know the actions of Wheatley's mother after she discovered the loss of her child, but I assume that she must have grieved tremendously and the pain probably never went away.

No bond is stronger than that of a mother and child. The mother carries the child in her womb for nine months, making that child a part of her body and spirit. Then after the birth, a typical mother feeds and nurtures that child to maturity. In turn, the child looks to the mother for guidance, security, and love. Therefore, a goddess-mother may be like any average mother who cares for and loves her children; what distinguishes the two is that the goddess-mother exercises divine power. Imagine Wheatley at seven years old, standing on a slave block, mostly nude, probably shivering with shock and/or cold. What thoughts were going through her head? How traumatic it must have been to her, losing her mother not to death but to slavery. It must have been another blow to realize that she would never see her mother again. Wheatley eventually learns that one way to cope is by composing poetry.

Given her own maternal instincts (she later gave birth to three children) and her study of ancient classicism, Wheatley would have been prepared to utilize the mother-goddess motif to give her mother divine qualities and thence to voice expression of her profound loss. Implicit in that loss is the concept of motherhood equating home and security. In Wheatley's case, she also missed Gambia and her short, carefree childhood. One important way that Wheatley utilizes her various poems to remember her mother is through the constant presence of goddesses. Because Wheatley was permanently removed from her mother since she was a little girl, she likely idolized and deified her because she was not physically accessible. As memories fade, people tend to remember beloved people and places through rose-colored glasses. In other words, people tend to recall the past not as they were, but as they positively imagined them to be, especially if they were traumatized as was Wheatley. In Wheatley's world of servitude, her distant mother very likely became a deity and Gambia became paradise. In her poem "An Hymn to Mo[u]rning,"[2] she honors her mother as a goddess without insulting the whites:

> Attend my lays, ye ever honour'd nine,
>> Assist my labours, and my strains refine;
> In smoothest numbers pour the notes along,
> For bright *Aurora* now demands my song. (56)

The "honour'd nine" that Wheatley refers to are the Muses, the goddesses of the arts. It is typical in classical poetry to invoke the Muses for inspiration. However, in this poem, the Muses are more than mere inspiration, for they aid Wheatley in writing poetry. Later, as is often the case in this poet's work, Calliope, the muse of epic poetry, plays the harmonious lyre while her sisters "fan the pleasing fire" of encouragement and support (lines 13–14). Wheatley mentions Calliope specifically because she appears to need her help more than that of her other eight sisters in writing this particular poem. Indeed, all these ladies are working very hard to help Wheatley; the Muses seem to be her ever helpful friends. Still, it is more than divine intervention that drives these goddesses to assist her. Obviously, in Wheatley's mind, they are fond of her and want her to succeed because she suggests they appear to do everything in their power to inspire and support her poem.

As well, this poem features another classical deity, Aurora, the Roman goddess of the dawn. Wheatley invokes the Muses because she claims that Aurora commands her to write poetry, like a mother telling a child to do a task. Furthermore, Aurora is more than a goddess; she may be read as a representation of Wheatley's mother. Wheatley's mother, like Aurora, greeted the morn.

Devona Mallory

Wheatley's mother did so by prostrating herself in front of the sun, and Aurora completed the task with her presence. Despite the slightly different methods, each has the same outcome. Aurora, like the goddess-mother Frymer-Kensky mentions above, touches nature with a gentle wind, as a mother would soothingly caress a child. Then, also as a mother would do, she protects Wheatley and her poetry writing by shading her "from the burning day" (line 12). Lastly, Aurora, like any mother, creates something that delights her child, which includes "[t]he bow'rs, the gales, the variegated skies / [which] [i]n all their pleasures in my bosom rise" (lines 15–16). Indeed, the Muses also symbolize an aspect of a mother figure because of their sheltering and nurturing of Wheatley physically, emotionally, and artistically. The fact that the names of the goddesses are italicized suggests Wheatley wanted readers to acknowledge a certain amount of importance regarding their appearance and actions. The emphasis on their names suggests their significance in her life.

Another poem, "On Recollection," continues this preoccupation with the goddess-mother. When one recalls something, it is a reflective moment in memory. It seems natural that, when people are sad and depressed, they may try to remember something pleasant in order to make themselves feel better. In Wheatley's case, she remembered her mother in another way by writing a poem:

> Mneme begin. Inspire, ye sacred nine,
> Your vent'rous Afric in her great design.
> *Mneme,* immortal pow'r, I trace thy spring:
> Assist my strains, while I thy glories sing:
> The acts of long departed years, by thee
> Recover'd, in due order rang'd we see:
> Thy pow'r the long-forgotten calls from night
> That sweetly plays before the fancy's slight.
> (lines 1–8)

What makes this poem significant is the appearance of Mneme. Mneme, the older form of Mnemosyne, is the goddess of memory and the mother of the Muses. In this poem, Wheatley does not ask for inspiration; she demands it with the opening line "Mneme begin. Inspire, ye sacred nine." She shows pluck and confidence in commanding the goddess-mother to invoke her memories as when she calls herself the "vent'rous Afric." Here, again anticipating Frymer-Kensky's model, Wheatley imbues Mnemosyne with enough power to do the tasks she wants done, which is namely helping her to recall "the acts of long departed years" (line 6). Wheatley, referring to herself as African, clearly suggests she wants to recall memories of her childhood in Africa, and by extension, Mnemosyne symbolizes the lost mother she wants to keep remembering.

Additionally, Wheatley states that while we sleep, Mnemosyne "pours" memory as if it were "the ample treasure of her secret shores" (line 10). Mnemosyne's act is very similar to the memory that Wheatley shared about her mother pouring out water; therefore, this line suggests further that Wheatley was remembering her mother and her homeland subversively. She could not confidently allow her slaveowners to know that she remembered more about her mother than she had told them. Also, by transposing the memory of her mother from morning to a sleep-filled night, Wheatley emphasizes that freedom enhances the subversive component of her poetics, for during the sunshine-filled day, she reverts back to being a slave.

Besides Mnemosyne and her daughters the Muses, Phoebe, the goddess of the moon, makes her appearance in line 12. According to Wheatley, Phoebe, along with the other goddesses, helps "the high-ratur'd poet," which of course is Wheatley. Also, Wheatley praises Mnemosyne as the one who never forgets a good or bad deed. For those who are good, she graciously takes care as she does of Wheatley by sounding "sweeter than music to the ravish'd ear" (line 22). The mention of "Maro" in the next line renders an epithet of the Roman poet, Virgil. Wheatley claims, therefore, that the divine songs conveyed to her by Mnemosyne are sweeter than those evoked by the earthly, revered Virgil. With these lines, she places the goddess-woman over any man.

What links Mnemosyne to Wheatley's mother, besides her being the mother of the Muses and the power she possesses over Wheatley's memories, are her specific actions. Mnemosyne, like Aurora in the previous poem, makes sure that Wheatley achieves her artistic endeavors because she has the capacity to do so. Any mother would help her children achieve their goals if it were within her power, even if that mother has to tell her children what to do, just as Wheatley summons Mnemosyne to tell her daughters to help Wheatley.

Unfortunately, Wheatley's memories of her mother were also bittersweet. The fact that she was taken from her mother at such an impressionable and young age must have continuously plagued her throughout her life. It was slavery that tore Wheatley from her mother, and it was slavery that forced her to remember her mother on the sly in her poetry. Besides images of a very nurturing mother, the last stanza of "An Hymn to Mo[u]rning" may refer to slavery:

Devona Mallory

See in the east th' illustrious king of day!
His rising radiance drives the shades away—
But Oh! I feel his fervid beams too strong,
And scarce begun, concludes th' abortive song.
(lines 17–20)

Here, at first, Wheatley celebrates the act of writing poetry and being encouraged by her mother's circle. Despite this initial praise of the "king of day," however, Phoebus Apollo, the god of the sun, and the aforementioned twin of Phoebe, with his "fervid beams too strong" (line 19), drives Aurora away. Phoebus' forceful, aggressive rays or ways parallel the overpowering American slaveowners that drive Aurora or Wheatley's mother away from her. This poem can then subversively suggest that she did comment forcefully on being taken from her homeland and forced into servitude. Notably, only female goddesses help Wheatley, never the male ones. Represented by the sun, it is the "king of day" that destroys whatever Wheatley attempts to accomplish.

Ironically, like her mother before her, Wheatley had to bow down to the sun after the dawn flees. Significantly, while the morning shadows that Aurora provides enhance her writing, the appearance of the sun stops it completely when she says "[a]nd scarce begun, concludes th' abortive song" (line 20). Furthermore, this passage may allude to the loss of her mother when the sun's "rising radiance drives the shades away" (line 18). Those shades, provided by Aurora, may well symbolize the caring and endearing mother protecting her child from harm, just as Wheatley's mother attempted to accomplish. Ultimately, Wheatley's mother could not save her daughter from slavery, and Aurora could not protect her from those same forces when she tried to write poetry.

To continue to build on the sun's link to slavery in this poem, the sun's "fervid beams" represent the concept of paternalism in slave culture (lines 17–21). Her white slaveowners protected her physically for their benefit and supported her artistically because she seemed to justify benevolent slavery, but they also shielded her from her culture and from freedom. Wheatley's "protection" came at a high cost; her slaveowners took good care of her, taught her how to read and write, and allowed her to create, but they expected her complete submission and gratitude as payment for all the "wonderful" things they had done to/for her. Yes, Wheatley was treated very well for a slave, but the fact was, she was *still* a slave. As payment for the Wheatley family taking care of her, she was forced to write her poetry in an idiom they would recognize, which was the classical mode. In fact, she did not have the freedom to critique aggressively what she wanted to say without raising suspicion, hence the necessity of remembering her mother and homeland in the guise of Greek and Roman mythology.

In Wheatley's "An Hymn to Mo[u]rning," the pleasant situation that Aurora/her mother and the "morning" brings quickly changes to the grief of "mourning" when Phoebus drives Aurora/her mother away. Phoebus' actions parallel the forcefulness of slavery that took Wheatley away from her mother. Also, "Mourning," my spelling of Wheatley's "Morning," suggests that Wheatley acknowledges her mother's spiritual presence while at the same time she mourns her physical loss. Wheatley was, perhaps subliminally, letting her mother know that she missed her.

In another part of the poem "On Recollection," Wheatley also discusses the impact of slavery on the maternal goddess of memory:

> But how is Mneme dreaded by the race,
> Who scorns her warnings, and despise her grace,
> By her unveil'd each horrid crime appears,
> Her awful hand a cup of wormwood bears.
> Days, years misspent, O what a hell of woe!
> Hers the worst tortures that our souls
> can know. (63)

The race that dreads Mnemosyne is the white race. It dreads her because in her role as memory, she constantly reminds them of the evil deeds they do with regards to enslaving Africans, like Wheatley. So in return they "scorn her warnings, and despise her grace" (line 26). Additionally, the fact of Mnemosyne's sadness over knowing that slavery is wrong is demonstrated in the lines, "[d]ays, years mispent, O what a hell of woe / Hers the worst tortures that our souls can know." Wheatley's mentioning of eighteen years passing probably refers to her age at the time she wrote the poem. Following this sort of reading makes sense, especially when she discusses the follies that occurred within her lifetime. Those follies are, of course, being kidnapped into slavery and being separated from her mother and Africa. Furthermore, this train of thought accords with her lines in "Recollection" about shame and mourning.

As evident in the above lines, Mnemosyne can be understood to represent Wheatley's mother. Not only did Wheatley suffer from being separated from her mother, Wheatley's mother must have been devastated by being separated from her daughter. A prime example of this phenomenon is the classic Greek myth of the mother and daughter goddesses Demeter and Persephone, a myth surely familiar to Wheatley. Demeter is the goddess of the grain who is responsible for making crops as well as causing nature to flourish. One day, while Persephone is picking flowers, she is kidnapped by her uncle, Hades, the god of the dead, and taken down to his underground kingdom to become his bride. Demeter is so sad and distraught by the loss of her daughter that nothing grows, and snow falls across the land. To save the earth and all its living creatures, Persephone is allowed to join her mother for half the year. When Persephone is with her mother, spring and summer prevail, and the mother and daughter live happily. When Persephone returns to the underworld, however, Demeter's grief brings to the world fall and winter (Husain 76–79; *Oxford Classical Dictionary* 447–48, 1142–43; *Oxford Companion* 177, 422).[3] This myth, of course, explains the seasons, but it also enacts the strong bond that can exist between a mother and her daughter—the bond even separation and slavery cannot sever. Unfortunately, unlike Demeter and Persephone, after her capture, Wheatley never saw her mother again. So it would be reasonable that she would remember her in the most honorable and idealized way—as a goddess. Tapping into idealized versions of motherhood at the time certainly would have served Wheatley well. While Wheatley does not, in her extant poetry, use the Demeter and Persephone mother-daughter pair, she may well have done so in such a poem as the as-yet not discovered "To Penelope," listed in her regrettably unpublished volume projected in her October 30, 1779, "Proposals" (190–92).

Along these lines, Demeter could have represented Wheatley's mother and Wheatley Persephone. Traditionally, just as in the case of Demeter bringing Spring and Summer to the earth when she is with Persephone and Fall and Winter when her daughter is away, light symbolizes goodness, revelation, and happiness, while darkness connotes evil, gloom, and what is hidden. The classical parallel to Wheatley's life coincidently calls up Hades. He may, in his kidnapping of Persephone, represent the evil darkness of male domination and enforced slavery—an event to which Wheatley could certainly relate. However, the opposite obtains in Wheatley's world since slaves typically worked in the daytime.

The Persephone-Demeter comparison proves to be especially instructive when examining several additional poems by Wheatley. As seen in "An Hymn to Mo[u]rning," the "shades" of Hades' underworld also invoke nighttime and the unconscious. Still, when Persephone eventually becomes the Queen of the Dead and balances out the oppression found in Hades, she represents both Wheatley and her mother—the victim and the avenger. Wheatley becomes the mother by "birthing" her poems. Physically, Wheatley has lost her mother, but strikingly she comes to life again in Wheatley's poetry. The cycle of loss, birth, and rebirth continues in a uniquely creative way. Another poem, "Thoughts on the Works of Providence," enhances this idea of regaining her mother at night:

> When action ceases, and ideas range
> Licentious and unbounded o'er the plains,
> Where *Fancy's* queen in giddy triumph reigns
> Hear in soft strains the dreaming lover sigh
> To a kind fair, or rave in jealousy;
> On pleasure now, and now on vengeance bent,
> The lab'ring passions struggle for a vent.
> What pow'r, O man! thy *reason* then restores,
> So long suspended in nocturnal hours? (47)

It is only at night and during sleep that Wheatley can take the journey to the underworld of her "unbounded" unconscious mind to let the inspired memories of her mother flow from her pen. Along these lines, in her text, *Women Who Run with the Wolves: Myths and Stories of the Wild Woman Archetype*, Clarissa Pinkola Estés, analyzes the wild woman myth by utilizing Jungian psychoanalysis.[4] She defines this term:

> The word wild here is not used in its modern pejorative sense,
> meaning out of control, but in its original sense, which means to
> live a natural life, one in which the *criatura*, creature, has innate
> integrity and healthy boundaries. These words, *wild* and *woman*,
> cause women to remember who they are and what they are about.
> They create a metaphor to describe the force which funds all fe-
> males. They personify a force that women cannot live without. (8)

Through her poetry and the "nocturnal hours," Wheatley allows her wild woman to roam free as well as turning her mother into a goddess-mother to honor her memory.

According to Monica Sjöö and Barbara Mor, feminists view the Demeter-Persephone relationship as "a paradigm of contemporary woman, struggling to escape the death clutch of patriarchy in a search for her original, fruitful

Devona Mallory

self" (167).[5] Women go to the underworld to rediscover their "creative, visionary power," "soul," and the damaged child within. Then women can come to terms with males without subjugating themselves to patriarchy (167). They also contend in clinical studies about the child identifying with the mother that "successful overcoming of problems—i.e., mature development—does not come from severing the early infantile sense of unity with the Mother, but from reestablishing it" (30).

Furthermore, in her role as the Queen of the Dead, Persephone connects with the dark queen-goddess of Africa, Wheatley's homeland. This connection demonstrates the link, at least in Wheatley's mind, to her mother. In fact, classical myth derives from Africa:[6]

> . . . researchers into early mythic history . . . see not only the
> black African origins of the Great Mother but to the extent to
> which early matriarchal Africans traveled throughout the ancient
> world, spreading the Black Goddess . . . then it is easy to under
> stand the existence of these Black Madonnas. They are not "psy
> chological symbols of the dark side of the mother of Christ"—or
> not solely, or originally. They are solid iconic remains of the an
> cient time when the religion of the Black Goddess ruled Africa
> and from thence, much of the rest of the world. (32)

A prime example of this concept occurs in the last poem to be considered, "An Hymn to Evening," which creatively and intricately encapsulates these ideas of the nurturing dark goddess-mother and the brutal sun or light god of slavery. However, Wheatley, because of her status, is very cautious in her comparisons. The first stanza demonstrates this tendency:

> Soon as the sun forsook the eastern main
> The pealing thunder shook the heav'nly Plain;
> Majestic grandeur! From the zephyr's wing.
> Exhales the incense of the blooming Spring.
> Soft purl the streams, the birds renew their notes,
> And through the air their mingled music floats. (58)

What is productive in the case of Wheatley's poetry is that in darkness one can cloak or disguise what one is actually saying. In the lines quoted above, the sun may symbolize the patriarchal light of slavery that threatens to overpower her with its beams of bigotry. Obviously, when the sun goes down, the "pealing thunder" announces its disappearance while the zephyr's or the west wind's wing gently flaps, spring exudes a pleasant scent, the streams calm, and the birds sing in harmony. These actions demonstrate that the sun negatively dominates the rest of nature as well.

Second, as her imagery suggests, while the piercing morning sun symbolizes slavery and America, the calming but equally effective night represents freedom and Africa, thereby allowing for the personal and creative freedom not only for Wheatley but for all earthly and heavenly creatures as well. The next stanza further drives this point:

> Through all the heav'ns what beauteous dies are spread!
> But the west glories in the deepest red:
> So may our breasts with ev'ry virtue glow,
> The living temples of our God below! (lines 7–10)

As the moon rises, its beauty complements but does not overpower the world around it. The red sky that the west glorifies echoes her passionate attachment to sundown. This passion is so apparent that she wants the world below to feel this joyful harmony as well—to see how beautiful the world can be without slavery. For, if the world follows the lead of the heavens, peace will reign throughout the whole universe. In heaven, all of nature is equal. Wheatley writes:

> Fill'd with the praise of him who gives the
>   light,
> And draws the sable curtains of the night,
> Let placid slumbers sooth each weary mind,
> At morn to wake more heav'nly, more refin'd,
> So shall the labours of the day begin
> More pure, more guarded from the snares of sin.
> (58–59)

Here, even though Wheatley still cloaks herself in darkness, her message in this stanza is more explicit. The word "him" refers to Phoebus who, in Wheatley's mind, provides light, but whose absence provides darkness for all. While she honors Phoebus this time, she also prays to him that he will end "the labours" of slavery; if he labors to confine slaves, he assumes the role of the slaveowner. In the context of this poem, Wheatley hopes that the gentle night will convince Phoebus to sooth the savage beast of oppression and deflate "the snares of sin," or more specifically, the evils of slavery. In addition, his reoc-

Devona Mallory

currence still prevents Wheatley from writing because it is his presence that kills the creativity the nighttime brings. These lines also suggest Wheatley's ambivalence toward her masters. She hates being a slave and losing her mother, but at the same time she is allowed to write. Instead of a joyful communion with divinity and nature, moreover, the sun reminds her of the work that comes with being a slave. In other words, at night she is free to be herself, but in the light she must conform to her enslavement.

Still, the night has another meaning. In the last two lines of the poem, Wheatley encapsulates her praise of Africa and freedom by stating "Night's leaden sceptre seals my drowsy eyes / Then cease, my song, till fair Aurora rise" (lines 17–18). By going to sleep, Wheatley hopes that Phoebus/slave-owner will end slavery for herself and the other slaves by the time she wakes up to Aurora, the goddess of the dawn. Also, Wheatley switches the meanings of light and dark for the overall imagery of darkness, which corresponds to the idea of remembering Africa. Traditionally, lightness symbolizes goodness and racial whiteness while darkness indicates evil and racial blackness. For centuries, Africa was called "the dark continent" because its people were considered backward, unintelligent, and even evil—a blatant excuse to justify slavery. In Wheatley's poem, however, darkness does not connote evil; it connotes equality and liberty. It is the sunlight that possesses negative qualities, with the exception of Aurora, for she gently eases people into the light, unlike the harsh sun. These three poems feature Wheatley's demonstration of her clever ability to cloak the praising of her homeland under the guise of classic poetry so as not to elicit suspicion. Like the evening she meditates upon, she cloaks her poetic message. Indeed, many of her poems may be read as blueprints for her subversive but extremely relevant and powerful prayer for hope and liberty.

Besides the poems explicated above, Wheatley assumes the role of goddess-mother in her elegies, poems that honor the recently departed. Elegies were a common poetic form in classical literature (*Oxford Companion* 208). In Wheatley's case, the recently departed may not be merely references to the deceased; they may be an attempt by the African American artist to console parents who have been separated, beyond their control, from their children. For instance, the subjects of many of Wheatley's extant elegies are parents who have lost their children. These titles include: "On the Death of a Young Lady of Five Years of Age," "To a Lady and Her Children, on the Death of the Her Son and Their Brother," "To a Gentleman and Lady on the Death of Lady's Brother and Sister, and a Child of the Name Avis, Aged One Year," "On the

Death of J. C. and Infant," and most notably the one about a classically mythological mother and her children entitled, "Niobe in Distress for Her Children Slain by Apollo, from Ovid's *Metamorphoses,* Book VI. And from a View of the Painting of Mr. Richard Wilson."

In most of these poems, Wheatley comforts those remaining to grieve for their children who have gone to heaven. Wheatley, through her elegies, perhaps tries to send a secret message to her mother saying that she was fine despite the travails that separated them forever. Assuming the role of the elegist also relates to the Frymer-Kensky model, in which the poet implies that the goddess-mothers were in charge of mourning the dead; therefore, Wheatley's utilization of the elegiac form may be read as yet another way in which Wheatley attempts to reconnect with Africa and her mother.

Losing a child or a parent to slavery is akin to losing one to death. We will never know exactly how Wheatley confronted her separation from her mother. As a mother, Wheatley also lost her children. In fact, she was found dead after giving birth to her last child. Therefore, she also knew how it felt to lose children (Mallory 1723). Hence, placing her long-lost mother on a divine pedestal helped Wheatley to endure her kidnapping, enslavement, and short life of hardship. The mythological goddess-mother represented a caring, nurturing, and protective mother, one who Wheatley had lost and surely tried to be with her own children. Through sophisticated poetic maneuvers, Wheatley could relive the few moments of her brief, happy childhood. On another level, her poetry demonstrates how the intrusive male god Phoebus, which can be seen to symbolize slavery, intrudes on her moments of happiness. Wheatley may have told her owners that she only had one memory of her mother; however, her poetry belies that statement.

NOTES

1. Here I am referring to the cult of the mother-goddess (goddess-mother) or "deae matres." Evidence of this cult appears in monuments and inscriptions in the Celtic and Germanic regions, extending from northern Italy to Britain during the period of the Roman Empire. Based on inscriptions on artifacts that served as food baskets, scholars believe these mother-goddesses were seen as fertility goddesses (*Oxford Classical Dictionary* 433). Furthermore, there is evidence of mother-goddess cults in other places such as Egypt and Syria. For further reading, see Marija Gimbutas's *The Lan-*

guage of the Goddess and Erich Neuman's *The Great Mother: An Analysis of the Archetype.*

2. The "u" is my addition. As part of my contention that Wheatley writes poems to honor her mother, explanation of this change will become apparent.

3. According to the myth, Persephone has to stay in the underworld part of the year because she ate the seeds of a pomegranate.

4. Pinkola Estés is a Jungian analyst who utilizes what she calls the "Wild Woman Archetype" to help traumatized women heal psychological issues. In her text, she analyzes such myths and legends such as "The Red Shoes, "Bluebeard," and "The Ugly Duckling" for mainstream empowerment and inspiration.

5. See Sjöö and Mor's *The Great Cosmic Mother,* specifically the chapter entitled, "Mother and Daughter, and Rebirth," wherein the authors consult Jill Johnston's *Lesbian Nation: The Feminist Solution,* and her 1960s *Village Voice* articles.

6. See the chapter titled "The Original Black Mother" in Sjöö and Mor's *The Great Cosmic Mother;* John J. Jackson, *Man, God and Civilization;* Sir E. A. Wallis Budge, *Egypt,* 197; and Leo Frobenius, *The Voice of Africa,* 345.

WORKS CITED

Budge, Sir E. A. Wallis. *Egypt.* London: The Home University Library, 1925.

Dictionary of World Myth: An A-Z Reference Guide to Gods, Goddesses, Heroes, Heroines and Fabulous Beasts. London: Duncan Baird, 1995.

Estés, Clarissa Pinkola. *Women Who Run with the Wolves: Myths and Stories of the Wild Woman Archetype.* New York: Ballantine, 1992.

Frobenius, Leo. *The Voice of Africa.* Vol. 1. London: Hutchinson, 1913.

Frymer-Kensky, Tikva. *In the Wake of the Goddesses: Women, Culture, and the Biblical Transformation of Pagan Myth.* New York: Free Press, 1992.

Gimbutas, Marija. *The Language of the Goddess.* New York: Thames and Hudson, 1989.

Husain, Shahrukh. *The Goddess.* Alexandria: Time-Life, 1997.

Jackson, John J. *Man, God and Civilization.* New Hyde Park: University Book, 1972.

Johnston, Jill. *Lesbian Nation: The Feminist Solution.* New York: Simon and Schuster, 1973.

Jordan, Michael. *Encyclopedia of Gods: Over 2,500 Deities of the World.* New York: Facts on File, 2003.

Mallory, Devona. "Phillis Wheatley." *The Greenwood Encyclopedia of African American Literature.* Ed. Hans Ostrom and J. David Macey Jr. Vol. 5. Westport: Greenwood, 2005. 1721–24.

McKay, Michele, and William J. Scheick. "The Other Song in Phillis Wheatley's 'On Imagination.'" *Studies in the Literary Imagination* 27.1 (Spring 1994): 73–84.

Neuman, Erich. *The Great Mother: An Analysis of the Archetype.* Princeton: Princeton UP, 1963.

The Oxford Classical Dictionary. Ed. Simon Hornblower and Antony Spawforth. 3rd ed. Oxford: Oxford UP, 1996.

The Oxford Companion to Classical Literature. M. C. Howatson. 2nd ed. Oxford: Oxford UP, 1989.

Shields, John C., ed. *The Collected Works of Phillis Wheatley.* New York: Oxford UP, 1988.

Sjöö, Monica, and Barbara Mor. *The Great Cosmic Mother: Rediscovering the Religion of the Earth.* San Francisco: Harper, 1991.

Wheatley, Phillis. *The Collected Works of Phillis Wheatley.* Ed. John C. Shields. New York: Oxford UP, 1988.

Devona Mallory

The Interaction of the Classical Traditions of Literature and Politics in the Work of Phillis Wheatley

Karen Lerner Dovell

Phillis Wheatley, the first published African American woman writer, draws upon the Western classical tradition to assert poetic authority, and to argue for slaves' rights to liberty.[1] In the mid-eighteenth century, classical poetics and literary conventions were strictly observed by those who wished to demonstrate cultural authority in the New World. In addition to literary classicism, political classicism was an important aspect of the "cult of antiquity" in the Revolutionary period.[2] Early Americans absorbed the political classical tradition from the literatures of Greek and Roman antiquity, and through the classical republicanism of the seventeenth-century British Whig tradition. Throughout the eighteenth century, classical tradition provided political exemplars and terms that became central elements in Revolutionary discourse (Reinhold 94–115).[3] Wheatley claims a place in this literary classical tradition; she also appropriates political classical conceptions of liberty, natural law, and virtue. Her use of the literary and political classical tradition presents a counter-discourse to Enlightenment racial theories. Wheatley's works contrast the professed ideals of political classical tradition and Revolutionary discourse with the material reality of her own status as both poet and slave.[4]

Wheatley's knowledge of the classical tradition was extensive. She was kidnapped from Africa at age seven, brought to America on the schooner *Phillis,* and sold to John and Susannah Wheatley, wealthy New England Congregationalists. In contrast to their treatment of their other household slaves, the Wheatleys permitted her to learn, and to receive instruction in Latin and the classics. She learned quickly to read and to speak English. Canonical classical texts were made available to her in the Wheatley home, and from the neighbors' libraries. She absorbed the classics and contemporary histories of antiquity, and began to write poetry and to publish in newspapers by the time she was fourteen.

Wheatley's works incorporate her classical education, the Congregationalist faith into which she was inducted as a slave, and her earliest memories of Africa. The juxtaposition of these elements in her works may be informed by Julia Kristeva's theory of intertextuality, which posits a symbiotic relationship between texts that alters discourses, as well as subject-positions (59–60).[5] As Aldon Nielsen notes, intertextuality in this sense refers not only to "direct textual sources"; it also suggests "the transposition of sign systems leading to a new positionality. From the moment Africans were forced to adopt English as their primary tongue in America, the sort of intertextuality described by Kristeva in her *Revolution in Poetic Language* was inevitable" (22–24). According to Aimable Twagilimana, African American writers have used intertextuality as one strategy with which they can "counter" the "erasure of identity, history, and memory" and the "ontological absence" which resulted from slavery (ix). Other critics find similarly dynamic, multiple subject-positions and discursive strategies in Wheatley's work.[6] This critical understanding recognizes agency in and through discourse, and illuminates Wheatley's inscriptions of discursive identity as poet, slave, citizen, muse, and her memory of Africa.

Wheatley's book of poetry and letters, *Poems on Various Subjects, Religious and Moral,* published in London in 1773 after Boston publishers had rejected the proposal in 1772, amply demonstrates her classical knowledge.[7] As Lucy K. Hayden notes, twenty-six of thirty-nine poems in Wheatley's book contain direct references to or allusions to classical myth (433). Wheatley also included her own, original translation of a section of Ovid's *Metamorphoses* in one of the two epyllia, or short epics, which appear in *Poems.* Her familiarity with classical poetics is apparent in her adaptations of the pastoral, Horatian ode, and elegy in her work (Shields, "Use of Classicism" 97–98). In addition to the works of Homer, Ovid, Virgil, and Pope, she is known to have read the work of John Milton, and owned her own copy of *Paradise Lost.*[8]

As a slave, Wheatley's classical knowledge was suspect. As Henry Louis Gates Jr. writes, "[s]ince the beginning of the sixteenth century, Europeans had wondered aloud whether or not the African 'species of men,' as they were most commonly called, *could* ever create formal literature, could ever master 'the arts and sciences'" ("Foreword" ix). For example, Thomas Jefferson, in *Notes on the State of Virginia,* wrote:

Karen Lerner Dovell

[The Roman's] slaves were often their rarest artists. They excelled too in science, insomuch as to be usefully employed as tutors to their masters's children. . . . But they were of the race of whites. It is not their [African slaves'] condition, then, but nature, which produced the distinction. (qtd. in Richard 96)[9]

In order to authenticate Wheatley's poems, John Wheatley assembled a group of "the most respectable characters in Boston," including the governor, Thomas Hutchinson, and John Hancock, to question Wheatley on her classical knowledge and confirm that her work was her own. They attested her ability in a prefatory note addressed "to the Publick," which was included in her book. Wheatley repeatedly associates herself, and Africa, with the classical tradition in her works, appropriating and displacing this cultural authority.

Prior to the Revolutionary period, this classical tradition provided a means of diverging from Great Britain and, by extension, with the whole of Western civilization. According to Carl J. Richard, knowledge of the classics gave the founders "a sense of identity and purpose, assuring [them] that their exertions were part of a grand universal scheme" (8). Early Americans believed that the westward progression of civilization, embodied in the classical concepts of *translatio imperii* and *translatio studii*, was destined to be carried out in America. As Anders Stephanson explains, *translatio imperii* was an "imperial theme" in the eighteenth century; it referred to "the agreeable double notion that civilization was always carried forward by a single dominant power or people and that historical succession was a matter of westward movement" (18). *Translatio studii* referred to the classical body of knowledge that accompanied this progression.

The concept of *translatio* was expressed in Bishop Berkeley's 1725 poem, "Verses on the Prospect of the Arts and Learning in America": "Westward the course of empire takes its way / The four first acts already past / A fifth shall close the drama with the day / Time's noblest offspring is the last." The *translatio* was associated with a covenantal sense of American national identity and purpose (Stephanson 17–20).[10] Patriot Whigs, responding to perceived abuses of power by Great Britain, saw these encroachments as signs of corruption, similar to that which took place in the Roman republic (Richard 52).

Recent historiography clarifies the complex relationship between the political classical tradition and American Revolutionary discourse. While prior scholarship emphasized the role of modern liberalism in this discourse, historians now advance the "republican hypothesis," which emphasizes the role of classical republicanism and political classical tradition in the Revolutionary period.[11] Bernard Bailyn, in his *The Ideological Origins of the American Revolution*, first identified the importance of political classicism in pre-Revolutionary American culture. Bailyn analyzed several hundred early American pamphlets concerning the Revolutionary cause, including "treatises on political theory, essays on history, political arguments, sermons, correspondence, [and] poems" (v). His research showed that in contrast to earlier assumptions, Revolutionary discourse developed from the classical republican belief that England's monarchy was corrupt, and would erode American liberty (v–vi, ix). The rhetoric of slavery and liberty, eventually used by American Whigs to describe their relationship with Great Britain, was derived at least as much from political classical tradition as from Enlightenment liberalism and covenantal Christianity.

In recognizing the significance of this classical political tradition, the republican hypothesis effected a shift in American historiography. Subsequently, historians acknowledge the classical background of the concepts of virtue, liberty, and natural law. Early Americans viewed all the classical discourses as part of the "tradition of liberty," drawing on Greek and Roman literary and political writings, and on classically based British Whig thought (Richard 52). The tradition of liberty was central to Revolutionary American discourse.

As both Shields and Betsy Erkkila discuss, Wheatley was a poet of the American Revolution. Shields asserts that her poems "should grant her recognition as certainly the most ardent female poet of the Revolution, if not, along with Philip Freneau, as one of its two most prominent poetic defenders" ("Struggle for Freedom" 240). According to Erkkila, Wheatley "transformed the revolutionary discourse on liberty, natural rights and human nature into a subtle critique of the color code and the oppressive racial structure of republican America" (201). Her appropriation of literary and political classical tradition contributes to this critique.

Wheatley's letter to Reverend Samson Occom, a Mohegan Native American minister, alludes to the classical conceptions of liberty and natural law that informed Revolutionary discourse, and connects them with natural rights for Africans: "I have this Day received your obliging kind epistle, and am greatly satisfied with your Reasons respecting the Negroes, and think highly reasonable what you offer in Vindication of their natural Rights" (176). She asserts that "the Chaos which has reigned so long [in Africa], is converting into beautiful Order, and reveals more and more clearly, the glorious Dispensation of civil and religious Liberty . . ." (176). Wheatley suggests the incongruity of slavery in her Bostonian cultural context: "How well the Cry for Liberty, and the reverse Disposition for the Exercise of oppressive Power over others agree,—I humbly think it does not require the Penetration of a Philosopher to determine" (177). As Anders Stephanson notes, the "embodiment of that central American anomaly, [the] slave master was also the quintessential exponent of standard Enlightenment ideas about rationality, human agency, and natural rights for everyone" (16). Wheatley writes eloquently that "in every human Breast, God has implanted a Principle, which we call Love of Freedom . . . and by the Leave of our Modern Egyptians I will assert, that the same principle lives in us" (177). In so doing, she argues for the humanity of slaves, and for their right to liberty.[12]

In calling for civil liberty for Africans, Wheatley implicitly asserts their innate personal and civic virtue. As Meyer Reinhold notes, the founders were "committed to the pursuit of virtue as the bulwark of freedom under a republic" (*Classica Americana* 144). According to a political vein found in the classical tradition, the promotion of virtue would forestall decay and ensure the historical existence of the republic. Classical virtue was related to the Aristotelian belief in *zoon politikon* (man is a political animal); in service to the republic, man achieves his highest and best capabilities (Pocock 98, 517–18).[13] The classical Stoic theory of natural law held that virtue was innate; virtue was attributed to an essentialized, inborn reason, and it was to be nurtured and expressed through service to the *polis*. Wheatley participated in the American discourse of revolution and liberty, which continually invoked these classical precedents and ideals, as completely as possible for one who had to mediate not only her own condition of slavery, but also the loyalist sympathies of her owner, John Wheatley.

Wheatley's classical knowledge contradicted the belief that slaves were not capable of virtue. The title of her book, *Poems on Various Subjects, Religious and Moral*, suggests the importance of secular as well as Christian moral instruction in pre-Revolutionary American culture. This secular aspect was taught through the study of classics as useful knowledge, in order to promote a virtuous republic. In Puritan New England, classical education was encouraged as a means of teaching virtue and morality (Reinhold 51–54). *Poems* begins with Wheatley's appropriation of the literary classical tradition; she subsequently claims political classical ideals as well.

In "To Maecenas," Wheatley addresses the Muses directly, asking why more Africans are not included in literary classical tradition. She cites Terence, a Roman playwright, poet, and one-time slave whose pen freed him, noting that he was an African:

> The happier *Terence* all the choir inspir'd
> His soul replenish'd, and his bosom fir'd
> But say, ye *Muses,* why this partial grace
> To one alone of *Afric's* sable race;
> From age to age transmitting thus his name
> With the first glory in the rolls of fame? (11)

Wheatley then boldly asserts to Maecenas, a patron of the arts, that she too will be a great poet: "I'll snatch a laurel from thine honour'd head / While you indulgent smile upon the deed." In calling attention to the singular presence of an African male slave within the literary classical tradition, and claiming a place for herself, she calls attention to the racialized and gendered limits of this tradition. Wheatley thus legitimates for her white audience the authority with which she makes her political claims for freedom. By asserting her place in the literary classical tradition, she connects herself to the *translatio,* and to the classical tradition of liberty. According to histories of antiquity, Terence was eventually freed due to his ability as a writer. Wheatley is "less happy" than Terence because, at this point, she "cannot raise the song"; she is not yet free.

In addressing the Muses directly, Wheatley's poems further convey her claims to a place in the classical tradition. In "Thoughts on the Works of Providence," she asks the "celestial muse" to "sustain" her "arduous flight" and "raise" her mind "to a seraphic strain" (43). Similarly, in "An Hymn to the Morning," Wheatley importunes:

> Attend my lays, ye ever honor'd nine,
> Assist my labours, and my strains refine;
> In smoothest numbers pour the notes along,
> For bright *Aurora* now demands my song. (56)

Wheatley claims the role of muse for herself, against the conventions of classical tradition, in "To His Honour the Lieutenant-Governor, on the Death of His Lady. March 24, 1773":

> *Virtue's* rewards can mortal pencil paint?
> No—all descriptive arts, and eloquence are faint;
> Nor canst thou, *Oliver,* assent refuse
> To heav'nly tidings from the *Afric* muse. (117)

Karen Lerner Dovell

In "An Hymn to Humanity," Wheatley also assertively refers to herself as "*Afric's* muse." She depicts herself as a source of inspiration who can recognize and convey virtue, and thereby associates herself with the classical tradition, specifically as an African poet and muse.

"An Hymn to the Morning," in alluding to the rising of the sun, suggests her earliest memories of Africa. Margaretta Matilda Odell, Susanna Wheatley's great-grand-niece, claimed in her memoirs that the only thing Wheatley remembered about her childhood in Africa was her mother's morning ritual of "pouring out water before the rising sun." As critics note, a pattern of references connecting the morning and the sun with Africa is evident in Wheatley's poetry (Shields, "Use of Classicism" 103–4).[14] In "An Hymn to the Morning," Wheatley's early memory associates the morning, "Aurora," the Roman goddess of the dawn, with Africa as well as with the muse. She invokes the presence of Apollo, the sun god, in this image: "See in the east the illustrious king of day! / His rising radiance drives the shades away" (57). Wheatley's use of pastoral images further connects Africa with the classical tradition, as she calls upon the Muses to "Attend my lays, ye ever honour'd nine / Assist my labours, and my strains refine." As Shields notes, Wheatley frequently "employed the pastoral mode [and] manipulated it in a subversive manner" ("Subversive Pastoral" 631). Wheatley's reference to the Muses who "refine" her "strains" suggests the "refinement" associated with incorporating the classical tradition into her verse.

Wheatley also alludes to "refinement" in one of her most frequently debated poems, "On Being Brought from Africa to America":

> Twas mercy brought me from my *Pagan* land
> Taught my benighted soul to understand
> That there's a God, that there's a Saviour too:
> Once I redemption neither sought nor knew.
> Some view our sable race with scornful eye,
> "Their color is a diabolic die." (18)

Here, Wheatley refers to Africa as a "Pagan land," and writes that it "twas mercy" that brought her to America. But her claims for her own association with the classical tradition, and the connection she makes between this tradition and Africa in other works, are reinforced in the admonishing final couplet: "Remember, *Christians, Negroes,* black as *Cain* / May be refin'd, and join th' angelic train." In addition to the Christian context of these words, her assertion that Africans "may be refin'd" also gestures toward classical knowledge and inspiration as hallmarks of culture. The poem signals a connection between Africa and the value ascribed to classical knowledge, and suggests that knowledge and "refinement" may also be found outside of the context of the Western, Berkelyean *translatio.*

In the poem "On Virtue," Wheatley again associates herself with the innate goodness of natural law and with the capacity for virtue:

> O Thou bright jewel in my aim I strive
> To comprehend thee. Thine own words declare
> Wisdom is higher than a fool can reach.
> But, O my soul, sink not into despair,
> Virtue is near thee. . . . (13)

Although "wisdom is higher than a fool can reach," virtue is "near" and attainable:

> Auspicious queen, thine heav'nly pinions spread
> And lead celestial *Chastity* along;
> Array'd in glory from the orbs above
> Attend me, Virtue, thro' my youthful years!
>   . . .
> Teach me a better strain, a nobler lay,
> O thou, enthron'd with Cherubs in the realms
>   of day! (13–14)

This poem implies a distinction between classical and Christian virtue, in that virtue "lead[s] celestial *Chastity* along." It suggests as well that wisdom alone is not enough to "comprehend" virtue; virtue is itself a form of knowledge that will teach her, as she writes in the final stanza, "a better strain." Wheatley thus aligns herself with virtue, natural law, and useful knowledge.

The interaction of the literary and political classical traditions in her work is evident in "On Recollection"; she identifies herself as a "vent'rous *Afric*" who claims poetic authority, and aligns herself with natural law and classical virtue. Here, Wheatley starts by addressing the muse of memory: "Mneme begin. Inspire, ye sacred nine / Your vent'rous *Afric* in her great design" (62). She subsequently promises to honor and give voice to memory:

Karen Lerner Dovell

> *Mneme,* immortal pow'r, I trace thy spring:
> Assist my strains, while I thy glories sing:
> The acts of long departed years, by thee
> Recover'd, in due order ranged we see:
> Thy pow'r the long-forgotten calls from night,
> That sweetly plays before the *fancy's* sight. (62)

In this poem, Wheatley inscribes herself as the beginning of African American history and tradition; her "poetic persona *is* the memory of her own 'sable race'— she is *Afric's* muse, and so she wields the weapon of racial memory" (Watson 126). Memory is "dreaded by the race" that "scorn her warnings and despise her grace"; as memory, Wheatley bears perpetual witness to the crimes of those who brought the slave trade to the colonies, and she will remember those who perpetuate it. Memory recognizes and rewards virtue: "*Mneme,* enthron'd within the human breast / Has vice condemned, and ev'ry virtue blest."

In the penultimate stanza, Wheatley addresses virtue directly:

> O *Virtue,* smiling in immortal green,
> Do thou exert thy pow'r, and change the scene,
> Be thine employ to guide my future days,
> And mine to pay the tribute of my praise. (64)

The power of virtue to "change the scene" suggests the classical understanding of virtue for the public good. Wheatley connects natural law with memory in the final stanza: "Of *Recollection* such the pow'r enthron'd / In ev'ry breast, and thus her pow'r is own'd" (64). The seeds of memory are contained within, as is the natural capacity for goodness, reason, and virtue; Wheatley claims ownership of this power, along with her power as a poet.

Wheatley's intertextuality draws on classical and Christian discourses; she deploys the classical and Christian values inherent in the republican conception of virtue to assert poetic authority. As Richard notes, in classical Stoic terms, "virtue was rewarded here, as well as in the next life, through self-respect and the respect of others." In mid-eighteenth-century American culture, fame was considered virtue's highest reward in this life, but not without some tension between classical and Christian virtue: "'fame' referred to the praise of one's few virtuous contemporaries and of posterity . . . the founders' emphasis upon fame as the principal reward of virtue was incompatible with Christian humility and the need to recognize that pride was folly" (Richard 186).

Wheatley addresses this tension between classical virtue and Christian humility in her epyllion, "Niobe in Distress for her Children slain by Apollo, from Ovid's *Metamorphoses*, Book VI, and from a View of the Painting of Mr. Richard Wilson" (101–13). According to Ovid, Niobe is excessively prideful concerning her wealth, and her parentage of seven sons and seven daughters. She claims to outdo the goddess Latona (mother of Apollo and Artemis), asserting she should be worshiped in Latona's place, since she has produced more children. For this sin of pride, Apollo and Phoebe slaughter all of Niobe's children; Niobe, in grief, is turned to stone. In early American literature, the Roman Empire itself was sometimes referred to as "the Niobe of nations" (Miles 341). While Wheatley does condemn avarice and deficient humility in this poem, she also demonstrates sympathy for Niobe's plight.

The painting mentioned in the title of Wheatley's poem, a rendering of the Niobe myth by the English landscape artist Richard Wilson (1713–1782), was titled "The Destruction of the Children of Niobe." In contrast to other depictions of the Niobe myth, this version, one of four painted by Wilson, foregrounds the deaths of the children, calling attention to Niobe's loss, rather than to her alleged sin.

As classicist Karl Kerenyi asserts, Niobe, a goddess from Asia Minor, was associated in Greek mythology with the "dark phase" of the moon, the principle of disorder and sin, the "primordial mother of the human race." Kerenyi also finds an association with Prometheus, who also overreached his place, and who "bore the human condition as something eternal." Kerenyi notes that "the throne of the Olympian Zeus, the Zeus of Phidias, was decorated" with images of the death of Niobe's children, and claims this myth suggests the centrality of their sacrifice to the construction of a divine order in classical antiquity. Niobe can be understood as representative, not of the sin of excessive pride per se, but rather as the bearer, like Prometheus, of the human condition, "the inevitability of human error and suffering" (61–70).

This understanding of the Niobe figure suggests another dimension to Wheatley's views on pride and virtue. Rather than accept her assigned place in the neoclassical order of things, Wheatley's counter-discourse inscribes her as "*Afric's* muse," the voice and memory of her people under slavery. Wheatley's main revision of Ovid's original version occurs toward the end, when Niobe is turned to stone; as Shields asserts, instead of "simply narrating Niobe's hurt pride" at her loss, Wheatley interpolates four lines in which she calls for vengeance from Jove ("Use of Classicism" 110). Wheatley also adds a line in which

Karen Lerner Dovell

Niobe's pleas to spare one child are echoed back to her, doubling her voice as well as the intensity of her pain:

> One only daughter lives, and she the least;
> The queen close clasp'd the daughter to her breast:
> "Ye heav'nly pow'rs, ah spare me one," she cry'd,
> "Ah! Spare me one," the vocal hills reply'd:
> In vain she begs, the Fates her suit deny,
> In her embrace she sees her daughter die. (112)

As Shields notes, "this resounding of the queen's grief throughout nature increases the intensity of her punishment" ("Use of Classicism" 110).

According to Lucy K. Hayden, the echo "intensifies the pathos" of Niobe's loss; Wheatley's Niobe, at this point in the poem, is both "more soft and tearful" and "more self-sacrificing and heroic" than in Ovid's version (438–43). Although the final stanza follows Ovid's original, Wheatley adds a footnote to explain that this section is "the Work of another Hand." Her version, then, concludes with the stanza cited above. In empowering Niobe with a voice, and underscoring her grief, Wheatley's poem suggests sympathy for Niobe's "folly of pride," and portrays her as ultimately virtuous. And after all, Wheatley insists, as Ovid does not, that Niobe is "all beautiful in woe" (101).

In "To Captain H—D, of the 65th Regiment," Wheatley praises civic virtue for the public good. Addressing the muse directly once more, Wheatley associates herself with the literary and political classical traditions, and assimilates them to the patriot cause:

> Say, muse divine, can hostile scenes delight
> The warrior's bosom in the fields of fight?
> Lo! here the christian, and the hero join
> With mutual grace to form the man divine.
> . . .
> Still to the field, and still to virtue true:
> *Britannia* glories in no son like you. (72)

The final line of the poem expresses Wheatley's praise of an American soldier. She explores the ideal of classical virtue in Revolutionary discourse by joining the "christian" with the "hero" in the "man divine." In conflating the republican and Christian sense of virtue, the poem reflects the conception of liberty derived from political classical tradition in pre-Revolutionary American culture.

In some respects, the political classical tradition and modern liberal thought were at odds in the Revolutionary period. The growth of commerce associated with liberalism was a matter of concern in the political classical tradition, which attributed the decline of Rome to the rise of commerce and individual interests in the classical republic. The tension between republicanism and liberalism in eighteenth-century American culture is most often described in terms of the conflict between virtue and commerce. According to political classical tradition, commerce was "the antithesis of 'virtue.' In a commercialized and professionalized world, men were not virtuous, [and there existed] a tension between 'virtue' and 'commerce' sufficiently ancient by 1776 to dispell any idea that a 'Lockean consensus' existed before that time" (Pocock, "Virtue and Commerce" 132). Although the rise of commerce was promoted in many ways, the tension between classical republicanism and liberalism, while not categorized as such at the time, suggests a conflicted sense of political identity in Revolutionary discourse. Liberal individualism and the rise of commerce contravened classical conceptions of virtue, natural law, and liberty, which were at odds with modern, civil political identity (Appleby 282).[15] Wheatley's position as a slave, a commodity in the American growth of commerce, further complicates this conflict, as two of her extant poems, "America" and "Liberty and Peace," suggest.

On one level of signification, "America" tells of the troubled relationship between Great Britain and the colonies. This relationship is described in accord with the tradition of liberty, in terms of mother and child, or master and slave. The child, "americus," feels the "iron chain" of the master/slave relationship, and Wheatley calls for "Brittania" to remember the "kindred" nature between America and itself. She depicts New England as "a wilderness" destined to be "a continent" in the first couplet, suggesting the covenantal paradigm of errand or mission that was embedded in the early American classical *translatio,* which would enable the transition from unruly primitive to civilized classical humanism.

But Wheatley also problematizes these ideas, introducing difference with the following two couplets:

> From feild to feild the savage monsters run
> E'r yet Brittania had her work begun
> Thy Power, O Liberty, makes strong the weak
> And (wond'rous instinct) Ethiopians speak. (134)

Karen Lerner Dovell

The first couplet seems, on first reading, to refer to Native Americans as they were then perceived, but the poem subsequently works against this racial slur and suggests several other connotations. The second couplet calls attention to the oppression of both Native Americans and Ethiopians, and recalls Wheatley's description of herself as "an *Ethiop*" in an earlier poem, "To the University of Cambridge in New England" (16). Classical liberty will empower them; even if it is not granted to them directly, by "wond'rous instinct" they will "speak." The couplet also suggests the benefits of useful knowledge inherent in political classical tradition, embodied here through "Liberty," and the capability of so-called savages to comprehend and benefit from this knowledge. The reference to "instinct" suggests innate capacity, implied by the classical conception of natural law.

The first line of the fourth couplet alludes to the previous reference to Ethiopians, and suggests a connection between the patriot cause and the situation for slaves:

> Sometimes by Simile, a victory's won
> A certain lady had an only son
> He grew up daily virtuous as he grew
> Fearing his strength which she undoubted knew
> She laid some taxes on her darling son
> And would have laid another act there on.
> (134)

The rest of the poem continues to compare America's relationship to Great Britain with slavery, as Wheatley implicitly calls into question the terms of classical liberty and virtue in this context. Moreover, the poem introduces commerce as a solution to the troubled relationships it depicts. Addressing "Brittania," Wheatley cites the example of Agenoria, the Roman goddess who calls men to action, and who "diligent imploys / her sons":

> Arise my sons with one consent arise
> Lest distant continents with vult'ring eyes
> Should charge America with Negligence
> They praise Industry but no pride commence
> To raise their own Profusion, O Britain See
> By this New England will increase like thee.
> (135)

This poem suggests that commerce will benefit both countries, working together; "diligent" and industrious employment will permit America to "increase like" Great Britain. The word "like" refers back to the simile mentioned earlier in the poem, connoting the potentially comparable benefits for America if it will be similarly just with its slaves. However, Wheatley also problematizes the "Profusion" of commerce, since it was of course dependent on slave labor in America at that time.

"Liberty and Peace," one of Wheatley's last poems, was written one year after the end of the Revolutionary War. This poem reflects the accelerating growth of commerce in this period, and connects it directly to the ideals of the classical political tradition. Wheatley begins by reiterating her discursive presence, firmly established throughout her earlier works, as the "prescient Muse" who "foretold" the triumph of liberty and freedom. Through this reassertion of poetic authority, first rendered in "To His Excellency George Washington," Wheatley again appropriates political as well as literary classical tradition: "Lo! Freedom comes. Th' prescient Muse foretold, / All Eyes th' accomplish'd Prophecy behold" (154). Freedom, or the goddess of Liberty, is depicted in classical as well as Christian terms; "laurel bind[s]" her hair, and she is also the "bright Progeny of Heaven." America, no longer the diminutive "americus," is now "Columbia," in which "kind Heaven" will "shine." In the following two couplets, Columbia, thus blessed, is now free to participate fully in the growth of commerce, associated with classical humanism as well as Enlightenment science:

> To every Realm her Portals open'd wide,
> Receives from each the full commercial Tide.
> Each Art and Science now with rising Charms
> Th'expanding Heart with Emulation warms. (154)

Wheatley goes on to assert that America, as "new-born *Rome*," will now "give *Britannia* Law," and condemns Britain for its excessive "Thirst of boundless Power." This phrase recalls the decay and corruption inherent in the degeneration of monarchies according to the classical political tradition. This degeneration was the cause of the failure of appeals to commonality between Britain and America, which Wheatley had called for in the earlier "America":

> The Muse's Ear hears mother Earth deplore
> Her ample Surface smoak with kindred Gore:

> The hostile Field destroys the social Ties,
> And every-lasting Slumber seals their Eyes.
> (155)

"Liberty and Peace" continues to describe, in epic terms, America's battle for liberty. Wheatley invokes Apollo in describing the war's conclusion; the classical god accompanies heavenly freedom:

> As for the East th'illustrious King of Day,
> With rising Radiance drives the Shades away,
> So Freedom comes array'd with Charms divine, And
> in her Train Commerce and Plenty shine. (135)

Wheatley deploys the image of Apollo, god of the sun, to mark the advent of prosperity and peace under the auspices of liberty. Given the association of Apollo, and the sun, with Wheatley's earliest memories, her classicism again recalls her ties to Africa, and connects her with revolutionary freedom. The interaction of literary and political classical traditions in Wheatley's work, together with her use of Christian and African references, intertextually inscribes her roles as poet, citizen, slave, and muse, and her memory of Africa.

NOTES

1. Recent criticism acknowledges Wheatley's appropriation of literary classical tradition. This essay continues to explore Wheatley's classicism, particularly with respect to her use of political classical tradition. See, for example, Paula Bennett, "Phillis Wheatley's Vocation and the Paradox of the 'Afric Muse'"; Lucy K. Hayden, "Classical Tidings from the Afric Muse: Phillis Wheatley's Use of Greek and Roman Mythology"; John C. Shields, "Phillis Wheatley's Use of Classicism" and "Phillis Wheatley's Subversive Pastoral." Aimable Twagilimana contends that Wheatley transforms literary neoclassicism in constructing discursive African American identity. See *Race and Gender in the Making of an African American Literary Tradition,* 46–47. Marsha Watson cites Wheatley's "active transformation" of "Anglo-European literary tradition," and asserts she transgresses conventional neoclassicism through the intertextuality of classical texts in her works. See "A Classic Case: Phillis Wheatley and Her Poetry." Carla Willard discusses

Wheatley's use of neoclassical praise conventions in "Wheatley's Turns of Praise: Heroic Entrapment and the Paradox of Revolution." With respect to political classical tradition, Phillip M. Richards cites the work of Bailyn, and contends that Wheatley's blend of "millennial and Whig strands of thought" was part of "Revolutionary rhetoric," which she deployed in her "attack on slavery." He situates Wheatley's work in the context of the "black appropriation of civic humanism, Puritanism and liberalism," and discusses her work with respect to liberty and natural rights. Richards focuses on Wheatley's poems in the context of republicanism, civic humanism, and Whig discourse in his "Phillis Wheatley and Literary Americanization."

2. In *Classica Americana,* Meyer Reinhold discusses the "cult of antiquity" that informed the construction of national identity, citizenship, and Revolutionary discourse:

> Evidence abounds for an American cult of antiquity during the
> eighteenth century, particularly during the second half: the ubiq-
> uitous classical quotations and tags; the common use of classical
> pseudonyms; the revival of classical place names, the constant
> adducing of classical parallels; even the use of classical names for
> slaves in the Southern states. Overshadowing all these was the
> tireless and purposeful reading by early Americans of the classics
> as a repository of timeless models for guidance in republicanism
> and private and civic virtue. (24)

3. More recently, John C. Shields makes clear the significance of classical discourse to the formation of American national and cultural identity, particularly with respect to the myth of Aeneas and to Virgil's *Aeneid* as an unacknowledged and effaced founding myth of the "American self." The "forgotten classical half of the American cultural self" is in tension with biblical discourse and the Adamic *mythos* (x). He "assert[s] that a distinctly American classicism dominated Early American thought and action during the period 1720–90" (155). See Shields, *The American Aeneas: Classical Origins of the American Self.*

4. In *The History of Sexuality,* Foucault asserts that "discourse can be not only an instrument and an effect of power, but also a hindrance, a stumbling-block, a point of resistance and a starting point for an opposing strategy" (1: 101, qtd. in McCabe 3). Arguably, counter-discourse allows for agency, both

Karen Lerner Dovell

in and through discourse. In "The Practical Theorizing of Michel Foucault: Politics and Counterdiscourse," Mario Moussa and Ron Scapp assert that although Foucault has been "criticized for lacking a theory of agency," his theory of counter-discourse encourages what they term "radical agency," through which the "formerly voiceless might begin to articulate their desires—to *counter* the domination of prevailing authoritative discourses" (88).

5. On Wheatley's use of intertextuality, see, for example, Nielsen; Twagilimana ix, 51–52; Shields, *American Aeneas* 225.

6. Bennett, Carole Boyce-Davies, and Paul Gilroy discuss Wheatley's work in the context of migratory and "transnational" poetic identity (Bennett 66). See Boyce-Davies, *Black Women, Writing and Identity: Migrations of the Subject;* see also Gilroy, *The Black Atlantic: Modernity and Double Consciousness.*

7. All subsequent references to Wheatley's works are taken from *The Collected Works of Phillis Wheatley,* ed. John C. Shields. *CW* refers to extant works not included in the original text of *Poems,* but included in the *Collected Works.*

8. On Milton's role in American political classical tradition, see Pocock, *Machiavellian Moment* 507. For a discussion of Milton's significance in African American literature and in Wheatley's work, see Carolivia Herron, "Milton and African-American Literature," *Re-membering Milton: Essays in the Texts and Traditions,* edited by Mary Nyquist and Margaret W. Ferguson.

9. On Enlightenment racial theories, see also David Bidney, "The Idea of the Savage in North American Ethnohistory"; Donald J. D'Elia, "Dr. Benjamin Rush and the Negro"; and John C. Greene, "The American Debate on the Negro's Place in Nature, 1780–1815," all in Shuffleton 97–102, 116–25, 103–15, respectively.

10. See also Gordon S. Wood, *The Creation of the American Republic, 1776–1787.* Shields originates the phrase "translatio cultus" to describe the transfer of Christian and classical discourses from Old World to New World; these discourses "carried with them cultural imperatives that ultimately determined the idea of the American self." See Shields, *American Aeneas* 3–37.

11. Though Bailyn does not use the term "republican hypothesis," later historians use it to refer to his theory and the scholarship engendered by his

work. Bailyn's work on the function of political classical tradition in American culture led to the historiographical revision that provides the context for my discussion of Wheatley's classicism. Bailyn's research resulted in numerous critical debates about the relative importance and effects of classical and liberal thought in eighteenth-century American culture, but historians agree that political classical tradition played a central, if not decisive, part in initiating the revolution. The following works rehearse key critical debates and conclusions about the republican hypothesis: Joyce Appleby, *Liberalism and Republicanism in the Historical Imagination;* Lance Banning, "Jeffersonian Ideology Revisited: Liberal and Classical Ideas in the New American Republic"; J. G. A. Pocock, *The Machiavellian Moment: Florentine Political Thought and the Atlantic Republican Tradition;* and Robert E. Shalhope, *The Roots of Democracy: American Thought and Culture, 1760–1800.* Frank Shuffleton provides a concise overview of the parameters and significance of these critical discussions in *The American Enlightenment,* ix–xxiii.

With respect to Wheatley criticism in this context, Betsy Erkkila cites Bailyn's work and contends Wheatley transformed the Revolutionary discourse Bailyn identifies. See "Revolutionary Women." Shields cites Wheatley as a poet of the revolution in his "Phillis Wheatley's Struggle for Freedom in Her Poetry and Prose." Helen Burke discusses Wheatley's use of "her new country's political as well as its poetical ideology" in writing of liberty and criticizing slavery, though not in the context of political classical tradition. See "Problematizing American Dissent: The Subject of Phillis Wheatley." Carla Willard also cites Wheatley's appropriation of revolutionary and republican discourse.

12. On the association between natural law and natural rights in political classical tradition and American Revolutionary discourse, see Richard 169–83.

13. Shields identifies civic virtue with Virgilian *pietas,* rather than Machiavellian *virtu;* he contends that *pietas,* a Roman virtue consisting of duty to God, family, and country, accounts for the dual presence of biblical and classical discourses that inform American identity and culture. Shields locates a "feminized *pietas*" in Wheatley's works. See *American Aeneas,* xxviii–xlv; 231–34.

14. See also Hayden 435.

15. Appleby uses the term "spiritual crisis" to describe Pocock's view of the conflict between classical and liberal thought in eighteenth-century

American culture. Appleby places more emphasis on the role of liberalism; Pocock privileges political classicism, and sees the conflict as acute.

WORKS CITED

Appleby, Joyce. *Liberalism and Republicanism in the Historical Imagination.* Cambridge: Harvard UP, 1992.

Bailyn, Bernard. *The Ideological Origins of the American Revolution.* Cambridge: Harvard UP, 1967.

Banning, Lance. "Jeffersonian Ideology Revisited: Liberal and Classical Ideas in the New American Republic." *William and Mary Quarterly* 43 (1986): 3–20.

Bennett, Paula. "Phillis Wheatley's Vocation and the Paradox of the 'African Muse.'" *PMLA* 133.1 (1998): 64–76.

Boyce-Davies, Carole. *Black Women, Writing and Identity: Migrations of the Subject.* New York: Routledge, 1994.

Burke, Helen. "Problematizing American Dissent: The Subject of Phillis Wheatley." *Cohesion and Dissent in America.* Ed. Carol Colatrella and Joseph Alkana. Albany: SUNY P, 1994. 193–209.

Erkkila, Betsy. "Revolutionary Women." *Tulsa Studies in Women's Literature* 6 (1987): 189–223.

Foucault, Michel. *A History of Sexuality.* Trans. Robert Hurley. 3 vols. Vol. 1. New York: Vintage, 1980.

Gates, Henry Louis, Jr. *Figures in Black: Words, Signs and the "Racial" Self.* New York: Oxford UP, 1987.

———. "Foreword: In Her Own Write." *The Collected Works of Phillis Wheatley.* Ed. John C. Shields. New York: Oxford UP, 1988: vii–xxvi.

Gilroy, Paul. *The Black Atlantic: Modernity and Double Consciousness.* Cambridge: Harvard UP, 1993.

Hayden, Lucy K. "Classical Tidings from the Afric Muse: Phillis Wheatley's Use of Greek and Roman Mythology." *College Language Association Journal* 35 (1992): 432–47.

Herron, Carolina. "Milton and African-American Literature." *Remembering Milton: Essays in the Texts of Traditions.* Ed. Mary Nyquist and Margaret W. Ferguson. Oxford, Taylor and Francis, 1987: 278–300.

Kerenyi, Karl. *Goddesses of the Sun and Moon: Circe, Aphrodite, Medea, Niobe*. Trans. Murray Stein. Dallas: Spring, 1979.

Kinneging, Andreas A. M. *Aristocracy, Antiquity, and History: Classicism in Political Thought*. New Brunswick: Transaction, 1997.

Kristeva, Julia. *Revolution in Poetic Language*. Trans. Margaret Waller. New York: Columbia UP, 1984.

McCabe, Tracy. "Resisting Primitivism: Race, Gender and Power in Modernism and the Harlem Renaissance." Diss. U. of Wisconsin, 1995.

Miles, Edwin A. "The Young American Nation and the Classical World." *The American Enlightenment*. Ed. Frank Shuffleton. Rochester: Rochester UP, 1993. 337–52.

Moussa, Mario, and Ron Scapp. "The Practical Theorizing of Michel Foucault: Politics and Counterdiscourse." *Cultural Critique* 33 (Spring 1996): 87–112.

Nielsen, Aldon L. *Writing between the Lines: Race and Intertextuality*. Athens: U of Georgia P, 1994.

Pocock, J. G. A. *The Machiavellian Moment: Florentine Political Thought and the Atlantic Republican Tradition*. Princeton: Princeton UP, 1975.

———. "Virtue and Commerce in the Eighteenth Century." *Journal of Interdisciplinary History* 3 (1972–73): 119–34.

Reinhold, Meyer. *Classica Americana: The Greek and Roman Heritage in the United States*. Detroit: Wayne State UP, 1984.

Richard, Carl J. *The Founders and the Classics: Greece, Rome, and the American Enlightenment*. Cambridge: Harvard UP, 1994.

Richards, Phillip. "Phillis Wheatley and Literary Americanization." *American Quarterly* 44 (1992): 163–89.

Shalhope, Robert E. *The Roots of Democracy: American Thought and Culture, 1760–1800*. Boston: Twayne, 1990.

Shields, John C. *The American Aeneas: Classical Origins of the American Self*. Knoxville: U of Tennessee P., 2001.

———. "Phillis Wheatley's Struggle for Freedom in Her Poetry and Prose." *The Collected Works of Phillis Wheatley*. Ed. John C. Shields. New York: Oxford UP, 1988: 229–270.

———. "Phillis Wheatley's Subversive Pastoral." *Eighteenth Century Studies* 27 (1993–94): 631–47.

———. "Phillis Wheatley's Use of Classicism." *American Literature* 52 (1980): 97–111.

Shuffleton, Frank, ed. *The American Enlightenment.* Rochester: Rochester UP, 1993.

Stephanson, Anders. *Manifest Destiny: American Expansion and the Empire of Right.* Ed. Eric Foner. New York: Hill and Wang, 1995.

Twagilimana, Aimable. *Race and Gender in the Making of an African American Literary Tradition.* New York: Garland, 1997.

Watson, Marsha. "A Classic Case: Phillis Wheatley and Her Poetry." *Early American Literature* 31 (1996): 103–31.

Wheatley, Phillis. *The Collected Works of Phillis Wheatley.* Ed. John C. Shields. New York: Oxford UP, 1988.

Willard, Carla. "Wheatley's Turns of Praise: Heroic Entrapment and the Paradox of Revolution." *American Literature* 67.2 (1995): 233–55.

Wood, Gordon S. *The Creation of the American Republic, 1776–1787.* Chapel Hill: U of North Carolina P, 1969.

The Trojan Horse: Classics, Memory, Transformation, and Afric Ambition in *Poems on Various Subjects, Religious and Moral*

Eric Ashley Hairston

I

In 1772, at the commencement of a revolutionary season, Phillis Wheatley sought to publish a collection of classically pastoral, epic, religious, and elegiac poetry. Revolutionary in her own right, she disrupted established assumptions about black literary authorship in eighteenth-century America and challenged broader European and Colonial doubts about African humanity and intelligence by producing a book of verse. So unique was her accomplishment that the primary obstacle to its publication was neither expense nor the quality of the verse but the suspicion of authorial fraud. Consequently, a historic authentication of Wheatley and her work and a subsequent public attestation by eighteen of Boston's most prominent white citizens launched the fledgling poet's career.

Scholars like John C. Shields, Karla Holloway, and Henry Louis Gates Jr. have fixed on the authentication as a historic test of African American intelligence and humanity. Gates suggests that interrogators pressed Wheatley to reveal the depth of her knowledge in the classical themes she deployed in her poetry ("Foreword" viii). The nature and depth of Wheatley's education has been at issue since the Colonial era. We know that it included "astronomy, some ancient and modern geography, a little ancient history, a fair knowledge of the Bible, and a thoroughly appreciative acquaintance with the most important Latin classics, especially the works of Terence and Ovid" (Mason xiii). A strong neoclassical stream also saturated the intellectual environment of Early America. Increasingly, scholars have noted the breadth of that stream in literary sensibility, religious expressions, the political philosophy of the Founding Fathers, and fine art like the sculpture of Horatio Greenough.[1]

Although many writers have repeated the standard account of Wheatley's education, few have substantially explored its historical and intellectual significance. William H. Robinson and John Shields have been the most thorough commentators, illustrating how carelessly we have read Wheatley. With these exceptions, scholars have not added significant detail to the early account of Wheatley's education. They have left unanswered the question of what value a slave could find in even a thoughtful use of the classics. Why would a young African slave address antiquity and invite its presence in her New World existence? Many contemporary scholars have also failed to consider her work in light of what a classical education has traditionally been said to produce: ingrained virtue, a strong sense of individual worth and power, rhetorical armament, martial inclinations, literary celebrations of warfare, and political and literary ambition. The historic underestimation of Wheatley's classical education has led scholars to misunderstand her importance and misjudge the depth of her poetry. In order to evaluate Wheatley's work accurately, reveal the power of her poetics, and understand her contribution to the African American literary tradition, scholars must reexamine her intellectual training and its influence.

Wheatley's first classical cues might well have come from her own name. Scholars have long presumed that Wheatley was named after the *Phillis*, the ship that transported her to Boston, but Wheatley's name also has classical mythological resonance as the name (Phyllis) of the abandoned, suicidal lover of Theseus' son Demophon (Bell 368). The name was a regular feature of the classical poetry of writers like Horace. It reemerged in neoclassical poetry and frequently appeared as an English Christian name by the sixteenth century. Phyllis (Greek "foliage") was a natural name within the pastoral genre and a recurrent name in English poetry preceding Wheatley's era. For instance, the 1919 *Oxford Book of English Verse* notes Thomas Lodge (1556–1625) wrote two poems to a beloved "Phillis" ("Lodge, Thomas"). We reasonably gather that Wheatley's education followed at least in part the standards of the exclusively male Latin grammar schools of the time. This educational model emphasized reading classical epics, histories, verse, and philosophy and translating between vernaculars and Latin. Their curriculum included Cato, Ovid, Cicero, Virgil, Horace, Terence, Homer, Isocrates, and Xenophon. Where Wheatley's makeshift education under the Wheatley children ended, there is good reason to believe somewhat more substantive Latin instruction began, in order for her to attain the oft-quoted "thoroughly appreciative acquaintance" with major Latin classics.

Eric Ashley Hairston

Beyond the more generic classical references, Wheatley made a significant investment in the work of Horace, Homer, Virgil, Terence, and Ovid. In *Poems,* John Wheatley's letter to the publisher stated that Wheatley's English and biblical skills came from study in his household, and her writing came of her own curiosity. Of her Latin learning, he wrote that she "has a great Inclination to learn the Latin Tongue, and has made some progress in it." Robinson has pointed to the case of a local Boston instructor in Latin and French, a Mr. Delile, as a possible tutor. As the 1773 publication emerged in Boston in 1774, the *Boston Weekly News Letter* included the rapturous Delile's request that four celebratory lines of Latin verse appear beneath the frontispiece of the book of poems. Shields has proposed that, as Wheatley closely followed Mather Byles's 1744 *Poems on Several Occasions* in the construction of her 1773 *Poems,* and because Byles liked to advise budding young poets and lived across the street from the Wheatleys, she may have enlisted Byles as her tutor (Wheatley, *Collected Works* 275; Robinson 42).

Scholars agree more uniformly that Wheatley was frequently in contact with learned men and women from Boston and its environs. These learned people, either through curiosity or genuine interest, took part in her education. Clergymen, politicians, and tutors visiting the Wheatley household routinely brought gifts of classical and contemporary texts to the young prodigy, attention from the literati that early biographer Margaretta Odell notes (13–15). In her 1784 elegy on the death of clergyman Samuel Cooper, Wheatley admits that he was a literary mentor, "A Friend sincere, whose mild indulgent grace / Encourag'd oft, and oft approv'd her lays." Cooper was the pastor of the Brattle Street Church and the minister who baptized Wheatley into the Old South Church in 1771.

There is evidence that Wheatley had good access to libraries that contained significant holdings in the classics and other literature. Reverend Thomas Prince left his renowned library to Wheatley's Old South Church upon his death in 1758. With the Wheatley family's staunch Congregationalist standing, Phillis Wheatley's exceptional circumstances, and her attendance at the church and baptism into the Old South Church's congregation in 1771, it is reasonable to suppose that she had access to its rich library holdings. The more than two thousand volumes that survived a fire at the church now reside in the Boston Public Library and include works by Horace (his *Odes,* e.g.) as well as works by Homer, Virgil, Ovid, Lucan, Caesar, Suetonius, Plutarch, Dante, Milton, Pope, and a host of Early American religious writers. This library alone would have been enough to form the classical, literary, religious, and historical foundations for Wheatley's work. The only local libraries that rivaled Prince's were those collected by Byles and Governor Thomas Hutchinson, both of whom attested Wheatley's authorship. Wheatley is unlikely to have used Hutchinson's library, since a Colonial mob destroyed it in 1765, when she was twelve. Although Wheatley penned her first, nonextant verse in 1765, there is no indication in what remains of Hutchinson's diaries and papers that they met in her youth.

Mather Byles, who knew Prince well, had inherited the bulk of the Mather family library, which contained between fifteen hundred and three thousand volumes in Cotton Mather's lifetime and included extensive holdings in the classics and theology and works by such American colonial writers as John Adams (the poet) and Joseph Seccombe. Mather, who had a formidable command of the classics, added significant numbers of classical texts to the library (Bercovitch 66).[2] Byles shared Cotton Mather's familiarity with the classics, and like Mather, who reportedly gave away as many as one thousand books in one year, Byles made a habit of lending books. He was also an active figure in Boston, a notorious wit, practical joker, and satirist, which makes his love of Alexander Pope unsurprising. Byles wrote to Pope in 1727 and asked for "the favour of a few lines . . ." (Eaton 102). Although he had nothing to say to Byles, Pope did send him a copy of his *Odyssey* when it was published. Byles and Wheatley also shared an interest in Pope's classical translations. There is record of Byles lending the book, so the text did circulate in Boston (Eaton 104–6). Both Wheatley's critics and supporters have pointed to Pope as one of her models, and his translations of Homer were among her favorite reading. While Wheatley was in England, the Earl of Dartmouth gave her money to buy books, and she bought her own copy of the 1766 Pope translation of the *Odyssey* and the nine-book set of Pope's *Works*.

Wheatley knew Cooper, Byles, and Hutchinson personally, and they are almost certainly among the visitors to whom Odell refers. Most of the influential men who signed the attestation knew each other well or were related to each other by blood or marriage, so they represented a remarkable block of support for Wheatley. Many had literary and theological interests that overlapped Wheatley's. Any one of these men could have been among Wheatley's continuing supporters, and some are recorded as mentors of varying importance and subjects of Wheatley's poems and letters.

Eric Ashley Hairston

II

Whatever Wheatley's connections to the Boston and Harvard elites, the attempt to publish her poems in America failed for racial and political reasons. Perhaps because few believed that she could create verse, she was unable to secure sufficient numbers of subscribers. Equally problematic was the fact that the angry population of Boston in the early 1770s was in no mood for genteel poetry, especially from a slave.[3] In England, Wheatley's reception was much warmer, and her poems were significantly more successful. Although Wheatley was a rarity, she had a larger classically and religiously educated audience in England than in Boston, one that was familiar with the structure, course, and expectations of a classical education, including the virtuoso performance. Moreover, they were immensely curious about her African presence and performance in such an elite intellectual and social space, due in part to successful marketing of the prodigy and the poems.

Kirsten Wilcox suggests that Wheatley's real agency in *Poems* ended with writing the verses. She was forced to arrange or see *Poems* arranged to mute her political and social opinions. Moreover, she had no hand in attending to the details of *Poems'* marketing and publication. Wilcox's reading downplays significant facts about Wheatley's assessment of the publishing environment and her own political and social position, for there is evidence that Wheatley was not only a gifted poet but also reasonably astute in the legal and financial ways of the world. In her October 18, 1773, letter to David Wooster, she indicates that she has secured her freedom. According to the letter, her manumission is in part "at the desire of [her] friends in England." She notes that the legal "[i]nstrument is drawn, so as to secure me and my property from the hands of Executvs.[,] administrators, &c. of my master, and secure whatsoever should be given me as my Own" (Wheatley, *Collected Works* 170). More interesting is that Wheatley's newfound freedom influenced the strategy for marketing her poems. She seems to have had both full knowledge of the plan for marketing and publication and a role and stake in its creation and execution.

> I beg . . . that you use your interest with the Gentlemen and
> Ladies of your acquaintance to subscribe also, for the more sub-
> scribers there are, the more it will be for my advantage as I am to
> have half the Sale of the Books. This I am the more solicitous for,
> as I am now upon my own footing and whatever I get by this is
> entirely mine, & it is the Chief I have to depend upon. I must also

request you would desire the Printers in New Haven, not to reprint that Book, as it will be a great hurt to me, preventing any further Benefit that I might receive from the Sale of my Copies from England. The price is 2/6d Bound or 2/Sterling Sewed. If any should be so ungenerous as to reprint them the genuine Copy may be known, for it is sign'd in my own handwriting. (Wheatley, *Collected Works* 170–71)

Wheatley seemed interested in the basic economics of publication. She was personally invested in the marketing of the poems, because she would gain half of the proceeds. Moreover, she was worried about protecting herself against unauthorized copies of her book and unabashedly concerned about the impact bootleg copies would have on her profits. Wheatley's nineteen-year-old entrepreneurial acumen is remarkable, but it also suggests both that the same marketing and profit concerns would have affected which poems composed the London edition and that Wheatley is likely to have influenced those decisions. She certainly would have had reason to choose the poems carefully, if she had any inkling that marketability, high sales, fame, and public pressure might help pay for her freedom, as they seem to have done. William H. Robinson notes that as the publication emerged, John Andrews, a Boston merchant and early fan of Wheatley's work, wrote to William Barrell in Philadelphia (42). He reported ". . . after so long a time have at last got Phillis' poems in print. . . . These don't seem to be near all her productions. She's an artful jade I believe and intends to have the benefit of another volume . . ." (Andrews). Andrews's comments point to a shrewd and ambitious poet, not the puppet imagined by Wilcox.

Wilcox attributes much of the agency in the marketing process to Susannah Wheatley, who doubtless orchestrated Wheatley's meetings with Bostonians and some of the London notables. This critic points out that Susannah Wheatley's marketing strategy for Phillis Wheatley and her poems provided Wheatley access to the noble and literate public to create publicity and a literary name for the African American poet. Selina Hastings, Countess of Huntingdon, arranged for Wheatley to have a series of audiences with significant British nobles and citizens. Wheatley's letter to Wooster reveals that she met with the Earl of Dartmouth, Alderman Kirkman, Lord Lincoln, a Dr. Solander, Lady Cavendish, Lady Carteret-Webb, rhetoric professor Dr. Thomas Gibbons, Israel Mauduit, Benjamin Franklin, and "Greenville" (for Granville) Sharp, among others. Sharp also escorted her on a tour of London (Robinson 35). In both Boston and London, the "series of drawing-room performances before Susanna Wheatley's ever-widening circle of influential friends" and the meetings with British nobles encouraged people to speak her name among the male names of the literary elite and "give her name meaning in the context of print" (Wilcox 11).

The Boston publication proposal did not showcase Wheatley's classically influenced work. Rather, it included her more provincial work, regularly referring to local Boston and New England affairs. Wilcox aptly notes that the book of poems offered to the English publisher reflects the kind of literary expectations a refined, educated audience maintained for an author attempting to make a name for himself (or herself). As Wilcox observes, "London publication brought with it certain belletristic expectations that affected both what Wheatley printed there and how her literary authority would be construed" (17). As true as this observation may be, the changes reflected more than superficially belletristic concerns or attempts to mute Wheatley's opinions. Wilcox's position assumes that replacing poems addressing local Boston issues with classically influenced verse (e.g., "Niobe in Distress" and "To Maecenas") silenced opinion, as though the classics are merely window-dressing—politically neutral and socially unthreatening. Intellectual history does not support that assumption. The classically influenced poems projected Wheatley's voice beyond provincial Boston into a broader Western discursive space, regularly employing the classics artistically and politically and known by various European elites, which may well have amplified Wheatley's positions. The Wooster letter, moreover, suggests that Susannah Wheatley was not the exclusive force behind the creation of the marketable Phillis Wheatley. At the very least, the poet was capable of comprehending the salient issues involved in advancing her fortunes, and Wheatley's words suggest that she took action to safeguard her interests. Additionally, Susannah Wheatley was not in London with Phillis Wheatley as she made the grand tour of private parlors and tourist sights. Neither was Selina Hastings in London to guide Wheatley. While the countess may have arranged for her to meet with English nobles and subjects, whatever advances Wheatley made by diplomacy, charm, wit, guile, and intelligent conversation were her own.

Wheatley traveled with her owners' son, Nathaniel, who has remained largely voiceless in the critical history surrounding Wheatley and her *Poems*. He was so voiceless that Benjamin Franklin expressed annoyance that, during his visit with Phillis Wheatley, Nathaniel did not come downstairs to greet him (Franklin 172–73). Some have suggested that the question of Wheatley's liberty was so uncertain in the aftermath of the Somerset legal decision that

Nathaniel was not comfortable meeting with Phillis's visitors in England. Wheatley's reputation and open discussions of slavery in England might well have exposed him to difficult inquiries about her.

The marketing for the text, including Wheatley's 1773 London tour, specifically presents Wheatley as a practitioner in the line of literary tradition, offering a poetic display unusual for one who was a black slave. Wheatley emerges as the "practicing poet concerned with the display of her belletristic mastery and engaged with other kinds of literary and artistic productions" that Wilcox suggests (18). But she also emerges as a visibly ambitious and self-aware black poet—one who would not only perfect her craft but also use its conventions and its audience to her own ends. Bell, the London publisher and associate of the countess, broadcasts Wheatley's access to elites and unexpected knowledge as part of her allure, allowing subscribers to share in her access to noble and learned classes. He is quick to note that Wheatley "wrote upon a variety of interesting subjects, and in a stile [sic] rather to have been expected from those who, to a native genius, have had the happiness of a liberal education" and was "conversed with by many of the principal Nobility and Gentry of this country, who have been signally distinguished for their learning and abilities . . ." (Wilcox 11–12). Like the Roman playwright Terence, whom she celebrates in "To Maecenas," Wheatley displays a mastery of the higher arts beyond her station and is called to sit at the side of the nobles as a result. When *Poems* is shipped back to the colonies, it has the imprimatur not only of Boston Brahmin but also of the nobles of the British Empire and the tradition of classical education, a combination that helps to win her manumission.

Although many scholars from Thomas Jefferson onward have failed to recognize value in Wheatley's use of classical literature, figures, and themes, it is clear from history that classical education animates imagination, intellectual adventure, and both political and poetic ambition. We cannot dismiss poetic ambition in Wheatley, since it is a primary concern of poets from the classical era through the Renaissance and well beyond Wheatley's time. Poetic virtue, classical or Christian, has always competed with or been accompanied by poetic ambition. Renaissance versifiers from Petrarch to Milton openly contended with that tension throughout their works. For Wheatley to use the classics as a tool to enhance her name while she publicly meditated on virtue would not be unnatural for a poet. Moreover, the classics support poetic ambition and adventure in a way that Christianity does not. Piety and humility provide Wheatley with a specific aura of Christian virtue and a shield against

Eric Ashley Hairston

excessive criticism, but Christianity does not emphasize pride, ambition, and ostentatious display as virtues. The classics arm her with intellectual weapons and opportunities to mount both ambitious ventures and openly display her prowess. The London-based *Gentleman's Magazine and Historical Chronicle*'s lament that youth, innocence, and piety, combined with genius, had not freed her highlights the key combination of piety, innocent virtue, and genius that empowered Wheatley (456). As she later pointed out, the influence of her friends in England hastened her freedom.

Poetic ambition would also not necessarily be overridden by the marketing interference of a slaveholder like Susannah Wheatley. Wheatley's access to classical education produced something entirely new in the nation, a black intervention in Anglo-American literature and thought not again matched among African American writers until the middle of the nineteenth century. The wonder and power of this "millennial, if not quite apocalyptic force" of a moving African American pen could not have escaped Wheatley's sensibilities (Gates, *Figures* 4). Wheatley's letters to David Wooster and Samson Occom, John Andrews's epistolary assessment of her as "an artful jade," and her facility in charming and using British and American elites indicate that, beyond the notoriety her classical applications gained, her study authorized her to live and write in a fashion unimaginable to black slaves and most whites. It also fired her ambition to approach and transgress intellectual and social boundaries of gender and race.

III

If classical education held such promise to fructify ambition, produce poetic power, and create an alternative to traditional constraints of race and gender, then we should expect to see significant uses of classical texts, authors, and themes in Wheatley's poetry. The amount of classical influence visible in Wheatley's poetry is certainly prodigious. Of the thirty-nine poems in the 1773 volume (of which thirty-eight are by her), at least twenty-five (64 percent) contain classical allusions, ranging from the mere mention of the Muses to Wheatley's translation of Ovid's myth of Niobe from the *Metamorphoses*. As Shields notes, some form of the word "muse" appears at least forty-one times in Wheatley's poems (Shields "Phillis Wheatley's Use of Classicism" 102). "To Maecenas," "Goliath of Gath," and "Niobe in Distress" immediately reveal their debt to major textual antecedents and writers like Homer, Virgil, Horace,

Terence, and Ovid, but other poems possess classical connections also. If we include not only the classically inflected work but also the poems in which Wheatley neoclassically personifies Christian themes or admirable qualities, then virtually all her poems reflect direct or indirect classical influence.

Wheatley's poems do a great deal to challenge, complicate, and transgress the normal boundaries and requirements of her eighteenth-century world. "To Maecenas" presents us with both tradition and transgression. The title immediately signals Wheatley's knowledge of Horace, recalling Horace's poetic conversations with his patron, Maecenas, which he initiated with his first ode. One can reasonably conjecture that among her gift texts, loans, and library volumes, Wheatley encountered Horace. Horace was a standard of eighteenth-century classical training, from Boston Latin School through Harvard College. He was seen as both a source of classical virtue that made good contemporary morality and as a font of practical advice for living (Reinhold 151). He would have been one of the classical authors foremost in the minds of those who attested Wheatley's poetic skill. Almost all of the men who signed the attestation in *Poems* were Harvard graduates who would have shared specific texts as the foundation for their educations—the grammar school authors in further depth, plus Sallust, Caesar, and the Greek New Testament (Reinhold 26–28). Horace provides an example of how tracing what texts were available to Wheatley gives us insight into what encouragements she might have had and what classical influences we should expect to find in her poetry.

Shields has adeptly alerted us to what other scholars have missed routinely, the Horatian connections to "To Maecenas" and "Ode to Neptune" ("Wheatley's Use" 100). He does not report, however, the interesting fact that two of Horace's *Odes* actually include references to "Phyllis." It is doubtful that either link would have eluded Byles, Hutchinson, and others of Wheatley's fans steeped in Horatian texts. Nor would they have failed to entice, intrigue, and even encourage Wheatley. Reading the *Odes*, Wheatley would have encountered "To Xanthias" and might have been inspired by Horace's account of the virtuous and beautiful slave, "Phyllis."

> *Nescias an te generum beati*
> *Phyllidis flauae decorent parentes;*
> *regium certe genus et penatis maeret iniquos.*
> *Crede non illam tibi de scelesta*
> *plebe delectam, neque sic fidelem,*
> *sic lucro auersam potuisse nasci matre pudenda.*

Eric Ashley Hairston

How do you know that your blond Phyllis isn't
Descended from highborn parents? Why, she must
Have come down from kings! Surely your Phyllis grieves

Because the unkind gods have brought her down
From what she was to this her present situation.
You can be sure of this: a person like her,

So without guile or greed, so faithful and selfless,
Must be the worthy child of a worthy mother.
(Horace 112–13)

Among other things, the poem diminishes the shame of slavery and celebrates
ancient Phyllis' attributes of guileless grace, lack of greed, faithfulness, and
selflessness—traits celebrated in Wheatley's own poetry. Wheatley might also
have found in the *Odes* an equally intriguing poem, the remarkably named "To
Phyllis." In this poem, Horace seeks to entice a young "Phyllis" away from her
beloved and into his arms.

Horace's signature, "To Maecenas," also introduces an element of transgression. Gaius Maecenas—minor poet, soldier, trusted personal and political
agent of Caesar Augustus, and wealthy patron—was the legendary protector of
Horace and Virgil, who was famously victimized by Roman power. Horace's
opening lines celebrate Maecenas' aid as he navigated the dangerous political
waters of a Roman republic running rapidly toward empire.

> *Maecenas atavis edite regibus,*
> *O et praesidium et dulce decus meum,*
> *sunt quos curriculo pulverem Olympicum*
> *collegisse iuvat metaque fervidis*
> *evitata rotis palmaque nobilis*
> *terrarum dominos evehit ad deos;*
> *. . . Me doctarum hederae praemia frontium*
> *dis miscent superis, me gelidum nemus*
> *Nympharumque leves cum Satyris chroi*
> *Secernunt populo, si neque tibias*
> *Euterpe cohibit nec Polyhymnia*
> *Lesboum refugit tendere barbiton.*
> *Quodsi me lyricis vatibus inseres,*
> *sublime feriam sidera vertice.*

> Maecenas, you, descended from many kings,
> O you who are my stay and my delight,
> There is the man whose glory it is to be
> So famous even the gods have heard the story
> Of how this chariot raised the Olympic dust,
> The dazzling wheel makes the smoking turn;
> . . . What links me to the gods is that I study
> To wear the ivy wreath that poets wear.
> The cool sequestered grove in which I play
> For nymphs and satyrs dancing to my music
> Is where I am set apart from other men—
> Unless the muse Euterpe takes back the flute
> Or Plyhymnia untunes the lyre.
> But if *you* say I am truly among the poets,
> Then my exalted head will knock against the stars.
> (Horace 3–5)

Like Horace, Wheatley gives her Maecenas the mantle of nobility, but hers is the prince of poets. What inspiration and talents the great poets possess, Maecenas' "equal genius shares / In softer language, and diviner airs." Wheatley also hungers after the same literary aid and renown that Horace desires from the Muses and Maecenas, but she seems not to expect a crown of laurels, despite her talent or success. The ivy crown of learning that Horace desires is curling round Maecenas' head in Wheatley's poetry, and as a slave, she must get by guile and theft what should be hers by merit.

> Thy virtues, great Maecenas! shall be sung
> in praise of him, from whom those virtues sprung:
> While blooming wreaths around thy temples spread.
>
> I'll snatch a laurel from thine honour'd head,
> While you indulgent smile upon the deed
> (Wheatley 11–12).

Wheatley incorporates a number of additions to the Horatian ode in her "Maecenas," among them a pastoral flourish, a demonstration of her familiarity with classical epics, an assessment of her own position as an enslaved poet, and a very pointed request for protection.

Eric Ashley Hairston

Shields has observed that as early as George Puttenham's 1589 *Arte of English Poesie* we see that the pastoral, which Wheatley employs, often serves as a political device and a sufficient mask for far deeper concerns than singing shepherds or woodland gods. Also, African American writers have long employed signifying to infuse otherwise innocuous words, allusions, or conventions with multiple politically and culturally charged meanings.[4] In this context, the Augustan convention of *recusatio,* a feigned inadequacy to the epic deployed in non-epic poetry, fails to capture the full range of Wheatley's African American poetics in "To Maecenas."[5] In the poem, Wheatley couches her ambitious pursuit of literary laurels in pastoral terms, suggesting some of the imagery from Virgil's *Eclogues.* Wheatley casts Maecenas "beneath the myrtle shade," reclining in some poetic Elysium when she interrupts him. She expresses awe at the work of the ancients, with lightning streaking the skies and thunder that "shakes the heav'nly plains."

This respectful admiration within the pastoral setting is predictable and safe—the humble servant singing in the glade. But, after walking into the poetic countryside to seek Maecenas' aid, Wheatley goes on to declare her intent to rival the ancients and sing of virtues, even with her alleged "grov'ling mind" and "less happy" state. Wheatley goes still a bit further to declare her intent to "snatch" a laurel while Maecenas and her readers look on "indulgent smil[ing] upon the deed." Immediately after boldly declaring her intent to commit the grand theft of poetic voice and literary power, Wheatley resumes her humble pose and closes with a pastoral image of flowing streams, reposing naiads, celestial bodies, and her own grateful appreciation of Maecenas' aid. Wheatley uses the pastoral mode both to court her audience's support and brashly stake out poetic territory among the great poets of virtue and political commentary. The verse continues with Wheatley's description of the features of Homer's verse and his potent abilities:

> While Homer paints lo! circumfus'd in air,
> Celestial Gods in mortal forms appear;
> Swift as they move hear each recess rebound,
> Heaven quakes, earth trembles, and the shores resound
> (9–10).

Beyond celebrating Homer's ability to animate the word, she also indicates her deep emotional reaction to his poignant scenes. Relegating the poem to mere *recusatio* would make Wheatley's choice of scenes meaningless, but to a black slave writing under physical threat, with the threat of censorship, and with ambitions for access, critique, and possibly liberty to mask and manage, the choice of authors, scenes, characters, and exploits can reasonably be expected to have more intent, meaning, and political value.

The scene she selects from Homer is fascinating, since it is an episode involving masking and assumed identity. Wheatley celebrates the famously tragic episode in book 16 of the *Iliad*, when Patroclus, eager to join the battle and rally the Greeks, asks to fight using Achilles' armor. Patroclus takes the field only to be slain by Hector, who ignobly mocks him as he delivers a death blow, strips him of Achilles' armor, and attempts to decapitate the body and feed it to the Trojan dogs. Patroclus, eloquent even in death, cuts Hector with his final poetic lines. Wheatley earnestly desires to join the literary fray, donning as much of the armor of the ancients as she can, assuming the role of a poet, and braving the dangers of her position as a slave to offer as many eloquent lines as she can.

In the midst of her praise, Wheatley indicates the special power over the human soul she sees in the array of gods and legendary epics, a power so great in the case of the ancients that even in her era the world still drew its ideals and virtues from the poetic tales of both immortals and mortal struggles. She also reveals that she desires to count herself among the great poets and acquire their power. She understands that if "[she] could rival thine [Homer's] and Virgil's page / Or claim the Muses with the Mantuan Sage" the "same beauties" and "same ardors" in her own soul might well enable her song "in bolder notes [to] arise" and "all [her] numbers pleasingly surprise" (10). Mirroring the talents of the ancients, Wheatley might protect herself with the skill of Maecenas or own the same educative cultural influence that Homer or Virgil achieved. She might exert that influence on the Africans who constituted "all [her] numbers" or generate the pathos in her white readers that Homer produced in his "gentler strains." We may well query if Wheatley cloaks her desires and hides her ambitions for freedom, abolition, or Christian equality in a Homeric Trojan horse. At the pinnacle of artistic possibility would have been her ability to produce poetry that would contain the eternal, redeeming virtues that generations of scholars could imbibe and use to redeem a less than virtuous world. One can easily argue that the *Iliad*, *Odyssey*, and *Aeneid*, at the very least, have served precisely this end in the West, as have many of the subsequent texts directly descended from the ancient epics.

Eric Ashley Hairston

Beyond the triumphant epics of antiquity, the authors to whom she alludes provide ways of critiquing safely lessons that Wheatley learned well. The poets Maecenas protected, like Virgil, often suffered under the Romans. Unlike Wheatley, Virgil was not a "belov'd" "babe" snatched from his home; tradition indicates that he had his ancestral home confiscated by Caesar Augustus. Within that tradition, his *Aeneid* is a work partly designed to regain his home by favor and flattery. Further, as scholars like Allen Mandelbaum have pointed out, despite the early critical tendency to glorify the *Aeneid,* the epic that canonized the ascension story of the empire also contains an undercurrent of pain and complaint. We might see "the ache and the bite of the *Aeneid,* ever less— as we read more—a triumphant poem in the praise of the *imperium* of Caesar Augustus." Mandelbaum notes, "for me, it was chiefly through Ungaretti that I saw in the *Aeneid* the underground of denial—by consciousness and longing—of the total claims of the state and history: the persistence in the mind of what is not there, as a measure of the present" (Virgil vii).

What exists neither in Wheatley's "To Maecenas" nor any of her other poems is unbridled enthusiasm for British or American civilization. Nor does she embrace the earthly church with abandon. Just as Virgil refuses fully and uncritically to embrace the Roman *imperium,* Wheatley retains the position of an instructor in virtue, a lecturer on piety and Christianity, and a messenger of recollection. She periodically reminds her readers that she is "less happy," "an Ethiop," and in need of defense. Wheatley does seem quite painfully aware in "To Maecenas" that she is in a precarious position as an African slave. She ends her celebration of Horatian and Virgilian poetic power with a plaintive assessment of her predicament: "But here I sit, and mourn a grov'ling mind / That fain would mount and ride upon the wind." She later laments that Maecenas is free to burn with the "immortal fire" of poetry, but the "less happy" Wheatley "cannot raise the song, / the fault'ing music dies upon my tongue." In the final two stanzas, Wheatley praises Maecenas and implores him to "Hear me propitious, and defend my lays" (11–12).

Wheatley does not ask for protection merely on the merits of her own verse or the basis of her desire to rival the ancients. She offers an example of another African who has given similar evidence of literary talent and proven a boon to his patron. In the fifth stanza, the "less happy" poet reminds the reader and Maecenas that Terence, the Roman dramatist, "all the choir inspir'd, / His soul replenish'd, and his bosom fir'd." She makes a special note beneath the poem that "He was an *African* by birth," and continues to ask

But say, ye, Muses why this partial grace
To one alone of *Afric's* sable race;
From age to age transmitting thus his name
With the first glory in the rolls of fame? (11).

At least two remarkable developments emerge from this passage. Wheatley is the first African American writer to deploy European heraldic elements to describe and valorize African heritage. Sable, the heraldic tincture of constancy and grief, defines Africanity as fidelity, *gravitas*, and mourning—characteristics visible in *Poems*. Furthermore, Wheatley seizes on and underscores Terence's African birth in Carthage to create a classical literary forebear of African descent.

Suetonius Tranquillus, whose works were widely known by Latin scholars, details Publius Terentius Afer's life in the fragmentary work *De Viris Illustribus*. In the section, *De Poetis*, he provides a biography of Terence (*De Vita Terenti*). The singular evidence of his race comes from Suetonius' description of Terence: *Fuisse dicitur mediocri statura, gracili corpore, colore fusco* (He is said to have been of moderate height, slender, and of dark complexion; Suetonius 460). *Fusco* is variously translated as "swarthy," "dark," or "dusky." Betty Radice, for instance, translating Terence's plays, describes him as "slight, dark, and good looking" (Terence 12, 342–43). Wheatley clearly intends to claim Terence as an African by geography and "by birth." Enlightenment scholars regularly claimed North African Romans as white; Kant and Hume left no room for blacks of antiquity. Jefferson argued that unlike Roman slaves, blacks gave no evidence of intelligence, and he included Terence as an example.

Wheatley would have received her information about Terence from Suetonius or a mentor who was familiar with Suetonius, and she chose to make an issue of *colore fusco*. Her reasons for doing so are understandable. Terence was one of the most widely studied and respected classical writers during the Colonial period. In *Classica Americana: The Greek and Roman Heritage in the United States*, Meyer Reinhold points out that Terence was the only dramatist of antiquity read with any regularity in America. John Adams lectured John Quincy Adams to read Terence because "Terence [was] remarkable, for good morals, good Taste, and good Latin." He also recommended him to his grandchildren in 1816 that "[t]he six plays of Terence are valuable [for a number of reasons, including] the Maxims and Proverbs, which are now and have been for 2000 years common place expressions of all civilized nations" (Reinhold 151). But the issue of *colore fusco* is not easily settled. Terence was not widely

Eric Ashley Hairston

imagined to be African in the sense that Colonial slaves were African, and letters and commentary from Jefferson to Adams and beyond declare or assume that Terence was African by geographic birth and not by race. Even twentieth-century translators have often gone out of their way to dismiss the possibility of racial Africanity (part of a larger problem of scholars in classics and other disciplines dealt with in excruciating and controversial detail in Martin Bernal's *Black Athena* and responding texts).[6] African American writer Joel Augustus Rogers, who created two volumes on historical figures of African ancestry, made a philological decision to translate in favor of blackness. He argued that he

> called Terence a Negro for the following reasons: he was from Africa; he was a slave; and Suetonius (A.D. 98–138) describes his color as 'fusco' (dusky, very dark). Had he been, say of a mulatto color, Suetonius might have said he was 'subfusco.' For instance, Ammianus, fourth century historian, says of the Egyptians of this time, 'Homines autem Aegyptii plerique *subfusculi* sunt et atrati' (The men of Egypt are, as a rule, somewhat swarthy and dark of complexion).
>
> Terence was also called 'Afer.' The *Century Dictionary* says of this, 'The ordinary terms for African Negro or Africans were Ethiops and Afer.' *L'Encyclopedie Franciaise* [*sic*] says similarly, 'The Latin, Afer, which was both ethnic and geographical, sufficed at a time when Africa was little known to designate its inhabitants by that characteristic which was almost typical of them and most apparent, namely color.' (1: 118–20)[7]

With her Latin training, it appears that Wheatley made a specific philological choice in translating *colore fusco,* perhaps for the reasons Rogers noted. Wheatley was certainly aware of Terence's influence in her world as a model of moral excellence, a font of good sense, and a source of excellent Latin. As a fellow African, Terence also released Wheatley from the bonds of uniqueness, provided a racial literary ancestor, and granted a racial link to the classical world. Houston Baker insists that these links between authors, the "sound of precursors," orient African American writers and allow them to comment thoughtfully on issues of race (Baker and Redmon 137). By penning Terence into her eighteenth-century discourse, Wheatley connected herself to a world beyond American slaveholding culture and found an experience that gave new meaning to her own. In Terence, she could identify a fellow African slave who employed the pen (or stylus) to defy the limitations of slavery and gain his freedom.

The acknowledging of Scipio Moorhead's now famous portrait of Wheatley also demonstrates the presence of another black prodigy and more evidence of black intelligence. But the verses to Scipio Moorhead operate as more than just an admiring and instructive poem, for Scipio (Publius Cornelius Scipio Aemilianus Africanus Numantius, or Scipio Africanus the Younger) is also the name of one of Terence's patrons and friends, the general responsible for ending the Punic Wars and conquering Terence's Carthage.[8] It cannot have escaped Wheatley's mind that the destroyer of Carthage and adopted grandson of the initial conqueror of Roman Africa would become the patron and friend of a Carthaginian slave. If Terence was, as has been popularly held, born in Carthage after the end of the Second Punic War, then selecting him was a consummate signifying gesture—the invocation of the incisive, insightful comedies (which regularly included precocious and provocative slave characters) of an African antecedent native to the empire that nearly dethroned Rome and changed human history. The studious Wheatley must have been aware of the biographical similarities between Terence's position and her own. Handsome young Terence, dressed in rags, so impressed the comic master, Caecilius Statius, that he was called to sit at dinner with the honored guests—a beginning similar to Wheatley's that would have resonated both with the poet and many of her learned readers.[9]

Like a contemporary Terence, Horace, or Virgil, Wheatley created within her book of poems the role of Maecenas, her indulgent patron. However, because she cultivated fruitful acquaintances and relationships with a number of powerful men and women, those individuals could have freely imagined themselves as Maecenas. In addition to creating a desirable identity for her readers, one that could encourage even greater support from them, she could also thank her actual, indulgent patron in the process. The question of who Wheatley's Maecenas was remains unanswered, but it was the aegis of the many patrons or mentors who collectively played Maecenas that made it possible for Wheatley to address audiences otherwise outside her reach. The imprimatur of the Harvard alumni who signed her attestation provided the authorization for her to lecture the scholars who were the target in the poem, "To the University of Cambridge, in New-England."

Wheatley seems fully invested in following the ancients' example by exhorting the students to virtue. The poem is third in the volume behind "On Virtue," continuing the theme of piety, morality, and practical advice that

Eric Ashley Hairston

Horace and Virgil help her establish in "To Maecenas." She immediately identifies her own motivation as the "intrinsic ardor [that] prompts [her] to write." The belletristic flourish of the Muses descending to assist her verse quickly reinforces her authority to speak, but their appearance also precedes her admission that she is from the "land of errors and *Egyptian* gloom." The first lines take in hand the practical problem of trying to address virtue as an African woman slave by pitting the mythological convention of enlightened literacy against the myth of African benightedness. The intrinsic virtue that inspires the poet, the high literary convention of the Muses, and the Christian redemption of the "Father of mercy" disrupt the powerful social conventions of race, slavery, and gender that might otherwise silence her. What emerges from the Trojan horse of piety, humility, and classical convention is a lecture.

When she turns her verse to the students, the lesson she offers is one of preserving virtue against sin. In making her case, she argues that, like blooming plants, they are vulnerable to destruction.

> Ye blooming plants of human race divine,
> An *Ethiop* tells you 'tis your greatest foe;
> Its transient sweetness turns to endless pain,
> And an immense perdition sinks the soul
> (Wheatley, *Collected Works* 16).

Wheatley lectures as a pious preacher of Christian virtue and a classically educated poet with the spiritual and intellectual authority to instruct the students, many of whom are barely older than she. She also overtly signals her race with one of the terms routinely used to identify black Africans in the classical world. "Ethiop" leaves no doubt that an African is the author and lecturer in the poem. Moreover, by making reference to "Egyptian gloom," Wheatley accomplishes two things. First, she affirms her Christian orthodoxy by embracing her redemption and separation from pagan Africa. However, by illustrating this point with Egypt, she also subtly reminds readers of Egyptian civilization's place in the classical world. This place ranges from the writings of Herodotus, to Memnon's position in the *Iliad*, to the Pharoahs, stretching to Ptolemaic Cleopatra, whose ethnic identity has been a subject of debate among scholars (Rabinowitz and Richlin 23–42). As she does with Terence, Wheatley writes Africa back into the classical world with her poetic reference to Egypt.

"Ethiop" also carries with it a resonance beyond the Roman identification with Africanity. It recalls Psalm 68:31: "Princes shall come out of Egypt; Ethiopia shall soon stretch out her hands unto God." With Ethiopian and

Egyptian references, she foreshadows nineteenth-century African American Ethiopianist and Egyptological movements within black nationalism. Wilson J. Moses describes the black nationalist impulse embedded in these movements as both separatist and resting on the idea that European civilization was more advanced (10–11). However, Phillis Wheatley deploys African Terence, the Egyptians, and "Ethiop" to establish blacks' place in the ancient and Christian worlds as equals. Blacks have a place in the ancient world, and Wheatley employs that vehicle to move toward both Africans' restoration in history and personal advantage. She rhetorically and incredulously inquires why Terence would be the only talented African. While affinity for elite Western culture does suggest her familiarity and comfort with European civilization, her Christian rejection of pagan Africa also suggests strong affiliation with the culture. Her continual positioning of herself as a lecturer, teacher, and pious critic of the culture, however, militates against concluding that she believed in white cultural superiority. In "To the University," for instance, Wheatley refers to the students' advantages as mere "privileges" that they should improve and refine while they exist. There is no evidence in her poetry that she desired anything other than to recover Africans' place in the free world—certainly not separation.

IV

While the aegis and influence of a collective Maecenas gave Wheatley freedom to write, there is reason to believe that Wheatley signaled to an individual who had given her special aid. At least a portion of the title of Maecenas must go to Mather Byles, who shared with Maecenas a short poetic career. Byles's library was available for Wheatley, and his influence is visible in a number of features Wheatley's poetry shares with his *Poems on Several Occasions.* Both Byles and Wheatley included hymns ("An Hymn to the Morning" and "An Hymn to the Evening"), poems recognizing artists ("To PICTORIO, on the Sight of his Pictures" and "To S. M. a Young African Painter"), and a treatment of the biblical David and Goliath story ("Goliath's Defeat" and "Goliath of Gath"). Moreover, Byles joined the classical muse and the Christian heaven in his elegy "To a Friend on the Death of a Relative," a conscious combination that Wheatley makes throughout her poetry. John Shields notes this syncretism of classical and Christian themes in Wheatley, and this relationship between the Christian and classical is visible in Wheatley's version of the Goliath story.

Eric Ashley Hairston

While Byles's "Goliath's Defeat" follows the biblical story closely, Wheatley's account reflects classical influence throughout. "Goliath of Gath" recalls the epic and violent accounts of battles in the works of Homer and Virgil, even as it addresses the classic Christian story. Like Homer and Virgil, her first lines call to the gods and the Muses and announce her tale.

> Ye martial powers, and all ye tuneful Nine,
> Inspire my song, and aid my high design.
> The dreadful scenes and toils of war I write,
> The ardent warriors and the fields of fight:
> You best remember, and you best can sing
> The acts of heroes to the vocal string:
> Resume the lays with which your sacred lyre
> Did then the poet and the sage inspire
> (Wheatley, *Collected Works* 31).

Immediately, there is a remarkable combination of Christian and classical pagan elements. Wheatley's invocation to martial powers suggests not only Mars but also the host of Olympians who participated in wars of both the *Iliad* and *Aeneid*. Next, Wheatley arrays the forces of Israel and Philistia, following Virgil's and Homer's pattern of metaphorically describing soldiers' ranks as natural forces. She spends considerable time giving detailed descriptions of the combatants' deportment and armor, again matching Homer and Virgil. Wheatley emphasizes elements described in the "Essay on Homer's Battels" that precedes book 5 of Pope's translation of the *Iliad*, Wheatley's working volume. Pope focuses on Homer's attention to the variety of deaths of the warriors, the record of the "Age, Office, Profession, Nation, Family &c." of the characters, and the attention to characters' clothing "and the Singularity of his [Goliath's] Armor" (Pope 252–53).

There is reason to characterize this biblical tale as an epic foray, an *epyllion* or short epic, by the ambitious poet (Wheatley, *Collected Works* 258). While both the Bible and Byles record Goliath's insults to the Israelites, Wheatley's boastful, insulting Goliath echoes the mocking Numanus Remulus of Virgil's *Aeneid* book 9: 576–604. Ascanius, the young son of Aeneas, who has not been involved in battle, hears Numanus' taunts against the Trojans and their gods.

> . . . For Numanus
> had stalked before the front lines, shouting things
> both worthy and unworthy to be spoken . . .

and boasting as he swaggered, bellowing:
'Twice conquered Phrygians, are you not ashamed
to be hemmed in again by siege and ramparts,
to set up walls between yourselves and death?
Look, those who want to take our brides by battle!
What god brought you to Italy or what insanity?'
(Virgil 234–35)

Numanus continues, bellowing that the Trojans dress like women (with "robes of saffron," and bonnets with ribbons) and adore dancing and laziness. Finally, he advises the Trojans to "leave arms to men, you have had enough of swords." Goliath sounds little different, swaggering and mocking.

The monster stalks, the terror of the field.
From Gath he sprung, Goliath was his name . . .
He strode along, and shook the ample field,
While Phoebus blazed refulgent on his shield.
Through Jacob's race a chilling horror ran,
When thus the huge enormous chief began:
"Say, what the cause, that in this proud array,
You set your battle in the face of day?
One hero find in all your vaunting train,
Then see who loses, and who wins the plain.
For he who wins, in triumph may demand
Perpetual service from the vanquished land:
Your armies I defy, your force despise,
By far inferior in Philistia's eyes:
Produce a man and let us try the fight,
Decide the contest, and the victor's right"
(Wheatley, *Collected Works* 31–33).

Like the *Aeneid*'s Ascanius, who lets fly an arrow through Numanus' head, the young David chides the mocking enemy and then brings down the great warrior, after pious words, with his first martial projectile. With Goliath's shattered brain and severed head, among other scenes, Wheatley also matches the regular gore of classical battle scenes.

Just o'er the brows the well-aimed stone descends;
It pierced the skull, and shattered all the brain—
Prone on his face he tumbled to the plain.

Eric Ashley Hairston

Goliath's fall no smaller terror yields,
Than riving thunder in aerial fields:
The soul still lingered in its loved abode,
Till conquering David o'er the giant strode:
Goliath's sword then laid its master dead,
And from the body hewed the ghastly head . . . (40).

Pope's translation of Homer's *Iliad* book 16 provides a good comparison. "Next *Erymas* was doom'd his Fate to feel, / His open'd Mouth receiv'd the *Cretan* Steel: / Beneath the Brain the Point, and drown'd the Teeth in Gore: / His Mouth, His Eyes, his Nostrils pour a Flood; / He sobs his Soul out in the Gush of Blood" (Pope 259). The combination of Christian and classical elements is especially vivid in the battle scenes echoing the epics of Homer and Virgil, and we can identify lines of poetic influence on Wheatley from the classical writers and Pope. However, looking at *Poems* as a conversation between Wheatley and Byles, like that between Horace and Maecenas in the *Odes,* further illustrates how the classics can unlock Wheatley's poetics.[10]

Twenty-five years ago, John C. Shields provocatively argued that Wheatley's frequent references to the sun and solar progress—Phoebus Apollo, Aurora, "round the central sun," and so on—signified a remnant memory of African solar worship mixed with Islam (103–4). Furthermore, he argued Wheatley was affected by her enslavement to the point that her circular, solar references were evidence of both memories of syncretized African animist and Islamic religious practices and the Jungian Mandala Archetype. Odell's biography reports that Wheatley recalled her "mother poured out water before the sun at his rising." We can reasonably accept with Shields that the Islam of the Arabic invaders, who conquered and converted remnant Roman African civilization at the tip of a scimitar, blended with a local animist and fetishist tradition in some cases. However, with only a reference to a single, fragmentary memory, we can yet resist the temptation to rest the entire discussion on these tantalizing conclusions about what Wheatley's memory and circular themes mean for her work and psychological state.

Shields is unconvinced that Christian sources for this circular or solar imagery provide sufficient explanation. However, Christian relationships between the Son and the sun, to which Shields alludes, are not the only historic Christian uses of solar or circular imagery. From the early preoccupation with the music of the spheres, concentric ranks of angels, and the celestial order to the Dantesque circles of *Inferno, Purgatorio,* and *Paradiso,* or even the

Renaissance fascination with the ovoid form as a representation of perfection (we should remember the prevalence of egg shapes in Renaissance painting), circular and spherical forms have been central to Christianity and Western literary representations of order. Moreover, the Age of Reason in which Wheatley lived and wrote was permeated with a Newtonian sense of clockwork organization in Nature, created by a mechanistic God. Ordered reason and virtue were thought to unlock the secrets of the rational Creation. Among the era's neoclassical literary creations, solar imagery and the representative gods of sun, moon, dawn, and dusk were commonplace enough to be subjects of the wit of the day. Richard Steele's *Tatler* No. 106 (for December 13, 1709) includes a humorous report of a poet desiring to go into business, selling his literary wares. Among his offerings are "about fifty similes that were never yet applied, besides three-and-twenty descriptions of the sun rising, that might be of great use to an epic poet" (Steele).

Also, one of Wheatley's candidates for Maecenas, Mather Byles, includes a substantial amount of solar imagery in his *Poems on Several Occasions.* For instance, Byles's "To the Memory of a young Commander slain in a Battle with the Indians, 1724," includes references to dawn, radiant streams from the sun, and shining stars. His "To PICTORIO, on the Sight of his Pictures" speaks of "An hundred Journies now the Earth has run, / In annual Circles, round the central Sun." His poem on "Eternity" includes the line "Before this System own'd the central Sun; / Or Earth its Race about its orbit run. . . ." These lines are strikingly similar to Wheatley's verse in "On Recollection:" "Now eighteen years their destined course have run / In fast succession round the central sun." Wheatley is surrounded by a culture obsessed with neoclassical balance and reason, Christian conventions of godly order, and a Western tradition in which the sun-centered universe long endured as a metaphorical analog of Christian order radiating out from the Creator God.

If we are inclined to apply contemporary knowledge and intelligently speculate about Wheatley's cultural influences or psychological state as a slave, then the Jungian explanation of Wheatley's psychological state may bear reconsidering. Time has rendered the Jungian Mandala Archetype a somewhat Byzantine explanation for attributes that can also be elegantly explained by sound contemporary psychiatric trauma theory. The mandala form is essentially the basic form for the entire Jungian model of the psyche, with the Mandala Archetype as the emerging archetype for the psyche in need of wholeness and healing.

Eric Ashley Hairston

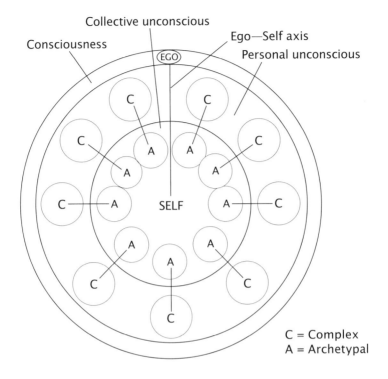

Jungian Psychic Apparatus: self, archetypes, complexes, collective and personal unconscious, consciousness, and the ego. From Anthony Stevens, On Jung, an updated edition with a reply to Jung's critics. Copyright 1990, 1999 Anthony Stevens. Published in the U.S. and Canada by Princeton University Press. Reprinted by permission of Princeton University Press.

The Jungian mandala and Mandala Archetype, as appealing as they are to some contemporary spiritual and cross-cultural projects,[11] exist primarily as theory, with little practical application to contemporary psychiatric analysis or therapy. Its most significant remnant is the Myers-Briggs Type Indicator personality test. Both the Freudian and Jungian projects deconstruct the rigid rationality and order of the Enlightenment, exposing the influence of the subconscious mind, proving that Woman or Man is not even master of her or his own house, much less a rational evaluator of an ordered universe. To descendants of Freudian analysis, however, contemporary neuropsychological or psychobiological approaches give more practical analyses of the function of the subconscious and the effects of environment, biology, and experience on the conscious mind.

In assessing the psychological landscape of Wheatley's poetry, we might take into account Margaretta Odell's report that Phillis Wheatley suffered from a kind of short-term memory loss. The Wheatleys had to place a candle or lamp nearby so she could record her inspirations whenever they emerged, even in the middle of the night, because she could not retain her immediate thoughts for extended periods. This inability could indicate the aftermath of significant trauma, which a seven-year-old child experiencing the Middle Passage no doubt endured. Contemporary psychiatry clearly articulates a series of neuropsychological responses to various kinds of trauma, and a range of memory impairments is among them (Sadock and Sadock 807–9). Contemporary researchers have found that early childhood trauma has marked, cumulative, and often permanent effects on the developing brain. Using magnetic resonance imaging and electroencephalography, researchers have determined that childhood trauma does visible damage to the hippocampus, one of the primary verbal and emotional memory centers in the brain, as well as to the amygdala and other brain structures. Moreover, this part of the brain impacts the production and dispersal of neurotransmitters. In short, childhood trauma can open a Pandora's box of problems, not the least of which can be various forms of memory impairment in registration, retention, and recall (Teicher 68–75).[12]

Wheatley's literary productions and artfulness in the social and business arenas related to publication give ample evidence of her reason, intelligence, and talent. However, it strains reason to imagine that Wheatley emerged from the Middle Passage unscarred, given what we now know of trauma. It is extremely likely that some remnant memories of her African life, abduction, and Middle Passage captivity haunted Wheatley, and her poetry offers evidence of the experience. The poem to the Earl of Dartmouth strongly suggests that her "love of Freedom sprung" from the trauma of being "a babe belov'd" who was "seiz'd" from her father. Although the pain is displaced onto the parents in the poem, Wheatley intimates that the true horror of the event can be understood by those with "feeling hearts alone." In fact, Wheatley's poetry is filled with a pattern equally recognizable and resonant as the circular, the theme or pattern of memory. She uses the classics to explore memory, especially as it relates to virtue. In "On Recollection," Wheatley extends earlier themes of virtue, piety, and reflection on sin and judgment. In this poem, she describes memory's role as a repository of reasons to resist the temptation to do evil and illus-

Eric Ashley Hairston

trates memory's capacity to terrify evildoers as they meet judgment. Wheatley calls to Mnemosyne, often called the mother of the Muses, to initiate the verse. Then she calls on all nine Muses to animate this particular verse and inspire "[their] vent'rous *Afric* in her great design."

> MNEME begin. Inspire, ye sacred nine,
> Your vent'rous *Afric* in her great design.
> *Mneme,* immortal pow'r, I trace thy spring:
> Assist my strains, while I thy glories sing:
> The acts of long departed years, by thee
> Recover'd, in due order rang'd we see:
> Thy pow'r the long-forgotten calls from night,
> That sweetly plays before the *fancy's sight*
> (Wheatley, *Collected Works* 62).

As an adventurous African, Wheatley seems intent upon revealing acts of the past, enshrined in memory and cinematically played in dreams. Wheatley points to the "pomp of images" given in dreams to the "high-raptur'd poet," and the "heav'nly phantom" that "paints the actions done / by ev'ry tribe beneath the rolling sun" (62–63).

Carla Williard argues that Wheatley was used as a tool by colonial audiences who needed evidence for their own social or political projects—patriot publications, royalist papers, and even race theorists like Thomas Jefferson. Moreover, since none of these audiences had the positive qualities that Wheatley attributed to them, she created ideal, "fictive audiences" in the forms of speaking heroes, like Wooster and Whitefield (who owned slaves), to act out the qualities she desired (Williard). Although Williard credits Wheatley with attempting a "heroic entrapment" of audiences, she does not contend with the classical models Wheatley deploys who are not part of her audience. Nor does she address poems like "Goliath of Gath," "Niobe in Distress," and "On Recollection," which address pride and obduracy in the face of God's will, the obvious presence of evil, or recollection that recalls and illuminates good and evil. The revelatory and echoing capacity of recollection is double-edged, "sweeter than music to the ravish'd ear, / Sweeter than Maro's entertaining strains," but "dreaded by the race, / Who scorn her warnings and despise her grace." Again we can note an intriguing commentary on race and power visible within Wheatley's verse. Mneme is portrayed as a combination of memory and conscience, both classical in origin and vaguely Christian in application.

Recollection seems to be the forceful arm of conscience, the internal moral compass that "enthron'd within the human breast, / Has vice condemn'd, and ev'ry virtue blest." Moreover, the voice of memory is sweeter even than that of Virgil's lauded verse when great and virtuous acts are recalled, but for the race guilty of vice and crime, memory's voice is dreaded and "her awful hand a cup of wormwood bears" (63).

The "race / Who scorns her warnings and despise her grace" could apply broadly to the world of sinners, in which Wheatley includes herself.

> Now eighteen years their destin'd course have run,
> In fast succession round the central sun.
> How did the follies of that period pass
> Unnotic'd, but behold them writ in brass!
> In Recollection see them fresh return,
> And sure 'tis mine to be ashamed, and mourn (63).

But Wheatley clearly repents of her folly and appeals to Virtue to guide her. That still leaves the unrepentant and unnamed race, "the wretch who dar'd the vengeance of the skies," to face the final reward of evil and perish as they recall their sins and repent too late. Emerging from Wheatley's apparent Trojan horse of pious introspection may be an attack on white slaveholders, who make excellent candidates for this unnamed group. The race arrogantly and unrepentantly engaged in evil is, like Goliath, unmoved by conscience, God's word, or recollection. Moreover, they may be unresponsive to the virtuous words of Wheatley, the "high-raptur'd poet" armed with Mneme's revelation of history, guided by Virtue, and capable of "chang[ing] the scene." Their fate is clear, unless they turn to virtue as the poet has. As she does with the students at Cambridge, Wheatley takes the opportunity to instruct the reader in virtue. She begins with a standard flourish, invoking the Muses to aid her, and she displays her own piety by interspersing meditations on her own virtue between criticisms directed outward. In "On Recollection," Wheatley emerges as being in league with or possessed by the Muses, their "vent'rous Afric." But, the "vent'rous Afric" of "On Recollection" is not the only transformation we see in Wheatley.

This theme of transformation—from benighted soul to Christian poet, Negro black as Cain to member of the angelic train, thief of laurels to poetic Patroclus, and "vent'rous Afric" to infant muse—may be the most thoroughgoing theme in *Poems*. Despite the obvious presence of the circular and solar or even recollection and Memory, the longest sustained classical project

Eric Ashley Hairston

in *Poems* is a verse translation of an author focused on transformation. Ovid's *Metamorphoses* provides the original text for Wheatley's "Niobe in Distress." The Latin Ovidian metanarrative is the dominant secular force at play in the writings of Dante, Petrarch, Shakespeare, *ad infinitum*. Not surprisingly, an Ovidian myth, which in some translations ends "[a]nd, as will happen, new tales bring back old" (*Metamorphoses*, book 6), serves as the basis for one of Wheatley's longest poems. The 224-line meditation "Niobe in Distress" is an extended poetic treatment of the pride and later mourning of the Phrygian queen, described as "all beautiful in woe" (Mason 48), who dared to count her splendor equal to the gods. After all her family and splendor are destroyed, she turns to stone.

Wheatley's treatment of the Niobe myth is also likely the first translation of any kind by an African in America. It certainly appears to be the first African American philological project in the classics. Translating the work of a major classical author is an ambitious undertaking by an African American slave in any case, but Wheatley's ambition is considerably more developed than Ovid's. She alters the Ovidian narrative to add her own signature in making another, longer and more personal foray into the frontiers of the epic, crafting an epyllion in "Niobe" that brings her within sight of her epic idols.

Ovid opens with Niobe's arrogant disregard for the lesson of her friend Arachne, her boasting, and her usurping of Latona's glory. Wheatley, on the other hand, invokes the Muses and focuses on the wrath of Apollo before addressing Niobe. Apollo's and Phoebe's indignant slaughter gets special treatment from Wheatley, who embellishes Ovid with additional lines:

> With clouds incompass'd glorious *Phoebus*
>   Stands;
> The feathered vengeance quiv'ring in his hands.
> . . .
> Then didst thou, *Sipylus,* the language hear
> Of fate portentous whistling in the air
> (Wheatley, *Collected Works* 106–7)[.]

Wheatley also removes the touch of mercy Apollo showed to Niobe's Ilioneus, who prayed to all the gods to spare him. His brothers had died of arrows that tore out flesh, spouted "streams of purple gore," and left blood "darting upward." Ovid wrote that Apollo was moved by Ilioneus' appeal, and Pope's account, which Wheatley almost certainly consulted, showed the touch of sympathy and mercy.

Ilioneus, the last, with terror stands,
Lifting in pray'r his unavailing hands;
And, ignorant from whom his griefs arise,
Spare me, o all ye heav'nly Pow'rs, he cries:
Phoebus was touch'd too late, the sounding bow
Had sent the shaft, and struck the fatal blow;
Which yet but gently gor'd his tender side,
So by a slight and easy wound he dy'd. (Ovid 177)

Wheatley coldly declares, "Thou too, O Ilioneus, are doom'd to fall, / The fates refuse that arrow to recal" (Wheatley, *Collected Works* 104).

Wheatley's alterations of Ovid amplify the wrath and vengeance of the gods who punished Niobe's excessive pride in her fine lineage and progeny. Unlike the comparably long "Goliath of Gath," "Niobe" does not have a premiere role for the humble warrior to launch powerful words and stones at a boastful giant; rather, it contains a self-reflexive warning about recklessly succumbing to comfort and poetic pride. "Niobe" emphasizes in its treatment of Ilioneus, whose prayerful but "unavailing hands" do not forestall his slaughter, that even piety, which has been part of Wheatley's aegis, does not always save the pious. Written in reaction, partially, to a painting by Welsh artist Richard Wilson, "Niobe in Distress" seems to contain and display all of Wheatley's fears about her essential vulnerability. The excessive mourning that Niobe displays also suggests that the added folly of immobilizing grief is something that neither the reader nor the author can afford. If Niobe errs in not learning from Arachne's ignominious downfall, then the readers and writer of so many elegies can err if they fail to learn from the lives of the departed and "take [them]" (as Wheatley suggests in her elegy on Whitefield, 23) for their lessons of faith or folly.

Interestingly, Apollo is the god associated with music, poetry, and finer cultural attainments, and he is the agent of Niobe's destruction. Unfortunate Niobe is excessively proud of her productions, fourteen children of beauty and strength. Also, when ordering Latona's worshipers to disband, she commands them to remove the laurels they wear to honor the goddess. Here, snatching a laurel, which is Wheatley's announced intent in "To Maecenas," is a precursor to annihilation. For Wheatley, the balance between ambition and endearing piety is an important and precarious one. Excessive pride is not a quality she can afford to display. In "Niobe in Distress," Wheatley outlines the dangers of self-praise in "Niobe" by contrasting the celebrated and proud queen—

Eric Ashley Hairston

> Niobe comes with all her royal race,
> With charms unnumber'd and superior grace:
> Her Phrygian garment of delightful hue,
> Inwove with gold, refulgent to the view, (104)

—with the devastated Niobe of the final stanza who is bereft of even the freedom of movement, that which Phillis was generally allowed as a pampered slave.

Wheatley's commentary on the lessons of death and mourning is particularly useful in considering her elegies. Many of them encourage mourners to focus on the virtues of the departed, and she often uses the classics to illustrate those virtues and their heavenly reward. Even in an elegy like "To a Gentleman and Lady on the Death of . . . a Child of the Name Avis . . . ," Wheatley mines the smallest classical vein for its value. In "Avis," she plays on the unfortunate child's Latinate name for both metaphors of heavenly flight and birdlike feeding on the eternal fruits of heaven, Wheatley's version of ambrosia.

> Thine *Avis* give without a murm'ring heart,
> Though half thy soul be fated to depart.
> To shining guards consign thine infant care
> To waft triumphant through the seas of air:
> Her soul enlarg'd to heav'nly pleasure springs,
> She feeds on truth and uncreated things (85).

The elegiac form that Wheatley relied on to memorialize Avis, console mourning families, and extol the real or imagined virtues of the dead may itself be construed as a classical influence. The elegy functioned as more than a funeral poem for classical writers, and it routinely expressed political positions. The primary Augustan tension was between the elegy as individual and indulgent versus Cicero's and Octavian's vision of Roman unity or *tota Italia* (the whole of Italy). Wheatley's elegies created community by drawing local Boston together in corporate mourning for admirable or pitiable members of the community. But she also used the elegy as a Trojan horse to make herself a valued member of the community—as elegist and fellow mourner—in an era when blacks, especially slaves, would normally be excluded from the community. Moreover, with the prerogative of the elegist, she *interprets* the virtues of the deceased. Wheatley's elegy to Whitefield is constructed seemingly to echo the teachings of the preacher, but it also allows her to echo her own sentiments of Christian equality voiced just two poems before in "On Being Brought from

Africa to America": "Remember, *Christians, Negros,* black as *Cain* / May be refin'd, and join th' angelic train" (18). The elegy admonishes the people of America to heed Whitefield's words. To her own race Wheatley declares that the Savior he offered is their Savior too.

> Take him, ye *Africans,* he longs for you,
> *Impartial Saviour* is his title due:
> Wash'd in the fountain of redeeming blood,
> You shall be sons, and kings, and priests to God (23).

Wheatley's focus on recollection, impious pride, death, and mourning also suggests that she is particularly aware of the dangers she and others face from their own folly and from simple fate. It is clear that Wheatley had reason to be vigilant about her balance of piety, ambition, and pride. Wheatley's poetic critiques and classical adventures did not go unchallenged, as the long history of criticism during and after her era attests. And, while she admits the limits of her poetic freedom and ability in such poems as "On Recollection," "On Imagination," and "Niobe in Distress," she insists that she is neither an African aberration nor a fraud. She subversively situates a poem of praise for fellow slave and artist Scipio Moorhead among the last poems. Furthermore, she includes a lighthearted but intriguing commentary on her own knowledge as the endpiece(s) of her work. "A Rebus, By I. B." and "An Answer to the Rebus" demonstrate both that Wheatley is again under examination and that she is transformed from the supplicant of "To Maecenas."

By the end of *Poems on Various Subjects, Religious and Moral,* Wheatley has joined the ranks of the Muses. In the "Rebus" and the "Answer," Wheatley responds to a series of classical tests, now believed to have come from James Bowdoin, one who attested her authorship and who became the founder of Bowdoin College. According to Wheatley, "[t]he poet asks, and *Phillis* can't refuse / To shew th' obedience of the Infant muse" (124). Wheatley demonstrates her memory of classical, Christian, and heraldic lore in this set of poems. Wheatley suggests herself as a tenth muse, as was said of Anne Bradstreet by her brother-in-law, but clearly she thinks of herself as an African muse.

Colonial British and American readers accepted Wheatley's poetry as it appeared—an appropriately respectful, properly attested, belletristic literary oddity that left white readers in control of their relationship with the black writer. Wheatley's relationship with the ancient poets and the Muses developed throughout the text of the poems, from her attempts to rival Homer and

Eric Ashley Hairston

Virgil and snatch the laurel of a mature poet to her appeal to the Muses to aid *their* "vent'rous Afric" and her evolution into an infant muse. But her relationship with her audience also developed, literally and in the literary world of *Poems on Various Subjects, Religious and Moral*. She allowed herself—gave herself—to be transformed by each Maecenas, reader of an elegy, fellow Christian, celebrant of the classical masters, or examiner of her classical acumen into something unique but greater than the limited and despised form of the black slave.

This overall transformation reveals the strategic ambush of Wheatley's literary Trojan horse. The scheme that was Wheatley's verse—not mere pastoral, mere *recusatio,* nor mere mimicry—carried her inside the literal and intellectual walls of white, Colonial American, and British societies. Wheatley used the classical models, pastoral repose, Christian and poetic humility, and wealthy patrons—familiar and accepted elements of belletristic literature and Colonial culture—to achieve extraordinary access to Colonial elites, mask her ambition, acquire the power to critique Colonial civilization, and secure her freedom. In "To Maecenas," the poet begged the solicitude of the reader, pled the weakness of her poetic voice, and longed for the power of the epic masters—playing down any sense of her own power. But in the same poem, she used the classics to penetrate the white intellectual world and Terence in particular to inject a resonant black presence there that authorized her own presence. Subsequently, she used her impeccable Christian credentials to lecture young students at Cambridge and celebrate redeeming virtue. She parlayed her virtuous verse into commentary on freedom and enslavement and a direct appeal to King George, and rewrote the rolls of heaven to include blacks in the "angelic train." The audience for whom she mourned the dead also found itself including her in the local community, but subject to her assessment of the virtuous life. She moved beyond Horace to position herself near the epic masters, whose lasting influence she envied, by transforming the David and Goliath story into an epyllion (taking care to chastise an unrepentant race seeking to enslave others) and then daring to alter Ovid into a second epyllion. By the end of her woven verse, the young poet, who needed authentication, protection from patrons, and guidance from ancient teachers, had not only successfully arrogated to herself the role of teacher but "Infant muse"—herself a source of poetic afflatus.

NOTES

I am grateful to Allen Mandelbaum and Pat Johansson for early inspiration and John C. Shields for more recent encouragement.

1. Sacvan Bercovitch, *The Puritan Origins of the American Self* (New Haven: Yale UP, 1975), 56–87. A later treatment of the subject can be found in John C. Shields, *The American Aeneas* (Knoxville: U of Tennessee P, 2001).

2. Bercovitch 66. As an example of Mather's and other Puritan divines' substantial investment in the classics, Sacvan Bercovitch points out that Mather's *Magnalia Christi Americana* is rife with Christian and Classical parallels and comparisons. Mather "alludes to the Roman epic [the *Aeneid*] more frequently, more consistently, than to any other work (except for the Bible), from his opening invocation, a direct paraphrase of Virgil's" to the last section, concerning the wars of Og-Philip, which he entitles "Arma Virumque Cano."

3. John Andrews, "To William Barrell," 29 May 1772, Andrews-Barrell Letters, Massachusetts Historical Society, Boston. "It is about two months since I subscribed for Phillis's poems, which I expected to have sent you long ago, but the want of spirit to carry on anything of the kind here has prevented it, as they are not yet published. . . ."

4. See Henry Louis Gates Jr., *The Signifying Monkey: A Theory of African American Literary Criticism* (New York: Oxford UP, 1988).

5. Philologists might dismiss "To Maecenas" as merely imitating the Augustan convention of *recusatio,* but only if they fail to consider the African American literary convention of signifying, the practical risks to black writers, the scope of Wheatley's ambition and self-promotion, or the practical limitations of Wheatley's classical education. Even if Wheatley recognized the *recusatio* as conventional, pretended humility executed through a Homeric foil, that she merely mimicked the *recusatio* and registered little or no meaning in the characters, texts, or authors she chose seems implausible given her broader poetic commentary on slavery, freedom, and virtue. It would have been yet another mechanism through which she could signify and transmit meaning particular and peculiar to her state as an enslaved African—thus transforming the classical model into a Trojan Horse. Unlike Horace and others who used the *recusatio* and truly did not brave the epic

Eric Ashley Hairston

mode, the allegedly humble and imitative Wheatley ventured at least to the brief epic or epyllion in "Goliath of Gath" and "Niobe in Distress for her Children Slain by Apollo," just as she dared to lecture to university students, flatter George Washington, and speak through her poetry directly to King George III.

6. Betty Radice took care to deny Terence's racial Africanity. She even denies that he is of North African origin. "Even the surname Afer is no proof that Terence was of North African origin; witness the distinguished orator, Gnaeus Domitius Afer. Terence has been conjectured to be a Semitic Carthaginian, a Berber, or the son of one of Hannibal's captives from South Italy, and so racially either Greek or Italian."

7. Joel Augustus Rogers, *World's Great Men of Color,* ed. John Henrik Clarke, vol. 1 (New York: Simon and Schuster, 1996), 118–20. A. J. Brothers and Robert Graves both challenge Terence's black Africanity. Graves's *Comedies of Terence* (Chicago: Aldine, 1962), ix, classifies him as "probably a Berber." The 1896 *Harper's Dictionary of Classical Literature and Antiquities* (New York: American Book Co., 1896) states "Terence was a native of Carthage (though his cognomen, Afer, suggests that he was of African [Libyan], not Phoenecian heritage." Elsewhere, the dictionary classifies Libyans and Aethiopians as two indigenous African peoples, but Libyans are imagined to be "Caucasian."

8. The son of Aemilius Paulus, Scipio Aemilianus was adopted as a child by Publius Cornelius Scipio Africanus' son, Publius Scipio. After razing Carthage with his armies and selling the inhabitants into slavery, he was honored by Rome with the name "Africanus" (like his grandfather by adoption) and later honored also as Numantius. Publius Cornelius Scipio Aemilianus Africanus Numantius, or Scipio Africanus the Younger, was the leader of the Scipionic Circle, which supported many other literary figures like Terence. "Cornelius, Scipio Aemilianus Africanus Numantius, Publius," *The Oxford Classical Dictionary,* 3rd ed., rev. Simon Hornblower and Antony Spawforth, eds. (New York: Oxford UP, 2003).

9. The all-too-early endings of the two figures are as ironically similar as their beginnings. Terence died around the age of twenty-six and Wheatley was approximately thirty-one at her death.

10. Byles's lines in Lucan's style and poetry and letters to Alexander Pope present us with earlier conversations between generations of poets. We

have one line of influence from Pope to Byles to Wheatley, but Wheatley also took inspiration directly from Pope's work.

11. Mandala-type forms appear in many cultures, giving the Jungian theory a special place in various projects that seek unifying themes across humanity.

12. Martin H. Teicher, "Scars that won't heal: The neurobiology of child abuse," *Scientific American*, 286.3 (2002): 68–75. The more generally accessible description of the medical findings at a number of research sites around the nation can be found in *Scientific American*. However, the in-depth research analyses are available in M. D. De Bellis, M. S. Keshavan, D. B. Clark, B. J. Casey, J. N. Giedd, A. M. Boring, K. Frustaci, and N. D. Ryan, "Developmental Traumatology, Part 2: Brain Development," *Biological Psychiatry* 45.10 (1999):1271–84, and Martin H. Teicher, "Wounds That Time Won't Heal: The Neurobiology of Child Abuse," *Cerebrum* 2.4 (2000): 50–67.

WORKS CITED

Andrews, John. Letter to William Barrell. 29 May 1772. Andrews-Barrell Letters. Massachusetts Historical Society, Boston.

Baker, Houston A., Jr., and Patricia Redmon, eds. *Afro-American Literary Studies in the 1990s.* Chicago: U of Chicago P, 1989.

Bell, Robert E. *Women of Classical Mythology.* New York: Oxford UP, 1991.

Bercovitch, Sacvan. *The Puritan Origins of the American Self.* New Haven: Yale UP, 1975.

Bernal, Martin. *Black Athena: The Afroasiatic Roots of Classical Civilization.* 2 vols. New Brunswick: Rutgers UP, 1987.

"Cornelius, Scipio Aemilianus Africanus Numantius, Publius." *The Oxford Classical Dictionary.* Ed. Simon Hornblower and Antony Spawforth. 3rd ed. Rev. ed. New York: Oxford UP, 2003.

De Bellis, M. D., M. S. Keshavan, D. B. Clark, B. J. Casey, J. N. Giedd, A. M. Boring, K. Frustaci, and N. D. Ryan. "Developmental Traumatology, Part 2: Brain Development." *Biological Psychiatry* 45.10 (1999): 1271–84.

Eaton, Arthur Wentworth Hamilton. *The Famous Mather Byles: The Noted Boston Tory Preacher 1707–1788.* Boston: W. A. Butterfield, 1914.

Eric Ashley Hairston

Franklin, Benjamin. *The Works of Benjamin Franklin.* Ed. John Bigelow. Vol. 6. New York: G. P. Putnam's, 1904.

Gates, Henry Louis, Jr. *Figures in Black: Word, Signs, and the "Racial" Self.* New York: Oxford UP, 1987.

———. "Foreword." *The Collected Works of Phillis Wheatley.* Ed. John C. Shields. New York: Oxford UP, 1988. viii–xxii.

———. *The Signifying Monkey: A Theory of African American Literary Criticism.* New York: Oxford UP, 1988.

Gentleman's Magazine and Historical Chronicle 43 (September 1773): 456.

Horace. *The Odes of Horace.* Trans. David Ferry. New York: Farrar, Strauss and Giroux, 1997.

"Lodge, Thomas." *Oxford Book of English Verse, 1250–1900.* 1919 ed.

Mason, Julian D., Jr., ed. *The Poems of Phillis Wheatley.* Chapel Hill: U of North Carolina P, 1966.

Moses, Wilson Jeremiah. *The Golden Age of Black Nationalism 1850–1925.* Hamden: Archon, 1978.

Odell, Margaretta. *Memoir and Poems of Phillis Wheatley.* Miami: Mnemosyne, 1969.

Ovid. *Metamorphoses of Ovid.* Trans. Sir Samuel Garth, John Dryden, Alexander Pope, Joseph Addison, and William Congreve. 1742. New York: Heritage, 1961.

Pope, Alexander. *Poems of Alexander Pope.* Ed. Maynard Mack. Vol. 7. New Haven: Yale UP, 1967.

Rabinowitz, Nancy Sorkin, and Amy Richlin, eds. *Feminist Theory and the Classics.* New York: Routledge, 1993.

Reinhold, Meyer. *Classica Americana: The Greek and Roman Heritage in the United States.* Detroit: Wayne State UP, 1984.

Robinson, William H. *Phillis Wheatley and Her Writings.* New York: Garland, 1984.

Rogers, Joel Augustus. *World's Great Men of Color.* Ed. John Henrik Clarke. Vol. 1. New York: Simon and Schuster, 1996.

Sadock, Benjamin J., and Virginia A. Sadock, eds. *Comprehensive Textbook of Psychiatry.* Vol. 1. Philadelphia: Lippincott, Williams, and Wilkins, 2000.

Shields, John C. *The American Aeneas: Classical Origins of the American Self.* Knoxville: U of Tennessee P, 2001.

———. "Phillis Wheatley's Use of Classicism." *American Literature* 52.1 (1980): 97–111.

Steele, Richard. *The Tatler.* Ed. George A. Aitken. Vol. 2. 13 Dec. 1709. London: Ballantyne, Hanson, 1898.

Suetonius. *Suetonius.* Trans. J. C. Rolfe. Loeb Classical Library. Cambridge: Harvard UP, 1970.

Teicher, Martin H. "Scars that won't heal: The neurobiology of child abuse." *Scientific American* 286.3 (2002): 68–75.

———. "Wounds That Time Won't Heal: The Neurobiology of Child Abuse." *Cerebrum* 2.4 (2000): 50–67.

Terence. *The Comedies.* Ed. Betty Radice. New York: Penguin, 1976.

———. *Comedies of Terence.* Ed. Robert Graves. Chicago: Aldine, 1962.

Virgil. *The Aeneid.* Trans. Allen Mandelbaum. New York: Bantam, 1983.

Wheatley, Phillis. *Collected Works of Phillis Wheatley.* Ed. John C. Shields. New York: Oxford UP, 1988.

Wilcox, Kristen. "The Body into Print: Marketing Phillis Wheatley." *American Literature* 71.1 (1999): 1–29.

Williard, Carla. "Wheatley's Turns of Praise: Heroic Entrapment and the Paradox of Revolution." *American Literature* 67.2 (1995): 223–56.

Eric Ashley Hairston

Empowerment through Classicism in Phillis Wheatley's "Ode to Neptune"

Patrick Moseley

Even the most recently initiated Phillis Wheatley scholar can pinpoint the charge most often leveled against the young African American poet: that she is, at the end of the day, at best a clever rhymester but always a derivative hack. Of course, the nature of these claims has changed since her volume *Poems on Various Subjects, Religious and Moral* first appeared in 1773. During Wheatley's own time, gentlemen such as Thomas Jefferson held firm to the belief that " . . . in imagination they [blacks] are dull, tasteless, and anomalous" (140), and therefore devoid of the very faculty on which a poet relies, while early-twentieth-century critics such as William J. Long fault Wheatley for her "pious platitudes, colorless imitations of Pope, and murmurs of a terrible theology" (qtd. in Watson 104). It is the charge of imitation of Pope in particular and neoclassicism in general that more recent critics seem to repeat. Perhaps, as Marsha Watson suggests, Wheatley is guilty by default—that too many readers view her work through a "post-Romantic lens," coloring every component of neoclassicism as "baroque, insincere, and repetitive." Watson suggests that, as critics, we must meet Wheatley where she lives, which is to say that without a fundamental understanding of neoclassical aesthetics, we can never judge Wheatley's work (or even Pope's, for that matter) fairly (Watson). The poetics of the era valued "order, concentration, economy, utility, logic, restrained emotion, accuracy, correctness, good taste, and decorum" (Harmon 342), and, especially, in Early American Literature, the *art* of imitation.

Indeed the virtue of good imitation was certainly instilled into Wheatley by her more than likely mentor, Mather Byles. An ardent admirer of Alexander Pope, Byles held firmly to the belief that a good poet "merge[s] his individual genius with the art of imitation" (Kyper 188). Perhaps, as Watson seems to suggest, the only way to do justice to Wheatley is to adopt a critical stance that "takes into account the fact that the realities of Wheatley's life are as inseparable from her poetry as are the dictates of neoclassic aesthetics . . . [and] the major texts of the western European literary tradition" (107).

Then again, perhaps not. With Watson's first assertion I am a bit hesitant: the realities of Wheatley's existence as a young woman ripped away from her parents in her native Gambia and held in the bonds of slavery are significant and, more often than not, shed light on her poetry. Inseparable, though? Certainly not: such an approach assumes that Wheatley's poems would be of little or no interest if it were not for the fact that they had been composed by a little black slave-girl. As for the assertion that we must recognize that Wheatley was a neoclassicist, and as such must criticize her accordingly, I patently disagree. The fact is, Wheatley might have more in common with Wordsworth and Keats than she does with Pope or Dryden; a preference for the heroic couplet, in other words, does not necessarily make a neoclassicist. But it is the last assertion, that we should read Wheatley in terms of the major works of the Western European tradition, in which I have the most interest in this essay. However, as opposed to the eighteenth-century British tradition with which Watson is largely concerned, I concern myself mainly with Wheatley's use of classicism, especially in her appropriation of Virgil's *Aeneid*.

While Wheatley's classicism is not uncharted territory, the topic has by no means been exhaustively mapped out and, as such, demands further exploration. Sometimes mentioned, though never thoroughly treated, is the short, three-stanza poem, "Ode to Neptune"—eighteen seemingly inconspicuous lines placed in the middle of her first and only collection ever published. This short work commands attention because of a number of peculiarities: it is the only work in the volume in which Wheatley specifically uses the word "ode"; it is one of only two works whose composition is specifically dated, and the only one to mention specifically where that composition took place; it is one of the few works in which she abandons heroic verse; and perhaps most importantly, it is one of the most *inter* and *intra*textually rich works Wheatley ever produced. I should clarify that when I use the term "intertextuality," I mean it in the more traditional sense in which "a text comes to rest on a prior text which functions as a stable force which is retrieved and made present by a study of allusion . . . and reference" (Preminger 620). As for "intratextuality," I view the entire volume of poems as a single text, in which images, poetic forms, and terms often reappear. Thus, the volume is a tightly woven tapestry, and as such

Patrick Moseley

no one poem in it, I would argue, can be fully appreciated without reference to the others.

In what follows, then, I argue that in "Ode to Neptune" Wheatley employs and tweaks the classical form of the Horatian ode, and in the space of eighteen lines manages not simply to allude to, but to appropriate Virgil's *Aeneid,* writing herself into the narrative as two characters at once: both as Aeneas as well as his goddess mother Venus. But just as important as *what* she does in this poem are the questions of how and why. An answer to these questions requires an exploration of Wheatley's own theory on the transcendent capabilities of the imagination, and an examination of the context of Wheatley's plight as a young woman held in the bonds of slavery and the ordeals she was forced to endure in order to get, at long last, her collection into print and finally to gain her freedom.

I

In the first sextet of "Neptune," Wheatley describes the weather conditions in Boston that make for a particularly dangerous sea voyage: " . . . raging tempests shake the shore, / While Ae'lus' thunders round us roar, / and sweep impetuous o'er the plain" (76). The poet then offers a plea to the "tyrant of the main [Aeolus, keeper of the winds]" (76) to be still while her Susanna embarks on a trip across the Atlantic. If the winds are "impetuous," they are not only violent, but also impulsive and irrational. As such, there is no way to appeal to their reason, requiring a plea to a higher authority, which in this case is Neptune, the god of the sea. Virgil's epic begins in the same manner. Juno bribes Aeolus, the keeper of the winds, to set them loose in order to make travel not only perilous, but deadly for the Trojans' voyage to Hesperia, the land to the West. Her plan works, for Aeneas, because of inclement conditions, loses all but seven of his ships before the appearance of Neptune, who is enraged that the winds would have the audacity to cause such a "fracas and . . . frenzy" (1: 177) on what is his domain. "Has pride of birth made you so insolent" (1: 187), Neptune asks, immediately ordering the winds to be gone, thus settling the conditions.

Wheatley's second stanza describes the newly calmed conditions in terms of classical imagery: "The blue eyed daughters of the sea / With sweeter cadence glide along" (76). Not only does the water no longer churn, but " . . . Sol sheds benign his ray, / And double radiance decks the face of day" (76), recalling Virgil's description wherein Neptune "brings quiet to the swollen waters, sets / the gathered cloud to flight, calls back the sun" (201–2). While these descriptions in the first two stanzas invite a connection between Wheatley's ode and Virgil's epic, the final sextet in "Neptune" provides a more clear parallel.

The first four lines describe the calm traveling conditions near and into the final destination, Britannia.

> To court thee to Britannia's arms
> Serene the climes and mild the sky,
> Her region boasts unnumber'd charms,
> Thy welcome smiles in every eye. (77)

What first commands attention is Wheatley's gendering of England as feminine: after Aeneas and what remains of his crew take advantage to settle on the shores of Libya, Aeneas and Achates journey from their camp to Carthage, which, just like Britannia in "Ode to Neptune," is a feminine-gendered city.[1] Also of interest is Wheatley's use of the verb "to court," which leads the reader to draw another connection to Virgil's epic. In order to ensure Aeneas' and his fellow Trojans' safety while in Carthage, Venus plans to "catch the queen by craftiness, / to girdle Dido with a flame [of love], so that / no great god can turn her back . . ." (4: 942–44). Both Wheatley's Susanna and Virgil's Aeneas are the objects of feminine courtship. But Venus' measure is a purely preventive one, since the Carthaginians are already sympathetic to the exiled Trojans' plight; even before Aeneas reveals his presence to the queen, he overhears her telling his fellow Trojans, "Whatever you may choose . . . I shall send you safe / with escort, I shall help you with my wealth" (4: 801–4). One may then say that welcome had already smiled "in every eye," even before Venus' trickery.

In the final couplet of Wheatley's ode, the poet writes, "Thy promise, *Neptune* keep, record my pray'r / Nor give my wishes to the empty air" (77), recalling Venus' request of the Sea-god in book 5. "Let them reach / Laurentine Tiber if what I beseech / is just, if fate has given them those walls," the goddess asks. Neptune answers that he will do his part to ensure Aeneas' safe arrival at Italy, and as Virgil later relates, "the fleet / runs safely on its way across the sea—/ even as father Neptune *promised*" (1139–41; emphasis added).

Although Wheatley's choice to relate Susanna's journey in terms of Aeneas' perilous voyage to Carthage en route to Italy is apparent upon close reading, less conspicuous is how the poet actually writes herself into the narrative, taking on the persona of Venus. The first indication that Wheatley is a character in her own work comes in the second line: Aeolus' thunders roar "round us,"

Patrick Moseley

not just around Susanna's point of departure. Second, her choice of the posses-sive pronoun in the phrase "my Susanna" denotes a close connection between her and the voyager. We are invited to make the connection between this rela-tionship and the one between Venus and Aeneas; in each case the former acts as protector of the latter. Of course, in 1772, Phillis Wheatley had no children, and the three that she would eventually have would all die shortly after birth. The personal connection between Wheatley and the traveler will be discussed at length later in the essay, but for now, suffice it to say that Wheatley, just like Venus, had more than a vested interest in her charge's safe arrival.

In the second stanza, Wheatley describes the "*Pow'r*" (Neptune) as "propi-tious"—willing to comply with the poet's wishes after hearing the lay, which indicates that the poet has risen to higher status than the average mortal. However, that the god, here, in this stanza is called a "Power" instead of by his proper name is significant beyond the fact that the word "Neptune" would not fit the scansion of the line. Had she addressed the god by his name, the implica-tion would be that the poet is of equal status with Neptune. Furthermore, this power is *willing* to help, not forced or obliged to do so. Wheatley enjoys high status, but has not yet ascended to the level of god; she is, in other words, not yet Venus.

The final couplet, however, reveals a remarkable hierarchical ascent. She addresses directly the god of the sea to remember his promise to keep the seas even and calm; the ode is "my pray'r," not Venus'; notice, as well, that she ad-dresses Neptune by name. Once again, Wheatley's grammatical structure comes into play as we see that she orders Neptune to keep his promise as she employs the imperative mood: "Thy promise, *Neptune* keep, record my pray'r, / Nor give my wishes to the empty air." Although it was common practice in this time period to italicize proper nouns, the emphasis serves another func-tion, connecting the second and third stanzas. From first to second to third stanzas, then, a remarkable ascent takes place in Wheatley's persona: in the first she is a mortal caught in the midst of a storm; in the second, she rises to a liminal space, somewhere between human and goddess; and in the third, she rises not just to the level of deity, but to one in the position to command. A mere "paean to the god of the seas" (*Aeneas* 236), this poem clearly is not. All the while, however, Wheatley serves the same function as Venus: to ensure the safe arrival of a beloved individual at her or his destination.

Shields notes that Wheatley's poetry displays "a tension between horizon-tal human movement and vertical semidivine motion" ("Struggle" 258). Given the remarkable transformation of Wheatley as a character in her ode, we would have to place this work among the most vertically oriented in the entire collection. But "Ode to Neptune" illustrates a complete transcendence of the horizontal as Wheatley's persona travels increasingly higher on the vertical scale, not just to a position of semidivine, but to divinity and further. To appreciate this movement fully, we must explore the intratextual connection between "Ode to Neptune" and "On Imagination," in which the poet describes the process in which the imaginative faculty allows for the transcendence of temporal reality.

That, in "On Imagination," Wheatley invokes the muse for help describing the powers of imagination denotes the importance of the faculty itself and how highly she regards it. In fact, she does not invoke *a* muse, but all of them: "From Helicon's refulgent heights attend, / Ye sacred choir, and my attempts befriend" (65). Although she asks, in the third stanza, who could possibly describe imagination's power or its "swiftness," Wheatley immediately dives into her subject—a move that displays supreme confidence in her poetic abilities. Imagination, she asserts, allows not just her, but anyone (the poet uses the first-person plural pronoun, we) to " . . . surpass the wind, / And leave the rolling universe behind" (66), on its "pinions." Two observations bear mentioning here: first, by using the metaphor of flight, Wheatley indicates that imagination allows one to ascend, to travel vertically. Second, imagination allows the poet to "surpass the winds," foreshadowing ("On Imagination" appears before "Ode to Neptune") Wheatley's ascension above Aeolus' thundering winds in "Neptune."

From the heights the imagination allows her to attain, the poet can either "in one view . . . grasp the mighty whole / Or with new worlds amaze th' unbounded soul" (66). Wheatley's imagination in "Neptune" allows her to do the former, as she rises to a level where she has a god's-eye perspective on the world, viewing Boston, the expanse of the Atlantic, and Britannia all at once. She also sees Sol's "double radiance" as light reflected off of the calm ocean—a view one would not be able to behold from the surface of the water. Stanza four describes the heterocosm imagination allows the poet to construct; Wheatley can make "Fair Flora . . . resume her fragrant reign, / And with her flow'ry riches deck the plain" (66), despite the fact that, in reality, "Winter frowns." The final stanza, however, reveals imagination's flaw: its ephemeral nature. Winter, or temporal reality, must finally reassert itself and end the poet's all-too-brief moments of rapture as "northern tempests damp the rising fire" of

Patrick Moseley

imaginative bliss. The poet, knowing perfectly well that imagination cannot maintain such heights, resigns herself to the fact and "reluctant[ly] leave[s] the pleasing views" (68). The horizontal will always triumph in the end.

Or will it? Not according to what we see in "Ode to Neptune," at least. In order to clarify this suggestion, it may be helpful to attend to the poem's form. As Shields demonstrates in "Phillis Wheatley's Use of Classicism," "Ode to Neptune" is a garden-variety Horatian ode, insofar as it is, true to the definition provided by the author in *The Princeton Encyclopedia of Poetics:* "stanzaic and regular . . . personal rather than public, general rather than occasional, tranquil rather than intense and contemplative rather than brilliant" (qtd. in Shields 101). Yet what is more important than the fact that Wheatley uses the form is that she employs the form in much the same manner as does Horace, demonstrating a more than passing knowledge of his works. In *Apollo and the Nine: A History of the Ode,* Carol Maddison observes a particular narrative progression in Horace's works: "The development of the Horatian ode is linear rather than circular. We never return to the beginning" (33). Wheatley follows Horace's example in "Neptune," using the power of imagination not only to ascend to the height of a goddess, calm the impetuous winds, and dole out orders to the god of the sea, but to maintain the vertical thrust indefinitely. This short ode, then, occupies a space unprecedented by any other work in the volume of *Poems,* insofar as it is the practical application of the theories set forth in "On Imagination." However, the imaginative faculty here (and only here) raises the poet to a position where the claims of reality can no longer lay hold of her, for, as is discussed in depth below, Phillis Wheatley had, by the time of this poem's composition, made an important step in making a fundamental change in her own reality.

II

To identify Phillis Wheatley as Aeneas in "Neptune" is more difficult than to identify her as Venus, if for no other reason than that the poem is subtitled "On Mrs. W—'s Voyage to England." At first glance one would think that "Mrs. W." is none other than Phillis's mistress, Susanna Wheatley. But as William H. Robinson has found, there is no evidence to suggest that Mrs. Wheatley ever, let alone on October 10, 1772, embarked on a trip across the Atlantic. Her name was not among those in the log; furthermore, the captain of the *London Packet,* Robert Calef, wrote to her twice from London during the specific time period. Robinson has discovered, though, that, included with a 1773 volume of *Poems,* is "a handwritten note saying that this poem was dedicated to a 'Mrs. Susanna Wright,' a celebrated artist who worked in wax" (*Writings* 273). One might then be tempted to conclude that "Mrs. W." is the Pennsylvania Quaker poet, Susanna Wright; both she and Phillis were contemporaries and practiced the same craft. Still, three undeniable facts preclude this conclusion: first, although born in England, Wright would take only one trip across the Atlantic, and that was in 1722 when she first came to Pennsylvania. Second, having never married, Wright remained a "Miss" all her life. Finally, although she wrote poetry and raised silkworms, working in wax was never one of her hobbies (Waldrup 110–16). In all likelihood, I would suggest, Wheatley's Susanna W was never a Susanna in the first place; perhaps the woman Wheatley had in mind was Mrs. Patience Wright, who was certainly famous, especially in Boston, for her uncannily lifelike wax statuary.[2]

After the death of her husband in 1769, Patience was forced to find a way to support herself and her four children. Opportunities would have been few and far between, the best bet probably being to take in boarders at her New York home; instead, she decided to take a childhood hobby of waxwork and turn it into a career. She gained fame almost immediately after embarking on her first sculpture circuit tour of the colonies in 1771. Perhaps the oldest (starting in 1733) and most prestigious stop on the circuit was Boston. Given that Phillis was granted an unusual amount of latitude for a slave, it is not unlikely that she would have been taken to see an artistic event of such magnitude. Just as likely too would be the possibility that the sculptor would have visited the Wheatley household on the corner of King Street and Mackerel Lane. Margaretta Odell writes in her biography that the Wheatley home was often frequented by notables from the Boston community and visiting elites. However, even if Wheatley had not seen Wright's artwork in person, she certainly could have kept abreast of that artist's activities through the news: a number of stories about Wright appeared in the *Boston News-Letter.* On June 20, 1771, Wheatley's local newspaper ran the story of Wright's house nearly burning to the ground. Phillis also would have read in this feature that nearly all of her sculptures had either been destroyed or damaged with the exception of the statue of George Whitefield.

As soon as Patience repaired the damage done to a number of the sculptures, she and her sister, Rachel Wells, took the show on the road one last time in America, stopping once again in Boston. Wright had close connections with Boston's elite; particularly close was she with Jane Mecom, sister of Benjamin

Franklin. Given the fact that Franklin was a lifelong friend of Mather Byles, who was in all likelihood the poetic mentor of Phillis Wheatley, it seems all the more likely that Phillis and Patience knew each other firsthand.

But perhaps the most substantial evidence linking Wright and Wheatley is their mutual relationship with the Reverend George Whitefield. Phillis had a personal relationship with the great awakener, who probably stayed in the Wheatley household during his last tour through the colonies. Wright, in all probability, knew him as well, insofar as Patience's sister, Rachel Wells, sculpted a likeness of him sometime in 1770. Grimsted contends that it was through Whitefield that the Wheatleys first came into contact with Selina Hastings, the Countess of Huntingdon. Whitefield may well have put Wright and her sister into contact with the countess as well. What is known for sure is that, later in her life, Wright and the countess had a close relationship, as both owned homes in London and at Bath; furthermore, sometime in early 1774, Huntingdon sat for Wright to sculpt her likeness. The point is, Wright and Wells may well have been among Hastings' protégés four years earlier—a fact of no little significance considering that "By the early 1770s Susanna Wheatley was opening her home to all of the countess's minister protégés who came to Boston" (Grimsted 384).

In any event, on February 3, 1772 (the middle of what was known as the storm season), Patience Wright boarded *The Nancy* and sailed for London where she hoped to spread her fame, and, of course, make more money. Like the story of Wright's house catching fire, the *Boston News-Letter* carried the news of Wright's departure. Leaving aside, for a moment, the discrepancy regarding the first name, Patience Wright meets all the appropriate characteristics of "Mrs. W.": she was famous for her works in wax, sailed for England in 1772, and most important, probably had some sort of personal relationship with Wheatley. Moreover, Wheatley certainly would have observed the striking similarities between Wright's experiences and those of Virgil's Aeneas. Just as Aeneas fled Troy with no possessions but his household gods while his city was burning to the ground, the only possessions that survived the fire consuming Wright's home were her works of art—those personal expressions of her own devotion and culture. Just as Aeneas was welcomed with open arms into Carthage and by its leader, Wright was well received by London and its culturally elite.

I would also argue that Wheatley must have seen Patience Wright as a role model. Many critics assert that Wheatley saw her poetry, her art, as that which would eventually free her from the bonds of slavery; I agree, and I would go a step further by saying that Phillis Wheatley, like Patience Wright, planned to make a career out of her calling at least as early as 1772, the time of "Neptune"'s composition. This intention, if openly expressed by a slave, would not have met with approval in pre-Revolutionary Boston (or post-Revolutionary, for that matter); it would have been exactly the sort of transgression that would have resulted in the revocation of her writing privileges. Thus, Patience Wright's first name may have been consciously changed to Susanna, but not simply because it scanned better (which, of course, it does), but with this one substitution, Wheatley changes the temper of the poem entirely; what might have been seen as an openly defiant expression of empowerment is transformed to a submissive expression of a young slave's devotion to her mistress.

Here again, Wheatley displays her uncanny understanding of the classical form of the Horatian ode. As Maddison notes, "The beginning of a Horatian ode frequently contains an address to the friend . . . for whom the poem is *nominally* written. . . . In speaking of his friends, too, Horace is never personal" (33–34; emphasis added). With this poetic form, Phillis could subtly divert her readers' attention from the true persona and subject matter, allowing the largely white readership to believe that "Ode to Neptune" is nothing more than a paean to Susanna Wheatley. Phillis's mistress, then, is not Wheatley's Aeneas, nor, for that matter, is Patience Wright's voyage Wheatley's ultimate concern. Referring once again to Horace's use of the ode, while the addressee often inspired the lay, more often than not, the subject matter was personal to the poet (Maddison 33). Consequently, while the sculptor and her journey serve as a representative character in the poem, the real hero of Wheatley's representation of Virgil's epic is the author herself.

Wheatley and her entire race without question were caught in the throng of "impetuous winds" in Boston, for even the most "reasonable" of Enlightenment thinkers blew—pardon the pun—hot air about the alleged natural inferiority of blacks. While David Hume wrote that "There never was a civilized nation of any other complexion than white, nor even any individual eminent either in action or speculation" (252), Immanuel Kant believed that "The Negroes of Africa have no feeling that rises above the trifling. . . . Not a single one was ever found who presented anything great in art or science" (110–11). This type of racist thinking kept Wheatley from publishing her 1772 volume in Boston. Wheatley ran three proposals on February 29, March 14, and April 18, 1772, in the *Boston Censor:* "A Collection of POEMS, wrote at several times, and upon various occasions, by PHILLIS, a Negro Girl, from the strength of her own Genius, it being but a few years since she came to this Town an uncultivated Barbarian from Africa" (qtd. in Robinson, *Black New England Letters* 50).

Gates estimates that the publishers would have required at least three hundred subscriptions before printing the volume. John Andrews, Boston merchant and admirer of Wheatley's poetry, suggests in a letter to William Barrel that, due to racist reasons, few were subscribing: "It's about two months since I subscribed for Phillis' poems, which I expected to have sent you long ago, but the want of spirit to carry anything of the kind here prevented it, as they are not yet published" (qtd. in Robinson, *Black New England Letters* 50). In *Black New England Letters*, William H. Robinson states the case more bluntly: "Boston whites . . . refused to subscribe to her volume, which they could not or would not believe had been written by a black slave girl" (51). It must have been clear to both Phillis and her most ardent supporter, Susanna Wheatley, that publication in Boston would be an impossibility; instead, Phillis would have to be courted by Britannia.

Indeed, "welcome smiled in every eye" in Britannia to some extent, inasmuch as by 1772, no slave having stepped foot on English soil could be forced to return to the colonies. The reception of black literary efforts must have been more congenial as well, considering that James Gronniosaw's slave narrative had been published there earlier that same year. And with the help of her patroness, Selina Hastings, Wheatley found a publisher willing to print the volume—Archibald Bell, who was sympathetic to printing works by "Methodists" with connections to Whitefield and the countess. However, one more hurdle lay in Phillis's path: Bell required a letter of attestation certifying that the poems included in the collection were works of the young woman's own imagination. Thus, as Henry Louis Gates explains, eighteen of the most prominent Bostonians gathered together with the young poet "sometime before October 8, 1772" to verify the poems' authenticity (Gates 5).

Although there is no extant record of these proceedings, Gates speculates that, in all probability, Wheatley would have been examined on her knowledge of the classics. But more important than the specific proof of authorship Phillis may have been required to provide is the impact the final decision would have, not just on the young poet, but on the entire African race. Gates captures perfectly this significance:

> If she had indeed written her poems, then this would demon-
> strate that Africans were human beings and should be liberated

from slavery. If, on the other hand, she had not written, or could not write her poems, or if indeed she was like a parrot who speaks a few words plainly, then that would be another matter entirely. *Essentially, she was auditioning for the humanity of the entire African people.* (27–28; emphasis added)

That she carried the burden not only of her own fortunes but the fortunes of an entire race is a situation not at all unlike the one Aeneas faced. One cannot help but recall the striking image of Aeneas fleeing the ruins of Troy as he carries his father, Anchises, on his back and leads the remainders of his Dardan race to a new life on a far distant shore, a land to the West. Certainly this connection would not have been lost on Wheatley, and judging from her appropriation of the epic in "Ode to Neptune," it was not.

Wheatley passed the examination and her interrogators signed the letter "assur[ing] the World, that the Poems . . . were (as we verily believe) written by Phillis, a young Negro Girl . . ." (*Poems* 7). Also commanding attention is a phrase in the same paragraph stating that Phillis was "under the Disadvantage of serving as a Slave in a Family in this Town." This statement must have been an overwhelming embarrassment to her master, John Wheatley; even if he had considered granting Phillis's manumission before, the matter would now be all the more pressing. Given that Wheatley would now, at long last, have a collection of her poetry published, and that stirrings of her own manumission were in the air, the composition date of "Ode to Neptune," October 10, 1772, just two days after the estimated date of the meeting, can not be underemphasized. Her own "household gods," the physical manifestations of personal devotion, would free her and by extension force the white readership to rethink their notions on "Afric's blameless race." Wheatley was for the first time, empowered; it comes as little surprise, then, that she would compose her ode in terms of the *Aeneid*—a work that relates one race's long, perilous journey from disenfranchisement to cultural domination.

With all the obvious similarities between the burdens carried by Wheatley and those carried by Aeneas, there is one distinct difference we should observe. Aeneas was not alone in his journeys from Troy to Italy. Along the way, he had his mother, Venus, exhaust all her efforts to ensure his safe arrival. Wheatley, on the other hand, did not enjoy the luxuries of divine intervention along her journey to be recognized as a poet, or even as a human being. Wheatley, in other words, had no choice but to play Venus to her own Aeneas; and like Venus, Wheatley had to be, to a certain extent, deceptive if she was to gain the recognition that she so clearly deserved. While Venus' trickery involved instilling the flame of love into Dido's heart, Wheatley's deception came in the form of a subtle subversive poetics.

The intratextual connection between "Ode to Neptune" and "To Maecenas" illustrates the nature of Wheatley's subtlety. Like Horace in his first book of *Odes*, Wheatley opens her *Poems* with a piece entitled, "To Maecenas," in which she promises to achieve fame in her craft. Although the jury is still out on the matter regarding who exactly Wheatley's Maecenas is, the poet claims that she will "snatch a laurel from thine honour'd head, / While you indulgent smile upon the deed" (12). Shields has commented on the importance of Wheatley's choice of the verb, "snatch"; while a white poet might be able simply to take or seize the laurel, a young slave girl would have to be more surreptitious in her efforts. While the action of snatching "indicates that she recognizes the uncertain reception awaiting her poetic efforts," it also emphasizes her "subversive voice," and dedication to possess the laurel even if she has to crown herself (*Aeneas* 121–22). In any event, Wheatley, in this poem which opens her volume, makes a promise not only to achieve poetic maturity, but also to gain recognition—a promise not unlike the one Horace makes in *his* "To Maecenas" opening his first book of *Odes*.

Horace asserts that his ultimate goal is to be given "ivy, the reward of learned brows" (29). Unlike Wheatley, however, this poet informs his Maecenas of the results such a crowning would have on him. "If you enroll me among the lyric bards," Horace claims, "my soaring head will strike the stars" (35, 40). Horace's uncertainty that he may be enrolled among the poets of his age recalls the same uncertainty Wheatley faces as a poet unable to procure a public forum for her work. But it is Horace's proclamation of what will happen to him if he is enrolled that draws a striking connection to Wheatley's "Ode to Neptune": he promises to reside "among the gods above" (30). As has already been demonstrated, "Neptune" is a work whose vertical thrust is unparalleled by any other attempt in the volume. Wheatley's imagination raises her to a height from which she can take on the persona of Venus, and address other gods in the imperative mood. That she does so in a poem written so shortly after she was at long last "enrolled among the lyric bards," after finally being "legitimized" by eighteen of the most prominent Bostonian citizens, is significant. In a very real sense, she had finally snatched the laurel, and "Ode to Neptune" demonstrates the veracity of that claim in specifically Horatian terms: she commands her head or her imagination to "soar," thereby confirming the opening promise made in Horace's "To Maecenas."

III

Although I maintain that "Ode to Neptune" is an enthusiastic expression of empowerment occasioned by the promise that her volume would finally be put in print, it would be disingenuous to suggest that Wheatley, by any stretch of her imagination, thought that her predicaments both as poet and seeker of freedom were, as of October 10, 1772, behind her. Just as Carthage was a brief respite on Aeneas' way to his final destination of Italy, London was merely a stopping point for Wheatley on her own poetic journey back to Boston. In Virgil's epic, Neptune does not make his promise to allow safe passage for the Trojans until the fifth book—not, in other words, until Aeneas and his crew had already set sail from Carthage. Just as important, Neptune has no power beyond his own domain of the seas. Aeneas would still have to face numerous challenges on his own after dropping anchor on the banks of the Tiber; moreover, it would take generations before the Romans would raise themselves to a position of cultural and political domination. So while Wheatley ends her ode on a note of imaginative rapture, having ascended to the level of goddess, she is also careful to end her own version of the epic at a point of only half completion. While both Wheatley herself and her volumes of *Poems* would return safely to Boston Harbor, her struggles both as a human and as a poet were certainly not at an end. Indeed, one could safely assert that those struggles continue to this day in academia between her apologists and her all-too-misguided detractors who insist that Wheatley's poetry is derivative.

More often than not, I would imagine, those accusations of imitation leveled against Wheatley are an outgrowth of an overall misunderstanding of Early American poetry in general—that what was written in the American colonies was a bastardization of the so-called superior literature produced on the other side of the Atlantic. Phillis Wheatley was not a neoclassicist, but a classicist; she did not need John Dryden to translate Virgil for her, nor did she need Alexander Pope to tell her why the ancient Roman poet was significant. And to come to this realization does not (to borrow one of Wheatley's most eloquent phrases) "require the penetration of a philosopher to determine" (*Collected Works* 177). To recognize the employment to which she puts ancient classical texts, however, does require some effort. Wheatley does not mine the classics for common tropes in order to display some sort of false erudition, nor, as some critics suggest, does she goes back to the literatures of Ancient Greece and Rome to window-dress her poetry. "Ode to Neptune," to point to just one instance, moreover, attests to the fact that she clearly made the epic content of

Patrick Moseley

Virgil and the poetic form of Horace thoroughly her own, in her effort to express authorial as well as personal empowerment.

NOTES

1. Of course, names of cities in the Latin language are feminine nouns. What bears mentioning here is that Carthage is not only feminine in a grammatical sense, but also feminine in a more figurative sense, insofar as it is founded and ruled by Dido.

2. For biographical information on Patience Wright, see Sellers.

WORKS CITED

Gates, Henry Louis, Jr. *The Trials of Phillis Wheatley: America's First Black Poet and Her Encounters with the Founding Fathers.* New York: Basic Civitas, 2003.

Grimsted, David. "Anglo-American Racism and Phillis Wheatley's 'Sable Veil,' 'Length'ned Chain,' and 'Knitted Heart.'" *Women in the Age of the American Revolution.* Ed. Ronald Hoffman and Peter J. Albert. Charlottesville: UP of Virginia, 1989. 338–444.

Harmon, William C., and Hugh Holman. *A Handbook to Literature.* 8th ed. Upper Saddle River: Prentice Hall, 2000.

Horace. *Odes.* Trans. David West. Oxford: Clarendon, 1995.

Hume, David "Of National Characters." 1882. *David Hume: The Philosophical Works.* Ed. Thomas Hill Green and Thomas Hodge Grose. Vol. 3. Germany: Scientia Varlag Aalen, 1964.

Jefferson, Thomas. *Notes on the State of Virginia.* Chapel Hill: U of North Carolina P, 1995.

Kant, Immanuel. *Observations on the Feeling of the Beautiful and Sublime.* Trans. John Goldthwait. Berkeley: U of California P, 1991.

Kyper, Peter Thomas. "The Significance of Mather Byles in the Literary Tradition of America: A Study of His Poems on Several Occasions and his Literary Criticism." Diss. Auburn U, 1974.

Maddison, Carol. *Apollo and the Nine: A History of the Ode.* Baltimore: Johns Hopkins UP, 1960.

Preminger, Alex, et al., eds. *The New Princeton Encyclopedia of Poetry and Poetics*. Princeton: Princeton UP, 1993.

Robinson, William H. *Black New England Letters: The Uses of Writings in Black New England*. Boston: Boston Public Library, 1977.

———. *Phillis Wheatley and Her Writings*. New York: Garland, 1984.

Sellers, Charles Coleman. *Patience Wright: American Artist and Spy in George III's London*. Middletown: Wesleyan UP, 1976.

Shields, John C. *The American Aeneas: Classical Origins of the American Self*. Knoxville: U of Tennessee P, 2001.

———. "Phillis Wheatley's Struggle for Freedom." *The Collected Works of Phillis Wheatley*. New York: Oxford UP, 1988. 229–70.

———. "Phillis Wheatley's Use of Classicism." *American Literature* 52 (1980): 97–111.

Virgil. *Aeneid*. Trans Allen Mandelbaum. New York: Bantam, 1981.

Waldrup, Carole Chandler. *Colonial Women: 23 Europeans Who Helped Build a Nation*. Jefferson: McFarland, 1999.

Watson, Marsha. "A Classic Case: Phillis Wheatley and Her Poetry." *Early American Literature* 31.2 (1996): 103–33.

Wheatley, Phillis. *The Collected Works of Phillis Wheatley*. Ed. John C. Shields. New York: Oxford UP, 1988.

Phillis Wheatley's Use of the Georgic

Eric D. Lamore

The first African American to publish a book in the English language, Phillis Wheatley was captured from her African homeland at the age of seven or eight and survived the horrific Middle Passage in the ship bearing the name, *Phillis*. This African American artist arrived in colonial Boston in 1761 with "no other covering than a quantity of dirty carpet about her" (Odell 12), and managed to accomplish what can be characterized as spectacular linguistic growth. Wheatley, with no prior knowledge, mastered the English language in some sixteen months time, and was able to read "the most difficult Parts of the Sacred Writings" (Wheatley vi). Not content with her acquisition of the English language or with her ability to handle the principal text of the Judeo-Christian religious tradition, this African American artist's impressive capacity to master linguistic systems advanced even further through her study of Latin. As John Wheatley, a member of the family who purchased Phillis when she arrived in the colonies, remarks in a "Letter sent by the Author's Master to the Publisher," "She has a great Inclination to learn the Latin Tongue, and has made some Progress in it" (Wheatley vi).

This infamous "Letter of Attestation," the same document wherein John Wheatley comments upon Wheatley's interest in Latin, accompanied the 1773 *Poems on Various Subjects, Religious and Moral,* and "verified" "that the Poems specified in the following Page [the table of contents page for *Poems*], were (as we verily believe) written by Phillis, a young Negro Girl." Only one page before this report authenticating Wheatley's remarkable ability to acquire language looms the verbal and visual interplay found in the now-famous frontispiece to the 1773 *Poems.* Selina Hastings, the Countess of Huntingdon, dedicatee of the 1773 volume, recommended the inclusion of this frontispiece, which pictures Wheatley. Arguably, without the support of Hastings, who successfully secured publication for the volume with the publisher, Archibald Bell, in London after the initial 1772 proposal for *Poems* was rejected by a racist colonial community, Wheatley would have continued to struggle in locating a press that would print her poems. The importance of the frontispiece should not, however, be overlooked. For in this text, the visual portion of the frontispiece reveals the African American artist impressively captured in the liberated act of composition; yet the verbal text surrounding this visual image, "Phillis Wheatley, Negro Servant to Mr. John Wheatley of Boston," verifies that this African American artist still remained in bondage. Wheatley's position as an African American slave becomes emphasized for a second time on the very next page through virtually the same message: "By Phillis Wheatley, Negro Servant to Mr. John Wheatley, of Boston, in New England."

With the 1773 publication of *Poems on Various Subjects, Religious and Moral,* some, but not all, eighteenth-century commentators dismissed this complex African American artist and her poetic efforts to negotiate a number of oppressive variables: her status as an eighteenth-century writer of African descent, her status as a woman in a predominately patriarchal society, and her status as a slave. Thomas Jefferson, in his popular *Notes on the State of Virginia,* for instance, serves as one of the earliest and most scathing critics of Wheatley in his remarks that, "Religion indeed has produced a Phyllis Whatley [*sic*]; but it could not produce a poet. The compositions published under her name are below the dignity of criticism" (147). In Jefferson's assessment, the usage of religious imagery, as seen in her elegies and her biblical paraphrases, does not allow Wheatley the status of a legitimate eighteenth-century poet. Jefferson's position that " . . . in imagination they [individuals of African descent] are dull, tasteless, and anomalous" (146) clearly contributes to his racist dismissal of Wheatley.

Discourse on the alleged inferiority of individuals of color, however, began well before the publication, distribution, and absorption of Wheatley's 1773 *Poems.* As early as 1744, for instance, dialogue surfaced over an individual named Francis Williams, a free, classically educated, black Jamaican who penned a forty-six-line Latin ode. Because of his education and achievement in composing verse, Williams called into question several of the major tenets found in eighteenth-century racist ideologies attempting to justify the transatlantic slave trade. Apologists for the slave trade maintained that the act of relegating individuals of color below the level of whites justified the use of these "sub-humans" in the slave trade. On another racist level, the apologists argued that because individuals of color were unable to produce any extension of the

Eric D. Lamore

arts, including literature and music, these same individuals would be "rescued" from their native counties in order to live more "productive" lives in bondage.

Perhaps the most often cited and most troubling opinion arising from this immense commentary that attempted to legitimize slavery may be found in the writings of David Hume. In a footnote from his "Of National Characters," an essay that made up a portion of his *Essays and Treatises on Several Subjects*, David Hume claimed that, "in Jamaica indeed they talk of one Negroe as a man of parts and learning; but 'tis likely he is admired for very slender accomplishments, like a parrot who speaks a few words plainly" (Hume 86). In the language employed by Hume, we find an all-too-familiar rhetoric that forcefully dismisses the obvious accomplishment of Williams's writing. Throughout the poem, for instance, Williams consciously points out how his poem transgresses the racist notion that individuals of color were unable to produce literary texts. In one particular line, for instance, Williams names a muse "of blackest tint" and openly asks, "What! shall an Æthiop touch the martial string, / Of battles, leaders, achievements sing?" (qtd. in Carretta, "Who" 230).

As these two, brief examples illustrate, Williams positions the eighteenth-century reader in what was likely an uncomfortable poetic space because the writer of African descent inserts race into standard poetic conventions of eighteenth-century verse. Williams perfectly captures this troubled position he forces the reader to inhabit with the word, "What," followed by an exclamation point. The "muse," one of "blackest tint" as argued by Williams, will no longer assist only white poets; rather, the racialized muse will assist writers of African descent. Williams, in his construction of a "muse" of "blackest tint," Vincent Carretta usefully observes, "anticipated by nearly fifteen years Phillis Wheatley's similar move in her poem, 'To Maecenas' (1773), in which she associates herself with Terence, an 'African by birth'" (218). The exploration of the generic conventions found in epic "battles, leaders, achievements," in the words of Williams, may now be sung not only by poets such as Homer and Virgil but also by poets of African descent. What these two examples indicate, then, is the fact that Hume, when reading the ode written by Williams, was unable to acknowledge how his racist ideology misinformed his "reading" of Williams. Hume viewed the attempt by Williams in utilizing a genre that originated in the ancient classical tradition, the Horatian ode, and the language of the intellectual elite, Latin, as a clear failure—one synonymous with the mimicry of a parrot "who speaks a few words plainly."

This brief illustration of acknowledging a muse of "blackest tint" and a writer of African descent possessing the ability to pursue the epic strain, as seen in the ode by Williams, functions as a necessary, critical bridge to reflect productively on the relationship between the extant works of Phillis Wheatley and the ancient classical tradition. For, in "To Maecenas," Wheatley underscores the same concern first voiced by Williams. In "Maecenas," the opening poem of the 1773 *Poems*, Wheatley, at first, laments that "O could I rival thine [Homer] and *Virgil's* page, / Or claim the *Muses* with the *Mantuan* Sage" (Wheatley 10), but, in the very next couplet, she charts a bold poetic mission: "Soon the same beauties should my mind adorn, / And the same ardors in my soul should burn" (10). Later, in this same poem, Wheatley acknowledges that the Roman writer of comedies, Terence, "an African by birth" as identified in her footnote, has been "inspir'd," "replenish'd," and "fir'd" by the Muses, yet ponders, "But say, ye *Muses*, why this partial grace, / To one alone of *Afric's* sable race" (11). At the end of the poem, Wheatley promises Maecenas, almost sounding like a threat, that the African American poet will "snatch a laurel from thine honour'd head, / While you indulgent smile upon the deed" (12).

Within this complex, introductory poem, then, Wheatley may be seen to be tracing her progress as a poet; her first attempts at "rivaling" the works of Virgil and Homer may prove unsuccessful, but, with practice, the talented African American poet successfully incorporates into her own poetry the "same beauties" and the "same ardours" found in their works. These "beauties" and "ardours," according to Wheatley, grant the poet respect from "Maecenas" in that he allows this writer of African descent to "snatch" a laurel, the key signifier standing for mature poetic achievement in the ancient classical tradition. Given this reading of "Maecenas," one in which Wheatley projects the evolution of her ability to construct successful verse, we may wonder how exactly this African American poet, first, longs to achieve expression of the same poetic afflatus that moved Homer and Virgil, and then succeeds, according to her own testimony, in the very next line, in incorporating the same "beauties" and "ardours" of Virgil into her own verse.

Beyond the mentioning of both Homer and Virgil in "Maecenas," Wheatley clearly shows interest in ancient classical authors. Her translation and appropriation of Ovid as seen in the poem, "Niobe in Distress for Her Children Slain by Apollo, from Ovid's *Metamorphoses*, Book VI. And from a View of the Painting of Mr. Richard Wilson" and her "Ode to Neptune," the Roman god of the sea, help to explicate the extent of Wheatley's reading, absorbing, and incorporating motifs of and themes from the ancient classical tradition into her own poetry. While readers of Wheatley's poetry have already explicated this

Eric D. Lamore

African American poet's usage of ancient classical genres such as epic, epyllion (mini-epic), and subversive pastoral, along with her use of the Judeo-Christian Bible, they have heretofore overlooked the complex ways in which Wheatley utilizes dimensions of Virgil's *Georgics*.[1]

One problem in the relatively brief history of scholarship on the Early American georgic has been the fusing of the ancient classical genres of "pastoral" and "georgic." In an article on Timothy Dwight's georgic poem, *Greenfield Hill*, for instance, Larry Kutchen observes that "'georgic' remains an unrecognizable genre in criticism of American literature since readers tend to concentrate more on Virgilian pastoral and epic than on Virgil's second work, the *Georgics*" (126). As early as the 1964 publication of Leo Marx's *The Machine in the Garden: Technology and the Pastoral Ideal in America,* nevertheless, the differentiation in American literary criticism between the genres of pastoral and georgic appears to be nonexistent, even though there are clearly different poetics in the *Eclogues* and *Georgics,* the first and second works by the Roman poet, Virgil.

Despite the fact that Marx claims, on his text's very first page, that he plans to investigate the "pastoral ideal" in *The Machine,* he does not, in his investigation, concentrate fully on the genre of pastoral or the shepherd figure. In one particular chapter, entitled "The Garden," for example, Marx quotes a long passage from Englishman Richard Price to illustrate how "'the *pastoral idea* of America caught on everywhere in Europe'" (104; emphasis added). In another quote from Price, Marx includes the phrases "'independent and handy yeomanry,'" "'drawing plenty from the ground,'" and "'the hand of industry'" (Price qtd. in Marx 105). As enumerated above, however, these phrases echo the genre of georgic in their emphases on the yeoman (or farmer figure), the importance of industry, and the need for cultivating the ground. Marx uses Price's comments to conclude in his later treatment of Thomas Jefferson's *Notes on the State of Virginia,* another American georgic text, that "there is no question here of Jefferson's having been influenced by Price's version of the *pastoral ideal;* by this time it was in the air on both sides of the Atlantic" (105; emphasis added). According to Marx, then, the genre of "pastoral" obviously includes the farmer figure, the representative of georgic, not pastoral; Marx appears to hold that the two genres are virtually inseparable.

Georgic texts differ from the genre of pastoral in significant ways. While the pastoral tradition features the shepherd figure mourning after lost loves, piping on oaten flutes, participating in singing contests, and sometimes subversively commenting on the foibles of society, georgic texts showcase the farmer figure, an individual who is engaged in plowing fields, often tending bees, caring for livestock, and constructing ways to prevent infection and plague. Most notable, however, is the thematic departure among georgics from pastoral. While in pastoral texts, the theme "love conquers all" dominates, in georgics, the theme of "labor conquers all" rules.

As the scholarly work of William C. Dowling, Timothy Sweet, and David S. Shields has demonstrated, treatments of the Early American georgic have focused, not exclusively, but mainly on Timothy Dwight's *Greenfield Hill,* Thomas Jefferson's *Notes on the State of Virginia,* James Grainger's *The Sugar Cane,* George Ogilvie's *Carolina; Or, the Planter,* and J. Hector St. Jean de Crèvecoeur's *Letters from an American Farmer.* Despite the fact that Dowling does provide some of the historical and literary contexts behind the georgic genre in his *Poetry and Ideology in Revolutionary Connecticut,* his presentation, while embedded in the larger design of the book, focuses mainly on Timothy Dwight's *Greenfield Hill* and on a single state during the Revolutionary period, thereby leaving a clear space for more work on this Early American genre.

A second treatment of the Early American georgic may be found in David S. Shields's *Oracles of Empire: Poetry, Politics, and Commerce in British America, 1690–1750,* wherein the author claims that Virgil's *Georgics* "loomed in the imagination of provincial Americans" (70). This critic, however, drastically revises this statement in other areas of his text by maintaining that *The Fleece,* a georgic produced by British poet John Dyer, "supplied his [Dyer's] New World imitators with several themes" (65). Within the first one hundred lines of *Carolina; or, The Planter,* George Ogilvie, one of Dyer's "New World imitators" according to D. Shields, draws on two different Virgilian genres. Ogilvie identifies his audience as those " . . . to their household gods, / Raise foreign altars in these new abodes" (9). This physical relocation to the New World, as referenced by Ogilvie, directly parallels the advice by the Roman hero, Aeneas, to his father, Anchises, before fleeing Troy in book 2 of Virgil's epic, the *Aeneid:* "'And one thing more; you, father, are to carry / The holy objects and the gods of the household, / My hands are foul with battle and blood, I could not / Touch them without pollution" (48). After comparing the New World inhabitants' westward migration to the one presented by Virgil in the *Aeneid,* a mere sixty lines later, Ogilvie imparts an imperative command: "Attentive listen to the instructive muse, / Whilst she describes the scite [*sic*] you ought to / choose" (11). Assuming the guise of the "instructive muse," as

Eric D. Lamore

does Virgil through his *Georgics,* Ogilvie advises the transplanted European on how to locate a productive patch of soil in the New World. Instead of a "New World imitator," then, Ogilvie, in this small portion from *Carolina,* frames his New World experience through a balancing of Virgilian epic and georgic.

In a third and more recent study on the Early American georgic, *American Georgics: Economy and Environment in Early American Literature,* Timothy Sweet productively traces the key points in American literary scholarship that have prevented the separation of the genres of pastoral and georgic and establishes the notion of a "counter" georgic rhetoric employed by the Cherokee Indians in an attempt to resist their forced removal (122). As one recent reviewer has observed, the parameters of this study on "Early American Literature" "ends with texts that are not early" (Field 429). The final chapter includes readings that place James Fennimore Cooper, Henry David Thoreau, and George Perkins in the tradition of American georgic. This effort to map an extensive part of American literary history may be viewed as admirable, but the project suffers from confining the contents of Virgil's *Georgics* to around a page and a half. This limiting of his treatment of Virgil ultimately restricts this critical investigation on the Early American georgic, especially considering the fact that the texts of Thomas Jefferson and J. Hector St. Jean de Crèvecoeur, authors whose texts Sweet explicates, both illustrate an extensive knowledge of ancient classical texts, including Virgil's *Georgics,* in *Notes on the State of Virginia, Letters from an American Farmer,* and *Sketches of Eighteenth-Century America.*

Potential avenues for redirecting the study of the Early American georgic, then, may be found in critical studies that extend beyond the confines of a single Revolutionary state, and which focus on how writers drew upon Virgil's *Georgics,* a text that largely constructed the genre itself. Accomplishing these three parameters for shifting the study of the Early American georgic, moreover, may also be invigorated through analyses of how writers of African descent, specifically Phillis Wheatley and Olaudah Equiano,[2] carefully manipulate the genre of georgic and Virgil's *Georgics* to combat the institution of slavery.

To be sure, however, in the poetry of Phillis Wheatley, we cannot locate the rejuvenation of bees, the presence of a plague, didactic instructions on how to complete successfully various agricultural tasks such as plowing soil, breeding livestock, marrying vines, tending bees, and extracting honey from the comb, albeit one would easily find these characteristics of georgic in the reading of Virgil. In fact, the labeling of any of Wheatley's extant verse as "georgic" would simply be a misrepresentation of generic classification. An explication of the influence of Virgil's *Georgics*, then, calls for uncovering georgic manifestations in her verse, which comprise intricate components of the ancient classical genre derived from Virgil's text.

Elements of georgic may be located in such poems as "On Imagination," "Elegy on Leaving——," and in her numerous political poems. Discovery of these georgic manifestations proves significant toward continuing to understand the intimate knowledge this African American poet had of the Roman poet Virgil and of his *Georgics*. This ancient classical work, comprising four didactic books, advised Roman farmers on various acts of husbandry, and simultaneously glorified and critiqued Rome. As the second text produced by Virgil, the *Georgics* followed the composition of the ten pastoral poems found in the *Eclogues* and anticipated, in this poet's use of epic similes and the epyllion of the beekeeper, Aristaeus (in book 4), the twelve-book epic poem, the *Aeneid*. Wheatley's debt to Virgil's *Georgics*, moreover, recovers an additional layer in this artist's poetic catalogue wherein the poet manipulates elements from the ancient classical tradition to structure significant rhetorical and poetic strategies aimed at combating the institution of slavery and an oppressive colonial Boston. Probably making more than "some progress" in learning "the Latin Tongue," as John Wheatley maintained in his letter which accompanied the 1773 *Poems*, Wheatley's own reading of the *Georgics* provided her with tools to transgress discourses that attempted to relegate blacks to mere "parrots" of the ancient classical tradition.

These identifiable manifestations of georgic, as seen in the poems "On Imagination," "To a Gentleman of the Navy," and "Elegy on Leaving," in particular, assist Wheatley's construction of a subversive poetics that grants the African American artist, through her use of the imagination, temporary escape from the confines of an oppressive, urban environment to a peaceful, rural environment. With the inclusion of "Sylvanus," the Roman god of plowed fields, boundaries, and shepherds, Wheatley constructs in "On Imagination" a "scene of transport" pregnant with "rural joys" as she would later refer to these mental escapes in "Elegy on Leaving——." In the construction of this rural heterocosm or alternative rural world through the figure "Sylvanus," Wheatley successfully subverts categorization by her white captors as an oppressed slave, and anticipates a long tradition of the flight motif for the purposes of obtaining freedom in later African American literary writings and hymns.

A second application of georgic figures prominently in the poet's political verse. In this catalogue of political verse, Wheatley praises America as "a new-born *Rome*" (154) and frames George Washington as an American Augustus; yet, at the same time, the African American artist qualifies these praises by granting America's fight for independence by this "new-born *Rome*" to be legitimate only if this struggle includes marginalized groups, particularly her black brothers and sisters.

Traveling from Rome to Wheatley's African homeland, we may trace what may be called subversive attempts, in her extant poetry and prose, to recover remnants of her African origins. We get little help, nevertheless, from Margaretta Odell, Wheatley's first biographer, for in her biographical treatment of the poet, the 1838 *Memoir and Poems of Phillis Wheatley* (reprinted in 1969), Odell asserts that Wheatley "does not seem to have preserved any remembrance of the place of her nativity, or of her parents, excepting the simple circumstance that her mother *poured out water before the rising sun*—in reference, no doubt, to an ancient African custom" (p. 12 of the 3rd ed.; emphasis in original). Odell defends her claim with the evidence that experiencing the horrendous Middle Passage "might naturally enough obliterate the recollection of earlier and happier days" (13). Continuing to claim that Wheatley preserved only one memory of her African homeland, Odell continues that "the solitary exception which held its place so tenaciously in her mind, was probably renewed from day to day through this long season of affliction; for every morning, when the bereaved child saw the sun emerging from the wide waters, she must have thought of her mother, prostrating herself before the golden beam that glanced across her native plains" (13).

Even though Odell does grant Wheatley one residual memory of her African homeland, her account frequently generalizes and, therefore, does not concentrate on the key details found in the African American artist's poetry. Moreover, Odell's account categorizes Phillis as an obedient servant to the Wheatley family. By pushing the reader to contemplate "the innocence of her [Wheatley's] life," "the purity of her [Phillis's] heart," and "the ease and contentment of her domestic lot" (21), Odell attempts to construct a narrative for Phillis that emphasizes her alleged domesticity, thereby ignoring the forceful arguments, in the artist's poetry and prose, against slavery. The remarks from Odell attest to the fact that the *Memoir* remains oblivious that the African American artist consciously crafted in her work, as she developed more sophisticated rhetorical strategies, a resistive poetics that frequently combated her own status as a slave while she was held in bondage.

Because of the claim that Wheatley retained only a single memory from her life in Africa, Odell's narrative has been a principal factor in deterring readers from uncovering attempts, in the poetry of Wheatley, to reconnect, in whatever way possible, elements of her African homeland. Odell's characterization of Wheatley as a content, domestic servant, moreover, quickly crumbles with close readings of the African American poet's extant verse that assist in recovering attempts, in both the public and subversive veins, by Wheatley to resist her status in an oppressive, urban society in order to reside, mentally, in a rural environment. For, within the catalogue of Wheatley's verse, which presently stands at fifty-six poems with the recent addition of the poem, "Ocean," one may chart a progressive and impressive evolution of a serious artist who concentrates, throughout her entire poetic career, on the goal of liberating herself from all forms of oppression, and to help other individuals, regardless of race, secure a taste of the "Love of Freedom," a "principle," the artist argues, which "God has implanted" "in every human Breast" (177).

In an effort to attract an audience and a publisher for her poems, Wheatley and supporters of her poetry (e.g., her mistress Susannah) printed a proposal for an upcoming volume of her poems in the *Boston Censor* on February 29, 1772 (Robinson, *Black* 49–50). This proposal, however, as Robinson notes, failed "because of racist resistance from piqued Boston whites, who . . . could not or would not believe [the poems] had been written by a black slave girl" (52). Subsequently Wheatley was forced to seek a more sympathetic audience, so she traveled to London in hopes of securing a publisher for what would eventually become her 1773 *Poems*. Upon reflecting on this trip, which comprised a six-week stay lasting from June 17, 1773, to July 26, 1773, and resulted in her gaining access to and networking with a number of prominent individuals in London, Wheatley, in an October 18, 1773, letter to David Wooster, records that, "Since my return to America, my Master, has at the desire of my friends in England given me my freedom" (170). Obtaining freedom brought upon her life and work a drastic shift, particularly affecting how she referred to and represented Africa in her poetry.

Less than just two months after penning this significant missive to Wooster, Wheatley engaged in a public and poetic dialogue that resulted in what is likely the first praise of Africa by an African American artist. Wheatley begins this poetic exchange with "To a Gentleman of the Navy," wherein the poet boasts, "Had you appear'd on the Achaian shore / Troy now had stood, and Helen charm'd no more" (140). Wheatley calls upon Calliope, the muse of epic poetry, to assist her to praise those whom she identifies as "they," which a reader may infer, some nine lines later, as the title suggests, to be "these blooming

Eric D. Lamore

sons of Neptune's royal race" (141). Interestingly, Wheatley positions "these blooming sons of Neptune" as "heroes of the main" in their ability, among other qualities, to "plough the wat'ry main" (140). Here Wheatley links sailing to farming in her comparison that sailors may be viewed as aquatic farmer figures who plow the sea instead of the land. While a minor detail in this poem, this use of farming imagery in conjunction with sailing may be viewed as one manifestation of georgic in Wheatley's poetry.

Because of the details in Rochford's "painting" (i.e., poetic response), which refer to Phillis as "the lovely daughter of the Affric [sic] shore" and describe "the Affric shore" as a "happy land," Wheatley responds to "The Answer," published on December 5, 1774, in the *Royal American Magazine* in Boston, by, at first, lamenting that her "pen," "least favor'd by the tuneful nine," does not "rival" Alexander Pope nor Sir Isaac Newton. After this brief interval of self-deprecation, however, Wheatley launches into clear praise of her African homeland. Wheatley responds in the following manner:

> Charm'd with thy painting, how my bosom burns!
> And pleasing Gambia on my soul returns,
> While native grace in spring's luxuriant reign,
> Smiles the gay mead, and Eden blooms again,
> The various bower, the tuneful flowing stream,
> The soft retreats, the lovers golden dream,
> Her soil spontaneous, yields exhaustless stores;
> For phoebus revels on her verdant shores.
> Whose flowery births, a fragrant train appear,
> And crown the youth throughout the smiling year.
> (144)

It is important to note here that Wheatley, in this poem, refers to Gambia as "Eden." The fact that the soil "yields exhaustless stores" recalls not the genre of georgic but the prelapsarian state described in Genesis in which Adam and Eve do not need to perform any type of physical labor. In this reflection upon Gambia, Wheatley also includes elements from ancient classicism; the presence of "phoebus," the sun, on her native continent, aids in the creation of "a fragrant train" of flowers. "Phoebus," Wheatley adds, assists in the production of "bending harvest[s]" which "ripen into gold!" (144). The poet's blending of both ancient classicism and Judeo-Christianity emphasizes the artist's agrarian reflections of Gambia.

As John Shields has recently shown that Wheatley's poetic career is punctuated by two periods of maturity, a subversive, premanumission period and a postmanumission one, and because this poem was written shortly after her manumission, Wheatley did not need to rely on a subversive poetic strategy to offer praise of Gambia. When we analyze the poet's "On Imagination," however, Wheatley's strategy to reconnect with her homeland changes to one of subversion because this poem was written before this artist secured her manumission. While we will explicate shortly Wheatley's use of georgic for the purpose of reconnecting with her African homeland, analyses of eighteenth-century travel narratives written about Africa illustrate that this poet resided in an agrarian environment before her forced entry into the institution of slavery.

Details found in Anthony Benezet's *Some historical account of Guinea* and Michel Adanson's *A Voyage to Senegal, the Isle of Goree, and the River Gambia* provide crucial particulars in our attempt to understand this African American poet's relationship to her native Africa, or, more specifically, to learn about her relation to "Gambia," which "returns" to "her soul" in the poem, "Phillis's Reply to the Answer" (144). The publication and recorded observations dates found in Benezet and Adanson, moreover, become especially important when we attend to the first sentence of Margaretta Odell's *Memoir:* "Phillis Wheatley was a native of Africa; and was brought to this country in the year 1761, and sold as a slave" (430). The year in which Wheatley arrived in colonial Boston, 1761, falls close enough to the 1735 account of Francis Moor, the 1726 account of William Smith, both of whom Benezet quotes, and the February 1750 date recorded in Adanson's *Voyage* of his trip up the Gambia River to regenerate, at the very least, an initial picture of Wheatley's "Gambia." These portions from Benezet and Adanson, whether Wheatley did or did not actually read them, underscore that the eighteenth-century "Gambia," which the African American poet praises, constitutes an agrarian environment predominately inhabited by African farmers. The details found in "Phillis's Reply to the Answer" of a soil yielding "exhaustless stores" and a "bending harvest ripen[ing] into gold" (144), therefore, may be much more than what Julian A. Mason holds to be merely a "poetic pose" (Mason, *Poems* 87).

First published in Philadelphia in 1771 and then revised and updated in 1784 and 1788 editions in London, Benezet's account generously quotes from eighteenth-century African travel narratives "to give [readers] some account of the different parts of Africa, from which the Negroes are brought to America" (xiv), and, more importantly, to shatter skewed representations of Africa for

Eric D. Lamore

those readers who were unaware of commonly distorted perceptions about the "dark continent" and the eighteenth-century transatlantic slave trade. Within the introductory chapter, Benezet focuses on the geographical parameters of the transatlantic slave trade, which extend for some "three or four thousand miles" (5) to pinpoint the regions in Africa he (with assistance from others' accounts of Guinea) proceeds to describe in detail. Because of the accessibility from the Atlantic Ocean, the route from which the traders would arrive from Europe, Benezet includes the "river Gambia" (5), the geographical location found in "Phillis's Reply," as a part of the "same tract for which Queen Elizabeth granted charters to the first traders to that coast" (5). Considering the notion that slaves from this region were alleged to be "docile" and "tractable," the "river Gambia" area was especially appealing to slave traders accessing the African Coast. Observations on this area, therefore, become significantly extended in the *Short Account*.

Quoting from Thomas Astley's *A New General Collection of Travel and Travels*, Benezet utilizes testimony from Andrew Brue, a "principal factor to the French African company" (6), and a traveler who navigated both the Senegal and Gambia rivers. In his voyage to the Senegal River, which could be found about three hundred miles north of the mouth of Gambia River, Brue notes that productivity of the soil increases with the distance traveled inward: "the farther you go from the sea, the country on the river seems the more fruitful and well improved . . . abounding with Indian corn, pulse [edible seeds of leguminous plants], fruit, &c" (Benezet 6). "Vast meadows," Brue continues, "which feed large herds of great and small cattle, and poultry" (6) also constitute a portion of this eighteenth-century account of the Gambia River environment.

Similar to his findings from his voyage up the Senegal, Brue observes in his account that land surrounding "the river Gambia" was "well cultivated," and that "scarce a spot lay unimproved" because of the planting of rice on the "low lands" and millet and Indian corn on the "higher ground" (7). Benezet uses the testimony of Brue, therefore, to discount the claim that Africans were "incapable of improvement" and that their lifestyles were considered "destitute" and "miserable," all too common notions held by racist supporters of the transatlantic slave trade and the white people's attempt to colonize Africa. Continuing his discussion of the African regions violated by the transatlantic slave trade, Benezet identifies the "Jalofs, Fulis, and Mandingos" as the three principal peoples who inhabited these parts of Africa (7).

The "Fulis" (today's Fula or Fulani), Benezet continues, occupied "both sides of the Senegal" (7) and in "mix[ing] with the Mandingos" also "settled on both sides of the Gambia" (7). The "Fulis," Benezet writes, "are good farmers, and make good harvest of corn, cotton, tobacco, &c. and breed great numbers of cattle of all kinds" (8). Benezet quotes from A. Brue to describe the Mandingos as an African peoples whose "chief of the trade goes through their hands" (10). "Many [of the Mandingos] are industrious and laborious," continues Brue, "keeping their ground well cultivated, and breeding a good stock of cattle" (10). These observations of the Gambia and Senegal locales made by both Benezet and Brue emphasize that the land from which Phillis Wheatley was most likely taken while around the age of seven was heavily indebted to the profession of farming for sustenance.

Translated from the original French into English and published in London in 1759, a date that would have allowed Wheatley to read the text during her London visit to oversee the publication of her 1773 *Poems,* Michel Adanson's *A Voyage to Senegal* reinforces observations found in Benezet's *Short Account* and adds more details about the regions surrounding the Senegal and Gambian rivers.[3] Recorded during January 1750, Adanson notes in his *Voyage* that he "entered the river Gambia [on] the 20th" (156). An invasion of locusts at first prevents Adanson from collecting data from this region. Concurring with Benezet, Adanson notes that the "Mandingoes or Sofes" inhabit the land surrounding the Gambia River (163). Albeit in passing, Adanson, like Brue, observes that the African agrarian community "had got in their crop long before my arrival" (166), thereby reiterating the dependence on farming in this particular area of Africa.

Claiming this part of Gambia as "one of the finest stops [in] all of Africa" (164), Adanson remarks that "the soil is rich and deep, and amazingly fertile: it produces spontaneously and almost without cultivation, all the necessaries of life, as grain, fruits, legumes, and roots" (164). These observations, which are also quoted by Benezet in his *Short Account* (12), made by Adanson, who left the Gambian region on March 12, 1750, curiously parallel those of Wheatley in her "Reply"; both poet and traveler remark that the soil found in the Gambian region contains "spontaneous" capacities.

Additional material found in Benezet's *Some historical account of Guinea* and Michel Adanson's *Voyage* may give readers of Phillis Wheatley a more thorough understanding of how the Senegal and Gambia regions impacted this eighteenth-century African American artist. In chapter 1, the same section in

Eric D. Lamore

which the Philadelphia abolitionist notes the "Jalofs, Fulis, and Mandingos" were inhibitors of the Gambia River region, for instance, Benezet also observes: "Some of the Mandingos who are settled at Galem, far up the river Senegal, can read and write Arabic tolerably . . ." (10). Knowledge of Arabic in this vicinity may have impacted the African American poet because, as Margaretta Odell notes in her *Memoir,* Wheatley, shortly after arriving in colonial Boston, was "frequently seen endeavoring to make letters upon the wall with a piece of chalk or charcoal" (431). While Odell does not provide any further details on these "letters," which were inscrutable to the whites and may well have been Arabic characters, the geographical region coupled with the curious act of writing at an early age may offer yet another way in which Wheatley retained some memory of her African homeland.

Observing that African villagers are able to identify "a considerable amount of stars" (253), Michel Adanson remarks, "it is amazing, that such a rude and illiterate people, should reason so pertinently, in regard to those heavenly bodies" (254). While this classification of native Africans as a "rude and illiterate people" counts as yet another case of Adanson's racism permeating his text, the line, "The peerless monarch of th' ethereal train: / Of miles twice forty million is his height" (43–44) from "Thoughts on the Works of Providence," to point to just one example, shows a keen interest in astronomy in the poetry of Wheatley. The poet's interest in astronomy, therefore, likely derives from her African origins.

Another interesting detail found in Adanson's *Voyage* occurs shortly after the traveler's observation on astronomy. Traveling within this same region, Adanson notes in June 1752 that he was "not willing to lose opportunity of seeing their [the African villagers'] method of tillage" (262). Adanson's observations state that "all the inhabitants attended the lord of the village into the field, singing and dancing as on a great festival," this occasion including both singing and dancing as some members of this African agrarian society "carried their tabour and pipe, [while] others had no other tool or instrument than a small spade helved with a stick, which was bent in the middle, and long enough to prevent their being obliged to stoop to work" (262).

After dancing in a field for only a few minutes, the agrarian villagers "began to throw up the ground with their spades, in order to root out the weeds" (263). Observing the interplay of labor elaborated by music and dance allows Adanson to conclude that the "husbandmen" were also "professed dancers and singers" (263). Two days later, Adanson remarks, " . . . their task consists in digging with the same spade a few holes, into which they throw a few grains of millet, over which they immediately spread the earth with their feet" (263). Recalling that Adanson notes that the African agrarian community near the Gambia River "had got in their crop long before my arrival" (166), this planting and dancing ritual, one which was witnessed to the east of the African coast, may have been practiced, in one variation or another, in locales dependent on the success of crops closer to the Gambia River. If these same agrarian rituals were practiced by nations residing closer to the Gambia River, the geographical region from which Wheatley was captured and forced into slavery, she may have experienced firsthand these same rituals up until the age of seven or eight. The dependence on farming in these African nations, nevertheless, likely provides the reason that Wheatley includes details on the soil and crops in her praise of Gambia, as we have seen, and why the artist would have been attracted to Virgil's *Georgics*.

These two eighteenth-century African travel narratives document the clear dependence on farming in the Gambia and Senegal agricultural regions. Specifically, these narratives help to recover portions of the original landscape from which Phillis Wheatley was captured and forced into the institution of slavery. Even though Odell's *Memoir* holds that Wheatley retained only one memory of her African homeland, in several of her poems this African American artist praises her African home and punctuates her blackness. In "To the Right Honourable William Legge, Earl of Dartmouth," for instance, Wheatley refers to the "cruel Fate" which "Snatch'd [her] from Afric's fancy'd happy seat" (Wheatley 218). In a number of different poems, moreover, as James A. Levernier has instructed us, Wheatley refers to herself as "An *Ethiop*," a "vent'rous *Afric*," "*Afric's* muse," a member of "*Afric's* sable race," and even in "To Maecenas" as a fellow "African by birth," thereby in this last case associating herself with the Roman writer of comedy, Terence (175). The act of distancing herself from her African heritage, as seen in the phrases, "land of errors" and "Egyptian gloom" (Wheatley 15) in her early "To the University of Cambridge, in New-England," for instance, simply does not persist in her later extant verse.

While Adanson's and Benezet's texts documenting early-eighteenth-century African agricultural practices may help to explain why this classically trained African American poet would have been drawn to Virgil's *Georgics*, reading the original Latin of Virgil's *Georgics* would, nevertheless, initially pose a challenge to this aspiring poet and known student of Latin. Wheatley would

Eric D. Lamore

have had access to John Dryden's 1697 *Works of Virgil* before the publication of the 1773 *Poems*. However, she must have had a tutor for her Latin studies because her "owner," John Wheatley, admits in the "Letter of Attestation" that the African American artist made "some progress" in her Latin studies. Unlike the Wheatley twins who did not receive a classical education, Mather Byles, nephew of Cotton Mather, preacher at the Hollis Street Congregational Church, and signer of Wheatley's "Letter of Attestation," as posited by J. Shields, may have served as a likely Latin tutor to Wheatley and as the individual who introduced the African American poet to Virgil's *Georgics*. The colonial grammar school and Harvard University curriculums would have more than prepared Byles for assisting Wheatley in her own Latin studies. The fact that Virgil's *Georgics* was a colonial grammar school textbook makes it all the more probable that Byles would have assigned Virgil's text to his pupil.

Examination of one of the last two texts completed by Byles's uncle, Cotton Mather, before his death in February 1728, moreover, strengthens the likelihood that Byles would have encouraged Wheatley to consult Virgil's *Georgics*. Shortly after Mather Byles received his degree at Harvard in 1725, his renowned uncle published *Manuductio ad Ministerium*, a handbook for individuals preparing for the ministry and *Agricola. Or, the Religious Husbandman*, a work that, as the title page indicates, outlined the "Main Intentions of Religion, Served in the Business and Language of Husbandry" for "Families of the Countrey [*sic*]" (Mather).[4] Because of Cotton Mather's portrayal of himself as a "Father" to Byles in his personal diary, it is inevitable that Mather Byles, upon instruction from his famous uncle before his passing, would have thoroughly read *Manuductio* in order to prepare for his entry into the ministerial profession.

The contents found in the *Manuductio* support Mather Byles's encountering praiseworthy commentary on the *Georgics* by Cotton Mather. In the section on the importance of poetry in the *Manuductio*, Mather engages in a complicated dilemma whether or not to praise ancient classical poets or to condemn the reading of classical poetry in a text for ministerial students soon to become representatives of the Judeo-Christian religious tradition. At first, Mather encourages the divinity students to write poetry since the author "cannot wish you [the students studying to become ministers] a soul that shall be wholly unpoetical" (18). The prominent Boston minister advises that the students "try your young wings now and then to see what [poetic] flights you can make . . ." (19), and to "make a little recreation of poetry in the midst of your painful studies" (20). To establish a basis for the study of poetic technique, Mather wishes the divinity students to familiarize themselves with "old Horace" and his "art of poetry" along with the "beauties" found in the epic writings of Homer and Virgil (18).

Following these clear praises of ancient poetic texts, however, Mather offers a number of qualifications. Using the metaphors of taste and food to describe his aesthetic attitude toward acceptable and unacceptable poetic practices, a rhetorical technique also seen in Sir Philip Sidney, the English Renaissance aesthetician, in his 1595 *An Apology for Poesy,* Mather cautions the divinity students not to allow themselves "to be always poring [*sic*] on the passionate and measured pages." Mather clarifies that poetry "should be sauce, rather than food." The Boston minister presses the divinity students to avoid "a boundless and sickly appetite for the reading of the poems," and cautions students to practice moderation so they do not become "intoxicate[d]" by the "Circaean cup." The Puritan minister even warns the divinity students to "preserve the chastity of your souls from the danger you may incur, by a conversation with muses that are no better than harlots" (20).

Despite what may appear to be contradictory advice for students, Mather eventually locates value in Virgilian georgic in the *Manuductio:* "Wherefore if his *Aeneid* . . . may not appear so valuable to you . . . his *Georgics,* which he put his last hand to, will furnish you with many things far from despicable" (19). Confusion over the order of Virgil's works aside (Virgil published the *Georgics* after writing the ten pastoral poems found in the *Eclogues* and before penning the twelve books of the epic, *Aeneid*), this advice coming from an adopted "Father" would have been taken seriously by Mather Byles who, at the time, completed his degree from Harvard just one year before the publication of *Manuductio.* The publication date of *Manuductio* and graduation date of Byles align so closely that Byles would have probably been instructed to consult Virgil's *Georgics* through intimate conversations with his uncle about the ministry profession even before the publication of the volume and through his own reading of *Manuductio.*

Cotton Mather's enthusiasm for the *Georgics* may, therefore, very likely have encouraged Byles to pass along his uncle's fondness for this Virgilian text to Wheatley. In order to satisfy his pupil's interest in learning Latin well before the publication of her 1773 *Poems,* the literary tutor and mentor, Byles, may have even assigned Wheatley to explicate certain Latin passages from the four books in the *Georgics.* Recalling the remarks on the importance of agriculture and farming in and around the Gambia River in Michel Adanson's *Voyage* and Anthony Benezet's *Some Historical Account of Guinea* and given Wheatley's obvious intelligence, this aspiring Latin scholar would have been doubtlessly attracted to this ancient classical text.

Mather Byles, as well, acquired a number of theological and ancient classical texts when he inherited portions of the impressive Mather family libraries following the deaths of his grandfather, Increase Mather, and his uncle, Cotton Mather. Commanding that, "... my Books & Manuscripts may not be sold or embezeled [*sic*]" (qtd. in Tuttle 292), Increase Mather, in his will, gave one-half of his library to Cotton Mather, one-fourth to his son, Samuel, and the other fourth of the texts to the "fatherless grandson, Mather Byles" (qtd. in Tuttle 293). Even though Byles received one-fourth of his grandfather's library in 1723, this colonial poet and preacher would later inherit all of Cotton Mather's library following his death in 1728.

This pattern of passing down the Mather library to surviving family members becomes even more significant considering the fact that Increase Mather lists the text, "Rami Prælection. in Virgil. Georg" in his 1664 "Catalogue of Books" (Tuttle 289). This particular listing refers to a 1578 Latin commentary on Virgil's *Georgics* written by Peter Ramus, the famous father of Puritan logic. If Mather Byles did not inherit Ramus's commentary on the *Georgics* after the death of his grandfather, he would have likely become the owner of this text in the significant expansion of his library following the death of his uncle. The literary portion of Byles's estate, according to Julius H. Tuttle, "consisted of two-hundred and thirty-two volumes in folio, one hundred eighty in quarto, two-thousand three-hundred ninety-four in octavo, and twenty four smaller books" (297). This Early American library, enormous for the times, would have been readily available for Wheatley to consume. Mather Byles's extensive library and his uncle's endorsement of the *Georgics* likely allowed Wheatley to discover Virgil's agrarian poem.

Based on her probable reading of the *Georgics,* Wheatley would have recognized what is normally referred to as the "optimist" and "pessimist" schools of reading the *Georgics*. As Monica Gales notes, the more optimistic reading of Virgil's poem tends to focus on the repeated praises of Italy in book 2 and the diligent Roman farmer who, through his own industry, can stand for the political stability brought about by Augustus; on the other hand, the pessimistic school of reading points to the plague at the end of book 3, and the repeated hardships, such as intrusive and destructive insects and the weather, which prove detrimental to the Roman farmer, despite his relentless industry (Gale 108). What may seem to be a continually fluctuating poetic tone in the *Georgics,* however, would have reinforced Wheatley's penchant toward the construction of subversive verse. While Wheatley had learned to construct subversive pastoral verse through her reading of Virgil's *Eclogues,* this artist would have learned, as well, through her reading of the *Georgics,* to infuse her poetry with subversive georgic.

Wheatley's study of the *Georgics* would have led her to the discovery that Virgil refers to his homeland in this poetic work and, more importantly, how to disguise a reference to one's home through the employment of a subversive poetics. In book 2, for instance, Virgil remarks on a "plain that unfortunate Mantua lost" (27). Here, of course, Virgil refers to his boyhood village as the "unfortunate Mantua." After calling up his native farmland, which the poet had taken away from him by Marc Anthony's displaced Roman soldiers returning from the war, Virgil moves into a significant and sustained description of a farmer plowing:

> Or land where the plowman, all fired up, has clear-cut the woods,
> leveling the groves that have proved unfruitful through the years,
> removing the deepest roots of the birds' immemorial
> homes—forced from their nests, they seek the sky—
> there the untilled plain shines beneath the driving plow. (28)

This passage gives an example of what may be referred to as subversive georgic. As we discovered in just ten lines previous to this quoted section, Virgil longs for his homeland, which he was forced to leave because of political turmoil. The "deepest roots" of the "birds' immemorial homes" removed by the "leveling" of the "plowman," then, may be found to represent the Roman soldiers who displaced Virgil from his own rural home. The passage, moreover, may be referred to as subversive when one considers that, just as Virgil read portions from the *Aeneid* to Augustus Caesar, the poet also read most of the four books of the *Georgics* to Augustus. When Virgil's voice failed him, his literary patron, Maecenas, read the remainder of the poem to Augustus (Wilkinson 69). In order to lodge critiques against Augustus, therefore, Virgil had no other choice, if he wished to remain in Rome and not face forced exile, than to cloak these criticisms behind a seemingly "innocent" digression on birds' nests.

As an ambitious poet determined to learn her craft and at the same time a classics scholar, Wheatley, through her own reading of the *Georgics* and her

Eric D. Lamore

earlier lessons learned regarding Virgil's subversive pastoral in his eclogues, would have inevitably noticed this subversive vein throughout the four-book poem devoted to agricultural duties. Facing what was perhaps an even more hostile audience who attempted to extinguish the artist's freedom, and to force the poet into slavery for most of her life, Wheatley came to rely on an even more subversive poetics than Virgil, especially before her manumission, if she were to exercise any forceful critique against the institution of slavery. As James A. Levernier clarifies, "Any overtly militant statements [on the abolition of slavery] would certainly have been construed by the Wheatleys as an insult and could have resulted in severe consequences for the author" (173). Even though Wheatley was somewhat "free" in the sense that the artist utilized her active imagination as a means to escape from the world of slavery, before becoming legally "free," according to eighteenth-century Colonial law at least, Wheatley was not able to resist her status as a slave in any open praises of her African homeland. In this sense, both Wheatley and Virgil were required to construct subversive poetry if the artists wished to establish any type of reconnection to their respective homelands. The discovering of this parallel predicament in her reading of Virgil's *Georgics* would have contributed substantially to the African American artist's development of her own subversive georgic.

In the construction of her own subversive georgic, Wheatley progresses from her poem, "On Recollection," to the poem, "On Imagination." "On Recollection" begins with an imperative command to "Mneme," the goddess of memory and Mother of the Muses, to "begin." Wheatley hopes that the "sacred nine," or the nine Muses, will "inspire" the "vent'rous *Afric* in her grand design." At this point in the poem, it is difficult to determine what exactly Wheatley means by "her grand design." In three lines which follow this reference, nevertheless, Wheatley remarks that, "The acts of long departed years, by thee [Mneme] / Recover'd, in due order rang'd we see" (62). Recovering "long departed years," then, may be viewed as the "grand design" in this African American artist's poem.

Wheatley continues to invoke the goddess of memory in the third stanza of the poem, thereby further emphasizing the importance of her mental capacities. Wheatley begins the third stanza of the poem by, once again, italicizing the word, "*Mneme*." After this second invocation to the goddess of memory, Wheatley poses an important question: "How sweet the sound when we her [Mneme] plaudit hear?" (63). Wheatley immediately answers this question in the next line of the poem. According to the speaker, the sound of Mneme, or

Wheatley's usage of her own memory, is "sweeter than music to the ravish'd ear" and, more important, "sweeter than Maro's entertaining strains" (63). These extended associations with Mneme and Maro (i.e., Virgil) are essential to understand how Wheatley envisions her own poetics. By signaling a relationship between these two words, Wheatley continues to emphasize a relationship between her interior, mental processes with poetry of the Roman poet, Virgil.

Because of the extended emphasis placed on the personal and the poet's interior mental space (i.e., "my mind"), the lines from "To Maecenas," "soon the same beauties [in Virgil's poetry] should my mind adorn, / And the same ardors [in Virgil's poetry] in my soul should burn" (10), become closer to being realized in "On Recollection." Wheatley shifts, nevertheless, in the fourth stanza of "Recollection," to focus specifically on one of her memories she recovers with the help of "Mneme." As Wheatley posits, a duration of "eighteen years" has elapsed since her birth; this length of time does not, however, erase or extinguish obviously painful memories, ones including the Middle Passage and a permanent separation from her family. As the poet maintains, "In Recollection see them fresh return, / And sure 'tis mine to be asham'd, and mourn" (64). Wheatley remains "asham'd" of these particular memories, not because she does not long for her African country; rather, the artist "mourn[s]" the obvious brutality of the slave trade. The poet, as well, still feels shame when the "pow'r" of recollection calls up this particular memory because, as Odell claims, it reminds her of the fact that, when she was forcibly removed from her homeland, she arrived in colonial America with "no other covering than a quantity of dirty carpet about her" (Odell 12).

"On Recollection," written in late 1771, may also be read as a poem wherein Wheatley articulates the multifaceted powers of memory. In this poet's hands, for example, Wheatley extends her observation that the powers of recollection, when exerted, may "change the scene" (64). Wheatley continues this preoccupation with her own mental faculties in the poem which follows "Recollection" in the 1773 Poems, "On Imagination." In this highly important poetic composition, Wheatley goes well beyond explaining the function of memory to showcase fully the abilities of her imagination to construct, in her mind, an alternative world distinct from colonial Boston—one free from slavery. Even though the poet values the "pow'r" of recollection, Wheatley's vision matures, in the later 1773 "Imagination," wherein she indicates how her imagination may contribute forcefully to a reconnection with her African homeland. In

Eric D. Lamore

"Imagination," for example, the poet celebrates the power of the mental faculty by claiming that "We [by means of her imagination and that of her readers] on thy pinions can surpass the wind, / And leave the rolling universe behind." No longer does Wheatley rely solely on the "pow'r" of recollection; these lines highlight the ability of the imagination to transport the poet to a location where she does not physically reside. She continues, in the third stanza of this poem, to locate the possibility of transport via the imagination because this faculty may construct "new worlds" which "amaze th' unbounded soul" (66).

The importance placed on the imagination's ability to construct "new worlds" is not, however, a detail mentioned only in passing. In fact, Wheatley, in the fifth stanza of the poem, constructs an alternative landscape:

> Though *Winter* frowns to *Fancy's* raptur'd eyes
> The fields may flourish, and gay scenes arise;
> The frozen deeps may break their iron bands,
> And bid their waters murmur o'er the sands.
> Fair *Flora* may resume her fragrant reign,
> And with her flow'ry riches deck the plain;
> *Sylvanus* may diffuse his honours round,
> And all the forest may with leaves be crown'd;
> Show'rs may descend, and dews their gems disclose,
> And nectar sparkle on the blooming rose. (66–67)

In this significant stanza from "On Imagination," Wheatley at first notes, "Though Winter frowns" (66). Here she deliberately chooses the word "Winter" to refer to the oppressive segment of the Boston community who refused to support her first attempt to publish a volume of her poems in 1772. Despite this group's best efforts to oppress the African American artist, the exercising of the imagination, Wheatley maintains, allows the artist to resist any form of oppression. Additionally, "Winter frowns" likely refers, as well, to the physical environment surrounding Wheatley during the composition of this poem. At this point, the poet would have endured enough Boston winters to understand cold. It is plausible, then, to suspect that the Boston community received (or was receiving) snow at the time Wheatley wrote "On Imagination."

Regardless of how this first portion of the fifth stanza is read, this cold, urban environment undergoes a radical transformation. In cataloguing the metamorphosis of this cold, colonial Boston into a warm and lusty rural scene, Wheatley uses the subjunctive six different times in the fifth stanza (e.g., "fields may flourish," "the frozen deeps may break," "Flora may resume," "Sylvanus may diffuse," " . . . the forest may with leaves be crown'd," and "Show'rs may descend . . ."). Documenting several conditional statements signifies that Wheatley celebrates the productive and flexible nature of this faculty. This preoccupation with the word, "may," signals the potential for these distinct changes to occur, provided that Wheatley exercises her imagination. The word "may" should not be read as an indicator of Wheatley's difficulty in envisioning these alternative scenes. Rather, Wheatley uses the word to express the vastly different capabilities of the imagination when she calls upon the mental faculty to function.

Additionally, the details Wheatley provides concerning the powers of the imagination, later referred to as "the leader of the mental train" (67), signify that the physical space Wheatley reconstructs constitutes one of agricultural productivity. The first detail, after Wheatley establishes this rural versus urban motif, may be located in her comment that "the fields may flourish" (66). In this detail, Wheatley juxtaposes these "flourish[ing] fields" from a sterile urban environment plagued by winter. The inclusion of the lines, "*Sylvanus* may diffuse his honours round, / And all the forest may with leaves be crown'd" indicates that "Sylvanus" resides in this reconstructed agrarian world. While some commentators associate "Sylvanus" with "the wild land beyond the boundaries of cultivated fields" (*Oxford Companion to Classical Literature* 524), others affiliate the god "with forests and agriculture" and identify him with the "countryside" (*Oxford Classical Dictionary* 1408). Even though Wheatley adds that, "And all the forest may with leaves be crown'd" because of the presence of "Sylvanus," it is important to note that, as indicated above, the responsibilities of this classical figure were multiple. Therefore, in addition to the forest "crown'd" with "leaves," "Sylvanus" may also be read as the agent responsible for the "fields" that "flourish."

Because "On Imagination" was written before the artist secured her manumission sometime before October 18, 1773, the rural versus urban motif and the inclusion of "Sylvanus" in "On Imagination" may be read as subversive manifestations of georgic. While it is true that Virgil references Silvanus in his other literary works,[5] this figure is cited in book 2 of the *Georgics*, the same book wherein Virgil praises rural life through a critique of urban living. According to Virgil, the farmer who resides in the country does not concern himself with wealth, avoids the "Forum's insanity," and stays clear of "wild tribes, allied in war," to list just a few of the advantages in rural living. Moreover, as Virgil

Eric D. Lamore

adds, the farmer is "fortunate" to "know the gods of the countryside" (37), which specifically include the sister nymphs and Pan, and, most important, "Silvanus" (38).

Unlike the subversive georgic in Virgil's poem wherein the poet longs for "Mantua" in his four-line exposition on birds' nests that have been destroyed by a farmer, as we observed above, Wheatley patterns her longing for home through subversive georgic involving the presumably "innocent" point that "Winter frowns," and the presumably "innocent" inclusion of "Sylvanus." What appear to be minor additions on the surface, however, are no less than resistive techniques drawn from the ancient classical genre of georgic and applied to Wheatley's own predicament as a slave. These manifestations of georgic empower Wheatley in her effort to reside in an environment reminiscent of her African homeland, yet at the same moment to resist her status as a slave in colonial Boston.

These observations on Wheatley's use of georgic in "On Imagination" furthermore prepare for a parallel that may be drawn between this poem and the later "Phillis's Reply to the Answer." This later poem reflects on an African soil that "yields exhaustless stores" and the presence of "phoebus," the sun, who aids in the creation of "a fragrant train" of flowers. In "On Imagination," however, Wheatley, who was constructing verse while still in the bondage of slavery, disguises her references to the soil of Africa and African flowers which grow from the earth through the classical figures, "Sylvanus," the Roman god of cultivated fields, and "Flora," the goddess of flowers. "Sylvanus" and "Flora" in "On Imagination," therefore, refer to the same physical space the poet conjures in her admiration of a "spontaneous" "soil" and "flowery births" in "Phillis's Reply," a poem written after the poet had secured her manumission. The precise ordering of these two elements, soil and flowers, in two different poems, written before and after manumission, allow readers of Wheatley to recognize, in this artist's extant verse, what is likely another memory drawn of her African homeland.

In what may probably be her final poetic composition before her tragic and untimely death on December 5, 1784, the pastoral elegy, "Elegy on Leaving—," alludes to escaping to a rural area, however temporarily, from the confines of an oppressive Boston community. Within the first stanza of "Elegy," for instance, Wheatley bids "farewell" to "friendly bow'rs," "streams," "lawns," and "groves," characteristics redolent of the genre of pastoral. As Wheatley adds, these "groves" provide the African American artist "a kind retreat" away "from noon-tide rays." This detail of the poet herself reclining in an rural environment immediately calls up the opening line of "To Maecenas," the introductory poem of Wheatley's 1773 volume wherein Wheatley places the literary patron of Virgil and Ovid "beneath the myrtle / shade" (9). By no means a coincidence, this calculated maneuver of including, first, Maecenas reclined under a shade tree and, second, the poet herself escaping the sun's heat under a shade tree allows Wheatley to draw a complete circle encompassing the period of her poetic maturity.

As Wheatley admits in this highly personal poem, moreover, the "wood-crown'd hill," the "solemn pines," and the "aged oak's protecting arms" all provide her with opportunities to become "wrapt in thought" in order to avoid "crowds and noise." The rural retreat and praise of the rural versus the urban becomes even more significant in the second-to-last stanza. Here Wheatley writes:

> But, ah! those pleasing hours are ever flown;
> Ye scenes of transport from my thoughts retire
> Those rural joys no more the day shall crown
> No more my hand shall wake the warbling lyre. (156)

Perhaps the most overlooked phrase in Wheatley's poetic catalogue, the "scenes of transport" to which Wheatley alludes and mourns that she will now never be able to reenact this "rural transport," may be directly tied to "On Imagination," a poem in which Wheatley constructs an alternative world wherein she mentally escapes the confines of urban Boston to a rural environment comprising both "Flora" and "Sylvanus." The principal subject of "Elegy of Leaving—," then, is not only Wheatley herself, but also the creative process that this artist uses to write her own poetry. These "scenes of transport," as seen clearly in "On Imagination," figure prominently in Wheatley's resistive poetics. By referring to these "scenes" within this pastoral elegy, the subject of this elegy is not an individual who has recently died; rather, the source of lamentation in this pastoral elegy arises from the fact that this artist will not any longer be able to reside in the "rural joys" her imagination assists in reconstructing.

Wheatley's "scenes of transport" and her creation of a rural heterocosm become all the more significant when we note that Michel Adanson, in his *A Voyage to Senegal*, observes the presence of "fables[,] dialogues, and witty stories with which the negroes entertained each other . . ." (252). The presence of a native, African folklore culture in and around the community from

Eric D. Lamore

which Wheatley was physically removed may offer an additional interpretation to Wheatley's poems. In a text titled *Drums and Shadows: Survival Studies among the Georgia Coastal Negroes,* the Georgia Writers' Project and the Works Project Administration recorded the "folk culture" (v) of the "Georgia Coastal Negroes" (vi), and explored the "question of the nature and importance of African heritage in America" (vi).

In documenting the folklore of these regions in Georgia, the editors argue that "pronunciation of individual words, elision, and emphasis play almost equal roles in the Negro speech section," and, as a result, all transcriptions found in *Drums and Shadows* have been "faithfully transcribed" to preserve speech patterns (xv). The social anthropologists solicit information on the folklore found in an area, located southwest of Savannah, from an individual named Paul Singleton, who was "brought to Savannah in 1869" (17). Curiously, Singleton states, "'Muh daddy use tuh tell me all duh time bout folks wut could fly back tuh Africa. Dey could take wing an jis fly off'" (17). Mose Brown, also a resident of Tin City and neighbor of Singleton, reports that

> My gran use tuh tell me bout folks flyin back tuh Africa. A man
> an his wife wuz brung from Africa. Wen dey fine out dey wuz
> slabes an got treat so hahd, dey jis fret an fret. One day dey wuz
> standin wid some udduh slabes an all ub a sudden dey say, "We
> gwing back tuh Africa. So goodie bye, goodie bye." Den dey flied
> right out uh sight. (18)

Resisting a position in the institution of slavery, the "flying" African of these folk tales consciously chooses to return to Africa. In the "Introduction" to the text, Mary Granger notes that, "newspaper advertisements indicate that a large proportion of these early [slave] cargoes came from the Gambia River and the Niger River sections . . ." (xvii). As seen in Adanson's remark regarding the existence of "fables[,] dialogues, and witty stories" (252), these particular "flying home" testimonies suggest that an African folk tradition has been applied to the predicament of an African held in bondage.

Cultural anthropologists have found the presence of this "flying" African motif in other areas of Georgia as well. According to the social anthropologists, Thomas Smith, a resident of Yamacraw, reports, "Well den, duh descendants ub Africans hab duh same gif tuh do unnatchun ting. Ise heahd duh story uh duh flyin Africans an I sho belieb it happen" (28). Another resident, Carrie Hamilton, observes that

I hab heah uh dem people. . . . Muh mudduh use tuh tell me bout em wen we set in duh city mahket selling vegtubbles an fruit. She say dat deah wuz a man and he wife an dey git fooled abode a slabe ship. Fus ting dey know dey wuz sole tuh a plantuh on St. Helena. So one day wen all duh slaves wuz tuhgedduh, dis man an he wife say, "We gwine back home, goodie bye, goodie bye," an jis like a bud dey flew out of sight. (29)

As seen in these different Georgia communities, displaced Africans from the Gambia and Niger River regions employ the trope of the "flying" African as a resistive narrative tool to counter oppression. The cultural work performed by the Georgia Writers' Project and the Works Project Administration, indeed, recovers significant influences of African heritage in America.

The *Drums and Shadows* project, furthermore, allows for a preliminary mapping of this "flying" home motif in African American letters. As Susan L. Blake has stated, *Drums and Shadows* was used as one of the intertextual sources for the construction of Solomon, a "flying African" (Morrison 322), in Toni Morrison's *Song of Solomon* (Blake 79–80). Beyond Morrison's *Song of Solomon,* as we will soon discover, this "flying home" motif may be located in Robert Hayden's "O Daedalus Fly Away Home" and Ralph Ellison's short story, "Flying Home." More important, however, a tracing of this "flying home" motif in the works of two twentieth-century African American artists positions Wheatley, through the construction of a rural heterocosm in "On Imagination," as the originator of this trope in the literary history of African American letters. Because Hayden's, Ellison's, and Morrison's contributions to this "flying home" motif come well after the 1773 publication of *Poems,* Wheatley's mental flight home in "On Imagination" establishes this key trope in African American literary history.[6]

The ancient classical genre of georgic helped to cloak Wheatley's mentally constructed "flights" home, an act that resulted in an early manifestation of the "flying home" motif, but Wheatley utilized this ancient classical genre as well in construction of her political poetry written during the Revolutionary War. Similar to the line of argumentation that claims the poetry of Wheatley closely resembles the poetry of Alexander Pope, this "derivative" position may also be located in commentary on Wheatley's political poetry. In "Poetry and American Revolutionary Identity: The Case of Phillis Wheatley and John Paul Jones," to point to one example, Daniel J. Ennis claims that he explores " . . . the role of poetic discourse in the formation of eighteenth-century [American] identity" (86).

Eric D. Lamore

Drawing parallels between Phillis Wheatley and the Revolutionary hero John Paul Jones, Ennis posits that both Wheatley and Jones " . . . were both trying to overcome and/or ease given identities by fashioning new, specifically American identities" (68). Particular attention should be placed on Ennis's deliberate usage of the word "new" in multiple places throughout the article, particularly in the case of Wheatley. After investing some five pages to explicating Wheatley's political poetry and her "new" American identity, Ennis falls into a familiar critical trap by reducing his findings to a sweeping generalization that the poetry of Phillis Wheatley was not actually "new" but rather demonstrated that the African American poet's " . . . place in the public discourse during times of crisis is far more reminiscent of John Dryden—a man who knew much better than Pope the value of well-placed compliments to those in high places" (95–96). Even though Ennis may be applauded for attempting to redirect critical attention away from the relationship between Phillis Wheatley and Alexander Pope, the substitution of Dryden for Pope fails to counter the "derivative" vein of argumentation.

Interestingly, before explicating Wheatley's poems, Ennis observes that " . . . like Virgil lyrically immortalizing Augustus . . . Wheatley recognizes that the success of a panegyric is actually a function of reception, not aesthetics . . ." (92). Here this critic unwittingly captures a potentially significant connection between the poetry of Wheatley and the Roman poet Virgil. Such a comparative analysis between Virgil and Wheatley would have prevented the "derivative" misstep asserted in the conclusion of the article. Immediately after establishing this potentially fecund connection, however, Ennis fails to mention which work from Virgil wherein he finds the comparative relationship between Wheatley and Virgil. Nor do Ennis's readers ever discover exactly which poems found in Wheatley's extant verse are "reminiscent" of Dryden, because the article comes to an abrupt stop after this remark. Using Ennis's imprecise connection between Virgil and Wheatley as political poets, we find ourselves, nonetheless, even better prepared to pursue Wheatley's use of the Roman poet Virgil in her political poetry.

By tracing the progressive publication pattern of "America" (1768), "To His Excellency General Washington" (1775), "On the Capture of General Lee" (1776), and "On the Death of General Wooster" (1778), all published before "Liberty and Peace" (1784), one discovers a clear preoccupation with the ancient classical genre of georgic and Virgil's *Georgics* in the construction of these political poems. The packaging of a revolutionary war as an internal familial struggle, including the detail of "fields of flight," and positioning

General George Washington as an American Augustus signify that Wheatley molded significant parts of her political poetry upon the ancient classical genre georgic. These details in Wheatley's political poems just pointed out, therefore, uncover a second manifestation of georgic in Wheatley's extant poetry.

In the poem "America," Wheatley first employs the trope of the family. Using the phrases "A certain lady" to represent Great Britain and "an only son" to stand for the colonies, this once-compact familial unit starts to encounter problems as the "virtuous" son grows up too quickly for the mother who "fear[s] his Strength." Attempting to quench the strength of her son, the mother "laid some taxes on her darling son," but then promises to "remove" the taxes after the son "amend[s] his manners." The son, later identified as "americus," pleads to his mother that "you have no cause to Chide," and weeps that he "feel[s] this Iron chain" (134).

Wheatley remains consistent in her use of this familiar trope because the poet utilizes the trope of the familial unit in "Liberty and Peace," a poem written in 1784. Compared to the earlier "America," coming from the early period of her juvenilia, "Liberty and Peace" offers a much more complicated representation of the American struggle for independence. In "Liberty and Peace," Wheatley condemns Britannia's "Thirst of boundless Power," a phrase repeated in "To His Excellence General Washington," and orders the British to "submit to Heaven's decree," one, according to Wheatley, "That bids this Realm of Freedom rival Thee!" As seen in the seventh line of this poem, Wheatley attempts to confute the Loyalist stance in her position that "Heaven" stands on the side of the American Revolutionaries. At this point in the poem, Wheatley reverts to the trope of the family. The poet describes the fighting between the British and Americans with the lines, "fraternal Arms engage, / And mutual Deaths, all dealt with mutual Rage" (155). As in the poem "America," the phrase, "fraternal Arms engage," recalls Wheatley's continued interest in the trope of the family. The phrase, "fraternal Arms," as well, positions this fight between Loyalists and Patriots as a revolutionary battle occurring within the same family.

Wheatley has adapted here, for her own purposes, salient portions from Virgil's book 1 of the *Georgics*. Following a large didactic section devoted to instructions about how best to plow fields, Virgil launches into a detailed description of a Roman civil war, fought between the legions headed by Brutus and Cassius and those led by Mark Antony and Octavian, this conflict having occurred at Philippi in 42 BC after the assassination of Julius Caesar. This Roman civil war at Philippi featured "Romans in battle," and, as Virgil notes,

Eric D. Lamore

resulted in Roman blood soaking "the broad Balkan plains" (19). Virgil projects that, "And a time shall surely come that, in those countries, / the farmer working the soil with his curved plow / shall discover javelins . . . / or clank on helmets with his heavy hoe / and wonder at the huge bones found in uncovered graves" (19). Similarly, the once-friendly familial unit comprising British and American soldiers, as we have seen in Wheatley's "America" and "Liberty and Peace," has turned violent.

In fact, as Wheatley mentions in her "To His Excellency General Washington," the aggressive fighting between the British and the American colonists takes place not on foreign lands, as Virgil notes in his *Georgics,* but on "hostile Fields," a "hostile Field," and "fields of fight" (155) in Colonial America. The continued emphasis on the word "field" implies that the Revolutionary War has temporarily rendered a physical space that formerly yielded agricultural products now unproductive and, therefore, useless. In fact, Wheatley, closely paralleling the Roman poet in his *Georgics,* writes that "mother Earth deplore[s]" the war because "Her ample Surface [becomes] smoke[d] with kindred Gore" (155). Because of the fighting in "fields of fight" and the "kindred Gore" on the surface of "fields," a reader is pressed to doubt that the surface of these colonial American fields will, after the war, be productive in generating crops. If any American crops are to be harvested at a later point after this battle in the "fields," the reader may also surmise that the American farmer will likely encounter remains from the "mutual deaths" that, according to the poem, plague both sides immersed in the conflict. Wheatley, therefore, has relied on Virgil's *Georgics* to offer a dramatic and emphatic portrayal of the American battle for independence.

While Wheatley frames the gruesome details of the Revolutionary War with the help of Virgilian georgic, the African American poet, in an earlier political poem, has already discovered a clear solution to the conflict. As we have observed, Wheatley refers to America as "new-born *Rome*" (154) in the 1784 poem, "Liberty and Peace." This fusion of the ancient classical and the American may, however, be applied to the earlier 1775 poem, "To His Excellency General Washington" in an attempt to explicate Wheatley's extensive praise of our first president-to-be. In fact, Wheatley continues to rely on the ancient classical tradition and Virgil's *Georgics* in her representation of George Washington as an "American Augustus" in "To His Excellency."

Unlike the majority of the Wheatley family, who remained Loyalists throughout the Revolutionary War, Phillis supported the revolutionary cause. From as early as her March 1770 poem, "On the Death of Mr. Snider,

Murder'd By Richardson," wherein Wheatley refers to "Snider," the first casualty of the Revolutionary War, as "the first martyr for the common good" (136) to her final political poem, "Liberty and Peace," published in 1784, Wheatley aligned with the Revolutionary cause, and, in particular, positioned the role of Washington as a focal point in the colonies' fight against Great Britain. Beyond the obvious praise of Washington in the poem "To His Excellency," which we visit shortly, Wheatley extended her praise of the general in a missive dated October 26, 1775, wherein she enclosed the poem, "To His Excellency," and noted, "Your being appointed by the Grand Continental Congress to be Generalissimo of the armies of North America, together with your fame of your virtues, excite sensations not easy to suppress" (185).

As evident in the poem "To His Excellency," Wheatley indeed articulates the "sensations" she refers to in the cover letter accompanying her handwritten copy of the poem that she sent to Washington. Significantly, these praises given to Washington by Wheatley in "To His Excellency" closely parallel ones given to Augustus Caesar by Virgil in book 3 of the *Georgics*. At the beginning of book 3, Virgil hesitates in imparting didactic instructions on how to select productive horses and cattle, how to breed livestock, and how to tend sheep and goats in order to sing his praises of Augustus. In particular, Virgil expresses admiration for Augustus largely because of his successful rebuilding of Rome following its own internal struggles for power after the assassination of Julius Caesar.

Because Virgil wishes to "soar triumphant from the lips of men" to glorify the achievements of Augustus, this digression in the third book is commonly read as preparation for the writing of the *Aeneid*. The Roman author specifically intends "to build a temple of marble" wherein the poet will "place [Augustus] Caesar in the center, a god in his temple" (40) among "victorious Romulus," "the names of nations sent down / by Jove," including Aeneas, Apollo, and statues of Priam. These doors on Augustus' temple documenting the evolution of Roman history, Virgil boasts, will be made of "ivory and solid gold." At the end of this rhapsodic introduction to the third *Georgic*, Virgil promises he will "arm himself to tell of [Augustus] Caesar's fiery / battles and assure his name's praise through as many years / as Caesar is distant from the birth of Dawn's consort" (41).

Unlike Virgil, who points to a future poetic endeavor to immortalize Augustus (i.e., the *Aeneid*), Wheatley capitalizes on the present political moment in Colonial America to salute Washington. She admits that Washington

Eric D. Lamore

is already "Fam'd for thy valour, for thy virtues more," yet the poet adds emphatically, "Hear every tongue thy guardian aid implore!" (146). Similar to Virgil's ambitious goal to "soar triumphant from the lips of men" (40), Wheatley follows in her own attempt to spread the virtues of Washington to "every tongue." The fact that "To His Excellency" was published in the March 20, 1776, edition of the *Virginia Gazette* and in *The Pennsylvania Magazine* or *American Monthly Museum* in April 1776 (Wheatley 305) assisted her attempt to publicize the virtues of Washington to "every tongue." As Virgil plans to address the decisive "battles" in which Augustus participated, the poet similarly boasts that, through the command of Washington in "fields of fight" " . . . Columbia's [i.e., America's] arm prevails" and "Britannia," or Great Britain, "droops" its "pensive head" only to "lament thy thirst of boundless power too late" (146). The celebration of decisive military victories, then, is prominent in both Virgil's and Wheatley's poetic productions about military and political figures.

Wheatley closes the poem with two significant couplets in which the poet refers to Washington as "great chief," ensures that "the goddess" will "guide" his "ev'ry action," and grants the general a "crown, a mansion, and a throne / With gold unfading, WASHINGTON! be thine" (146). As Virgil promises Augustus "ivory and solid gold" on the doors of his temple, the adjective "unfading" in the construction of Washington's crown, mansion, and throne results in a permanent dedication for the American Revolutionary hero in Wheatley's poetic space. Wheatley not only attempts to enroll Washington permanently in her poetry but she also wishes to celebrate him with a position as monarch of America, seen most prominently in the "throne" that Wheatley includes in her list. Washington, according to Wheatley, will then have no competition, as does Augustus in Virgil's poem, in securing power in Revolutionary America.

In the political poems, "America" and "To His Excellency General Washington," then, Wheatley argues that America should be viewed as a reincarnation of classical Rome and George Washington as an American Augustus. Of course, these poetic positions would have been palatable for revolutionaries attempting to fashion favorable public identities in their justification for severing their relationship with Great Britain. As seen in this catalogue of Wheatley's political poetry, however, this artist did not subscribe to the idea of constructing exclusively praiseworthy verse for the revolutionaries' political cause.

In a February 11, 1774, epistle to Samson Occom, a Native American (Mohegan) minister, Wheatley, within months of securing her manumission, writes that " . . . in every human Breast, God has implanted a Principle, which we call Love of Freedom; it is impatient of Oppression, and pants for Deliverance . . ." (177). Wheatley then moves in this widely published missive to identify that the same individuals, who keep the African and Native American races in bondage, are guilty of severing the important relationship between "Words" and "Actions" (177). As Wheatley notes, "This I desire not for their Hurt, but to convince them of the strange Absurdity of their Conduct whose Words and Actions are so diametrically opposite" (177). By locating the opposition between "Words" and "Actions" of mostly white revolutionaries, Wheatley exposes the hypocrisy behind the revolutionaries' irresponsible rhetoric, which frequently used the tropes of the "family" and "slavery" to justify separation from Great Britain (Erkkila 161).

The usage of the ancient classical tradition and portions from Virgil's *Georgics* in Wheatley's political poetry, then, may be seen as a calculated rhetorical maneuver. In her writing and publishing of "On the Death of Mr. Snider Murder'd by Richardson," "America," "To His Excellency General Washington," and "Liberty and Peace," that is, Wheatley deliberately positions the colonial reader to receive her poetry favorably. With the publication of "On the Death of General Wooster" (1778), however, Wheatley, as a self-identified African American artist, but one simultaneously concerned for the acquisition of freedom "in *every* human Breast" (177; emphasis added), significantly shifts her position and tone in her political poetry to remind those in power that the rhetoric of "liberty," used so often by the white revolutionaries, should include other, marginalized races.

In an obvious attempt to extinguish racist ideologies and to subvert a racial hierarchy that devalorized and denigrated individuals of color, Wheatley inserts a clear racial message in "On the Death of General Wooster" for the same colonial readers already conditioned to absorb Wheatley's praise for the Revolutionary cause. Beginning the poem with the observation that Wooster "perish'd in his Country's cause" (149), Wheatley then moves to focus on the "expiring hero" as she envisions him about to perish. What is stunning in this particular poem is the fact that Wheatley actually inserts dialogue into the mouth of the dying Wooster. Perhaps an even more deliberate and critical attack on racist ideologies than her comment in "On Being Brought from Africa to America," that, "Remember, *Christians, Negros,* black as *Cain,* / May be

Eric D. Lamore

refin'd, and join the Angelic train" (18), Wheatley here inserts dialogue into the mouth of the expiring but reflective General Wooster just before he passes:

> "But how, presumptuous shall we hope to find
> Divine acceptance with th' Almighty mind—
> While yet (O deed Ungenerous!) they disgrace
> And hold in bondage Afric's blameless race?
> Let virtue reign—And thou accord our prayers
> Be victory's our's, and generous freedom theirs."
> (149–50)

As the dialogue makes clear, Wooster wishes for "victory" for the revolutionaries but also reminds eighteenth-century readers that, if they wish to achieve "acceptance with th' Almighty mind," they should grant "generous freedom" to "Afric's blameless race."

Recalling the aforementioned line, "Sometimes by Simile, a victory's won," Wheatley capitalizes on this idea in the dialogue spoken by Wooster. As Wooster, through the help of Wheatley, maintains, a victory for the revolutionaries should bring about "freedom" for "Afric's blameless race." In this regard, Wheatley succeeds in her "simile" argument; African Americans should also participate in the attainment of "liberty." Read in concert with such political poems as "America" and "To His Excellency General Washington," however, "On the Death of General Wooster" operates on another, more ambitious, poetic level. By inserting this significant dialogue into the mouth of the white General Wooster, Wheatley purposefully dismantles her previous political world comprising America as a "new-born *Rome*" and Washington as an American Augustus for the sole purpose of freeing "Afric's blameless race" from bondage. Indeed, if America is to be legitimately praised as a "new-born *Rome*," and if Washington is to be viewed as an American Augustus, Wheatley maintains that the African race must be released from bondage and included in the democratic project; only then may theory and practice merge.

Keenly aware of the rhetorical effectiveness found in the classical genre of georgic, Phillis Wheatley, classics scholar, Early African American writer, and skilled rhetorician, adapted, not simply lifted, salient portions from Virgil's *Georgics* in order to construct a resistive poetics. These manifestations of georgic in the poetry of Phillis Wheatley complicate the already-alluded-to strained relationship between Thomas Jefferson and Phillis Wheatley. While we have previously touched upon Jefferson's denouncement of Wheatley and the African American race in *Notes,* the most troubling part about Jefferson's critique is the fact that certain parts of his *Notes* may be catalogued within the genre of the Early American georgic. In query 19, "The Present State of Manufactures, Commerce, Interior and Exterior Trade" from *Notes,* for instance, Jefferson boasts of the importance of "industry" and the American husbandman: "But we have an immensity of land courting the industry of the husbandman. . . . Those who labour in the earth are the chosen people of God, if ever he had a chosen people" (170). The presence of georgic in both authors' texts shows how truly misinformed a reading Jefferson gave of this African American poet, since these two individuals had, surprisingly, something in common.

NOTES

1. For treatments of Wheatley's use of epic, consult the chapter, "The American Epic Writ Large: The Example of Phillis Wheatley," in John C. Shields's *The American Aeneas: Classical Origins of the American Self,* and Robert Kendrick's "Re-membering America: Phillis Wheatley's Intertextual Epic." For a discussion of Wheatley's use of subversive pastoral, see Shields's "Phillis Wheatley's Subversive Pastoral." Sondra O'Neale's essay, "A Slave's Subtle War: Phillis Wheatley's Use of Biblical Myth and Symbol," remains the best treatment on Wheatley's incorporation of the Judeo-Christian Bible in her poetry.

2. Numerous critical readings focusing exclusively on Olaudah Equiano's use of the Bible have positioned the discourse the Judeo-Christianity as hegemonic in Equiano Studies. In a seldom-cited essay, "Possible Gustavus Vassa/Olaudah Equiano Attributions," however, Vincent Carretta observes that "ten letters signed 'Gustavus Vassa' appeared between 24 July 1777 and 10 July 1778 in the pro-government London newspaper the *Morning Post, and Daily Advertiser*" (103) which "reveal a familiarity with French and Latin and Classical history not found elsewhere in Vassa/Equiano's work" (106). As Carretta submits, "I know of no one else who published under the pseudonym Vassa during the last quarter of the eighteenth century" (104).

Carretta's key observations enable an examination of how Equiano, as early as the first edition of the *Narrative* (1789), strategically employs elements of classical georgic, most likely taken from John Dryden's 1697 trans-

Eric D. Lamore

lation of Virgil's *Georgics,* to attack, in the first three chapters of the *Narrative,* the institution of slavery and the eighteenth-century transatlantic slave trade. Despite the fact that Equiano draws a parallel between the "pastoral" (25) state found in Genesis and his African agrarian community, emphasis placed on the "industry" found in his African community, the incorporation of an African agrarian civil war, and a reference to his reconstructed Eboe agrarian community as a "theatre of war" (25) may also be located in Virgil's *Georgics.* Equiano cleverly buries his use of the ancient classical genre through a footnote intended to direct the reader to "See Anthony Benezet's *Account of Africa* throughout" (25), and thereby avoids the potential critique for using (and overusing) the ancient classical tradition.

3. Lines from Wheatley's most recently discovered poem, "Ocean," may establish that this African American poet read and seriously critiqued Adanson's *Voyage.* In one particular section of the *Voyage,* for instance, Adanson boasts killing a "nguiarkol" (228), an African bird, the visitor of Africa describes, which possesses characteristics similar to "an eagle" (228). Killing of the bird by Adanson provokes a strong reaction from the Africans who accompany him:

> I killed one of them, which made my Negroes look upon me with a very bad eye, because they fear and reverence this bird: they even carry their superstition so far, as to place it among the number of their *marabous,* that is, of their priests, whom they look upon as persons sacred and divine. (228)

In his description of the bird, Adanson comments that the "Jaloffs," one of three African communities that Benezet identifies residing near the Gambia River (7), refer to this eaglelike bird "by the name of nguiarkol" (227). Curiously, Wheatley's "Ocean," a poem penned on her trip from England to America, a trip that resulted from the Boston community rejecting her proposal based on racist reasons, contains a scene in which "C—f's hand" shoots and kills "an Eagle young and gay" (Mason, "Ocean" 79). These parallels found in the texts of Adanson and Wheatley do not appear to be accidental. "C—f," the first and last letters of the ship captain's last name, "Calef" (Mason, "Ocean" 80) may stand as a substitute for Adanson, an individual, in the above scene, entirely disrespectful of African customs and beliefs, and the "Eagle" may be cloaked as the African "nguiarkol." This presumably "innocent" detail in "Ocean," then, may serve as another example of subversion in Wheatley's poetic arsenal and an inclusion of her African heritage in her poetry.

4. In addition to failing to notice the impact of georgic among the early chapters of Olaudah Equiano's *Narrative,* Cotton Mather's 1727 *Agricola. Or the Religious Husbandman: The Main Intentions of Religion Served in the Business and Language of Husbandry* may be categorized as an omission in the scholarly treatments focusing on the Early American georgic. Written just one year after the penning of *Manuductio ad Ministerium,* wherein the author praises Virgil's *Georgics* in his text for soon-to-be ministers, *Agricola* can be read as more complicated text than what Perry Miller sees as a product of "daily spiritualizing," an exercise practiced by Puritan ministers to convince a stray congregation that the presence of God may be seen in daily activities (404–5), and what Denise D. Knight, in *Cotton Mather's Verse in English,* sees in "The Rain gasped for," a poem found in *Agricola,* as Mather's attempt to "reinforce the Puritan notion that everything on earth, including drought, is a result of God's divine providence" (23).

Penning such as "Singing at the Plow," "The Sower a Singer," "The Song of the Sithe," "The Songs of God, Singing among the Trees of God; Full of Sap, and of Songs before Him," and "The Songs of Harvest," Mather looks to Virgil as a guide to christianize the didactic messages found in the *Georgics.* Hence, Mather's claim in *Manuductio* that Virgil's *Georgics* will "furnish you [an upcoming minister] with many things far from despicable" (19) becomes accomplished through the writing of *Agricola.* A reading of *Agricola* that departs from both Miller and Knight, then, focuses on Mather's rhetorical mastery in blending ancient classical and Judeo-Christian discourses for the purpose of "christianizing" rural farmers in colonial Boston. Extending this argument just a bit further, one can observe that Mather alludes to the "evil" "Imagination" in the first chapter of *Agricola* (5–6). This one example highlights how this Puritan minister, similar to the classical figure Proteus, strategically shifts his rhetorical mission based on his audience. The "public" denouncing of the imagination differs greatly from a clear reliance on this faculty to blend, in *Agricola,* the discourses of ancient classicism and Judeo-Christianity to advance "Religious Husbandry."

5. In fact, Virgil refers to Silvanus once in both the *Eclogues* and the *Aeneid.* Silvanus makes a brief appearance in the tenth eclogue wherein he spreads his "rustic glories on his brow" by "waving" his "fennel flowers" and "tall lilies" (91). Moreover, in the tenth eclogue, Gallus includes the

Eric D. Lamore

name "Phyllis" as one of his lovers (91). This provocative naming of "Phyllis" would have surely resonated immediately with Wheatley who, as we have noted, was named after the slave ship that transported her to Boston. An association with this classical lover, instead of the slaver, would have infused her name with dignity. Nevertheless, in the tenth eclogue, Virgil associates Silvanus with "flowers" and "lilies," not the "fields" we find in Wheatley's "On Imagination."

In the *Aeneid*, Silvanus appears in book 8, a highly important point in Virgil's epic in which Aeneas and his fellow Trojans have landed on the shore and successfully determined that Latium will become the future site of Rome. Shortly before the decisive battle starts, Aeneas and his men rest in a location where "Silvanus' honor, god of the fields, / God of the fold" resides" (199). While it is also tempting to speculate on the importance of this additional reference to Silvanus in the *Aeneid* to our discussion of Wheatley's "On Imagination," it is important to note that, in these two references to Silvanus, we do not see a juxtaposition between the rural and the urban as we do in book 2 of the *Georgics* and in Wheatley's "On Imagination." Out of the four total times Virgil refers to Silvanus in his poetry, he includes the figure twice in his *Georgics*, a deliberate act that positions this ancient classical deity within the realm of georgic. Even though both Horace and Ovid, whom Wheatley also read, include Silvanus in their poetry, it is more likely, based on the rural versus urban motif in both Virgil and Wheatley, that this African American artist drew from the *Georgics* for her inclusion of Silvanus.

6. A complete tracing of this motif in African American letters, which figures so powerfully within Negro spirituals of the nineteenth century, lies beyond the scope of this project; however, brief analyses of Robert Hayden's "O Daedalus Fly Away Home" and Ralph Ellison's short story "Flying Home" help to establish that this motif of flight has mutated slightly throughout African American literary history but still registers as a critical protest against oppression.

Included in the *Collected Poems of Robert Hayden*, the title of the twenty-two-line poem, "O Daedalus Fly Away Home," solidifies that Hayden draws upon the ancient classical figure, Daedalus, a crafty inventor whose son, Icarus, perished because he flew too close to the sun as the father-and-son team attempted to escape from the labyrinth, to comment forcefully on the institution of slavery. Surrounded by the "drifting scent of the Georgia pines," "coonskin drum," and "jubilee banjo," an unidentified slave held in bondage longs for "pretty Matilda." As the slave/speaker identifies "Night" as "juba" and "conjo," the speaker hopes to "weav[e] a wish and a weariness together / to make two wings" (19).

The packaging of a "wish" and "weariness together," according to these lines, would result in the creation of "two wings," the composition of an instrument the unidentified slave would use to reunite with his "pretty Matilda." The unidentified slave/speaker reinforces his wish for escape away from the institution of slavery by explicitly stating, "*O fly away home, fly away*" (19; emphasis in original), by asking, "Do you remember Africa?" and lamenting, "I knew all the stars of Africa" (19). At the close of poem, the speaker faces the same dilemma in his hope that "a wish and weariness together" may form "two wings" in order to "*fly away home, fly away*" (20; emphasis in original). In the context of "O Daedalus Fly Away Home," then, Hayden continues in the same poetic vein as Wheatley in drawing upon the classical tradition to voice the predicament of the African slave and his attempt at reconnecting with Africa.

Originally published in 1944 and reprinted in the more recent *"Flying Home" and Other Stories,* on one level, Ralph Ellison's short story, "Flying Home," may be read as a critical response to the failed African American flight program at Tuskegee Institute. This program, in theory, served to provide training for African Americans to become pilots yet, because of racially motivated reasons, this training system was never able to boast of producing a single graduate (Trimmer 129). On another level, however, the metaphor of flight becomes a central theme in the narratives of both Todd, an African American pilot, and, Jefferson, a poor, rural African American who first discovers Todd's plane and cares for the injured pilot.

Ellison's short story opens with Todd regaining consciousness after his plane crashes. Ellison notes that Todd had "been flying too high and too fast" (Ellison 155), resulting in an unsuccessful flight. While the crash registers as an unsuccessful flight for Todd and an unsuccessful venture in distancing himself from the African American community, the character, Jefferson, proves to be a bit more successful in his own "flights." As Ellison's Jefferson inquires about the intricacies found in the demolished plane and the status of other African Americans training to become pilots, this rescuer of Todd makes a curious off-hand remark: "Sho, I died and went to heaven . . . maybe by time I tell you about it they be done come after you" (156). Even though Jefferson hesitates to admit to Todd that the tale counts as a "lie"

Eric D. Lamore

or not, he quickly boasts about his ability to sprout wings after his "death": "Well, I went to heaven and right away started to sproutin' me some wings. Six feet ones, they was. Just like them the white angels had" (157). Shortly after his initial, exciting discovery that he possesses the ability to fly "just like them white angels," Jefferson learns from other black angels that "colored folks had to wear a special kin'a harness when we flew" (158). According to Ellison's Jefferson, "Ole Saint Peter" acquiesces to the fact the black angel may leave off his harness as long as he does not perturb heaven with his "one wing flyin.'" Despite the warning, Jefferson disobeys "ole Saint Peter" for a second time by "flyin' fast enough to shame the devil" (159), an act that results in his expulsion from heaven because, as "ole Saint Peter" claims, Jefferson poses as a clear "danger to the heavenly community" (160). As Jefferson adds, "They rushed me straight to them pearly gates and gimme a parachute and a map of the state of Alabama . . ." (160).

Because Jefferson reacts to the ending of his own story with "a burst of laughter" (160), we must keep in mind that the "heaven tale," as it might be named, functions as much more than comic relief. Jefferson launches into the "heaven narrative" to distract Todd from his injuries sustained from the crash. The "heaven narrative," moreover, comments forcefully upon Todd's own attempt at flight and entrance into a "white" profession. Moreover, this brief metanarrative in Ellison's short story shows that the "flying motif" has been adopted and slightly altered by the most successful twentieth-century African American writer. Unlike the poetry of Phillis Wheatley, wherein "flight" becomes accomplished through a flexing of the imagination, Ellison enables Jefferson to secure freedom in "heaven" due to his "death." By utilizing the Judeo-Christian concept of "heaven" in "Flying Home," Ellison places Jefferson in an environment in which he may have a better opportunity of escaping oppression and experiencing freedom. As Jefferson notes, "It was so good to know I was free at last" (158).

Even in a constructed heavenly realm, though, Jefferson's celebration of freedom, exercised through his encompassing flights, is only temporary because the flights disrupt a heavenly realm predicated upon racial difference and classification. The construction of a fictionalized account of a racist heaven allows Ellison to follow Wheatley in the collapsing of the same environment that grants the African American agent a taste of freedom. As Wheatley briefly experiences freedom in her "rural transports," according to the fictional world constructed by Ellison, an African American character cannot even experience freedom in the heavenly realm. As seen in the works of Hayden and Ellison, the problem of permanently securing freedom through flight, to one's home in the work of Wheatley and Hayden or in "heaven" in the work of Ellison, remains a contemporary motif in African American letters to offer a stinging critique lodged against forms of oppression.

WORKS CITED

Adanson, Michel. *A Voyage to Senegal, the Isle of Goree, and the River Gambia.* London, 1759.

Benezet, Anthony. *A Short Account on that Part of Africa, Inhabited by Negroes. With Respect to the Fertility of the Country; the good Disposition of many of the Natives, and Manner by which the Slave Trade Is Carried On. Extracted from several Authors, in Order to Shew [sic] the Iniquity of that Trade and the Falsity of the Arguments usually Advanced in its Vindication. With a Quotation from George Willis's System of the Laws, etc. and a Large Extract from a Pamphlet latterly Published on the Subject of the Slave Trade.* Philadelphia, 1762. London: Frank Cass and Co., 1968.

———. *Some historical account of Guinea, its situation, produce, and the general disposition of its inhabitants. With an inquiry into the rise and progress of the slave-trade, its natural and lamentable effects. Also a republication of the sentiments of several authors of note, on this interesting subject; particularly an extract of a treatise, by Granville Sharp.* Philadelphia, 1771. London: Frank Cass and Co., 1968.

Blake, Susan L. "Folklore and Community in *Song of Solomon.*" *MELUS* (1980): 77–82.

Carretta, Vincent. "Possible Gustavus Vassa/Olaudah Equiano Attributions." *The Faces of Anonymity: Anonymous and Pseudonymous Publication from the Sixteenth to the Twentieth Century.* Ed. Robert J. Griffin. New York: Palgrave Macmillan, 2003. 103–39.

———. "Who Was Francis Williams?" *Early American Literature* 38.2 (2003): 213–37.

Dowling, William C. *Poetry and Ideology in Revolutionary Connecticut.* Athens: U of Georgia P, 1990.

Ellison, Ralph. "Flying Home." *"Flying Home" and Other Stories.* Ed. John F. Callahan. New York: Random House, 1996. 147–73.

Ennis, Daniel J. "Poetry and American Revolutionary Identity: The Case of Phillis Wheatley and John Paul Jones." *Studies in Eighteenth-Century Culture* 31 (2002): 85–98.

Equiano, Olaudah. *The Interesting Narrative of the Life of Olaudah Equiano, or Gustavus Vassa, the African, Written by Himself.* Ed. Werner Sollors. New York: W. W. Norton, 2001.

Erkkila, Betsy. "Phillis Wheatley and the Black American Revolution." *Feminist Interventions in Early American Studies.* Ed. Mary C. Carruth. Tuscaloosa: U of Alabama P, 2006. 161–82.

Field, Jonathan Beecher. Rev. *American Georgics: Economy and Environment in Early American Literature* by Timothy Sweet and *Working in the Garden: American Writers and the Industrialization of Agriculture* by William Coulogue. *American Literature* 75.2 (2003): 429–31.

Gale, Monica. "Didactic Epic." *A Companion to Latin Literature.* Ed. Stephen Harrison. Malden: Blackwell, 2005. 101–15.

Georgia Writers' Project and Works Project Administration. *Drums and Shadows: Survival Studies among the Georgia Coastal Negroes.* Athens: U of Georgia P, 1940.

Granger, Mary. Introduction. *Drums and Shadows: Survival Studies Among the Georgia Coastal Negroes.* Athens: U of Georgia P, 1940. xvii–xx.

Hall, James C. "Folklore, Intertextuality, and *Song of Solomon.*" *Approaches to Teaching the Novels of Toni Morrison.* Ed. Nellie Y. McKay and Kathryn Earle. New York: MLA, 1997. 68–72.

Hayden, Robert. "O Daedalus Fly Away Home." *The Oxford Anthology of African-American Poetry.* Ed. Arnold Rampersad. Oxford: Oxford UP, 2006. 19–20.

Hume, David. "Of National Characters." *Political Essays/David Hume.* Ed. Knud Haakouseen. Cambridge UP, 1994. 78–92.

Jefferson, Thomas. *Notes on the State of Virginia.* New York: Penguin, 1999.

Kendrick, Robert. "Re-membering America: Phillis Wheatley's Intertextual Epic." *African American Review* 30.1 (1996): 71–88.

Knight, Denise D. "Introduction." *Cotton Mather's Verse in English.* Ed. Denise D. Knight. Newark: U of Delaware P, 1989. 11–27.

Kutchen, Larry. "Timothy Dwight's Anglo-American Georgia: Greenfield Hill and the Rise of United States Imperialism." *Studies in Literary Imagination* 33.2 (2006): 109–28.

Levernier, James A. "Style as Protest in the Poetry of Phillis Wheatley." *Style* 27.2 (1993): 172–94.

Marx, Leo. *The Machine in the Garden: Technology and the Pastoral Idea in America*. New York: Oxford UP, 1967.

Mason, Julian. "'Ocean:' A New Poem by Phillis Wheatley." *Early American Literature* 34.1 (1999): 78–83.

———. *The Poems of Phillis Wheatley*. Chapel Hill: U of North Carolina P, 1966.

Mather, Cotton. *Agricola. Or, the Religious Husbandman: The Main Intentions of Religion, Served in the Business and Language of Husbandry. A Work Adapted unto the Grand Purposes of Piety; And Commended therefore by a Number of Ministers, to be Entertained in the Families of the Country*. Boston, 1727.

———. *Manuductio ad Ministerium. The Native Muse: Theories of American Literature from Bradford to Whitman*. Ed. Richard Ruland. New York: E. P. Dutton, 1976. 18–22.

Miller, Perry. *The New England Mind: From Colony to Province*. Cambridge: Harvard UP, 1953.

Morrison, Toni. *The Song of Solomon*. 1977. New York: Vintage, 2004.

Odell, Margaretta. "Memoir." *Memoir and Poems of Phillis Wheatley*. 1838. Miami: Mnemosyne, 1969. 11–35.

Ogilvie, George. "Carolina; or, The Planter." Special issue of *Southern Literary History* (1986): 7–112.

O'Neale, Sondra. "A Slave's Subtle War: Phillis Wheatley's Use of Biblical Myth and Symbol." *Early American Literature* 21.2 (1986): 144–65.

Oxford Classical Dictionary. Ed. Simon Hornblower and Antony Spawforth. 3rd ed. Oxford: Oxford UP, 1996.

Oxford Companion to Classical Dictionary. Ed. M. C. Howatson. 2nd ed. Oxford: Oxford UP, 1989.

Robinson, William H. *Black New England Letters: The Uses of Writing in Black New England*. Boston: Public Library of the City of Boston, 1977.

Eric D. Lamore

————. *Phillis Wheatley: A Bio-Bibliography.* Boston: G. K. Hall, 1981.

Shields, David S. *Oracles of Empire: Poetry, Politics, and Commerce in British America, 1690–1750.* Chicago: U of Chicago P, 1990.

Shields, John C. *The American Aeneas: Classical Origins of the American Self.* Knoxville: U of Tennessee P, 2001.

————. *Phillis Wheatley's Poetics of Liberation: Backgrounds and Contexts.* Knoxville: U of Tennessee P, 2008.

————. "Phillis Wheatley's Subversive Pastoral." *Eighteenth-Century Studies* 27.4 (1994): 631–47.

Sweet, Timothy. *American Georgics: Economy and Environment in Early American Literature.* Philadelphia: U of Pennsylvania P, 2002.

Trimmer, Joseph F. "Ralph Ellison's 'Flying Home.'" *The Critical Response to Ralph Ellison.* Ed. Robert J. Butler. Westport: Greenwood, 2000. 129–39.

Tuttle, Julius Herbert. "The Libraries of the Mathers." *Proceedings of the American Antiquarian Society* 20.2 (1910): 269–356.

Virgil, *Aeneid.* Trans. Rolfe Humphries. New York: Macmillan, 1987.

————. *Eclogues. Eclogues, Georgics, and Aeneid I–VI.* Trans. H. R. Fairclough. Loeb Classical Library. Cambridge: Harvard UP, 1999. 23–95.

————. *Georgics.* Trans. Janet Lembke. New Haven: Yale UP, 2005.

Wheatley, Phillis. *The Collected Works of Phillis Wheatley.* Ed. John C. Shields. New York: Oxford UP, 1988.

Wilkinson, L. P. *The Georgics of Virgil: A Critical Survey.* 1969. Norman: U of Oklahoma P, 1997.

PART II

Placing Phillis Wheatley in Newly Applied Historical Contexts

Works of Wonder, Wondering Eyes, and the Wondrous Poet: The Use of Wonder in Phillis Wheatley's Marvelous Poetics

Jennifer Billingsley

Upon receiving an award in Gotthold Lessing's name, the political thinker Hannah Arendt reflected, "That a person appears in public at all, and that the public receives and confirms him is by no means a matter to be taken for granted. Only the genius is driven by his very gifts into public life . . . as if it were a natural phenomenon erupting into human society" (*Dark Times* 3–4). Arendt believed Lessing to be one of these natural phenomena and spent a lifetime attempting to discern others who through their work shed light on the affairs of all persons, even during the darkest of times when political regimes, dogma, or prejudice suppressed public discourse. She focused on the few courageous souls who still ventured into the public realm to enlighten mankind despite the grave consequences that awaited them.[1] Unknown to Arendt and so many others, the poet Phillis Wheatley, like Lessing, was one of these natural wunderkinds, although one who has suffered over the years from a continued sense of doubt concerning the range of her achievement rather than the overwhelming sense of curiosity that inspired Arendt in Lessing's work. Lessing's public welcomed and confirmed his genius, but the question of authenticity and a sense of doubt have afflicted the public reception and even the present-day perception of Wheatley's work.

Lessing himself discussed such men in the thirteenth and fourteenth centuries, men who predicted a new age for the gospel and believed "they could make their contemporaries, who had scarcely outgrown their childhood, without enlightenment, without preparation, men worthy of their *Third Age*" (215). He called each an "enthusiast" who "casts true glances into the future, but for this future he cannot wait. He wishes this future accelerated, and accelerated through him. That for which nature takes thousands of years is to mature itself in the moment of his existence" (215). For many of these natural geniuses, however, as well as for Wheatley, what they recognized as the best did not become the best in their lifetimes. Their hopes for their age were not realized in their lifetimes. Amid rampant denial and doubt, such men might become less committed to revealing to the world the truth they had discovered; yet, like those few before her, Wheatley remained committed to revealing the truth to her age, and so, like Lessing's examples, she did not make "a bad use of the present" (217). As a poet, she entered the public affairs of men, revealing and reminding them of the wonders of the world their reason concealed from them. Similarly, she yet remains an important figure as our understanding of African American and Early American literature matures, revealing and reminding us of the wonders and of the wonder itself our education conceals from us.

The poetry of Wheatley provides an incredible opportunity to view a literary artist's individual effort to form a new poetics. Like Edward Taylor before her, Wheatley formed her poetics privately, but for reasons quite different from Taylor's. Her status as a slave prevented her from nurturing her poetics under the auspices of a university education or within a literary circle as was the case among other poets. Instead, she was required to sharpen her poetics independent of the halls of academia and public scrutiny, relying on the private generosity of men like Mather Byles, who gave her access to his library and to the classical texts that inspired her poetics. Where Edward Taylor and Wheatley differ is in Wheatley's undeterred efforts to introduce her personal poetics to the public realm where she would be both heralded and denounced and subjected to a literary tribunal to verify that her work was indeed her own. In the end, this tribunal verified the authenticity of her work, and the attestation of her white, male judges accompanied the formal publication of her work in America. Since that judicious day of October 8, 1772, when Wheatley's poetry and poetics were submitted to public scrutiny, however, the contentious debate over Wheatley has never subsided. On the contrary, Wheatley has been tried and tried again for all types of social and racial infractions, and only of late have her defenders grown more fervent and effective. At last she may have found a public ready to read her work anew as Henry Louis Gates Jr. requires: "unblinkered by the anxieties of her time and ours" (89).

For Gates, Wheatley demonstrated "the creed that culture was, could be, the equal possession of all humanity" (90). Her use of the classical tradition certainly proves Gates's assertion. Douglas Bush described the multitude of classical symbols inherited by poets of the Renaissance and Romantic periods as a "public treasury" (vii). From this great treasury, Wheatley extracts her fantastic images and poetic forms. Consequently, part of the abuse Wheatley has endured over the years derives from the use of these classical symbols and the general anxiety produced by the neoclassical tradition taking place in Europe. For certain critics of the early to mid-twentieth century, the rigid, artificial forms of neoclassicism prevented Wheatley from truly expressing her own views and experiences within her poetry. Vernon Loggins lamented that "she wrote too rarely about herself" (89) and concluded that her genius was simply the genius of imitation (92). Arthur P. Davis provided a rebuttal to Loggins's assertion that she was detached and objective in her writing, but he could not bring himself entirely to dismiss Loggins's conclusion (192). For Davis, Wheatley's objectivity or detachment was not simply a neoclassical trait but a "congenital reserve" to guard her emotions (198). In both of these cases, each critic fails to read Wheatley's work on its own merit by perpetuating the prevailing "anxieties" concerning the neoclassical tradition, which had then fallen into ill repute, instead of trying to discern how Wheatley's personal poetics influenced the public affairs of men to remind society, as Gates notes, that culture was and is the possession of all mankind.

At last it is not an uncommon preoccupation for contemporary critics to find past cultural objects (classical or otherwise) feeding a sort of Arnoldian "cultural philistinism" (Arendt, "Crisis" 206). Cultural objects (as well as religious objects) of all types have a tendency to be used as currency to preserve or acquire a higher position in society. In this process of acquisition, the objects themselves exchange their initial value of inspiring understanding for something more vulgar, so it would be easy to denounce Wheatley as a "vulgar" poet for trying to use classical myths as cultural currency to improve her station. Yet this preoccupation that denounces this African American poet fails to recognize Wheatley's tremendous personal effort, not only to possess such cultural currency, but to spend that personal currency publicly while she remained a slave. Therefore to say her effort was derivative, detached, or guarded has now become disingenuous. Above all, when reading Wheatley, critics must supply a greater effort to understand their subject and thereby avoid this misstep.

Not only do critics fail to acknowledge the personal side of Wheatley's poetics, they fail to recognize that her poetics is not rooted in a neoclassical tradition at all, but in the classical tradition. Simply to discuss everything classical in neoclassical terms is disingenuous. American poets like Wheatley were not ingrained in a neoclassical tradition, attempting to mimic their European counterparts. Even the simple biography of Wheatley by Shirley Graham notes that her master's son Nathaniel taught her Latin as a child (74), though probably a bogus notion as critics such as Shields have posited that Mather Byles may have served as her Latin tutor. Too often modern critics forget that Early American education consisted of Latin schools. Educated Americans as a result were able to access ancient texts on their own accord and therefore did not have to rely on the "superior" knowledge of Europe to direct their own aesthetics.

At the moment when Americans began to identify themselves as Americans, Wheatley, like other Americans, looked to their classical past for a usable model. As a result, these Early Americans did not need to mimic English or Continental traditions to prove their worth. These Early Americans, including the founding fathers themselves, freely exercised their preference for the original, classical treasures. From their firsthand knowledge of the classics, they were not only able to acquire mythological symbols; they were able to appropriate ancient philosophy as well. This appropriation of ancient thought provided depth and coherence to the founding fathers' establishment of a new form of government[2] and enabled writers like Wheatley to construct and exercise a poetics of their own. Therefore, it is inaccurate to argue that Wheatley imitated the artificial structures of the neoclassical tradition; rather she consciously developed a philosophical position that helped to establish a new poetics out of the classical tradition. The inclusion of the classical faculty of wonder in her poetics is of interest here.

The appellations ascribed to Wheatley from her initial critical reception to the present reveal the persistent curiosity cultivated by this enslaved female poet: in the *Massachusetts Gazette* in 1773 she was a called "a most surprising genius" ("L" 21); Archibald Bell indicated that the London newspapers of 1773 proclaimed her "one of the greatest instances of pure, unassisted Genius, that the world ever produced" (28); William J. Snelling wrote in 1834 that she was "a precocious genius" and "an honor and ornament to her race and her kind" (64ff); Benjamin B. Thatcher in the same year wrote that "her compositions furnish abundant proof of a degree of native genius which is exceedingly rare among persons of any race, class or condition" (70); a century later, Vernon Loggins identified her as "one of the ornaments in American literature as well as one of the most interesting curiosities" (92); in 1972, R. Lynn Matson saw her as "a slave who enjoys all the benefits of a kind of enlightened family, a position to be guarded, and yet an enslaved muse" (115); for Terence Collins in 1975, she was a "showpiece novelty" (149); and finally more recent scholars, such as Charles Scruggs, have identified her as a "natural genius" (281), while Henry Louis Gates Jr. describes her as "auditioning for the humanity of the entire African people" (21). As these responses note, Wheatley's novelty as a "genius" erupted into early American society and continues to disrupt the standard critical narrative. Her novelty and the curiosity it affected, however, are not inadvertent, but may be interpreted to result from her application of wonder.

Howard Parsons considered the word "wonder" (Old English: *wundor*) to be a cognate of the German term *Wunde* (to wound). Therefore, he suggested wonder to be "a breach in the membrane of awareness, a sudden opening in a man's system of established and expected meanings, a blow as if one were struck or stunned." Wonder, then, is both an aspect of the event and an aspect of the observer's response to the event. For Parsons, "Wonder is the spark of excitation leaping across the gap between man and the world" (85). Although wonder remains widely unacknowledged in Wheatley scholarship, this concept provides vital insight into Wheatley's poetics and the possible critical response to her poetry. Her ability to create an object of wonder within her works as well as to make the concept part of her persona permits her to initiate a response of wonder within her readers. So applied, the concept of wonder constitutes a significant strategy, one not to be ignored.

In order to understand Wheatley's work, it is first necessary to understand the development of this faculty of wonder. Little has been noted of the faculty of wonder in American literature, but it has a long and detailed history. One of the earliest examples of wonder coming to us from the ancient, classical world is demonstrated in *Theaetetus* when Plato has Socrates conclude, "this wondering: this is where philosophy begins and nowhere else" (173). In the classical tradition, wonder was a basic faculty, the very prerequisite of thought. Aristotle agreed with Plato's sense of wonder and explained in his *Metaphysics*,

> For it is owing to their wonder that men both now begin and at first began to philosophize; they wondered originally at the obvious difficulties, then advanced little by little and stated difficulties about the greater matters, e.g. about the phenomena of the moon and those of the sun and the stars, and about the genesis of the universe. And a man who is puzzled and wonders thinks himself ignorant (whence even the lover of myth is in a sense a lover of wisdom, for myth is composed of wonders . . .). (1554)

Despite the great critical divide between the fate of myth and poetry in Aristotle's and Plato's philosophies, both ancient philosophers agreed that the mysteries of the material world inspired the faculty of wonder in mankind, which in turn beget serious questions concerning ontology, epistemology, and metaphysics, the basic questions of philosophy. For these earliest thinkers, wonder initiated thought itself, but the function of wonder would change as systems of thought were established and continuously revised through the ages.

For the medievalist Caroline Walker Bynum, "wonder" is an important topic in understanding the concepts of change and alterity in the twelfth and thirteenth centuries. Wonder also remains a serious topic in late Renaissance and baroque periods, a time span that is appropriately called the Age of the Marvelous (Kenseth 25). Except for an interest in the sublime, however, wonder still eludes most scholarship on the Age of Enlightenment, the age into which Wheatley was born. As strange as it may seem today, wonder played an equally important aesthetic role in this period and in periods since, for ideas rarely have expiration dates and exist on the shelf long after being considered fashionable or useful. In these earlier periods, during its eminence, interest in the miraculous and fantastic motivated both art and European voyages of discovery like those of Columbus. Women and men during the Age of the Marvelous discovered or reproduced marvelous objects that were intended to astonish the viewer, making the viewer question the reality of what was seen while also expecting a reason for it. These marvelous objects revealed a complexity not yet understood; their existence elicited evidence of a difference between the world perceived and the world conceived by the viewer.

Wheatley herself represented such an object of wonder during the Enlightenment: an African slave who could use language better than her master. As a result, before her work could even be published, it had to be authenticated, and even after being authenticated she would remain an object of wonder whom many would doubt. There existed and still exists doubters, exemplified by Thomas Jefferson who dismissed Wheatley as incapable of anything more than mimicry of white culture, if even that. As Parsons noted, wonderful objects may be so disruptive to an observer's "system of established and expected meanings" that they are denied factually, as Jefferson denied Wheatley's artistry rather than accommodate her in a modified system of meaning.

In order to understand wonder during the Enlightenment and how it affected Wheatley's reception and work, it is necessary to understand the evolution of wonder through these earlier periods in more detail. Bynum's work pro-

Jennifer Billingsley

vides a starting point in this endeavor. Her interest is not simply to catalog objects of wonder and the theories of wonder they represent; she explores the behavior of wonder itself (39). For Bynum, wonder is not only concerned with the object encountered; it is concerned with what human beings can and cannot know or understand. One wonders only at what one does not understand. For this reason, wonder is often associated with the ignorant or the primitive because "we wonder at what we cannot in any sense incorporate, or consume, or encompass in our mental categories; we wonder at mystery, at paradox . . ." (53). In medieval works, she identifies three characteristics of wonder. Wonder is always factual, singular, and perspectival (54). First, wonders are objects that astonish, because they must in fact exist in order to be experienced; they are situated in a material and temporal reality. Next, upon being found a credible object or event, wonder cannot be associated with a natural process; it must be an anomaly or singular event that cannot be reproduced. Finally, in Bynum's terms, wonder is perspectival, which means it is relative to the viewer. She uses the classical example of a Cyclops to understand this characteristic. We might marvel at a Cyclops who has one eye as much as the Cyclops might marvel at us upon seeing that we have two eyes (55). This cognitive component becomes significant to the discussion of wonder in Wheatley's work.

For Bynum, wonder became an "incentive to investigation" because the novel or bizarre that induces wonder seemed both to "exceed explanation and to indicate that there might be reason (significance—not necessarily cause) behind it" (72).[3] Bynum discovers that this reason that wonder implies is more often an implied moral significance, rather than merely a causal one. Wonders were often considered prodigies or portents; therefore, their existence indicated divine meaning. In this manner, wonder destabilizes accepted tautologies by triggering ontological as well as epistemological questions. In view of these shaken tautologies and new questions, Bynum concedes that "marveling at diversity can be the prelude to appropriation"; it is not an attribute of wonder itself, however (69). The need to possess the marvelous does become a significant part of the cultural forces until the Age of the Marvelous. Bynum recognizes the medieval period's positive emphasis on "uniqueness" and the potential of wonder to view the world in more complex terms (72).

This positive enthusiasm for the miraculous and fantastic survived the medieval period and indeed expanded during later periods to include most of Europe as new philosophical and scientific advances expanded the realm of wonder while a corresponding interest in classical civilization introduced texts (like Aristotle's *Metaphysics* and *Poetics*) and artifacts that illustrated ancient interests in the marvelous that served as the precedent for developing a new understanding of the marvelous (Kenseth 27).[4] With this new understanding, the marvelous became classified into three expanded categories: the supernatural, the natural, and the artificial (Kenseth 31). In this period, the supernatural, which was previously limited to the miraculous and fantastic phenomena of Christian mythology, began to reemploy more pagan myths. With the advent of greater travel and scientific discovery, natural wonders took on a new significance as well. Following Bynum's assertion that a natural process could not engender a wonder response, the natural phenomena of this category were deemed anomalies (nature's mistakes or, in Bynum's terms, singularities) (Kenseth 35). Human prodigies like dwarfs were included in this category as well as new species of animals and vegetation, like the then recently discovered penguins and coffee. Inevitably, it became a vogue during the period to collect such marvels for encyclopedias, for museums, and for private closets in order to view a compendium of "God's ingenuity." Previously, these natural wonders were studied "to learn about Providence, not nature" (Ashworth 131). The moral significance of wonderful objects, however, declined as reason contradicted their divine meaning.

As Bynum has noted, monsters and prodigies were considered portents of God's displeasure and therefore fell into the category of the supernatural; the new category of natural wonders, however, separated monsters and prodigies from these products of nature that were seen "as either nature in jest or nature in error" (Ashworth 132). As apparent aberrations, individuals such as Francis Bacon felt that such objects could reveal more about how nature works in comparison to ordinary objects. At the same time, artificial objects of wonder (paintings, sculptures, architecture, etc.) that were meant to demonstrate man's own ingenuity by reproducing instances of novelty that cultivated wonder similar to natural wonders became fashionable as well (Kenseth 38).

As wonder became the goal of the period's aesthetics, the exotic and bizarre became the subjects of artworks, and art that demonstrated technical achievement because of its size or its verisimilitude was considered a great feat that emulated God's virtuosity. These notions would eventually dissipate, however, and the excesses and oddities of such art came to be considered "meaningless exercises that ultimately had no edifying purpose" (Kenseth 55). The interest in natural wonders would also run its course. Aberrations would lose their significance as keys to understanding nature, and marvels would become fully naturalized and subsumed into ordinary natural processes, thereby losing the positive effects of wonder that Bynum identified (Ashworth 141). The Age of Reason had begun. As wonder evolved, objects of wonder would no longer evoke a more complex vision of the world. Before this paradigm shift occurred, though, these three categories of the marvelous altered nearly every field of knowledge and set the stage for the epistemological quandary that would pre-occupy the Age of Reason: what can woman or man truly know objectively once free from her or his superstitious past?

Before the Age of the Marvelous ended, the interest in the marvelous ar-rived on American shores. The prevailing vogue surrounding traditionally marvelous objects led to further assimilation of natural objects that in turn encouraged not only further scientific discoveries but voyages of discovery to satisfy the need to possess the marvelous. In this period of exponential travel, the native inhabitants of these exotic locations became the objects of wonder as well. Edward Said in *Orientalism* has accurately described how the Orient was transformed by the West into an exotic object defined by European tra-dition. Other cultures were equally susceptible to these cultural forces. The encounters of Europeans with the unknown, which led to wonder, also led to an insistent appropriation.

The voyage of Columbus as retold by Stephen Greenblatt in *Marvelous Possessions: The Wonder of the New World* illustrates this type of confronta-tion between the old world with the reality of a new world and the subsequent intellectual as well as material possession of that world. For Greenblatt, the culture with the technical ability to represent the other culture always pre-vailed, because "The unlettered peoples of the New World could not bring the strangers into focus; conceptual inadequacy severely impeded, indeed virtu-ally precluded, an accurate perception of the other. The culture that possessed writing could accurately represent itself (and hence strategically manipulate) the culture without writing, but the reverse was not true" (11). Because there were no categories to prescribe marvelous discoveries in the new world, those who traveled to the New World assumed the authority to ascribe new catego-ries. As a result, early discourse on America was "a record of the colonizing of the marvelous" (24–25). These travelers, like Columbus, who witnessed events and encountered objects never before experienced by their contempo-raries were forced to conceptualize the marvelous in order to communicate and represent their experiences upon their return home. As Greenblatt clarifies, "The native seized as a token and then displayed, sketched, painted, described, and embalmed is quite literally captured by and for European representation" (119). In this manner, then, wonder became increasingly significant. The ability to communicate a marvelous experience became the perceived prerequisite for assuming agency in the colonization and possession of other lands and cultures.

Inevitably, as this reconceptualization continued, wonder would become less and less wonderful, so to speak. At this point in history, Phillis Wheatley was sold on the block in Boston—at the point when wonder was considered a vice and skepticism, a virtue. As wonderful discoveries eventually became subsumed into the ordinary as they were naturalized and assimilated into new scientific systems, the Age of Reason disputed not only the value of wonder as a prerequisite of agency but the very facticity of an object of wonder, as seen in Jefferson's dismissal of Wheatley's poetry. In view of the earlier imperious use of wonder to master the marvelous, this change in direction ought to have been welcomed; however, possession of the marvelous did not change only the supposition for assuming such rights of possession. The supposition of reason's new moral significance justified the Western tradition's continued possession of the marvelous. Jefferson's dismissal of Wheatley reveals the transfer of authority from the agent of wonder to the agent of doubt.

In this context, the native inhabitants of a region, who were once considered marvelous objects themselves, were considered less than human because of their very capacity to wonder. Only a "primitive" could be awestruck seeing the inventions of the modern world. Only the "ignorant" could mistakenly attribute phenomena to something other than the laws of nature. Only "vulgar" people believed in superstitions and prodigies. Wonder devolved to its earlier Medieval version, but without its commensurate authority. Without access to a linguistic system to represent its culture textually, a native group was unable to refute these views—that is, until Wheatley. As a slave, Wheatley was considered primitive and therefore susceptible to superstitions and prodigies. Her genius, however, allowed her to tap into the faculty of wonder ascribed to her.

Her literary skills, although earlier cast into doubt by Jefferson's dismissal, which plagued her reputation, today are widely accepted. Still her literary skills even now are less important to readers than her background as a slave. It is this fact at which many marvel, partly, because slaves retain the classification as a "natural," "primitive" object of wonder incapable of higher reasoning. Just as the perception of slaves as "primitive" is limited, the conception of wonder as superstitious is also limited, as illustrated by the history already given. Wheatley knew better.

Jennifer Billingsley

The skepticism of David Hume represents the prominence of doubt and the precipitous fall of wonder. He posits, "No weakness of human nature is more universal and conspicuous than what we commonly call CREDULITY, or a too easy faith in the testimony of others . . ." (*Treatise* 78). Hume considers reason limited to experience and, therefore, the veracity of testimony is limited to the resemblance of that testimony to experience. Hume regrets that "we seldom regulate ourselves entirely by it; but have a remarkable propensity to believe whatever is reported, even concerning apparitions, enchantments, and prodigies, however contrary to daily experience and observation" (*Treatise* 78). Knowing, then, is based on the similarity of experience and a reliance on the probability of events based on that experience, which invalidates the faculty of wonder since wonders are aberrations and unpredictable.

Hume addressed the specific problem of miracles as an issue of human testimony in *An Enquiry Concerning Human Understanding*, stating,

> The reason, why we place any credit in witnesses and historians, is not derived from any *connexion*, which we perceive *a priori*, between testimony and reality, but because we are accustomed to find a conformity between them. But when the fact attested is such a one as has seldom fallen under our observation, here is a contest of two opposite experiences; of which the one destroys the other, as far as its force goes, and the superior can only operate on the mind by the force, which remains. (85)

Such testimony if accepted would lead to the "mutual destruction of belief and authority," and for Hume such testimony, if given even by Cato, would invalidate his great authority (Hume 86). In this attempt by Hume to solve the epistemological problem of what we can and cannot know, he simply eliminated the possibility of miracles and the corresponding sense of wonder, because the acceptance of miracles would lead to the end of common sense. Instead, he questioned the very validity (the facticity) of the testimony of witnesses of the miraculous.

Hume's skepticism appears to feed into Jefferson's skepticism regarding Wheatley's poetry.[5] Jefferson invalidated the testimony of the attestation, because in his experience he never found that "a black had uttered a thought above the level of plain narration; never [saw] even an elementary trait of painting or sculpture," and therefore Wheatley's poetry was beneath "the dignity of criticism" (140). Accepting Wheatley as a poet would mutually destroy both his belief system and his authority, so Hume's argument justified Jefferson's denial of the testimony given in the attestation. Jefferson would write, "Religion indeed has produced a Phyllis Whately [sic]; but it could not produce a poet" (140). He was not only framing Wheatley's religious poetry as derivative, but arguing that only a religious audience could testify and believe Wheatley to be a poet. Only an institution that recognized miracles and other marvelous phenomena could produce Wheatley. For Jefferson, reason remained superior, and the reasoning of Hume provided an excuse to deny the validity of Wheatley as a poet and intellectual being.

Wheatley is truly a paradox. Wheatley becomes an agent of wonder in the Age of Reason, thus leading to the immediate, strong reactions of both wonder and doubt. What is important is that Wheatley was not just an object of wonder. She assumes the agency of Columbus and the enthusiasm of the medieval period. She takes possession of the cultural apparatus that appropriated the new world and uses it for her own purposes in her poetry. She exercises the faculty of wonder in her poetry, making classical references and invoking the supernatural, utilizing natural wonders to invoke the sublime, and using even herself as one of these wunderkinds, thence investing race with a new sense of wonder in an attempt to redeem that original sense of wonder that induced observers to test their tautologies and view the world in more complex terms.

In *The Trials of Phillis Wheatley,* Gates describes the incredulity Wheatley encounters as part of a broader discourse among philosophers of the Renaissance and the Enlightenment. These philosophers, including Hume, were "vexed" by the African and how to accommodate the African within the family of man or as another species altogether (23). The trial of Wheatley illustrated this issue. Even the attestation of such eminent men could not convince everyone of Wheatley's literary achievement. Like Hume and Jefferson demonstrated, reason could not answer this question adequately, and further application of reason could not repair the inadequacies of reason. To avoid confronting established beliefs, reason became a vehicle of doubt. Through the application of doubt, reason simply annulled the question of Wheatley's creative aptitude by denying Bynum's first characteristic of wonder: the facticity of the object of wonder itself. In contrast, Wheatley successfully employs a strategy beyond the limitations of reason. For Wheatley wonder is that subjective faculty that can breach the gap between man and the world and help negotiate a new understanding of race and reality after reason fails.

Wheatley's work stands, therefore, in direct opposition to Hume's skepticism. For Hume as well as Lord Kames, wonder was simply a vulgar senti-

Jennifer Billingsley

ment, a feeling of awe, that had to be excised. However, Wheatley preferred to use wonder, just as Kant would later use the faculty of the imagination, to move beyond the limitations of reason. In "Thoughts on the Works of Providence," for example, Wheatley writes,

> Almighty, in these wond'rous works of thine,
> What *Pow'r,* what *Wisdom,* and what *Goodness* shine?
> And are thy wonders Lord, by men explor'd,
> And yet creating glory unador'd! (44)

In this example, Wheatley calls upon natural wonders to assist her poetic impulse and to induce her reader to wonder and view the world in more complex terms. In these lines from "Thoughts," the sun becomes the focal point of wonder, and thus the use of "shine" in the second line. The verse begins: "Ador'd for ever be the God unseen, / Which round the sun revolves this vast machine" (43). Like Aristotle, Wheatley viewed the phenomenon of the sun as an object of wonder that inspired notions of power, wisdom, and morality. Men first begin to puzzle over small things, but they advance little by little to puzzle over greater matters such as the genesis of the sun to even greater philosophical matters of power, wisdom, and morality as Wheatley begins to ponder here. In the context of "Thoughts," Wheatley focuses on a deliberate and gradual application of wonder rather than a simple sentiment used by a primitive poet. A series of similar accounts of wonder may be found throughout Wheatley's work.

Her very interest in the elegy reveals an interest in the tautologies surrounding death. Each elegy attempted to explain death, the great unknown, and death for her was a subject of wonder. In the first reference to wonder in her letters, she described her vigil at Mrs. Wheatley's bedside before she passed away. In a letter to Sir John Thornton, for example, Wheatley wrote that she "sat the whole time by her bed side, and saw with Grief and Wonder the Effects of Sin on the human race" (179). Her elegiac poetry continued to explore this same sense of wonder.

The clearest indication of this use of classical wonder is in the poem "To a Lady and Her Children on the Death of her Son and their Brother," wherein Wheatley described a child's spirit removed from its earthly bonds who in turn found joy, glories, and virtues unknown. She exclaimed, "What blissful wonders to his mind unfold!" (83). Blissful wonders here directly "unfold" in the child's mind. Then, in "An Hymn to Humanity," she wrote, "What wonders rise, what charms unfold / At his descent to earth!" (95). Again wonders "unfold" knowledge to the subject of each poem. The objects of wonder in these two examples are indeterminate, but they perform the same function. Wonders breach that membrane of experience of expected meaning to expose another level of meaning.

As previously noted, it was Socrates in his dialogue with his young friend Theaetetus who declared wonder to be the beginning of philosophy. Afterward, he explains, " . . . I dare say you will be grateful to me if I help you to discover the veiled truth in the thought of a great man—or perhaps I should say, of great men?" He directs Theaetetus to look around to "see that none of the uninitiated are listening to us—I mean the people who think that nothing exists but what they can grasp with both hands; people who refuse to admit that actions and processes and the invisible world in general have any place in reality" (Plato 173). Wheatley's application of wonder corresponds with Socrates' application, but her purpose differs. Socrates wants to distinguish two realms of perception to enlighten his young friend while Wheatley wants to make such a distinction to refute men like Jefferson. Socrates recognizes the "friction" and "intercourse" between the two sides of experience (senses) and thought. There are names for the things man experiences with his senses. For those invisible things "on the other side there is the race of things perceived, for each of these perceptions perceived things born of the same parentage, for all kinds of visions all kinds of colors, for all kinds of hearings all kinds of sounds; and so on, for the other perceptions the other things perceived, that come to be in kinship with them" (Plato 174). The purpose of thinking is to make these invisible things visible through dialogue. Wheatley's persistent use of wonder in her poetry is a dialogue itself.

It is not conclusive that Wheatley knew Plato or Aristotle, but it is not unlikely either. She undoubtedly knew wonder in a classical sense. Less than a century earlier, Cotton Mather's description of witch trials demonstrates this classical wonder. In *Wonders of the Invisible World Being An Account of the Trials of Several Witches Lately Executed in New England* (1692), he explained preternatural events in New England, attributing them to witchcraft and "invisible," evil spirits.[6] Mather's account is more metaphysical than spiritual, and his critic Robert Calef said as much in his rebuttal, *Wonders of the Invisible World*. But it is this type of metaphysics inspired by wonder that was also of interest to Wheatley.

In Aristotle's study of the subject, he considered "the artist wiser than the men of experience" (1553), because the artist has the capacity to pursue knowl-

Jennifer Billingsley

edge furthest from the senses (1554). The artist has the ability to free himself from the common perceptions of man. In fact, men begin to wonder in order to attain knowledge, but this aspiration to discover knowledge only occurs in the absence of necessity; as Aristotle notes, "we do not seek it for the sake of any other advantage; but as the man is free, we say, who exists for himself and not for another . . ." (1554–55). According to Aristotle, men willfully begin "by wondering that the matter is so (as in the case of automatic marionettes or the solstices or the incommensurability of the diagonal of a square with the side; for it seems wonderful to all men who have not yet perceived the explanation that there is a thing which cannot be measured even by the smallest unity" (1555). The release of Wheatley's subjects in "To a Lady and Her Children on the Death of her Son and their Brother" and "An Hymn to Humanity" from the necessities of life allows wonders to be "unfolded"—to know those invisible things furthest from their senses. To be free so to speak allows access to the metaphysical realm prohibited by experience.

Other examples of wonder cannot be as easily construed as the classical. In the elegy about Dr. Sewall, Wheatley wrote, "'Mourn him, ye youth, to whom he oft has told / 'God's gracious wonder from the times of old'" (21). This example demonstrates a more passive form of wonder, a form of wonder that belongs to a different tradition. Classical texts were not the only source that elaborated on the faculty of wonder. In *Leviathan*, Thomas Hobbes regarded wonder as a synonym for miracles. He asserted, "By *miracles* are signified the admirable works of God; and therefore, they are also called *wonders*" (293). Hobbes identified wonders with works of God. He explained,

> To understand, therefore, what is a miracle, we must first under-
> stand what works they are which men wonder at and call admira-
> ble. And there be but two things which make men wonder at any
> event: the one is, if it be strange, that is to say, such as the like of
> it hath never, or very rarely, been produced; the other is if, when
> it is produced, we cannot imagine it to have been done by natural
> means, but only by the immediate hand of God. (293)

Certainly, there are moments when this sense of wonder as a miracle is invoked in Wheatley's work as it is in "God's gracious wonder from the times of old." This sense of wonder does not entice further speculation. Works of God instead are unknowable and beyond the capacity of man to understand or imagine. These wonders are not the prelude to metaphysics.

Another example of a usage of wonder that actually denies the classical element outright but at the same time summons miraculous wonder may be seen in "To a Gentleman on his Voyage to *Great-Britain* for the Recovery of his Health." Here Wheatley invokes not "the chant of gay *Elysian* scenes" (88) but the "great Ruler of the skies" (89). She asked this Ruler to "Exert thy wonders to the world again!" (89) and with healing power, "This equal case demands thine equal care, / And equal wonders may this patient share" (89). Here Wheatley is not calling upon a classical sense of wonder to invoke philosophical thought; she invokes the miraculous wonder Hobbes described that evolved out of the Judeo-Christian tradition. As demonstrated earlier, wonder throughout history remains inconstant. Wheatley's different conceptions of wonder reveal a subtle awareness of this inconstancy.

It would be premature, however, to consider even this use of wonder (the works emanating from God) as derivative and imitative. Acknowledging this sense of wonder as well as the classical sense of wonder was significant. It revealed a breadth of understanding within the poet. She is aware of the conflicting tautologies within wonder itself, and her use of both types of wonder appears to be one of those "courageous attempts to experiment, to flex and bend the available tools of imaginative literary discourse, in order to create something new—something not British or Continental or even classical, but American" (Shields, *American Aeneas* 348).

In perhaps her most important poem, "On Imagination," Wheatley provides a glimpse into her own literary process. In the poem, Wheatley coronates imagination as the "imperial queen" (65). Here wondrous works are not attributed to the hand of God, but to imagination; and, in reference to this imperial queen, she writes, "Thy wond'rous acts in beauteous order stand, / And all attest how potent is thine hand" (65). Wheatley recognizes works of wonder are not just from the "immediate hand of God." Aristotle noted in his *Poetics* that the poet can represent three different aspects of things: things "either as they were or are, or as they are said or thought to be or to have been, or as they ought to be" (2337). In addition, he identified three distinct levels of knowing for an artist: the objective, the subjective, and the ideal. For poetic ends, Aristotle believed, "there is not the same kind of correctness in poetry as in politics" (2337). One could sacrifice technical correctness if the design of the poem required it in order to succeed at representing one of these three aspects. Wheatley realized before Kant that the power of the imagination allows the poet not only to recognize other realms of knowledge but to represent those realms in his or her own work.

Jennifer Billingsley

The previous works of wonder considered above demonstrate an object-oriented wonder. Both classical and Judeo-Christian traditions defined different objects as wonderful. Hobbes determined that " . . . ignorant and superstitious men make great wonders of those works which, knowing to proceed from nature (which is not the immediate, but the ordinary work of God, other men admire not at all . . ." (294). According to Hobbes, objects that could be understood by reason could not be considered as wonderful because the source of wonder was God, and if the Deity could not be understood, neither could his work. Therefore, such wonders only required a faith in God. However, like the Romantics after her, Wheatley did not confine her sense of wonder to the unexplainable and miraculous; ordinary events and objects also invoked wonder for the artist. Accordingly, in "To S.M. a Young African Painter," she directs the artist to "Conduct thy footsteps to immortal fame! / High to the blissful wonders of the skies / Elate thy soul, and raise thy wishful eyes" (114). Here it is the responsibility of the artist to negotiate a sphere of wonders in addition to the works of wonder (miracles) of the Deity. By developing a category of natural wonders, the artist can develop her or his own unique aesthetic.

In the most recent addition to Wheatley's extant works, a poem called "Ocean," Wheatley notes, "let us view the wonders of the main" and then "Again with recent wonder I survey / The finny sov'reign bask in hideous play" as she peered out over the Atlantic Ocean upon her return from England (Mason 79). The poetic use of wonder might be considered a risky tactic for a serious poet because of its short shelf life and the potential for an audience to consider such a use "vulgar." The reader can only briefly wonder at novelty. For this reason, ordinary and familiar objects for Hobbes were not considered wonders; such objects could not create nor sustain an emotive affect of awe or terror. In regard to this quality of wonder, Lord Kames in *Elements of Criticism* (1763) noted the instantaneous nature of wonder and its equally sudden decay (48). It would be a remarkable and rare feat for a poet to capture the true sense of wonder in a poem and then to hold onto it. As Lord Kames noted, because wonder inspires by the novelty of strange objects, such novelty wears off, and, stranger and stranger objects, and, stronger and stronger evidence is required to induce further wonder (68). Therefore, only among the uneducated or lower class is wonder easily exploited, because it requires merely the slightest evidence to produce the greatest belief, in contrast to the doubt such tactics inspire in the cultural elite. The use of wonder is suspect in serious poetry for these reasons. However, what is not apparent in this aesthetic judgment is how fundamental wonder is to inducing thought itself. As a source of philosophy it should not be cast aside so quickly. It is perhaps this very feature of classical wonder that enables a poet like Wheatley to sustain a sense of wonder through the activity of thought.

Hobbes provides a good example of the subordination of the subjective faculties like imagination to sensory perception. Imagination for him is a *"decaying sense"*; "the imagination of the past is obscured and made weak, as the voice of a man is in the noise of a day" (8). For Hobbes, imagination and memory are the same thing. Imagination which may normally be considered an agent in thought is simply a subordinate to experience (8–9).[7] The following examples hint at Wheatley's compelling interest in the classical tradition. In her last extant poem, "An Elegy on Leaving," she described a vivid picture of a rural landscape, perhaps her native Africa, where she "pass'd in grateful solitude the day" that was broken briefly when "wrapt in thought I pensively have stray'd / For crowds and noise, reluctant, I forsake" (156). The grateful solitude again must be broken as she writes,

> But, ah! those pleasing hours are ever flown;
> Ye scenes of transport from my thoughts retire;
> Those rural joys no more the day shall crown,
> No more my hand shall wake the warbling lyre.
> (156)

In this poem, there is no weak, decaying sense of memory. The strength of her memory as well as her imagination has provided agency and respite, as in "On Recollection," when she called upon Mneme to assist her strains and concluded "Of *Recollection* such the pow'r enthron'd / In ev'ry breast, and thus her pow'r is own'd" (64). Whereas Hobbes subordinates subjective faculties to experience, the classical tradition subordinates experience to thinking just as Wheatley describes in these examples. It demonstrates Wheatley's next step in her poetic process. She moves beyond the sensory experience of objects of wonder and explores a subjective faculty of wonder within her poetry.

Wonder, like the sublime for Kant, confronts the epistemological problem of the marvelous at its core. Kant determined that contemplation (thinking) consisted of more than practical reason, which is based on experience. Contemplation of beauty required a separate faculty as well as contemplation of the sublime. In its simplest form, reason concludes that only sensory data (the purely objective) reveals the truth, but the sublime induces a supersensory experience that does not fit any definite idea and yet remains a meaningful

Jennifer Billingsley

experience. Such experiences for Immanuel Kant are too great for our faculty of comprehension:

> For when apprehension has gone so far that the partial represen-
> tations of sensuous intuition at first apprehended begin to vanish
> in the Imagination whilst this ever proceeds to the apprehension
> of others, then it loses as much on the one side as it gains on the
> other; and in comprehension there is a maximum beyond which
> it cannot go. (112)

The faculty of reason cannot appropriate the sublime without defining what is indefinite. Wonder, like Kant's analysis of the sublime, allows an observer to recognize an object outside the context of our reason. For Kant, the imagination allows an observer to be "moved" (120), to become conscious of a faculty of judging superior to nature. Wheatley's use of wonder also evokes a faculty superior to the natural order of things. What reason prohibits, imagination and wonder provide.

As impossible as it might seem to sustain wonder as Hobbes recognized, it is also seemingly impossible for any poet to "move" someone's mind, to use Kant's term from *The Critique of Judgment* (120), and to force a reader to reconsider her or his preconceived notions of death and nature. Only a serious poet would take on such a task. Like Wheatley, Kant felt the representation of the ocean inspired such a movement; however, Kant, like Lord Kames, felt the ocean must be viewed by a poet "merely by what strikes the eye" and nothing more (138). Only a true representation of the ocean or other scenes of nature could inspire the sublime and inspire a parallel of this movement within the observer. The ocean, however, was not necessarily a representation merely of the sublime for Wheatley; it conveyed personal wonder. Whereas Kant believed such objects contained aspects of the infinite that required a super-sensibility in the observer, an ultimate sense surpassing all other senses, Wheatley determined that only the faculty of wonder was required.

The ocean and other works of wonder did not represent the unattainable. This distinction shows that Wheatley understood and utilized the sublime in her poetry as both Phillip Richards and John Shields have argued successfully that she did. On the contrary, it means Wheatley's poetics were more complex and varied than previously accepted. Like Kant, she attempted to combine the seemingly contradictory notions of a work of God and the capacity of man to know and represent such a work. Wonder, like the sublime for Kant, confronts the epistemological problem of that ever-evolving boundary between mind and matter. In its simplest form, reason concludes that only sensory data (the purely objective) reveals the truth, but the sublime induces a supersensory experience that does not fit into any definite, preconceived idea. The faculty of reason, therefore, cannot appropriate the sublime without defining what is indefinite: "the Imagination reaches its maximum, and, in striving to surpass, sinks back into itself" (Kant 112). The faculty of wonder, however, allows an observer to recognize an object outside the context of reason, and an active sense of wonder allows that observer to bring such objects into the orbit of reason or even adjust reason to the orbit of the object. In Wheatley's words, wonders allow the mind to "unfold," not necessarily to collapse in on itself.

In the end, Kant concluded that sublimity "does not reside in anything of nature, but only in our mind, in so far as we can become conscious that we are superior to nature within, and therefore also to nature without us" (129). The evolving sense of wonder in Wheatley's works moves in the same direction away from an objectified wonder to a subjective wonder. This movement away from the objectification of wonder allowed her to sustain a sense of wonder in her poetics. In "To the Honourable T.H. Esq; on the Death of His Daughter," Wheatley notes, "She leaves her earthly mansion for the skies, / Where new creations feast her wond'ring eyes" (99). Here wonder is no longer outside the subject, but a part of her faculties. In another funeral poem on the death of an infant, she wrote,

> Planets on planets run their destin'd round,
> And circling wonders fill the vast profound
> Th' ethereal now, and now th' empyreal skies
> With growing splendors strike his wond'ring eyes[.] (69)

The notion of an object of wonder remains, but Wheatley introduces the idea of a subjective wonder in this poem. As lines from these two elegies attest, the power of wonder no longer resides in the object but in the subject's capacity to call upon it. As a result, it is in the power of the subject to sustain wonder because objects are no longer required.

It is curious to note here that Wheatley was not the first poet to use "wond'ring eyes." In book 8 of *Paradise Lost*, Milton observes,

> Straight toward heav'n my wond'ring eyes I turned,
> And gazed awhile the ample sky till raised

Jennifer Billingsley

> By quick instinctive motion up I sprung,
> As thitherward endeavoring and upright
> Stood on my feet. About me round I saw
> Hill, dale, and shady woods, and sunny plains. (184)[8]

Milton's use of wonder is significant because he utilized the same forms of the word and the idea as Wheatley would later do. Like Milton, Wheatley, who owned a copy of *Paradise Lost,* uses an active wonder, a wonder that resides in the observer and not simply in the works of God where philosophers like Hobbes were inclined to locate it.[9] Both Milton and Wheatley subscribe to a classical interest in wonder. In *Rhetoric,* Aristotle observes that "Learning things and wondering at things are also pleasant for the most part; wondering implies the desire of learning, so that the object of wonder is the object of desire; while in learning one is brought into one's natural condition" (2183). This desire for learning in order to be brought into one's natural condition is at the heart of Wheatley's strategy, and the above examples of wonder show this artist not only demonstrating the capacity to wonder, but finding her subjects becoming "wondrous" as a result.

Another example of an active, subject-oriented form of wonder appears in "An Hymn to Humanity," wherein she wrote, "The bosoms of the great and good / With wonder and delight he view'd" (95). Here Wheatley demonstrated the desire to learn. She continued to explore this desire in "To His Honour the Lieutenant-Governor, on the Death of His Lady," when she described Elisha as "Wond'ring he gaz'd at the refulgent car" (116). Then, in the earlier poem, "America," she wrote,

> E'r yet Brittania [*sic*] had her work begun
> Thy Power, O Liberty, makes strong the weak
> And (wond'rous instinct) Ethiopians speak
> Sometimes by Simile, a victory's won. . . . (134)

In this excerpt, Wheatley consciously recognized this aspect of wonder in her own race, not as a fault; but by pairing it with learning, she reforms the idea of wonder and her race. Whereas Hobbes defied the ability of men to realize the meaning of a work of wonder, Wheatley recognizes this very power in Ethiopians.

These examples reveal how the source of wonder moved from the object to the observer. There are even times when she stops wondering, as in "On

Virtue": "I cease to wonder, and no more attempt / Thine height t' explore, or fathom thy profound" (113). These examples demonstrate that wonder has become an integral part of her poetics. A final example of this active sense of wonder may be seen in her letters to the Reverend Samuel Hopkins on her sympathy concerning Philip Quaque's lack of success as a missionary. She wrote, " . . . Philip may not be the instrument in the Divine Hand, to perform this work of wonder, turning the African 'from darkness to light'" (182). Here Wheatley transferred the very works of wonder from the hand of the Deity to the hands of man. This sense of wonder runs contrary to the passive wonder described by Hobbes. By establishing the subjective faculty of wonder, Wheatley was close to taking her final step in using wonder to develop her complex poetics.

Thinkers like Lord Kames attempted to delineate a system of aesthetics that incorporated the ideas of the Age of Reason. As a result, contrary to Plato and Aristotle, Lord Kames dismissed supernatural wonder as simply a means of imposing vulgar convictions on weak minds, a rhetorical maneuver that contravened the use of reason. Thus, he dismissed the use of classical allusions. Natural wonders were suspect as well, because "to prefer any thing merely because it is new, shows a mean taste of which one ought to be ashamed: vanity is commonly at the bottom, which leads those who are deficient in taste to prefer things odd, rare, or singular, in order to distinguish themselves from others" (Kames 136).

What is interesting is the fact that Lord Kames shared the seventeenth- and eighteenth-century critic's anxiety concerning neoclassical forms. He argued, "fictions that transgress the bounds of nature seldom have good effect; they may inflame the imagination for a moment, but will not be relished by any person of correct taste" (403). He considered the introduction of classical figures in epics as such a transgression, because "The Marvellous is indeed so much promoted by machinery, that, it is not wonderful to find it embraced by the plurality of writers, and, perhaps, of readers" (405). For Lord Kames, the allegorical figures, like Phoebus (as a machine, e.g.), in ancient classical literature obscure the very notion of truth and morality. Despite these concerns, in "Ocean," Wheatley began to wonder at the view before her, describing the body of water in classical terms, and calling upon Neptune: "Yet when the mighty Sire of Ocean frownd / 'His awful trident shook the solid Ground'" (Mason 79). She did so despite Lord Kames's assertion not to. However, for Wheatley these allusions aided her tactic of inspiring wonder by returning her reader to that historical moment before objects of wonder were rational-

Jennifer Billingsley

ized. She was not writing to preserve correct taste. She intended to "inflame" the imagination and inspire thought. In doing so, Wheatley contradicted the prevailing aesthetic and should thereby not be considered derivative.

Lord Kames promoted an aestheticism for the free, disengaging English aesthetics from classicism. In contrast, Wheatley created a poetics of wonder that contradicted Kames's aesthetic and the aesthetics of race applied to her person. She exposed the commonplace experiences of her readers to a Socratic dialogue in hope of inciting new ideas. Despite her awareness of various senses of wonder, she did not try to obtain advantage or position by utilizing the classical tradition as a type of cultural currency. She was not trying to endear herself entirely to the poetic standards that came before her, nor to the standards that would follow; rather, she was trying to reproduce the subjective experience of nature as will the Romantics after her. She wanted to introduce her reader to a powerful vision that inspired a sense of wonder that would require them to think and perhaps begin to see alternative tautologies.

A poet does not have to refute a tradition in order to attain a novel approach. Lord Kames, however, expected the poet "in the first place, to make his own poem, without depending upon Phoebus for any part of it, or calling out for aid upon any of the muses by name" (423). He attempted to use ridicule, like Joseph Addison, to make his point understood, but expected that some of the female poets would not listen even then to his design "to condemn every poem to the flame in which Jupiter thunders, or exercises any other act of authority which does not belong to him." Furthermore, he argued, "The marvellous is indeed so much promoted by machinery, that is not wonderful to find it embraced by the plurality of writers, and perhaps of readers. If indulged at all, it is generally indulged in excess" (Kames 423). Wheatley does not cast off this tradition so slightly. Lord Kames condemned classicism to the fate of the marvelous, but his condemnation was wrong on both accounts as Wheatley demonstrates.

Despite Lord Kames's condemnation of classical references, Wheatley joined the ranks of those women who ignored his criticism and continued to call upon Phoebus and the Muses. Indeed, Wheatley incorporates Phoebus and the Muses in "To Maecenas," and in other poems she calls specifically upon Phoebus or the Muses: "The muses promise to assist my pen" ("To the University of Cambridge in New England" 15); "Celestial muse, my arduous flight sustain" ("Thoughts on the Works of Providence" 43); and "'Tis his to call the planets from on high, / To blacken *Phoebus,* and dissolve the sky" ("To a Lady on the Death of Three Relations" 51). Overall, Lucy Hayden has identified classical allusions in twenty-six of the thirty-nine poems published in *Poems on Various Subjects, Religious and Moral.* Hayden speculates that these classical allusions were subliminally a result of "residual knowledge of tribal gods that created in her an affinity for the Greek and Roman Pantheon" (435). In an article "Phillis Wheatley's Subversion of Classical Stylistics," Shields has taken this analysis a step further to suggest that Wheatley was consciously using such classical allusions taken from white culture to criticize subversively the white establishment.

The intellect that Shields recognizes in Wheatley is important to note. Too often, Wheatley is recognized as a genius while her work is maligned as derivative. If she were a genius, as testimony certainly attests, she was capable of more than simply responding emotionally to her servitude with bitterness and disdain. She was capable of responding intellectually to it and to the culture that justified it. This intellectual capacity should never be overlooked while reading Wheatley's poetry. Therefore, whether or not Wheatley read the condemnation of Lord Kames, the fact that she persisted in her use of classical references, despite having experienced the condemnation of her poetry as derivative, suggests a conscious, intelligent decision on her part to continue to appropriate classical references for her cause.

Lord Kames's condemnation of these classical references should be considered derivative in its own right. As Benjamin Kurtz asserts in his studies on the marvelous, the dispute over the marvelous was originally a dispute between Plato and Aristotle. Plato joined his own contemporaries in their criticism of Homer's impious account of the Greek gods (Kurtz 15). Homer presented an aesthetic and historical problem with his impossible and therefore fictitious account of the behavior of Greek gods, which created an impasse between philosophers and poets. In the *Republic,* the quarrel between philosophy and poetry came to a head, and Plato decided, "For if you grant admission to the honeyed Muse in lyric or epic, pleasure and pain will be lords of your city instead of law and that which shall from time to time have approved itself to the general reason as the best" (832). Plato felt poetry fostered emotions that made people worse rather than better; therefore, poets should not be admitted into the republic until they themselves could convince the republic otherwise. Although Lord Kames might agree with Plato for the most part, Wheatley is convinced that both poets and the account of classical gods were inherent to her cause.

Some additional examples from Wheatley's poetry reveal her final strategy. She begins by recounting God's works of wonder, the artist's works of wonder,

Jennifer Billingsley

and the development of a "wondering eye." She ends by becoming "wondrous" herself. In "Goliath of Gath," she describes David as the "wond'rous hero" after he demanded the people of Israel to battle Goliath and his armies (34). Like David, she calls the young African painter a "wond'rous youth" when she challenges him to pursue "each noble path" (114). The power of wonder has been transferred to the subject, and finally the subject itself becomes wondrous.

Not only have the works of an artist become wondrous, just as the African painter becomes "wond'rous"; at last the artist herself also becomes wondrous in the process. In "To a Gentleman of the Navy," Wheatley called her own poem "My wondrous theme" (140), to which the gentleman replied, "Her wondrous virtues I could ne'er express! / To paint her charms, would only make them less" (143). In "An Hymn to Humanity, To S.P.G. Esq," she even called herself the "Afric's muse" (97). Wheatley has become wondrous like Phoebus and David. She inserts herself into the pantheon of classical figures that Kames warned against, just as she snatched the laurel from the honored head of Maecenas. Not only does her work inspire wonder, her very person inspires wonder. Despite Jefferson's assertion, Wheatley exists as an anomaly as the first published slave poet—a classically educated slave who asserted herself in the public realm, even addressing George Washington. Wheatley as a wonderful figure implied to her readers that the reality of race still exceeded explanation. Her poetry and person then and now indicate a broader meaning of race not yet understood. Her poetics is one in search of agency in a world that did not offer any to those of Wheatley's caste, but through the faculty of "wonder" she found the means at least to try to transform her world.

The only critic to recognize a period of wonder in American literature is Tony Tanner, but he failed altogether to note Wheatley. Indeed, he failed to note the entire history of wonder in Early America. Tanner begins his study with the transcendentalists. For Tanner, the foundation of this interest in wonder was explained by Rousseau's primitive innocence. To save men from the "excesses of reason," Rousseau believed that the individual needed to be educated in natural surroundings apart from the corrupting influences of civilization in order to preserve a childlike vision of the world. In such surroundings, the individual was able to maintain a sense of harmony with nature and the universe, and as a result, to gain a superior mode of cognition without the interference of reason. For Tanner, this superior mode of cognition meant that "Wonder is substituted for judgment. Man seeks to re-enjoy the sleep of reason . . ." (5). After severing the connection between wonder and reason, Tanner placed wonder alongside the naïve, concluding that writers like Emerson and Twain preferred wonder to analysis.

Tanner's argument is, however, flawed. Of course, American writers faced distinct problems and needs, primarily the need "to recognize and contain a new continent" (Tanner 10), yet solving this problem by introducing a new, naïve interest in wonder does not account for the long history of wonder prior to the transcendentalists. Wonder played a role in the travel literature discussed by Greenblatt, Wheatley's work, and even works such as Cotton Mather's *The Wonders of the Invisible World: Being an Account of the Trials of Several Witches Lately Executed in New England.* Tanner's failure to acknowledge the pre-Revolutionary history of wonder reveals an important fallacy at the center of his critique which affects the central tenet of pairing wonder with a naïve vision in American literature.

Certainly, the dilemma for early American writers was to establish a foundation for a national literature on the new continent, but this dilemma informed Cotton Mather and Phillis Wheatley, as well as the later transcendentalists. However, Tanner's belief that the naïve vision allowed writers to develop a new way of appropriating reality with "minimum reference to previous familiarity and interpretive knowledge" (11) is simplistic. By ignoring earlier American writers, Tanner ignored the interpretive knowledge of writers like Wheatley. Tanner concluded that wonder provided a strategy for achieving a naïve vision which in turn allowed authors like Emerson and Twain the opportunity to rediscover and rewrite the new world for themselves. It appears that nineteenth-century American writers knew their predecessors better than we have supposed. However, their very interest in wonder shows that writers like Emerson and Twain did not deny this interpretive knowledge, but used it as the foundation for a continuing effort to explore the new world.[10] The relationships between early American writers are far more complex than depicted by critics like Tanner, just as the history of wonder is far more complex than his text allows. For this reason, it is imperative to understand Wheatley's works in more depth in order to understand her descendants, like Emerson and Twain as well as Herman Melville and even Alejo Carpentier much later, who also make use of wonder.

In addition, for Tanner to assert that wonder is opposed to analysis is to dismiss this core value of wonder in the classical tradition—the very tradition that informed the education of early Americans. The emphasis on the faculty of wonder as a naïve strategy is entirely an arbitrary decision. Between classical

Jennifer Billingsley

wonder and naïve wonder, classical wonder is a more accurate source of wonder in American literature, especially in Wheatley's work. For Wheatley, the faculty of wonder destabilizes accepted tautologies by triggering ontological questions as well as epistemological ones, but it does not make these tautologies obsolete. It does not negate analysis. Like Bynum's description of medieval wonder, the prevalence of "wonder" throughout Wheatley's poetry reveals an enthusiasm for the capacity of wonder to open up new thought-provoking realms, and the fact that "wonder" appears so often in her poetry and twice in her known prose attests the importance of wonder as part of her poetics. Although Wheatley's marvelous poetics has been largely ignored by critics, in time criticism may finally recognize her contribution to American literature and to the phenomenon of wonder in American letters.

As previously noted, classical artifacts and texts served as important precedent in the development of the marvelous aesthetics in the late Renaissance and baroque periods. Classical discourse also influenced the American Revolutionary moment as Carl Richards described, but as Shields has asserted, a "radical shift in discourse" followed that led to the diminution of classical works and languages as part of the American education system (*American Aeneas* 258). This shift may be viewed in part as a final attempt to disengage the culture from the influence of the marvelous aesthetics, and as an attempt to remove American culture from its seemingly "primitive" or "vulgar" state. It also explains Tanner's attempt to disengage American literature from pre-Revolutionary writers, as though American literature began with the transcendentalists. This preoccupation with finding the birth of American literature is another anxiety to shed. It is more important to recognize the relationships between authors and their literary ancestry than to disparage such ties by creating arbitrary boundaries.

In a time when wonder has lost its virtue, the use of wonder may seem inconsequential. Mary McCarthy once noted that hope suffered a similar fate. Today it floats around sentences without any real meaning. In fact, when someone says "hopefully," the word means the opposite, "the absence of hope" (87). So it is with wonder as well. While it would appear that wonder has now lost its rhetorical value, the poetics of Wheatley reveals a viable form of wonder from our past. Her poetry serves as reminder that words like "wonder" matter: that each word has a history and a reason for its place in speech. Perhaps if wonder were returned to its primary form, terror would not hold so rhetorical a sway over the public mind. Perhaps the public treasury is not entirely bankrupt with such figures as Wheatley safely secured within.

Wheatley was driven into the public life in hope of making her age worthy of the freedom they aspired to by not denying slaves their own freedom. Although the Age of Reason would deny this revelation, she still attempted to educate men and preserve herself in the process by contradicting the very claims of what men can and cannot know, and produce from this wonder the understanding to which her age so long aspired. Lessing observed,

> Education gives to Man nothing which he might not educe out
> of himself; it gives him that which he might educe out of himself,
> only quicker and more easily. In the same way too, Revelation
> gives nothing to the human species, which the human reason left
> to itself might not attain; only it has given, and still gives to it, the
> most important of these things earlier. (195)

At last Wheatley still draws our attention for what she can reveal about the wonderful and the marvelous.

NOTES

1. Arendt possessed such courage as well. As a German Jew, she was forced to flee Nazi Germany after being detained for publishing an article on anti-Semitic language. She was astounded at the ease with which German intellectuals went along with Nazi dogma. Rather than focusing on the many who did not stand against such sweeping ideology, however, she spent her life trying to understand the individuals who sacrificed truth for power.

2. Carl Richard provides an important account of the founding fathers' vast knowledge of ancient texts and their subsequent use of such texts in the formation of a new government. With the recent movement to view the country as a Christian nation, this fact is often ignored, but it is doubtful that the founding fathers could have conceived the government in its present form without their classical background. The same depth of thought and understanding is also present in the authors of the period. They were not simply imitating neoclassical forms. Their preferences reveal a greater understanding at work. John Shields decries this simplification of history in *The American Aeneas*, arguing: "This myth of an allegedly universal, derivative literary culture has been largely responsible for the loss of a usable past within the history of Early American letters" (374).

Jennifer Billingsley

3. Bynum reminds her readers at this point in her text of our postmodern anxiety of knowing anything with certainty and that the particular is often considered a triviality. With this in mind, she calls upon students to be cautious and slow to appropriate texts and artifacts to a theory. It is better to concede that things are always a little beyond our theories and fears, because "Every view of things that is not wonderful is false" (75).

4. Three examples of classical texts that regained interest were Ovid's *Metamorphoses* and Aristotle's *Rhetoric* and *Poetics*. Ovid was obviously important to Wheatley's "Niobe in Distress." Aristotle's influence is less obvious, but will play a part in the developing philosophy and subsequent aesthetics (Kenseth 27).

5. For a discussion of how Hume's ideas of race and his identification of African Americans as "subhuman" and "incapable of reason" dismiss even the ability for literary achievement by the African American race, see Gates (23–27).

6. Cotton Mather and Robert Calef (*Wonders of the Invisible World*) debated witchcraft and the wonders that convinced the public of its presence in Puritan society. They debated whether wonders not created by God could actually exist and whether wonders could be explained rationally. To ignore these types of texts is to ignore another explanation for the appearance of wonder in post-Revolutionary America.

7. Hobbes wrote, "This *decaying sense,* when we would express the thing itself (I mean *fancy* itself), we call *imagination,* as I said before; but when we would express the *decay,* and signify that the sense is fading, old, and past, it is called *memory.* So that *imagination* and *memory* are but one thing, which for diverse considerations hath diverse names" (8–9).

8. It is important to note that the same forms of the word "wonder" are used by Milton and Wheatley, e.g., wonder, wondering, and wondrous. One exception, however, is wonderful. Milton used this variation of wonder in Book 3: "For wonderful indeed are all his works" (99).

9. Milton did, however, use wonder to describe the works of God as well. He wrote of the "Unspeakable desire to see and know. / All these His wondrous works (but chiefly Man, / His chief delight and favor, him for whom / All these His works so wondrous He ordained)" (*Paradise Lost,* Book 3, 662–65).

10. Founding a new tradition is often confused with beginning anew. Founding means creating order out of chaos, establishing standards, and

providing direction for the future. Virgil's account of the founding of Rome provides the best example. He utilized both Roman and Greek mythology to provide Rome with a foundational myth. On the other hand, the Adamic myth is not a foundational myth. It establishes something entirely new. It does not conceive of a common past. Indeed, it ignores the past altogether. This observation is made in Shields's *The American Aeneas*.

WORKS CITED

Arendt, Hannah. "The Crisis of Culture." *Between Past and Future.* New York: Penguin, 1968. 197–226.

———. *Men in Dark Times.* New York: Harcourt Brace & World, 1968.

Aristotle. *The Complete Works of Aristotle.* Ed. Jonathan Barnes. 2 vols. Princeton: Princeton UP, 1984.

Ashworth, William B., Jr. "Remarkable Humans and Singular Beasts." *The Age of the Marvelous.* Ed. Joy Kenseth Hanover: Hood Museum of Art and Dartmouth College, 1991. 113–44.

Bell, Archibald. " . . . one of the greatest instances of pure, unassisted Genius, that the world has ever produced." *Critical Essays on Phillis Wheatley.* Ed. William H. Robinson. Boston: G. K. Hall, 1982. 28–29.

Bush, Douglas. *Mythology and the Romantic Tradition in English Poetry.* New York: W. W. Norton, 1965.

Bynum, Caroline Walker. *Metamorphosis and Identity.* New York: Zone, 2001.

Calef, Robert. *The Wonders of the Invisible World.* Boston: T. Bedlington, 1828.

Collins, Terence. "Phillis Wheatley: The Dark Side of the Poetry." *Critical Essays on Phillis Wheatley.* Ed. William H. Robinson. Boston: G. K. Hall, 1982. 147–58.

Davis, Arthur P. "Personal Elements in the Poetry of Phillis Wheatley." *Phylon* 14.2 (1953): 191–98.

Gates, Henry Louis, Jr. *The Trials of Phillis Wheatley.* New York: Basic Civitas, 2003.

Graham, Shirley. *The Story of Phillis Wheatley.* New York: Julian Messner, 1949.

Greenblatt, Stephen. *Marvelous Possessions: The Wonder of the New World.* Chicago: U of Chicago P, 1991.

Hayden, Lucy K. "Classical Tidings from the Afric Muse: Phillis Wheatley's Use of Greek and Roman Mythology." *CLA Journal* 35 (1992): 432–37.

Hobbes, Thomas. *Leviathan.* Indianapolis: Hackett Publishing, 1994.

Hume, David. *An Enquiry Concerning Human Understanding.* Ed. Tom L. Beauchamp. Oxford: Clarendon, 2000.

———. *A Treatise of Human Nature: Being An Attempt to Introduce the Experimental Method of Reasoning into Moral Subjects.* Ed. L. A. Selby-Bigge. Oxford: Clarendon, 1964.

Jefferson, Thomas. *Notes on the State of Virginia.* Ed. William Peden. Chapel Hill: U of North Carolina P, 1955.

Kames, Henry Holm. *Elements of Criticism.* Honolulu: UP of the Pacific, 2002.

Kant, Immanuel. *The Critique of Judgment.* Trans. J. H. Bernard. Amherst: Prometheus Books, 2000.

Kenseth, Joy. "The Age of the Marvelous: An Introduction." *The Age of the Marvelous.* Hanover: Hood Museum of Art and Dartmouth College, 1991.

Kurtz, Benjamin P. *Studies in the Marvelous.* New York: Haskell House, 1972.

"L." "An accomplished mistress of her pen . . ." *Critical Essays on Phillis Wheatley.* Ed. William H. Robinson. Boston: G. K. Hall, 1982. 21–23.

Lessing, Gotthold Ephraim. "The Education of the Human Race." *Literary and Philosophical Essays.* Ed. Charles W. Eliot. New York: P. F. Collier and Son, 1910. 195–217.

Loggins, Vernon. " . . . one of the most interesting curiosities." 1931. *Critical Essays on Phillis Wheatley.* Ed. William H. Robinson. Boston: G. K. Hall, 1982. 88–92.

Mason, Julian. "'Ocean': A New Poem by Phillis Wheatley." *Early American Literature* 34 (1999): 78–83.

Mather, Cotton. *The Wonders of the Invisible World.* 1693. New York: Burt Franklin, 1866. Vol. 1 of *The Witchcraft Delusion in New England.* Ed. Samuel G. Drake. 3 vols. 1970.

Matson, R. Lynn. "Phillis Wheatley—Soul Sister?" *Critical Essays on Phillis Wheatley.* Ed. William H. Robinson. Boston: G. K. Hall, 1982. 113–22.

McCarthy, Mary. "Language and Politics." *Occasional Prose.* New York: Harcourt Brace Jovanovich, 1985. 83–100.

Milton, John. *Paradise Lost*. New York: W. W. Norton, 2005.

Parsons, Howard L. "A Philosophy of Wonder." *Philosophy and Phenomenological Research* 30.1 (1969): 84–101.

Plato. *Plato: Complete Works*. Ed. John M. Cooper. Indianapolis: Hackett Publishing, 1997.

Richard, Carl J. *The Founders and the Classics: Greece, Rome, and the American Enlightenment*. Cambridge: Harvard UP, 1994.

Richards, Phillip M. "Phillis Wheatley, Americanization, the Sublime, and the Romance of America." *Style* 27.2 (Summer 1992): 194–221.

Scruggs, Charles. "Phillis Wheatley and the Poetical Legacy of Eighteenth-Century England." *Studies in Eighteenth-Century Culture* 10 (1981): 279–95.

Shields, John. *The American Aeneas: Classical Origins of the American Self*. Knoxville: U of Tennessee P, 2001.

———. "Phillis Wheatley's Subversion of Classical Stylistics." *Style* 27.2 (Summer 1993): 252–72.

———. "Phillis Wheatley and the Sublime." *Critical Essays on Phillis Wheatley*. Ed. William H. Robinson. Boston: G. K. Hall, 1982. 189–205.

Snelling, William J. "A Review of Wheatley's *Poems on Various Subjects*." *Critical Essays on Phillis Wheatley*. Ed. William H. Robinson. Boston: G. K. Hall, 1982. 63–65.

Tanner, Tony. *The Reign of Wonder: Naivety and Reality in American Literature*. Cambridge: Cambridge UP, 1965.

Thatcher, Benjamin B. " . . . abundant proof of a degree of native genius . . ." *Critical Essays on Phillis Wheatley*. Ed. William H. Robinson. Boston: G. K. Hall, 1982. 69–74.

Wheatley, Phillis. *The Collected Works of Phillis Wheatley*. Ed. John Shields. New York: Oxford UP, 1988.

Queering Phillis Wheatley

Tom O. McCulley

I

I first became interested in attempting a queer discussion of Phillis Wheatley after reading her poem, "To S.M. a Young *African* Painter, on Seeing His Works." John Shields notes that "[b]oth Mason . . . and Robinson . . . identify 'S.M.' as Scipio Moorhead, black slave of the Reverend John Moorhead. Robinson also suggests that the black painter may have executed the engraving of Wheatley's portrait for the 1773 *Poems* frontispiece" (*Collected Works* 295). Having become acquainted with Wheatley's subversive use of the poetic conventions of her time, I found that a close reading of "S.M." revealed it to be a "queer" text. This African American "slave girl," who by all intents and purposes should not even have had a *voice,* writes about an African American slave man who should also not have had a *voice.* Using a subversive style that at once co-opted the language of her oppressors, Wheatley raised African American artists' voices above the work of the white folk who owned them and onto a revolutionary plane.

I return to "S.M." later, but suffice it to say that Wheatley's concluding lines (27–34) in "S.M." demonstrate a keen awareness that she will only be able to give *voice* to her inherent "otherness" outside of the normative expectations of her reading public.[1] Wheatley writes, "There [the 'realms above' which stand both for 'heaven' and 'freedom'] shall thy tongue in heav'nly murmurs flow, / And there my muse with heav'nly transport glow: / No more to tell of *Damon's* tender sighs, / Or rising *Aurora's* eyes, / For nobler themes demand a nobler strain, / And purer language on th' ethereal plain" (115). In other words, once Wheatley and "S.M." have achieved freedom, either through death or decree, they will be free of the need to couch their separate artistic languages (words for her, painting for him) in discussions of the idealized rustic character (Damon) that their masters would make of them, or in imagistic references to Africa ("Aurora's eyes")[2] Until then, as Wheatley notes, she must shut her muse down since "the solemn gloom of night / Now seals the fair creation from my sight" (115).

II

On one level, it is Wheatley's keen awareness of herself as a body outside of the normative expectations of her society—an awareness clearly visible in "S.M." and other poems—that opens the doorway for an attempt to read her works in the light of Queer Theory. First, however, it is necessary to establish an idea of Queer Theory that moves beyond the restrictions placed on that term by an interpretation that would limit Queer Theory to lesbian and gay studies, or to the idea of sexuality itself.

Eve Kosofsky Sedgwick's *Epistemology of the Closet* and *Tendencies* and Judith Butler's *Gender Trouble: Feminism and the Subversion of Identity* and *Bodies That Matter: On the Discursive Limits of "Sex"* are widely credited with bringing the ideas behind Queer Theory to the forefront.[3] For the purposes of brevity I do not gloss these four works here except to state that their primary scholarly objectives are to move away from the restrictive idea that "queer" can only be situated within the limitations of the lesbian, gay, bisexual, or transgendered body. As Sedgwick writes, " . . . a lot of the most exciting recent work around 'queer' spins the term outward along dimensions that can't be subsumed under gender and sexuality at all: the ways that race, ethnicity, postcolonial nationality criss-cross with these and other identity-constituting, identity-fracturing discourses . . ." (*Tendencies* 9). The important idea in Sedgwick's writing is that Queer Theory, like other acts of performative language, has the ability both to create and destroy its very call to identity. It would appear to be necessary, then, for Queer Theory to be in a state of constant creation/destruction in order for it to achieve meaning outside of the normative expectations placed upon any "theory" within the linguistic confines of literary study.

In relation to a queer reading of Phillis Wheatley, Sedgwick's idea of performativity is especially important. As she states,

Tom O. McCulley

> I want to go further with an argument implicit in *Epistemology*
> *of the Closet:* that both the act of coming out, and closetedness
> itself, can be taken as dramatizing certain features of linguistic
> performativity in ways that have broadly applicable implications.
> Among the striking aspects of considering closetedness in this
> framework, for instance, is that the speech act in question is a
> series of silences! (*Epistemology* 11)

Phillis Wheatley was a "slave girl" who was made, on some occasions, to perform her speech acts for an audience almost always made up of "others" including white men and women slaveowners, or, in some cases, other African Americans who had not been given her access to *voice* and who could not, therefore, be anything other than an "other" to her more eloquent ways. Phillis Wheatley enacted "performances" that were performative acts of linguistic self-identity re-created with subtlety from the very language of her oppressors. Phillis Wheatley used silences and the act of silencing her own "muse" (remember the end of "S.M.") to draw attention to the fact that her particular *voice* was not allowed to be heard in all its glory, a glory on par with or even more sophisticated than her white "masters." Phillis Wheatley was, I would argue, "in the closet" in ways that can and should echo profoundly within the corridors of Queer Theory. That Wheatley used her "closet" as a form of protection, and that she used the defining language of the closet forced upon her by the normative expectations of identity-destroying words like "black," "slave," and "female" to redefine herself outside of that closet was, as June Jordan so aptly puts it, the beginning of "The Difficult Miracle of Black Poetry in America."

Donald Hall provides another way of looking at Queer Theory. In his article "Introduction: Queer Works," Hall posits that the term "Queer" works to "stimulate public discussion among individuals who otherwise might never have confronted issues surrounding sexual and social non-conformity or acknowledged the many forces opposing individualistic expressions" (3). Hall proposes that the etymology of "queer" comes from roots that mean "across, traverse, to twist, and athwart," and that the term "Queer Theory" has acted as a catalyst for moving beyond gender/sexual specifics in relationship to a "Queer approach" to literary and cultural studies. Hall argues that Queer Theorists have adapted a strategy of confrontation that moves across the very rules and regulations used by a heterosexist society to confine and limit Queer Theory's possibilities. Citing the TV show *The Simpsons* as an example of how this strategy works, Hall writes, "In slippery and often sophisticated ways, *The Simpsons* implies that one of the best tactics available for society's iconoclastic and disgruntled is simply to turn society's own rules and expressions against it, to call its bluff, to 'queer' it brashly" (4). Hall goes on to locate specific instances where the creators of *The Simpsons* use the expectations of "foundational and fixed" identity categories to "open up ideas of agency" by playing against the normative expectations of those categories (7). For example, in one episode, "Blue Collar," Homer suddenly burst into a song about loving another man.

Unlike Sedgwick's performative acts of speech, then, Hall's approach points more toward a definition of Queer Theory that is as elusive as it is fixed. As Hall points out, one of the challenges facing Queer Theory is that society's expectations for the word "queer" are constantly altering in relation to its awareness of what this new theory means and how it can effect change in perceptions about identity and politics. Hall, drawing on Elspeth Probyn's comment that the boundaries of Queer Theory are "eminently porous," insists that such a lack of precise definitions might work toward the good: "[P]recision has always been an elusive goal . . . one often engendering hypocrisy and encouraging rigid exclusions; textual studies have always been political, but often only surreptitiously and dishonestly so; and identity, my friends, is (substantially, at least) a set of fictions that we tell ourselves or have been told is 'natural'" (9).

When a rigid definition of a term like "black slave girl" is applied to Phillis Wheatley, it is easy to see how Hall's concerns about "identity" are justified. Some who have studied Wheatley have produced accusations that Phillis was everything from a purely imitative poet to an unrepentant "Uncle Tom." The fact that scholars such as Henry Louis Gates Jr., James A. Levernier, and John C. Shields have spent their careers disproving such accusations speaks directly to Hall's point about the political nature of literary studies. Only after the waters surrounding Wheatley became muddied by scholars who no longer accept the normative prescriptions of the terms "black," "slave," and "girl" did her true stature as an "African" "American" "female" "poet" begin to emerge. In other words, to use Hall's terminology, it was only after scholars "queered" Wheatley by admitting to the "eminently porous" nature of the terms used to define her that her power as an "other" voice in the normative expectations established by her use of the poetic modes of her day began to be celebrated for the "miracle" they constituted.

Garry Leonard, in his introduction to the "Praxis" section of the special 1997 issue of *College Literature* devoted to Queer Theory and Lesbian and Gay

Tom O. McCulley

Studies, ties Queer Theory to desire. He holds that Lesbian and Gay Studies express desire as experiential while Queer Theory explores desire in the abstract sense of a need to examine the "other" that all humans hold. In both cases, desire is expressed against the binary of "normal" versus "perverse" or "legitimate" versus "ob-scene" (196). Leonard then states that society's presumptions of "normalcy" must, by their very being, depend on what is "abnormal" to give shape to the unexamined empiricism that passes as "truth" for many people.

It is not difficult here to relate Leonard's identity category and desire to one of Wheatley's most famous poems, "On Being Brought from Africa to America." A more detailed examination of this poem follows shortly; I mention it here simply to point out that Wheatley's use of identity categories and desire parallels Leonard's discussion of Queer Theory. In "On Being Brought," Wheatley capitalizes on the identity category of "black": "Some view our sable race with scornful eye, / 'Their colour is a diabolic die'" (18). Her intent is to reveal the absolute "whiteness" or empirical assumptions behind the Colonial belief that slaves were brought to America for their own good since it exposed them to the possibility of salvation through Christianity. Wheatley addresses the issue of seeking Christian Salvation in her own words when she states, "I redemption neither sought nor knew." To the benighted reader of Wheatley's poem it might seem that a desire for salvation has produced a categorically "white" slave who has been saved from an inherent "blackness" of both skin and soul. However, keeping in mind the subversive uses of language that Wheatley so skillfully employs, it eventually becomes clear that her "desire" in this poem is to return to a place where "Christian Salvation" was not necessary and where she could define her spiritual journey for herself. In fact, this poem is one of Wheatley's clearest protestations against the wholly unequal treatment given to black slaves at the hands of those who would claim to be "enlightened" through Christian love—a treatment that included an assumption (carried out to some extent by contemporary evangelical missionaries) that a black slave could not have a desire for a spirituality of her or his own.

In contemporary society, the symbiosis between Queer Studies and the unequal treatment of lesbians and gays within the academic structure that views "Queer Theory" as a hot commodity is evident in a number of ways. As Helene Meyers points out in her essay, "To Queer or Not to Queer: That's Not the Question," at the same time that Queer Theory came out on campuses, few of the institutions that were promoting its development had clearly stated antidiscrimination policies that specifically protected lesbian and gay students and even fewer extended health care and other spousal benefits to domestic partners of faculty and staff (Meyers 171–73). While much has changed since 1997, the fact remains that full antidiscrimination protection for lesbians, gays, and transgendered persons remains an ongoing struggle. Meyers uses Urvashi Vaid's idea of "virtual equality" as "a state of conditional equality based more on the appearance of acceptance by straight America than on genuine civic parity" (Vaid xvi) to point out that the commodification of Queer Theory without an accompanying change in the actual status of gay and lesbian academics has led to a situation whereby Queer Theory is, in fact, shoring up heterosexual "superiority" (Meyers 176–77). In other words, what is passing, under the guise of Queer Theory as equal freedom of expression and protection for lesbian and gay academics is, in fact, not reality as it is being played out on college campuses. Leonard, using Foucault's ideas about desire, knowledge, and power, states, "there is no ideal sexuality distorted by the necessary but regrettable imposition of repression; instead, the construction of 'sexuality' into gender, and the constitution of 'knowledge' as 'truth,' both occur in order that 'reality' might be seen as independent of the exercise of power, when, in fact, any given 'reality' reflects and reifies the very apparatus of power that configures and maintains its own culturally intelligible status as 'real'" (197).

Given that her owners purchased Phillis at the age of seven or eight, it is clear that the Wheatleys would not have imbued their "black slave girl" with any kind of sexuality at all. As Phillis grew into young womanhood, it is apparent, as evidenced by her poetic output, that her linguistic prowess also grew. It is not so hard to imagine, then, that Susannah Wheatley, Phillis's "everyday" contact with her owners was able to create a "reality" in which Phillis's sexual awakening was subsumed, perhaps in Susannah's mind, by Wheatley's keen interest in language and writing. In other words, in her owners' minds, Phillis Wheatley was probably being given the status of a gifted daughter even though she was, in fact, a piece of purchased property.

Phillis's poems point out again and again that she was keenly aware of the "virtual equality" of her own existence. What is not clear, however, is whether the Wheatleys ever moved beyond the constructed reality of their "talented daughter" and accepted as fact the power structure they wielded over Phillis. In fact, Phillis's letters point out that Mr. Wheatley only granted Phillis her manumission after fierce prompting from Phillis's social and literary connections in England. In fact, once a fully sexualized Phillis Wheatley emerged from the "talented daughter reality" created by her owners, she became little more than a servant—a piece of property that was disposed of, albeit reluctantly, upon the death of Mr. Wheatley's wife, Susannah.

Finally,[4] Fadi Abou-Rihan writes about an "other" identity as being equated with the term "world traveler" in "Queer Marks/Nomadic Difference: Sexuality and the Politics of Race and Ethnicity." Abou-Rihan uses a definition from Maria Lugones to explain that travelers are always both an "other" and "themselves" when they encounter "new worlds." In this sense, travelers physically "travel" in strange lands and also "travel" metaphysically in that they are aware of their internal "difference" as that difference is played out on the unfamiliar stage of "an other place" (255). A Queer Theorist, like a "black slave girl," is a traveler in the strange world of heterosexist terminologies wherein she/he is marked by multiple identities—lesbian or gay, male or female, black or white—all leading to an overall identification with the "other" as the "self."

In other words, Queer Theory is situated in a space that instantly "others" an already "othered" identity, an identity defined by the normative expectations placed on the "traveling" Queer Theorist by the cultures of lesbian and gay activists and the diverse cultures of academia. In such an environment, the "othered other"[5] faces a daunting task when it comes to constructing a self that is outside of the normative expectations placed on it not only by the dominant white male culture, but also by the "other" cultures that strive to define the "othered other" in their own terms. Abou-Rihan has it, " . . . for any individual with multiple marked identities, the political project of dismantling barriers of racism and ethnocentrism begins with the very problematic construction of identity and its relation to differing, and often discordant, communities and political projects" (256). Abou-Rihan, drawing on the work of Audre Lourde, goes on to posit that the only way the "othered other" can survive is to "dwell in the house of difference" (257). This dwelling, by its very nature, is a nomadic one, consciously inhabited by an ever-shifting array of identities whose only commonality is a resistance to the normative processes being applied from the outside. In Lourde's mind, such a space becomes an invitation to "play" in the stream of "trying to become" instead of remaining static in the normative fixed position of "being." Such positioning makes the nomadic dweller of such a space, then, a world traveler, one who inhabits different "worlds" while all the while maintaining a keen awareness of the "othered" self within those worlds.

How better to describe the articulate–female–slave–poet–cultural critic–black–African–Christian–classical scholar–servant–provocateur that was Phillis Wheatley? Like the "traveling" Queer Theorist, Wheatley had to lead a nomadic life in order to inhabit the multiple possibilities that her unique position offered. That critics for years overlooked Wheatley's ability to occupy multiple spaces at once is a testament to her ability to do just that. If Wheatley only inhabited one of her identity choices, such habitation would surely have led to physical, intellectual, and/or spiritual death. Like the "traveling" Queer Theorist, Wheatley's only option, if she was to be given a voice at all, was to move beyond the fixed state of normative presumptions imposed by colonial expectations and to create a nomadic identity. As Abou-Rihan explains the term "nomadic identity," "By this I mean an identity which not only goes beyond the refusal to raise the flag of this or that social marker or political standard, but also, and at least partially, as one which actively betrays the institutions, regulations, and codes typical of one-dimensional identity politics" (259).

If nothing else, the above discussion reveals that arriving at a comprehensive contained definition of Queer Theory is difficult, if not impossible. In 1995, *PMLA* pointed out that Queer Theory was so new that most of its practitioners were graduate students. Never the radical creator of new literary trends, *PMLA* went on, in an article authored by Lauren Berlant and Michael Warner, to articulate a decidedly conservative view that the whole idea of "Queer Theory" was premature and that something like "Queer commentary" was probably more appropriate (343). In 2001, when this essay was first written, not much had changed. In 2007, as this essay is being edited, the movement to include Queer Theory into discourses concerning literature and culture on campuses across the nation is present, especially in a number of "Introduction to Theory" books, but I would argue that it is not flourishing.

I do not believe the answer to Queer Theory's ultimate place in academic and cultural discourses has been fully written—yet. Such placement is not the focus of this paper. What is important today, to borrow the title from the May 1995 article from Berlant and Warner, "What Does Queer Theory Teach Us about *X*?" is the ongoing exploration about identity/identities that Queer Theory demands. Queer Theory, today more than ever, offers a gateway into exposing the ways that normative institutions still uphold the power of the straight white male majority both within and outside of academia. Queer Theory remains a fresh tool for exploring how language holds the power to perform acts of naming outside of normative institutions. Queer Theory provides the groundwork for understanding that one of the best ways to exact change is to turn linguistic utterances inside out in order to reveal their strengths and weaknesses to those who most believe in their viability.

Tom O. McCulley

Given my obvious casting about for some loose definition of Queer Theory, perhaps it seems odd to state that I think it is an excellent tool with which to explore the unique position held by a "black slave girl" named Phillis Wheatley who stood "queer" and alone (*"and she was the first one,"* June Jordan keeps telling us, over and over again) at the birth of a new nation. In fact, I believe Queer Theory provides the perfect expression for how Phillis mirrored that nation's expressed desire for freedom for all its people back onto itself in ways that directly speak to the attempts by lesbians and gay men to do the same today.

III

A Queer reading of all of Wheatley's texts would encompass a book-length project and would, for a better feel of how Queer Theory might be applied to Early American writing in general and to slave writing specifically, need to include explorations of other extant writing from slaves in Colonial America. For the purposes of this present essay, I have chosen to attempt a Queer reading of three of Wheatley's poems, two of which have been mentioned above: "To S.M. a Young *African* Painter, on Seeing His Works," "On Being Brought from Africa to America," and "On Imagination."

"To S.M." was the first poem to inspire me to attempt a Queer reading of Phillis Wheatley. When I understood that "S.M." was another slave, it occurred to me that Wheatley had to step outside of her usual role of writing for her white audience and adapt the role of "other" more specifically than ever before. In terms of Queer Theory, "S.M." points to a unique moment of recognition when the "queer other," that body outside of the normative practices of mainstream society, occupies a space and time with another "queer other" who stands in opposition to the same mainstream society, and in opposition to the "self" that "queer other" identifies. As with her own identity, Wheatley saw in Scipio an embodiment of an "other" who could easily meet and exceed the standards set by colonial society for his artistic endeavors. For as she states, "Still may the painter's and the poets fire / To aid thy pencil, and thy verse conspire! / And may the charms of each seraphic theme / Conduct thy footsteps to immortal fame!" (114).

As stated earlier, it is with the last part of "To S.M." that Wheatley truly "queers" the relationship between the traditional use of her language, the expectations of her readers, and the true meaning behind her lines. She writes, "But when these shades of time are chas'd away, / And darkness ends in everlasting day, / On what seraphic pinions shall we move, / And view the landscapes in the realms above?" (115). The queered other, in this case the male "S.M." who works with paints instead of words, has now become part of a "we," and not only a "we," but a "we" who can rise above the "shades of time" to view a future world outside of the normative label of slave and master, black and white. Once outside of the restrictive labels prescribed by colonial America— labels that demand that Scipio be demeaned as the idealized rustic Damon and that she be limited to referring to her beloved Africa by using images of Aurora, much in the same way that labels demand that a Queer Theorist be gay or straight, male or female—the two "queered" souls are free to perform a linguistic dance of creation whereby they can use the "nobler themes" of "purer language" to foster new identities.

However, Wheatley was anything but naïve. The last two lines of "S.M." recognize and accept that she is, indeed, still bound by the temporary physical realities of her position as slave to the dominant dialectic and that for the time being, at least, the release of her "queered" soul must be "sealed" by the solemn gloom of that dialectic. After envisioning a time and place where she and "S.M" might be recognized as *voiced* individuals, Wheatley offers a denouement, "Cease, *gentle muse!* the solemn gloom of night / Now seals *the fair creation* from my sight." In the very moment of creation, in the moment when subversive language has been used to envision, if not equality with her white "masters," then at least a possibility for an equality of expression, Wheatley embraces and accepts a momentary physical reality wherein she is a named piece of property owned by another. She is the "othered other," the one who sees beyond her actual reality, but is at the same time linguistically imprisoned by that reality.

If Wheatley was not naïve about her physical position in the world, she was certainly not prone to surrendering that position by granting naming rights to other. Instead, Wheatley was especially ingenious in her use of "acceptable" language as a form of protest . One way to overcome a physical reality that seeks to suppress more metaphysical longings is through stealth. Other slave writers like Jupiter Hammon, George Moses Horton, and Frederick Douglass used "stealth" language in a variety of ways to comment on the condition of African slaves in America. As Sondra O'Neale points out, Wheatley may have been the stealthiest of all. As O'Neale states, "While Wheatley did not have to acquire [her] language skills stealthily, she was subject to authentication for proper classical and evangelical content. Within such constraints Wheatley—

Tom O. McCulley

as did Hammon, Horton, and Douglass—found the Biblical myth, language and symbol to be the most conducive vehicles for making subtle, yet effective statements against slavery" (145).

"On Being Brought from Africa to America" exemplifies both the use of biblical language as protest language and what I have called Wheatley's position as an "othered other." For a Queer theorist, "On Being Brought" is a gold mine for the kinds of fluid identities, self-aware commentary, guerrilla linguistics, and cultural critiques that make up the crux of what Queer Theory is all about. Like the Queer person who stands outside of the mainstream while still painfully aware of his or her place within it (the "othered other"), Wheatley uses "On Being Brought" to challenge directly the normative presumptions of a colonial society that used Christianity to "justify" its ownership of slaves. In fact, as O'Neale states, Wheatley used white Christian presumptions about a racial superiority to condemn those very assumptions by pointing out that in the Christian belief system, all believers are equally called to salvation.

Wheatley Queers the very first line of "On Being Brought" by reflecting back onto white Christians the idea that their concept of mercy is what brought her out of her "Pagan" land and "Taught my benighted soul to understand / That there's a God, that there's a *Saviour* too."[6] Shields, O'Neale, and others have pointed out that Wheatley's separation of God and Saviour, given her other subversive uses of language, can only be deliberate. From a Queer Theory standpoint, this line can be seen to drip with sarcasm, though sarcasm was not usually employed by Wheatley, who was ever conscious of her white masters' ability to take away her voice. Still, as O'Neale so aptly states, it is hard to overlook the idea that Wheatley is pointing out that she was aware of a god before having one explained to her by white Christians.

The italicized emphasis on Saviour can be read in multiple ways. A favorite comeback for lesbian and gay activists faced with the chant that "Jesus Saves" is "Yes, but can He save me from YOU?" A Queer reading of Wheatley's line, "there's a *Saviour* too," does not seem to be that far removed from such a comeback. Another reading is that Wheatley, in her role as a "benighted soul," simply did not need to be "saved" before arriving in America as a slave. This reading is buttressed by the next line in the poem, "Once I redemption neither sought nor knew." In the fluid exchange of identities apparent in the first four lines of the poem, then, Wheatley has moved from the "othered" status of pagan to the "othered other" status of a black African supposedly worshiping in the normative religion of the dominant culture, to the further "othered other" status of an educated African slave who is aware enough of her own bodily integrity to reclaim her pagan status by co-opting the very language used by her "Christian" oppressors. Wheatley has, in essence, queered her own queerness through a masterful use of self-referentiality.

The second half of Wheatley's "On Being Brought" further queers the poem by disrupting the normative colonial culture whose justification for slavery is personal salvation for the slaves. Playing off universal Western themes of black equals bad and white equals good,[7] Wheatley opts for the term "sable" to describe her race against those who view Africans with "a scornful eye" and refer to their blackness as a "diabolic die." A "sable" can be a kind of weasel, interesting in itself from a Queer point of view since the term "weasel" is often used in a derogatory sense to describe an "other" that is outside of the mainstream, but it can also stand for the blackest of black colors or for the fur of a sable, fur that is at once black *and* shimmering when caught by the light. Like those contemporary Christians who insist that they "hate the sin but love the sinner" when referring to lesbians and gays, Wheatley's Christians espouse a hatred for those blacks whom they supposedly "rescued" from damnation in hell as a result of their paganism.

In a final Queering of the normative colonial justification for slavery, Wheatley directly admonishes those Christians who have used a call to spiritual freedom to justify bodily slavery by reminding them that even *Negroes*, viewed by some as carrying the blackest mark of all—the mark of Cain—will, in heaven, be on the same "angelic train" as their white oppressors. To put it mildly, Wheatley's performative use of language as a "call to being" in "On Being Brought" and her deliberate "Queering" of accepted standard tropes is nothing short of a linguistic tour de force.

"On Imagination" mirrors Queer Theory's call to use performative language to reinvent the fractured identity of the "other" as that "other" works across and twists the expectations placed upon it by normative societal demands. The parallels in "On Imagination" between a linguistically gifted mind trapped in a "black slave girl's" restricted and labeled body and a "queer mind" trapped in a lesbian or gay man's restricted and labeled body are palpable. "On Imagination" opens with a traditional call to the Muses in the form of the "imperial queen," imagination, and her "potent" and "wond'rous acts" (65). In the second stanza, Wheatley moves beyond the usual call to the Muses and into something much more akin to a demand that the Muses work with her poetic voice in order "To tell her [Imagination's] glories with a faithful tongue, /

Tom O. McCulley

Ye blooming graces, triumph in my song" (66). In other words, like a Queer Theorist, Wheatley is demanding of language here that it lift itself above the normative restrictions of everyday existence and "call forth" a new existence tied to the act of (re)naming that is always present in relation to imagination.

Stanza three furthers the queer call for (re)creation of the "othered" identity by introducing imagination's powerful ability to capture the bodily senses and convince the mind that it is "experiencing" a reality that is not, in fact, tangible. In this way, the "captive mind" is at once involved in the fluidity of creation of an "other" space where both the "self" (the mind) and the mirror self ("some lov'd object [that] strikes her wand'ring eyes") can interact with freewheeling imagination's powerful ability to (re)create reality.

Stanza four opens with a question one would not expect a "black slave girl" to be able to answer, "Imagination! Who can sing thy force? / Or who describe the swiftness of thy course?" (66). If there are any advantages to being an "other," one of them might be, as Frantz Fanon[8] and others have suggested, that by default the dominant force controlling the "other," due to the bodily space of (its) superiority, rarely allows the "other" the subjective space of recognition and, therefore, rarely allows herself or himself to explore fully and understand the "other" over whom she or he has dominion. The "other," on the other hand, who is always aware of her objectified space and who always carries a desire for the subject who dominates that space, inherently grows to know that dominant "other" in ways in which the dominant "other" may never know itself. In Queer Theory, this lack of knowledge demonstrated by the dominant culture translates to the fact that while heterosexuals often have a low "homosexual IQ"—as a result, mostly, of heterosexuals' need to objectify the "homosexual lifestyle"—homosexuals, by their very existence as objectified "others" surrounded by and inundated with dominant heterosexual messages, often understand their heterosexual counterparts. In the case of Phillis Wheatley and other African slaves alive during the Colonial period, the same can be said regarding their white masters. By being forced to be involved with the details of their masters' lives while not being allowed to have a voiced presence in those lives, African slaves during the Colonial period were in essence full of an intimate knowledge of how their masters operated on a day-to-day basis. At the same time, those masters were often unaware of the everyday lives of their slaves beyond moments of contact where slaves were of use to them, causing the real lives of African Americans to remain invisible to the dominant culture.

In connection to Wheatley's "On Imagination," the question of "who can sing thy [imagination's] force?" is answered with a playfulness and directness by Phillis that is astounding. *I can,* she writes. *I can.* For it is the "black slave girl" in her restricted body who, like the queer who also stands restricted and labeled, can best and most easily break the fetters of normative culture and thereby soar with imagination to "Th' empyreal palace of the thund'ring God" and who can "leave the rolling universe behind" to "measure the skies, and range the realms above" (66).

The next two stanzas of "On Imagination" are a pure Queer celebration of the fact that by (re)creating fluid identity through imagination's eyes, the "othered other" can also place her bodily self, through imagination's control of the senses, into scenes where winter turns to spring, where passions bow before the throne of *fancy,* and where joy can rush—unobstructed by the normative demands of the dominant society—into an open heart (67). In the end, however, the queer heart is always aware of its "otherness" in the face of the normative dominant society, and "On Imagination" ends on a note of resignation. Just as the "queer other" persona of "On Imagination" catches a glimpse of the freedom she once felt under the blaze of Aurora's (Africa's) rising, just when she catches the sun's rays glancing off an African landscape, she is forced "reluctant [to] leave the pleasing views, / Which *Fancy* dresses to delight the *Muse*" (68).

Once again, Wheatley is confronted with the physical realities placed on her body, mind, and spirit by a repressive society. She writes, "*Winter* austere forbids me to aspire, / And northern tempests damp the rising fire." As Shields states, winter could stand for nothing less than the normative, cold, and *white* demands placed on Phillis's "black slave girl" body by the Wheatley's calls for her service (Shields, "Phillis Wheatley's Subversion"). Like any "queer" who for a brief moment believes that normative society might understand and accept the "otherness" it has imposed on him or her, Wheatley is abruptly reminded that while her queer imagination might rise above the restrictions of her body, colonial society can, or will, not. Her flight of imagination is over; the queered body is once again brought back down to earth: "They chill the tides of *Fancy's* flowing sea, / Cease then, my song, cease the unequal lay."

IV

What can a "black slave girl" who died in abject poverty in 1784 teach a blossoming Queer Theorist in the present? As I hope this preliminary investigation has shown—plenty! First and foremost, Wheatley has taught this writer that performative acts of language do have the power to create new and fluid identities outside of the normative restrictions placed on an "othered" body, even if there is a time limitation for such transformation. Second, by learning the language of the dominant normative discourse of one's time, a poet can achieve a "queering" of that very discourse in subtle ways that beg hegemonic constructions to look back upon themselves and question their very positions as controlling forces. Finally, as Wheatley so clearly stated in her February 1774 letter to a Native American "other," Samson Occom, Queer Theory can gain much from the idea that rubbing against and questioning the normative domination of a central culture has its intellectual and theoretical rewards. Queer Theory is nothing, in the end, if it is not about the freedom of the individual to "queer" society in ways that ultimately lead to freedom and equality. As Phillis Wheatley so aptly put it, "for in every human Breast, God has implanted a Principle, which we call Love of Freedom; it is impatient of Oppression, and pants for Deliverance; and by the Leave of our Modern Egyptians I will assert, that the same Principle lives in us . . . How well the Cry for Liberty, and the reverse Disposition for the Exercise of oppressive Power over others agree,—I humbly think it does not require the Penetration of a Philosopher to determine" (176–77).

NOTES

1. For detailed discussions of Wheatley's use of subversion in her poetry, see: Shields, "Phillis Wheatley's Subversive Pastoral"; McKay and Scheick, "The Other Song in Phillis Wheatley's 'On Imagination'"; Willard, "Wheatley's Turns of Praise: Heroic Entrapment and the Paradox of Revolution"; and chapter 2 from Russell Reising's *Loose Ends*, entitled "The Whiteness of the Wheatleys: Phillis Wheatley's Revolutionary Poetics."

2. Shields discusses the incorporation of Aurora as an homage to Wheatley's mother and as a reference to her African roots in "Phillis Wheatley's Struggle for Freedom in Her Poetry and Prose," "Phillis Wheatley's Subversive Pastoral," and *The American Aeneas: Classical Origins of the American Self.*

3. For discussions of Butler's and Sedgwick's importance to the "beginnings" of Queer Theory, see William B. Turner, *A Genealogy of Queer Theory;* Calvin Thomas, ed., *Straight with a Twist;* John C. Hawley, ed., *Post-Colonial, Queer;* and the Special Issue of *College Literature* 24.1 (February 1997) devoted to Queer Theory and lesbian/gay studies.

4. Further discussions of the meaning of "Queer Theory" consulted but not used in this paper include: Rosaria Champagne's "Queering the Unconscious"; Lauren Berlant and Michael Warner's "What Does Queer Theory Teach Us About X?"; Lee Edleman's "The Future Is Kid Stuff: Queer Theory, Disidentification, and the Death Drive"; and Jan Campbell's *Arguing with the Phallus*.

5. The term "othered other" is one of my own creation. In my mind, it reflects the status of a body that is out of the mainstream not only of the predominant culture, but of its own select minority as well. In my own case, the fact that I am gay makes me an "other" in context with the mainstream culture that surrounds me. The fact that I am a gay man in a long-term relationship and that I have raised a child and that I have grandchildren makes me an "othered other" in the sense that I do not, and cannot, fit into the prescribed role of the "other as gay man" as that role is set down by either the predominant culture or my own minority. In the case of Phillis Wheatley, the fact that she was a black slave made her an "other" in the predominant Colonial culture. The fact that Phillis was female further "othered" her "otherness." The fact that Phillis was articulate, that she was able to read and write in the normative language of the predominant discourse and, further, that she was able to manipulate that language toward her own ends made her an even more pronounced "othered other" in that she could not comfortably fit in any of the "real" world roles available to her.

6. My readings of Wheatley's poems have been influenced, though not dictated, by John Shields's "Phillis Wheatley's Subversive Pastoral"; Katherine Clay Bassard's *Spiritual Interrogations: Culture, Gender and Community in Early American Women's Writing;* Carla Willard's "Wheatley's Turns of Praise: Heroic Entrapment and the Paradox of Revolution"; Michele McKay and William J. Scheick's "The Other Song In Phillis Wheatley's 'On Imagination'"; Russell Reising's *Loose Ends;* and Helen M. Burke's "The Rhetoric and Politics of Marginality: The Subject of Phillis Wheatley."

7. See "The Whiteness of The Wheatley's: Phillis Wheatley's Revolutionary Poetics" in Russell Reising's *Loose Ends* (73–116).

8. See Frantz Fanon, *Black Skin, White Masks.*

Tom O. McCulley

WORKS CITED

Abou-Rihan, Fadi. "Queer Marks/Nomadic Difference: Sexuality and the Politics of Race and Ethnicity." *Canadian Review of Comparative Literature* 21.1–2 (March–June 1994): 255–63.

Bassard, Katherine Clay. *Spiritual Interrogations: Culture, Gender and Community In Early American Women's Writing.* Princeton: Princeton UP, 1999.

Berlant, Lauren, and Michael Warner. "What Does Queer Theory Teach Us about X?" *PMLA* 110.3 (May 1995): 343–49.

Burke, Helen M. "The Rhetoric and Politics of Marginality: The Subject of Phillis Wheatley." *Tulsa Studies in Women's Literature* 10.1 (Spring 1991): 31–45.

Butler, Judith. *Bodies That Matter: On the Discursive Limits of "Sex."* New York: Routledge, 1993.

———. *Gender Trouble: Feminism and the Subversion of Identity.* New York: Routledge, 1990.

Campbell, Jan. *Arguing with the Phallus: Feminist, Queer and Postcolonial Theory: A Psychoanalytic Contribution.* New York: St. Martin's, 2000.

Champagne, Rosaria. "Queering the Unconscious." *South Atlantic Quarterly* 97.2 (1998): 281–96.

College Literature 24.1 (February 1997). Special Issue. Queer Utilities: Textual Studies, Theory, Pedagogy, Praxis. College of Literature: West Chester University.

Edelman, Lee. "The Future Is Kid Stuff: Queer Theory, Disidentification, and the Death Drive." *Narrative* 6.1 (1988): 18–30.

Fanon, Frantz. *Black Skin, White Masks.* New York: Grove, 1967.

Hall, Donald E. "Introduction: Queer Works." *College Literature* 24.1 (1997): 2–10.

Hawley, John C., ed. *Post-Colonial, Queer: Theoretical Intersections.* Albany: SUNY P, 2001.

Jordan, June. "The Difficult Miracle of Black Poetry in America or Something Like a Sonnet for Phillis Wheatley." *Massachusetts Review* 27.2 (1986): 252–62.

Leonard, Garry. "Introduction: Praxis." *College Literature* 24.1 (1997): 196–201.

McKay, Michele, and William J. Scheick. "The Other Song in Phillis Wheatley's 'On Imagination.'" *Studies in the Literary Imagination* 27.1 (1994): 71–84.

Meyers, Helene. "To Queer or Not to Queer: That's Not the Question." *College Literature* 24.1 (1997): 171–82.

O'Neale, Sondra. "A Slave's Subtle War: Phillis Wheatley's Use of Biblical Myth and Symbol." *Early American Literature* 21.2 (1986): 144–66.

Reising, Russell. *Loose Ends: Closure and Crisis in the American Social Text.* Durham: Duke UP, 1996.

Sedgwick, Eve Kosofsky. *Epistemology of the Closet.* Berkeley: U of California P, 1990.

———. *Tendencies.* Durham: Duke UP, 1993.

Shields, John C. *The American Aeneas: Classical Origins of the American Self.* Knoxville: U of Tennessee P, 2001.

———. "Phillis Wheatley's Struggle for Freedom in Her Poetry and Prose." *The Collected Works of Phillis Wheatley.* Ed. John C. Shields. New York: Oxford UP, 1988. 229–70.

———. "Phillis Wheatley's Subversion of Classical Stylistics." *Style* 27.2 (1993): 252–71.

———. "Phillis Wheatley's Subversive Pastoral." *Eighteenth-Century Studies* 27.4 (1994): 631–47.

Thomas, Calvin, ed. *Straight with a Twist: Queer Theory and the Subject of Heterosexuality.* Urbana, IL: U of Illinois P, 2000.

Turner, William B. *A Genealogy of Queer Theory.* Philadelphia: Temple UP, 2000.

Vaid, Urvashi. *Virtual Equality: The Mainstreaming of Gay and Lesbian Liberation.* New York: Doubleday, 1995.

Wheatley, Phillis. *The Collected Works of Phillis Wheatley.* Ed. John C. Shields. New York: Oxford UP, 1988.

Willard, Carla. "Wheatley's Turns of Praise: Heroic Entrapment and the Paradox of Revolution." *American Literature* 67.2 (June 1995): 233–56.

Marketing a Sable Muse: Phillis Wheatley and the Antebellum Press

Jennifer Rene Young

While Phillis Wheatley *worked to shape her own identity*, the media had its different, sometimes contradictory characterizations of her. During her seventeen-year career, which spanned from 1767 to 1784, Wheatley employed four principal marketing strategies: her concerns for individual salvation, the developing hostilities between England and her adopted American colonies, the issue of slavery, and the public's growing curiosity about her. As an enslaved poet, she had to balance her imagistic language and political subtext with messages pleasing to a mostly white readership.

Several factors influenced Wheatley to write poems about religion and politics, including her experiences as a Middle Passage survivor, a Boston "servant" owned by a slaveholding Christian family, a baptized Christian, and an intellectual aware of American colonists who argued for freedom from English rule. Just as tensions leading up to the Revolutionary War (1776–83) served as setting for Wheatley's patriot poems, having owners, subscribers, and printers who were avid supporters of the Great Awakening impacted her religious work and the reception of it (see table 1).

Poems such as "On Messrs. Hussey and Coffin" (1767), "On the Death of Rev. Dr. Sewell [*sic*]" (1769), and "On the Death of Rev. Mr. George Whitefield" (1770) reveal the poet's religious inclinations. Wheatley had a great deal of public recognition by the time her broadside was published in 1770.[1] Her poems helped garner attention from the literary marketplace that largely focused on religious texts. As evidenced by a then-unpublished poem from 1767, "An Address to the Deist," her religious convictions are hard to ignore: "'Father forgive them,' thus the Saviour pray'd / Nail'd was King Jesus on the cross for us. / For our transgressions he sustain'd the Curse" (*Collected Writings* 72–73).

TABLE 1

1765	1775	1785

1450–1850 Mid-Atlantic slave trade [international trade]

1619 Slave trade begins in America

1730s Early printers (Bradford, Zenger, Franklin) pave way for publishing industry

1730–1750 Evangelical tour in England and America

Circa 1753 Phillis Wheatley is born in western region of Africa

1760 1 poem published for both Briton Hammon and Jupiter Hammon

1761 Phillis Wheatley is captured and sold to Boston family

    1767 Wheatley's first poem is published, "On Mssrs. Hussey and Coffin"

    1768 Robert Bell begins his publishing career in Philadelphia; Bell starts a "Circulating Library"

    1770–1780 Major importation of books, esp. the Bible [mainly German and English]

    1770 George Whitefield dies; transatlantic printings of Wheatley's elegy

    1771–1794 John Dunlap is editor of Pennsylvania Packet

    1771 Isaiah Thomas's Massachusetts Spy

    1772 Wheatley's first proposal / Her 1773 proposal is the only published volume

    1772 Lord Mansfield renders slavery illegal in London, England

    1773 Wheatley accompanies Nathanial Wheatley to London. She returns in September

    1773 Poems on Various Subjects, first published in London; Wheatley is freed

    1774–1785 25 newspapers began in New York, 22 in Pennsylvania, 8 in New Jersey

        1775 Thomas Paine is editor of Pennsylvania Magazine

        1776 Signing of Declaration of Independence

        1776 First edition of Paine's Common Sense

        1778 Jupiter Hammon's poem to Wheatley

        1779 Wheatley's third proposal

        1784 Wheatley's final proposal

        December 5, 1784 Wheatley dies in Boston

During the peak of her career, 1770–76, Wheatley's pious poems were emphasized more than her political ones. For instance, "On Being Brought from Africa to America" was reprinted several times in the *London Chronicle* in September 1773. Perhaps those who endorsed Wheatley thought this poem would have greater audience appeal. Her conversion supported the evangelical idea that grace was available to Christians and provided a stirring example of conversion in an unlikely candidate (see table 2).

The poet's career was particularly orchestrated by three women with strong Christian values: her patron, the Countess of Huntingdon (who also provided patronage for other African writers); her mistress, Susannah Wheatley; and one of her probable tutors, Mary Wheatley (the Wheatley's daughter).[2] These women believed in the poet's power as a Christian example, especially since they approved the use of Wheatley's poems to spread the message of the Great Awakening in general and Methodism in particular.

Her religious poetry appealed to many people, and Wheatley's political poems were pertinent to the public's concerns as well. William Robinson ("Quandry") and Antonio Bly attribute authorship of "On the Affray in King-Street, on the Evening of the 5th of March" to Wheatley. The poem celebrates several Boston civilians—one of them an African, Crispus Attucks—who died when British troops opened gunfire on a crowd of protestors on March 5, 1770. As Robinson and Bly point out, Phillis may have witnessed the scene since the Wheatley home was located on King Street where the massacre occurred. By the time her London printer, Archibald Bell, published *Poems on Various Subjects, Religious and Moral* in 1773, Wheatley had positioned herself as a Negro poet who wrote on important political events—like the repeal of the Stamp Act in "To the King's Most Excellent Majesty" or the British captain sent to pacify restless Bostonians in "To Captain H—D, of the 65th Regiment." And with over a dozen elegies in her 1773 volume, the poet also provided comfort through her words to grieving families of the Boston elite.

Some of Wheatley's poems and letters acknowledged her distaste for slavery, a professed love for Africans, and advocacy for emancipation. Her metaphors for bondage in "On Imagination" are described as "silken fetters" and "soft captivity." In "To the Earl of Dartmouth," the poem's speaker cries to be released from "mournful strain" and "the iron chain."[3] In "To S.M. a young African Painter," she celebrates the artistry of Scipio Moorhead—the enslaved artist who is credited as having drawn her portrait for the 1773 Poems frontispiece. Wheatley inserts a footnote in "To Maecenas" to be sure her readers

TABLE 2

Wheatley's Broadsides and Pamphlets

TITLE	TYPE OF PUBLICATION	PUBLISHER & DATE
"An Elegiac Poem. On the Death of that Celebrated Divine, and eminent Servant of Jesus Christ, the late Reverend, and pious George Whitefield, Chaplain to the Right Honourable the Countess of Huntingdon."	5-page pamphlet in 62 lines	S. Southwick, in Queen Street (Newport, Rhode Island): 1770
	Printed **9 times** as 62-line broadside in 1770	Boston: publisher unknown, 1770 [printed 5 times]
		S. Southwick, in Queen Street (Newport, Rhode Island): 1770 [printed 2 times]
		New York: Samuel Inslee and Anthony Carr, 1770 [printed 1 time]
		Philadelphia: William Goddard, 1770 [printed 1 time]
	Printed **twice** in 64-line broadside	London, publisher unknown, 1771
"Heaven the Residence of the Saints, A Sermon. Occasioned by the sudden and much lamented Death of the Rev. George Whitefield, A.M., Chaplain to the Right Honourable the Countess of Huntingdon [sic]. Delivered at the Thursday lecture at Boston, in America, Oct 11, 1770. By Ebenezer Pemberton, D.D. Paster [sic] of a Church in Boston. To which is added an Elegiac Poem on his Death, by Phillis, a Negro Girl, Seventeen Years of Age, Belonging to Mr. J. Wheatley of Boston."	Broadside with Ebenezer Pemberton's sermon and Wheatley's elegy	"Boston printed: London, reprinted, for E. and C. Dilly in the Poultry; and sold at the Chapel in TOT-Tenham Ct. Road. M. DCC. LXXI. Price sixpence" (printed in 1771).
"An Ode of Verses on the much-lamented Death of the Rev. Mr. George Whitefield, Late Chaplain to the Countess of Huntingdon; Who	64-line broadside, variant version	Boston: publisher unknown, 1771.
	printed for charity: "for the Benefit of a poor Family burnt out . . . near Shore-ditch Church (Boston)."	Priced "a Penny apiece or 5s."

TITLE	TYPE OF PUBLICATION	PUBLISHER & DATE
departed this life, . . . near Boston the Thirteenth of September, 1770, at Fifty-seventh Year of his Age. Compos'd in America by a Negro GirlSeventeen Years of Age. and sent over to a Gentleman of Character in London."		
"To the Hon'ble Thomas Hubbard Esq: On the Death of Mrs. Thankfull Leonard."	Broadside, 46 lines	Dated "Boston, January 2./ 1773," publisher unknown
Poems on Various Subjects, Religious and Moral First London edition DOES have an engraving of Wheatley, a title page, "Entered at Stationer's Hall" on verso title page (see Robinson, "Bio" 14) *This first London edition does NOT have a dedication to the countess, no "Preface," no brief biographical sketch signed by John Wheatley, no attestation of 18 Bostonians. (see Robinson, "Bio" 14)	**First ed.** Book, 39 poems, 38 written by Wheatley 1 (last one) written by "JB" (which may be James Bowdoin) **Second London ed., 2 versions:** 1. neatly bound edition 2. blue paperback sewn edition [this edition (both versions) contain a dedication, preface, sketch by J. Wheatley, and attestation.]	London: Printed for A.Bell, Bookseller, Aldgate; sold by Messrs. Cox and Berry, King Street, Boston London, printed for. A. Bell, date unknown
"An Elegy, Sacred to the Memory of that Great Divine, the Reverend and Learned Dr. Samuel Cooper . . . by Phillis Peters"	52-line broadside	Boston: printed and sold by E. Russell, 1784
"Liberty and Peace, a Poem by Phillis Peters"	This broadside is published after December.	Boston: printed by her in death Warden and Russell, 1784

know that Terence, the ancient Roman poet, is "African by birth," part of "Afric's sable race." In letters to her friend Obour Tanner, readers see a different side of Wheatley, one less constrained by majority views. She shares similar sentiments with her friend Samson Occom, the Mohegan preacher. Published in the *Connecticut Gazette* and the *Universal Intelligencer* in March 1774, the letter reveals a side of Wheatley that was not marketed to the presses:

> Otherwise, perhaps, the Israelites had been less solicitous for
> their Freedom from Egyptian Slavery; I do not say they would
> have been contented without it, by no means, for in every human
> Breast, God has implanted a Principle, which we call Love of
> Freedom; it is impatient of Oppression, and pants for Deliverance;
> and by the Leave of our Modern Egyptians I will assert, that the
> same Principle lives in us. (Wheatley, *Complete Writings* 153)

While advertisements for her 1773 volume praised the poet as an "unassisted genius," there were critics who sought to dismantle her career by questioning her intelligence and discrediting her poems. In "Wheatley's Turns of Praise: Heroic Entrapment and the Paradox of Revolution," Carla Willard argues that Wheatley's authentic slave voice was manipulated by conflicting claims over slavery, because Wheatley was bold enough to assert her own social criticisms (238).

Between 1785 and 1825, the pro-slavery and abolition movements in Europe grew larger, eventually dominating discourse in the Atlantic world. Wheatley's poetry was increasingly used to support pro- and antislavery arguments. Writers also involved Wheatley in the debate on the nature of the African. Her poetry was negatively marketed in segments of the Colonial press that had little interest in publishing abolitionist arguments.

Richard Nisbet, a writer from Philadelphia, harshly criticized Wheatley's poetry in his 1773 book, *Slavery Not Forbidden by Scripture.* Nisbet holds,

> A few instances may be found, of African Negroes possess-
> ing virtues and becoming ingenious; but still what I have said,
> with regard to the general character, I dare say, most people ac-
> quainted with them, will agree to. The Author of the address [by
> Benjamin Rush] gives a single example of a Negro girl writing a
> few silly poems, to prove that blacks are not deficient to us in
> understanding. (25)

Nisbet challenges his contemporary Benjamin Rush for praising Africans and their talent, especially as evidenced by Wheatley.

In his 1775 publication, Bernard Romans is another critic who did not praise Wheatley's writing. His collection, *A Concise Natural History of East and West Florida,* was printed for the author in two volumes. Romans characterized Wheatley as an intelligent African:

> . . . far be it from me to approve or recommend the vile usage to which this useful part of the creation is subjected by some of our Western nabobs, but against the Phyllis [*sic*] of Boston (who is the Phoenix of her race) I could bring at least twenty well known instances of the contrary effect of education on this sable generation. . . . (1: 105; cited in Robinson, Bio-bibliography 29)

Romans supported the pro-slavery argument by declaring Wheatley an exception that proves the rule: blacks, in his opinion, did not generally benefit from education. He used derogatory terms to argue in favor of the subjugation of blacks. While Bernard Romans perhaps derisively appointed Wheatley the "Phoenix of her race," he supported the pro-slavery argument because he calls her a "nabob," a negative term used by slaveholders. Evidence of Colonial readers' mixed feelings toward Wheatley is also revealed in an anonymous letter dated "January 29, 1778." This author slandered Wheatley in Boston's *Independent Chronicle and Universal Advertiser,* by ridiculing blacks in politics and in the arts (qtd. in Robinson, Bio-Bibliography 30).

Writers like Romans and Nisbet, in support of maintaining the slavery institution, believed that blacks lacked virtue and religious character. By the time *Notes on the State of Virginia* was published in Philadelphia in 1788, four years after Wheatley's death, Thomas Jefferson's assumption of the incompetence of slaves was both supported and negated by other American and European writers, using Wheatley's image and poetry as examples for disparate arguments.[4] His text, first published in London in 1782, was filled with echoed sentiments that had already been circulating. While slavery was not the central focus in Jefferson's *Notes,* his observations in "Query XIV. Laws" criticized the talents of black writers. He even identifies some by name including Phillis Wheatley and Ignatius Sancho. Jefferson's derisive comments contributed to the trend of thinking that would forever plague her identity and stigmatize her poetry.

Far outweighing the negative attention of pro-slavery arguments, there were many more abolitionists who used Wheatley's work to advance their antislavery campaign. With the abolition of slavery in London in 1772, the English were in the forefront of the abolitionist movement. As a result, most of the portrayals of Wheatley during her lifetime were from the English, not Americans. For the English, Wheatley and her career offered a powerful rebuke to slavery. Promoting Wheatley further supported England's growing hostility toward the American colonies.

"Recollection" is one of Wheatley's poems that has an explicit reference to her African past. This poem became very popular because of the intense interest in the nature of Africans generated by the debate over slavery. The poem was reprinted twice in British magazines—the *London Magazine* (January 1772), *Essex Gazette* (March 1773), and once in Isaiah Thomas's *Massachusetts Spy* (March 1773).[5] The poem focused on a fanciful memory and legacy of Wheatley's life as an "Afric." It is possible that Isaiah Thomas published "Recollection" to signify the capabilities of Wheatley as an author. While his views on slavery were not articulated in his biography, Thomas may have used "Recollection" to convey the dark hold that oppression had on Africans, especially those who demonstrated a talent for something greater than physical labor.

The debates regarding slavery included black writers as well. Jupiter Hammon, wrote a poem in 1778 with Wheatley as the central subject. The title suggests his support: "An Address to Miss Phillis Wheatly [*sic*] Ethiopian Poetess, in Boston, Who Came from Africa at Eight Years of Age, and Soon Became Acquainted with the Gospel of Jesus Christ." Hammon writes, "That thou a pattern still might be, / To youth of Boston town, / The blessed Jesus set thee free, / From every sinful wound" (205). Hammon's poem foreshadows the support of future black authors who see the importance of blacks entering the public sphere of print. Just as Wheatley had written a poem to Scipio Moorhead, the black artist who is said to have drawn her frontispiece, Hammon continues the tradition of celebrating what blacks can produce.

Several leaders used Wheatley's poetry and her self-education journey as part of their position against slavery. John Wesley and his Methodist followers were known for combining their idea of universal redemption with their antislavery position. Wesley even used his Methodist publication the *Arminian Magazine* to argue for abolition. Her poems and elegies appeared in the *Arminian* in 1784, and in later years when the magazine, housed in Philadelphia, became the *Methodist Magazine.*

When Wheatley's poetry was published in the 1790s, most of the presses were based in Philadelphia, a city that was one of the earliest to be involved

Jennifer Rene Young

with the American abolition movement. The Quakers, who were the earliest religious group to abolish slavery, established a large community there. Philadelphia was also home to the noted physician Dr. Benjamin Rush, and the statesman Benjamin Franklin, both of whom Wheatley knew. Wheatley had written a poem to Rush, evidenced by the titles in her 1772 proposal (Wheatley, *Complete Writings* 165); her 1779 proposal of poems, which did not garner enough subscriptions for publication, was dedicated to Franklin (167). In *An Address to the inhabitants of the British Settlements in America Upon Slave-Keeping,* published by Philadelphian John Dunlap (another one of Wheatley's congenial connections), Rush spoke fondly of Wheatley:

> There is now in the town of Boston a Free Negro Girl about 18 Years of age, who has been but nine years in the country, whose singular genius and accomplishments are such as not only do honor to her sex but to human nature. Several of her poems have been printed, and read with pleasure by the public. (Robinson, *Bio-Bibliography* 22)

Several members of the free black community, including Reverends Richard Allen, of the African Methodist Episcopal church, and Absalom Jones, of the Episcopal church, were also active in Philadelphia's political and social circuits.

In the years following her death, 1784–1825, Wheatley's volume, *Poems on Various Subjects, Religious and Moral,* went through seven editions: three from London presses and four from Philadelphia. While the majority of these editions were marketed respectfully, one publisher denigrated the poet's eminence. In 1787, J. French changed the title of Wheatley's volume to *Poems on Comic, Serious, and Moral Subjects;* added it to his list of "Satirical Publications"; and sold it for one shilling, instead of the several pounds sterling that it was worth.[6] Other book titles in French's list included "Picture Gallery of Popular Portraits," "Devil Divorced, or the Diablo-Whore," and "Court of Adultery, 2 Parts." J. French associated Wheatley's volume with a peculiar group of odd-titled texts. Being part of this "lyric repository" was damaging to her reputation since these writers were more characteristic of Grubstreet than the Republic of Letters, thus supporting Thomas Jefferson's allusion to Wheatley as one of Pope's "dunces."[7] Wheatley's image was inextricably linked to the vulgar, hack writers that Pope ridiculed in *The Dunciad.* The poet went from being applauded by the Countess of Huntingdon to being mocked by a London publisher.

There were also editors like Philip Freneau whose patriot magazine, the *National Gazette,* addressed Wheatley's poetry as entertainment, not eminent work. The following anonymous letter in 1791 encouraged readers to purchase *Poems on Various Subjects.*[8]

> . . . I observe the Publisher of the work has put himself to abun-
> dance of trouble to convince the public that the poems are genu-
> ine: and, indeed, they evidently require a great deal of apology of
> this kind to prevent a suspicion of their being sadly garbled. . . .
> I am treated with little else than some trite stuff 'on the death of
> George Whitefield' to the Rev'd Mr. Such and one of the decease
> of his wife. Or 'Verses to a Student in divinity on some of the
> Dogmas of Fanaticism'—to say the truth, I see little more merit
> in these poems than would be incident to any other collection,
> the work of some person that had been a good deal conversant in
> Watt's lyrics and [pamphlet] poems. Several impressions, how-
> ever, have been sold off as I am informed; not so much it is to
> be supposed for the real merit of poetry as the accidental circum-
> stance of its being the production of a sable Ethiopian.
> (Robinson, Bio-Bibliography 38)

This letter advances the author's curiosity about Wheatley as an African poet. It seems that many people bought her poetry because of the bizarre notion that an African could write. The presence of Wheatley in the *National Gazette* suggests the continued marketability of her persona, if not her work, as racist propaganda.

By the nineteenth century, there were several leaders writing against Jefferson's *Notes on the State of Virginia,* including Thomas Clarkson, Henri Grégoire, Gilbert Imlay, and Gabriel Stedman. And, just as black writers Jupiter Hammon and Ignatius Sancho had written pieces in support of Wheatley, the early 1800s revealed black writers, editors, and presses who would keep her poetry in circulation. An unknown publisher in Halifax, Nova Scotia, for example, published Wheatley's volume as an addendum to Olaudah Equiano's *Narrative* in 1813. This Halifax printing marks the first time Wheatley's poetry was packaged and marketed with another African writer. It would be twenty-five years before her volume of poetry appears with another black writer, the poet George Moses Horton. And, it is not until the start of *Freedom's Journal* in 1827 that poetry, articles, and graphics by blacks began appearing together in print.

Jennifer Rene Young

Though she died on December 5, 1784, Wheatley's poetry continued to circulate through volume editions and periodical printings. While Archibald Bell had published the first edition in London in 1773, her first American edition of *Poems* was not reprinted from British presses until a Philadelphia printing in 1785. With the support of the Society of Friends and other organizations, leaders against slavery began to organize and use writers like Wheatley as part of their evidence for African intellectualism and competency. From 1785 to 1816, publishers in London, Boston, and Philadelphia distributed at least six printings of Wheatley's volume. After the 1816 Philadelphia printing, *Poems* would not be reprinted until 1834.[9]

Fifty years after her death, George W. Light, a Boston publisher, turned *Poems* into a new edition. This edition, which was also reprinted in 1835, had a different title from the 1773 volume: *Memoir and Poems of Phillis Wheatley, a Native and African Slave.*[10] Little is known about Mr. Light except that he trusted Margaretta Odell, a Wheatley descendant, to write an authentic biography of the poet. In the introduction to the text, Light writes that Odell is "familiar with the name and fame of Phillis from her childhood" (28).

Odell's biography may be responsible for the majority of myths about Wheatley that still exist today. For instance, Odell speculated, "[Phillis Wheatley] does not seem to have preserved any remembrance of the place of her nativity, or of her parents, excepting the simple circumstance that *her mother poured out water before the sun at his rising*—in reference, no doubt, to an ancient African custom" (Odell 10). This indirect account did not help Wheatley's reputation as a literary poet concerned with pious and patriotic matters. Odell's unintentional mythmaking romanticized the poet's past and minimized her condition in bondage.

Odell's mythmaking also helped create an exemplary image for pro-slavery supporters. She highlighted Wheatley's devotion to her mistress, Susannah, making the poet seem as though she was content with slavery:

> . . . [Wheatley] never for a moment lost sight of that modest, un-
> assuming demeanor, which first won the heart of her mistress in
> the slave market. Indeed, we consider the strongest proof of her
> worth to have been the earnest affection of this excellent woman,
> who admitted her to her own board. Phillis ate of her bread, and
> drank of her cup, and was to her as a daughter. . . . (Odell 11)

One can speculate that Odell exaggerated in this passage, basing her information from either Wheatley's poetry or on stories she heard. On the other hand,

Odell's questionable recollection appears to have some truth. Wheatley did identify her mistress as family at some point. In a letter to John Thornton, a family friend in London, Wheatley wrote about her mistress Susannah who passed away in 1774: "By the great loss I have sustain'd of my best friend, I feel like One forsaken by her parent in a desolate wilderness" (*Complete Writings* 158). Although this letter would not be published until 1864, it supports Odell's assertions. Odell gave readers a sympathetic image of Wheatley's master and mistress. She also suggested that Wheatley had a less difficult life, because she was treated like a servant, not a slave. The kindness that her master showed Wheatley could be demonstrated as a positive, Christian example of slaveholding. If such is the case, these myths could have easily been available to use as positive testimony for slavery.

Odell also identified Phillis as the Wheatley family's favorite slave. She recounted the circumstances of Wheatley's return from visiting with a local Boston family:

> The weather changed during the absence of Phillis, fearful of
> the effects of cold and damp upon her already delicate health,
> [Susannah Wheatley] ordered Prince (also an African and a slave)
> to take the chaise, and bring home her protégée. When the chaise
> returned, the good lady drew near the window, as it approached
> the house, and exclaimed—"Do but look at the saucy varlet—
> if he hasn't the impudence to sit upon the same seat with my
> Phillis!" And poor Prince received a severe reprimand for forget-
> ting the dignity thus kindly, though perhaps to him unaccount-
> ably, attached to the sable person of "my Phillis." (13)

Probably imbued with fictionalizations, this story includes a quotation that Odell would have had to have recalled from her childhood. Published at least twice in a decade, this apocryphal biography would later be accepted as fact by subsequent authors. Though it may have been unintentional, Odell participated in the plantation tradition genre by creating a characterization of a slave too good to associate with other slaves and solely devoted to the family who owned her.

Other portions from Odell's *Memoir* likely proved devastating for Wheatley's poetic persona. The biographer recalled Wheatley's disposition and writing habits, which added to her exceptionality:

Jennifer Rene Young

The light was placed upon a table at her bedside, with writing materials, that if anything occurred to her after she had retired, she might, without rising or taking cold, secure the swift-winged fancy, ere it fled. . . . Mrs. Wheatley did not require or permit her services as a domestic; but she would sometimes allow her to polish a table or dust an apartment; . . . but not infrequently, in these cases, the brush and the duster were soon dropped for the pen, that her meditated verse might not escape her. (Odell 15)

Such differing accounts of Wheatley from Odell and others made her seem peculiar and singular in her role as a Negro poet. Such description could not have been helpful for abolitionists who argued that all slaves—not just special ones—could thrive as free blacks, capable of deciding to stay in America or immigrating to Liberia.

Wheatley's distorted image was also used in a mid-century novel to promote the antislavery movement. Assuming that the "Phillis" of the author's title is a version of Wheatley, the poet was characterized as a docile slave in Mary Henderson Eastman's *Aunt Phillis's Cabin,* written in 1852, the same year as the publication of Harriet Beecher Stowe's *Uncle Tom's Cabin.* Eastman used quotations from *Uncle Tom's Cabin* to advance her arguments on the moral, religious, and economic benefits of slavery. Though her story was not a bestseller like Stowe's, Eastman's *Aunt Phillis's Cabin* gave readers access to a negative image of Phillis Wheatley.[11] As Henry Mayer explains in *All on Fire,* Stowe's novel "spawned a commercial sideshow, [making] Uncle Tom the most frequently sold slave in the country" (427). Because *Uncle Tom's Cabin* was also "popular with racist defenders of slavery" (Mayer 428), texts like *Aunt Phillis's Cabin* further justified the rationale of the slave system. Eastman used Wheatley's namesake to identify the protagonist Phillis, though the character's life did not entirely resemble Wheatley's. Wheatley the poet was, however, well known in the literary marketplace, so readers buying pro-slavery or antislavery periodicals, novels, narratives, and essays would have been aware of her name, if not her poetry. Perhaps Eastman thought of Phillis Wheatley as a contented slave based on the flawed biographies that circulated from press and volume publications about her life. Therefore, if Eastman did construct her character for *Aunt Phillis's Cabin* from Wheatley's persona, she was misled by myths, not facts.

Eastman portrays the character, Phillis, as a content slave on a Virginia plantation. This character is described as a "tall, dignified bright mulatto woman" with twelve kids and a husband, Uncle Bacchus. Wheatley was not a mulatto woman, and the three children she and her husband John Peters cared for after their marriage in 1778 died in infancy. However, the implication could be made that the character "Phillis" was pious, docile, and loyal, characteristics that readers could readily locate in some of Wheatley's poetry or Odell's *Memoir*. In *Aunt Phillis's Cabin*, the fictitious master talks about his favorite slave: "Her price is above rubies. . . . I wish abolitionists would imitate one of her virtues—humility. . . . she is a slave here, but she is destined to be a saint hereafter" (Eastman 137). Wheatley's most famous elegy, "On the Death of George Whitefield," echoes the same sentiment mentioned by the fictitious slave master. In this elegy, Whitefield speaks as if quoted, "Take him, ye *Africans*, he longs for you / *Impartial Saviour* is his title due: / Wash'd in the fountain of redeeming blood, / You shall be sons, and kings, and priests to God" (*Complete Writings* 34–37). Wheatley uses the theme of salvation in her elegies and other poems such as "On Being Brought from Africa to America," "Recollection," and in one of her biblical paraphrases, "Isaiah lxiii. 1–8."

Phillis Wheatley's known loyalty to the Wheatley family which was misconstrued may have influenced Eastman's central figure. Instead of being a progressive leader, fighting with her pen, the character Phillis is a smart slave, content with her future on the plantation. When the character accompanied her master to a "free state" in the union, she encounters abolitionists who are willing to help her. Phillis the literary character responds,

> I want none of your help. My husband and children are at home;
> but if they wasn't I am an honest woman, and am not in the habit
> of *taking* anything. I'll never *take* my freedom. If my master would
> give it to me, and the rest of us, I should be thankful. I am not going
> to begin stealing, and I fifty years of age. (Eastman 103)

This passage has some resemblance to the poet's life. Accompanying her master's son, Nathaniel Wheatley, Wheatley did travel to London in 1773, a year after Lord Mansfield's decision to abolish slavery in the capital city. Despite spending time with abolition lawyer, Granville Sharp, and others who could have influenced her to stay in London, Wheatley returned to Boston to care for her ailing mistress. Also, Wheatley did not flee from her master's home. She was granted her manumission papers sometime in October 1773, a few months before copies of her volume were shipped from London to Boston for sale. She did not move out of her master's house as soon as she was emancipated either. Among other reasons, Wheatley stayed to care for Susannah (Carretta xxxii).

While abolitionists had their own techniques for using Wheatley's persona, the Jeffersonian stigma attached to her led to a new characterization of the poet, which seemed to have been overlooked by some abolitionists. For instance, *Frederick Douglass' Paper* (formerly known as the *North Star*) advertised the release of Eastman's book on September 3, 1852. The advertisement was accompanied by an anonymous literary review: "The story is rather pretty. We have no objection to 'Aunt Phillis.' And as may be imagined, she is the heroine. . . . The story will do neither good nor harm" (Douglass 1990). This review implies that the text is harmless for public consumption. Readers may have seen the correlation, but not the fallacy in Eastman's heroine.

Perhaps "Aunt Phillis" was used to contrast with "Uncle Tom." The editors of *Frederick Douglass' Paper* did not see the damaging representation that *Aunt Phillis's Cabin* had on Phillis Wheatley. Though *Douglass' Paper* did not relate Phillis the character to Phillis Wheatley the poet, the paper focused on validating *Uncle Tom's Cabin*. In defense of abolitionists, the editor writes, "The base attempt, to arraign the veracity of Mrs. Stowe, will, we hope, be dealt with by able pens, as it deserves to be" (Douglass 1990).[12]

In contrast to the poor depictions of Wheatley by those advancing proslavery arguments, Wheatley's work was praised by abolitionists in nineteenth-century newspapers and magazines. In the eighteenth century she was considered an occasional poet of national issues. English abolitionists like Thomas Clarkson and Gabriel Stedman praised her way of attacking American revolutionaries who refused to see the abolition of slavery in the same category as their own fight for independence. In the nineteenth century Wheatley was explicitly used in the abolition movement as an example of African American competence and intelligence.

For instance, Wheatley's "An Hymn to the Morning" was reprinted in three publications: *Freedom's Journal, The Liberator,* and *New England's Magazine.* Perhaps the editors were attracted to Wheatley's combination of classicism and nature. The last four lines of "Hymn to the Morning" reiterate her central point:

> See in the east th'illustrious king of day!
> His rising radiance drives the shades away—
> But Oh! I feel his fervid beams too strong,

And scarce begun, concludes th' abortive song.
(lines 17–20)

The popularity of Wheatley's "Hymn" indicated a demand for lyric poetry. Perhaps the editors selected her poems to demonstrate both their discernment of quality writing and the poet's execution of it.

Wheatley's marketability was particularly sustained by northern publishers and readers, especially in Philadelphia, Boston, and New York. By the early 1820s, outside of Philadelphia, Boston was the location for one of the most active Anti-Slavery Societies in the American colonies; Boston would grow to have an influential Colonization society, and the well-circulated abolition newspaper, *The Liberator*, was based there, though agents for the paper resided all over the country. While New England was an active area for the abolition movement, Wheatley's work was still circulated in other antislavery newspapers like New York's *Weekly Anglo-African*.[13] Publishers and writers used her poetry as proof of moral integrity, which could easily serve as logical reasoning against pro-slavery arguments.

Although most abolitionist journals were owned and operated by white men, there were a few between 1827 and 1865 that were partially or fully owned by black men. Her poetry was reprinted in both white- and black-owned publications. At different times during this period, several black newspapers led the charge in shaping how the abolition movement affected African Americans.[14] For example, John Brown Russwurm and Reverend Samuel E. Cornish published *Freedom's Journal* (1827–29) in New York. As the first black newspaper in America, the editors aimed to have a paper written by blacks for blacks. As the editors expressed, " . . . that a paper devoted to the dissemination of useful knowledge among our brethren, and to their moral and religious improvement, must meet with cordial approbation of every friend to humanity . . ." (Russwurm 1990). Proud of the poet's work, editors from *Freedom's Journal* printed Wheatley's biography on March 23, 1827, in addition to lines from her elegy, "On the Death of J.C. an Infant," and lines from "Hymn to the Morning." On November 9, 1827, the entire poem of "Hymn to Humanity" was printed, and *Freedom's Journal* published a letter on November 2, 1827, entitled "Letter, no. V to Rev. Samuel E. Cornish." Cornish had received the letter from one of his correspondents in Liberia.[15] The letter reads,

[Wheatley] has left behind her small volume of poems, as a rich legacy to our race; . . . if our brethren here, do not feel able or

Jennifer Rene Young

willing to erect a monument, let a general contribution be made
by us through the Union—let us evince to the world that we are
not insensible to the fame and renown which her writings have
conferred upon us—that we are proud of them. (Russwurm,
Freedom's Journal, vol. 1)

Though we do not know the writer's identity for certain, the letter was identified as one from Liberia's capital city, Monrovia. One may infer that the writer
is black, because he identifies Wheatley as a "member of our race." This letter
is similar to the public accolades Wheatley received from Ignatius Sancho and
Jupiter Hammon. The posthumous publication *Letters of the Late Ignatius
Sancho, An African* appeared in London in 1782. In one of those letters, Sancho
celebrates Wheatley's ability to "put art—merely as art—to the blush" (125).[16]
Also, Hammon praises Wheatley in his 1778 broadside, "An Address to . . .
an Ethiopian Poetess." This adulation happens again as Reverend Cornish receives correspondence from another black leader who positions Wheatley in
the same category as other black achievers.

In addition to her poems and biographical sketch, Wheatley was featured
in an article reprinted in *Freedom's Journal* from the *Abolition Intelligencer* on
May 18, 1827. The article, "The Surprising Influence of Prejudice," argued for
an end to slavery. The writer named several black intellectuals who had benefited from emancipation. Taken from the Bishop of France Henri Grégoire's
An Enquiry Concerning the Intellectual and Moral Faculties, the writer listed
several important blacks, including Antony Amo, Job Ben Solomon, James
Capitein, Toussaint L'Ouverture, and Phillis Wheatley.[17]

First published in 1789 in French, *An Enquiry* would not be translated until
1791 by a London publisher. By 1810, *An Enquiry* went through at least three
editions. Grégoire was interested in Wheatley's career earlier than most abolitionists. For instance, he composed biographical comments about Wheatley
in 1808 although scholarship later proved the biography to be false. His mistakes—concerning the poet's birth date, manumission date, year of marriage,
and death date—were translated from French into English, and the press continued to reprint these errors. Despite these errors, however, it is significant
that "An Hymn to Morning," "On the Death of J.C an Infant," and "To the
Earl of Dartmouth" were translated into French. Grégoire wrote, "I insert here
three of her pieces. The reader would do well to remember that, in judging the
works of a nineteen-year-old slave girl, indulgence would be an act of justice.
Besides, the translation is perhaps only a bad copy of a good original" (51).

Nevertheless, these three transactions no doubt multiplied the international readers who experienced Phillis Wheatley.

Grégoire admonished Jefferson for identifying Wheatley as inferior to her white, male contemporaries:

> Jefferson, who appears unwilling to acknowledge the talents of
> Negroes, even those of Phillis Wheatley, pretends that the heroes
> of the Dunciad are divinities, when compared with this African
> muse. If we were disposed to cavil, we might say, that to an as-
> sertion, it is sufficient to oppose a contrary assertion; we might
> appeal to the judgment of the public, which is manifested by the
> collection made of the poetry of Phillis Wheatley. (237)

Grégoire encouraged his readers to investigate Jefferson's claims by actually reading Wheatley's poetry as opposed to reading about it in biased sources. He wanted individuals not only to see Wheatley's work for what it is, but also to recognize the intellectual limits that oppression of slavery had on its victims.

Grégoire also acknowledged Wheatley's Christian values, and he commended her for showing her faith through her poetry: "Almost all her poetical productions have a religious or moral cast—all breathe a soft and sentimental melancholy. . . . We are particularly pleased with her odes on the works of Providence, on virtue, on humanity, to Neptune, to a young painter, of her own color" (238).

In the efforts to liberate the poet from derision, he refers to Wheatley's educational background: "Passionately fond of reading, and delighting in the perusal of the scriptures, she rapidly attained knowledge of the Latin language" (Grégoire 235). For those who doubted her originality, an issue called into prominence by the pro-slavery comments on Wheatley, Grégoire added:

> It was doubtless her acquaintance with the works of Horace,
> that induced her to commence like him with an Ode to Macenas
> [sic] whose protection poets secured by flattery. Their baseness
> throws a veil over his Augustus, by the same means, buried in
> oblivion the horrors of the Triumvirate. Phillis in this piece
> reminds us that Terence was her compatriot. It is not without
> merit; but we hasten to subjects more worthy of her muse. (238)

He combated Thomas Jefferson's earlier insistence that Wheatley and Ignatius Sancho were not capable of originality; they could only imitate (like parrots).

Jennifer Rene Young

Grégoire argued patronage as a central issue in "To Maecenas." He knew that Wheatley was not seeking the kind of protection and dependence that Horace once sought by means of flattery from the historical Maecenas. Her work with imagination and the sublime suggested Wheatley's desire to be a profound poet of reason, emotion, and logic. Grégoire attempted to qualify Wheatley as an intellectual and to negate arguments that suggest African abnormality. By providing a list of examples that pertain to her work as a religious poet, Grégoire acknowledged one of the marketing strategies that Wheatley constructed for herself.

Two other black-owned newspapers reprinted Wheatley's poetry: Philip A. Bel's *The Coloured American* (1837–41) and Frederick Douglass's *North Star* (1847–51), later renamed *Frederick Douglass' Paper* (1851–59). *Douglass' Paper* published "Hymn to Humanity" on August 31, 1855, along with "On Being Brought from Africa to America" and "Ode to Neptune."[18] Though primarily interested in the abolition of slavery, these newspaper publishers used Wheatley as an example of "mental and moral improvement." Black writers were beginning to be appreciated by the larger literary world as valuable contributors to American literature. The publications of black writers in the nineteenth century added to the exposure of African American achievement, which in turn helped maintain a positive reputation of Phillis Wheatley.[19]

Almost all of Wheatley's poems from her volume were published in 1832 in *The Liberator,* from 1831 to 1865. Published by Isaac Knapp who also published editions of Wheatley's volume, *The Liberator* was influential with agents across the country, particularly in Maine, Massachusetts, Vermont, Connecticut, New York, Delaware, New Jersey, Pennsylvania, Ohio, and Indiana, as well as in upper Canada, the British Dominions, Haiti, Liberia, and England. Worldwide reports on oppressed peoples were reprinted in that weekly newspaper. Thomas Hachey notes in *Voices of Revolution* that *The Liberator*'s circulation numbered no more than three thousand subscribers and that one-fourth of the subscribers were white (232).

Despite this low number of subscribers, readers often shared subscriptions, an act that added to the newspaper's appeal and increased the cultural circulation of Wheatley. *The Liberator* printed original letters and speeches debating the antislavery struggle across the nation. Many newspapers, including the *New York Times,* the *Emancipationist* (published by the Boston American Antislavery Society), the *Friend of Man* (published by the New York Antislavery Society) and *Liberia Herald* (the official newspaper for the newly formed African colony of Liberia) reprinted excerpts of letters from abolition-ist circles.[20] Pro-slavery presses like Washington, D.C.'s *National Intelligencer* also reprinted letters verbatim that were first in the pages of *The Liberator.* Raised Baptist and temporarily affiliated with the Friends, William Lloyd Garrison was committed to representing many sides of the abolitionist issue.[21] Though Wheatley's poetry did not have overt messages of abolition, Garrison probably reprinted her poetry as evidence of African capabilities.

Wheatley's poetry in *The Liberator* appeared in the backdrop of the grow-ing national debate of "free states" versus "slave states." Poet William Cullen Bryant expressed his discontent with the "plantation discipline" set forth by national laws. Appalled by the collective conscience of the Senate, Bryant wrote in the *New York Evening Post,* "Has it come to this, that we must speak with bated breath in the presence of our Southern masters?" (Mayer 453). Not grouped with hack writers, Wheatley's poetry appeared alongside poems like "The African Chief" by William Cullen Bryant, "The Fair Quakeress" by John Greenleaf Whittier, "Prison Sonnet" by Garrison, and "Childhood" by Mrs. Ann Maria Wells.[22] Serious about their craft and the significance of their words, these writers spoke out against oppression. The caliber of their work positioned Wheatley's persona in a positive venue. As Garrison wrote in his inaugural issue:

> I am aware that many object to the severity of my language; but is there not cause for severity? I *will be* as harsh as truth, and as uncompromising as justice. On this subject [of slavery] I do not wish to think, or speak, or write with moderation. No! No! Tell a man whose house is on fire, to give a moderate alarm; tell him to moderately rescue his wife from the hands of the ravisher; tell the mother to gradually extricate her babe from the fire into which it has fallen; but urge me not to use moderation in a cause like the present. (Vol. 1: 1n)

Garrison vowed to keep all of his articles at this level of urgency. On a weekly basis in 1832 almost all of Wheatley's poems from the 1773 volume appeared in the "Literary" section of *The Liberator.* Garrison included her poetry to continue the abolition strategies of moral reasoning, sympathy, African intel-lect, and inalienable rights.

Wheatley's poem "To Maecenas" was her first poem published in *The Liberator*'s literary section on February 11, 1832. In addition to being first in publication order for the 1773 volume, one may infer that "Maecenas" was chosen for its many classical allusions, its popularity, and its reference to the ancient black Roman poet, Terence. Furthermore, the poetic voice in "To Maecenas" pleads for literary recognition and praise. *The Liberator* editors granted Wheatley this aspiration by starting the column with her words. No biographical information was added. By 1832, Wheatley was a known poet, so the editors may not have felt the need to attach an explanation to her poem. Instead, the poem was printed with "Lament for the Slave," a poem by local Bostonian Alonzo Lewis.

Not until the next issue of *The Liberator* did the editor identify Wheatley as a former slave. Her poem in this February 18 issue was, "On Virtue," to which a footnote was attached to her last name:

> 'Sir, in my country—a land not destitute of poets, as we believe,
> —an African woman, the well known Phillis Wheatley, has pro-
> duced a volume of poetry, which while it displays want of educa-
> tion, and was written at hours stolen from the labors of slavery,
> and was the production of a mind weighed down by the shackles
> of servitude—for almost every poem commences with a lamenta-
> tion of her enslaved and abject condition—stands almost as the
> head of the poetry of the age in which it was produced.'
> —Speech of Samuel L. Knapp, Esq. (Vol. 2: 28n7)

Samuel L. Knapp, author of the first cultural history of the United States, *American Cultural History, 1607–1829* (1829), reminded readers of Wheatley's astuteness to express her views on liberation. According to Knapp, Wheatley served as an exemplar for the antislavery argument since she desired liberation for the country and for her own "abject condition." By reprinting this informa-tion, the editors of *The Liberator* reminded their readers of Wheatley's perse-verance, artistry, and aptitude.

Wheatley was published with another black poet in *The Liberator*. "An Hymn to the Morning" appeared with "Lines" from the black journalist Maria Stewart. Published on May 19, 1832, both poems discuss a degree of mental freedom that can exist, regardless of one's physical state.[23] The first part of "Lines" contains a quotation from the Bible. The verse reads, "Verily, I say unto you, it shall be more tolerable for the land of Sodom and Gomorrah, in the Day of Judgment, than for that city" (*Liberator* vol. 20, page 80). After the biblical passage, Stewart's four lines follow:

I all their rage and malice do despise,
For God my Saviour reigns above the skies;
On Him I will rely, in Him I'll trust,
Until this form of mine shall turn to kindred dust.

Stewart is the only known black literary poet, aside from Wheatley, to be published in the "Literary" section of *The Liberator* for 1832.[24] It is also important to note here that Wheatley's "Hymn" poem is published separately in volume 33, number 49, December 4, 1863, along with the popular poem "Thoughts on the Works of Providence." Garrison's decision to publish black writers together proved his belief that poetry by blacks was just as good as that by whites.

In volume 2, issue 7, of *The Liberator*, Abigail Mott wrote "A Short Account of Phillis Wheatley." Mott (1766–1851) included Wheatley in two of her books, *Biographical Sketches and Interesting Anecdotes of Persons of Colour. To Which is Added, a Selection of Pieces in Poetry* (1826) and the posthumous 1875 publication, *Narratives of Colored Americans*. Mott's biography included some incorrect information about the poet: "[The harsh treatment by her husband] affected her susceptible mind, and delicate constitution; she soon went into a decline, and died in 1780, about the 26th year of her age, much lamented by those who knew her worth" (*Liberator* 2: 28n7). Contrary to the information above, Wheatley died at the approximate age of thirty-one, on December 5, 1784. There was also not enough evidence to label John Peters as irresponsible, though the press amplified and reinforced this myth. Aside from Wheatley's alleged marital problems, Mott conveyed Wheatley's poetry in a way that supported the abolition of slavery. Lines from "To the Earl of Dartmouth" were reprinted in this biographical sketch. Mott wanted readers to know where Wheatley's "love of Freedom sprung" (line 21). Wheatley did not want others to feel the "tyrannic sway" (line 30) of slavery, which motivated her to write for change. Mott successfully characterized this revolutionary side of Wheatley, though most of the half-column article carried more myths than truths.

Wheatley's reputation and poetry were used in *The Liberator* to promote the abolitionist agenda in many forms. As a female poet, she dismantled the patriarchal element of literature by appearing as one of the few females in the "Literary Column" of this newspaper. Her religious slant contributed positively to the argument that Africans could reason. She often professed her Christianity. In "On Being Brought from Africa to America," the speaker commands the reader to "Remember, *Christians*, *Negros* [sic], black as *Cain*, /

Jennifer Rene Young

may be refin'd, and join th' angelic train" (*Complete Writings* 13). Also in "Thoughts on the Works of Providence," the speaker mentions God or some version of the divine close to two dozen times in the thirteen-line, multistanza poem. The speaker cries, "When wants and woes might be our righteous lot, / Our God forgetting, by our God forgot!" (*Complete Writings* 28). Wheatley used her belief system to combat the immoral slave laws and the masters who blindly followed them. Her life story may have served as propaganda for the newspaper's cause. Abolitionists needed funds for Sabbath schools, temperance societies, the Anti-Slavery Society, the Convention for Colored Delegates, and other public-interest groups. By publishing Wheatley's poems and her life story, people from around the world were encouraged to sympathize with the abolitionist cause, and in turn to help the movement in some way.

Despite the myths about Wheatley's life, the poet's image was renewed when in 1838 Isaac Knapp published an edition of Wheatley's poetry alongside the first published African American male poet: George Moses Horton (ca. 1798–1880), a slave from Raleigh, North Carolina. Entitled *Memoir and Poems of Phillis Wheatley, a Native African and a Slave—Also, Poems by a Slave,* Horton's twenty-one poems were originally entitled *The Hope of Liberty* when it was first published in Carolina by the secretary of the American Colonization Society, Joseph Gales, in 1829 (Horton 15). The title was changed to *Poems by a Slave* when two Philadelphia abolitionists published it in 1831. Divided into two sections, the first half of the book was a reprint of Wheatley's original volume; the second half contained Horton's memoir and third edition of poetry.

Neither the title page nor the table of contents indicated that Horton was the anonymous author of *Poems by a Slave.* Readers could not discover the author of that section of the book until they reached page 119. Even though Horton's poetry had been previously published in *Freedom's Journal* and *The Liberator,* editors used Wheatley's persona to promote and to endorse Horton. Indicating that she had "arrived" as a poet in the black literary canon, Wheatley's name was used to draw buyers to the text.

The editor's "explanation" in George Horton's book resembles John Wheatley's 1773 "Letter to the Publisher" that was printed on behalf of Wheatley. Horton's editors explain, "George knows how to read, and is learning to write. All his pieces are written down by others" (Knapp 120–21). By 1838, Isaac Knapp no longer worked with Garrison on *The Liberator,* yet he continued to publish abolitionist material. To endorse Horton, Knapp integrated his abolitionist position into his introductory comments:

Many persons have now become much interested in the promotion of his prospects, some of whom are elevated in office and
literary attainments. They are solicitous that efforts at length be
made to obtain by subscription, a sum sufficient for his emancipation, upon the condition of his going in the vessel, which shall
first afterwards sail for Liberia. It is his earnest and only wish to
become a member of that Colony, to enjoy its privileges, and apply
his industry and mental abilities to the promotion of its prospects
and his own. It is upon these terms alone, that the efforts of those
who befriend his views are intended to have a final effect. (119)

The passage was propaganda for colonization. The editor explained that the
sales from this text were to go toward the price of manumitting Horton and
deporting him to Liberia. Though Wheatley's poetry and persona are used
to reach a wider audience that may have sympathized with Horton's enslaved
condition, he did not raise enough money to buy his liberty. Despite several
attempts to secure his freedom, Horton would not be freed until 1865 when
he was almost seventy years old.[25] Wheatley's and Horton's poems could
have been considered a text in support of abolition since the volume included
poems such as "To Maecenas," "Farewell to America," and "To the Earl of
Dartmouth," and poems by Horton including "On Liberty and Slavery" and
"The Slave's Complaint."

Wheatley had another editor in this period who respected her attempt to
write belles lettres. George Duyckinck supported Wheatley by including her
poetry in his 1856 *Cyclopaedia of American Literature*.[26] The encyclopedia
was first printed in two volumes of two thousand pages under the direction
of George Duyckinck. After George died, his brother Evert Jr. updated and
published the *Cyclopedia of American Literature* again in 1866. Relinquishing
editorial control in 1872, Evert Duyckinck served an advisory role to the editions and proprietors of the third edition, which appeared in 1875. A brief biographical sketch, Wheatley's frontispiece from the 1773 *Poems* and excerpts of
her poetry were printed in these editions. In his preface, George Duyckinck
holds that

The poems themselves show as marked indications of the feeding-
grounds of the readers and imitators of verse in the eighteenth
century, as do those of Mistress Anne Bradstreet in the seventeenth. What in the earlier day was quaint, rude, and daring, in

Jennifer Rene Young

the latter is smooth, sounding and fluent. . . . Phillis Wheatley is
a very respectable echo of the Papal strains. (Duyckinck 382)

Identifying the poet as an imitator of Alexander Pope, Duyckinck commended
the author for writing "To Maecenas," saying: "[Phillis Wheatley] writes of
Homer with an eloquence evidently derived from the glowing translation of the
bright-eyed little man at Twickenham" (382). As John Wheatley mentioned in
his 1773 "Preface," Wheatley had studied Latin. Mr. Wheatley suggested that
Phillis read classical texts in the original Latin to help her further understand
authorial intentions of classical authors. Duyckinck may have mentioned her
educational background to confirm Wheatley's belonging in the encyclopedia.

Wheatley was part of this literary history because her poetry was published
and distributed in the middle of political debates about America's system of
slavery. George Duyckinck also explained the objectives of his *Cyclopaedia*
project:

> The history of the literature of the country involved in the pages
> of this work, is not so much an exhibition of art and invention,
> of literature in its immediate and philosophical sense, as a record
> of mental progress and cultivation, of facts and opinions, which
> derives its main interest from its historical, rather than its critical
> value. It is important to know what books have been produced,
> and by whom; whatever the books may have been, or whoever
> the men. (v)

Duyckinck provides readers with a sample of what he calls "American cultivation." He believed in publishing a variety of work from a diverse lot of writers,
who lived and wrote in America whether they were born in the country or elsewhere. Duyckinck saw Wheatley as not only American, but as a writer who deserved to be published in the encyclopedia alongside well-known writers such as
Thomas Paine, Benjamin Rush, Philip Freneau, and Thomas Jefferson. Women
writers were also included, namely Anne Bradstreet, Ann Eliza Bleecker, Lydia
Sigourney, Sarah J. Hale, and Mercy Otis Warren. The editor chose authors
who were either well known or whose works were often read.[27]

Wheatley's presence in the text suggested her value as a celebrity. The editor provided a brief biography to show the poet's significance:

> Among the attentions which [she] received in London was the
> gift from the Lord Mayor Brook Watson, of a copy of Foulis's

folio Glasgow edition of *Paradise.Lost,* which was sold after her death, in payment of her husband's debts. It is now preserved in the library of Harvard College at Cambridge. (Duyckinck 381)

Not only did readers learn of her upper-class connections, but the biographer applauded Wheatley's accomplishments. To justify her presence in the *Cyclopaedia,* he emphasized that she was known by British royalty and that her poetry was housed at Harvard College. In other parts of this *Cyclopaedia* entry, Duyckinck revealed his admiration for Wheatley. He indicated that she had "a few good lines" in "Niobe in Distress," noting lines 107 and 108 of the poem. He added, "there is one line which would do honor to any pen":

> With clouds incompass'd glorious Phoebus stands
> The feather'd vengeance quiv'ring in his hands. (384)

This segment of "Niobe" occurred right before Apollo's slaughter of Niobe's sons. Duyckinck commented that Wheatley had "touch[es] of the poetic flight" within her verses.

Duyckinck's *Cyclopaedia* reprinted the following poems by Phillis Wheatley: "Liberty and Peace," "To the University of Cambridge," "On the Death of the Reverend Dr. Sewall," "On the Death of George Whitefield," and "Farewell to America." The editor also included the printing of Wheatley's correspondence with George Washington, the first publication to do so. Before the *Cyclopaedia,* only Wheatley's letter and poem to Washington had been printed.[28] Though he did not offer an extensive critique of Wheatley's poetry, Duyckinck was impressed by her work, as he included so many pieces.

As her poetry continued to be published in the later 1800s, Wheatley became a subject of scholarly interest. With three editions of the *Cyclopedia,* the poet's literary exposure in America was also reestablished by Charles Deane, who edited *Letters of Phillis Wheatley* in association with the Massachusetts Historical Society in 1864. Identified as "The Negro Poet of Boston," Wheatley was credited in this book's editorial notes for her achievements. Deane's publication of her letters during the abolition movement supported the poet's importance as a figure of change and freedom. This publication demonstrated Wheatley's marketable value. Her popularity was so great that Wheatley's most private correspondences were considered noteworthy.

According to the reverse side of the title page, one thousand copies of *Letters* were printed for private use. In his notes, Deane acknowledged the

Jennifer Rene Young

Massachusetts Historical Society for sponsoring the project. He shared his excitement and pleasure in editing the collection: "[the letters] indicate much maturity of mind, and refinement and delicacy of feeling and character" (Wheatley, *Letters* 2). He promoted the poet as a flexible writer, one who could create art through letters, not just poetry.

Deane focused on the epistolary aesthetic of Wheatley's portfolio. Although few of her letters had been published before 1864, Deane was the first editor to publish an entire collection of her letters, which were all addressed to Wheatley's confidant, Obour Tanner. The emotion in the letters was reminiscent of the posthumous praise Ignatius Sancho gave Wheatley in 1784. Now that her letters were published, readers would be able to associate her with her contemporary Sancho, aside from Thomas Jefferson's derogatory comments. Deane did provide some insight into Wheatley's letter recipient, Obour: "[These letters] are addressed to a Negro friend in Newport, R.I. . . . probably serving in the same capacity as Phillis herself; and, from some expressions in the first letter, it may be inferred that they were both brought from Africa, and perhaps at the same time" (Wheatley, *Letters* 7). Deane participated in mythmaking by estimating the arrival of Wheatley and Tanner. Still, both women were survivors of the mid-Atlantic slave trade, a gruesome reality that could have strengthened their connection. Not only did the letters show their art of writing, but it also demonstrated their bond during uncertain times of slavery and the Revolutionary period.

The publication contained introductory comments as well as extensive footnotes on the provenance of Wheatley's letters. The footnotes and introduction further aided Deane's argument. Of the letters, Deane said the following at a meeting of the Massachusetts Historical Society in 1863:

> I have thought it desirable that they should somehow be preserved; for, so far as my observation extends, but few letters of this remarkable person are extant. [With the exception of the letter to Washington] . . . What judgment, therefore, has hitherto been formed of her literary attainments, and of the strength and general culture of her intellect, must have been derived chiefly from her poems. At a moment, too, when so much attention is drawn to the colored race, I feel that I need not apologize for occupying so much of the time of members as to call their attention to the letters of one of his class (who, nearly a century ago,

was the object of so much attraction both here and in England), and to read some portion of them to the meeting. (Wheatley, *Letters* 6–7)

Deane enumerated Wheatley's career publications and achievements. He believed that readers of Wheatley would have a better sense of this African American artist's spiritual character and political objectives through access to her letters. Not only did he remind the society members of Wheatley's letter to Washington, but he also acknowledged the public accolades that Wheatley received in London and Boston. With sponsorship from the historical society and his description of Wheatley's "famous reception" in London, Deane called attention to her life as a celebrated African poet. The Massachusetts Historical Society's decision to publish letters that one eighteenth-century servant wrote to another servant suggests the letter writer's literary merit.

While some literary critics wanted to compare the work of black writers to their white counterparts for abolitionist causes, other critics began to recognize, as the nineteenth century progressed, the difference in aesthetic accomplishment depending upon the writer's ethnicity and lived experiences. As many scholars have already noted, Wheatley's poetry was so marketable that it certainly contributed to the formation of the African American literary genre. By the late nineteenth century, writers like Charlotte Forten, Frederick Douglass, and Martin Delaney read and attempted to understand Wheatley's objectives. She was characterized as a competent and skillful writer by both the white and black presses. In the antebellum decades following her death, those who printed her poetry dictated how she would be perceived. Despite the turbulence of the slavery debates, Wheatley's image and poetry did not suffer too terribly. Editors and their well-intentioned representations helped keep Wheatley's work in circulation and her persona in high esteem, hence encouraging editors of literary anthologies and critics of African American literature to promote the work of Phillis Wheatley.

NOTES

1. William Robinson's *Phillis Wheatley: A Bio-Bibliography* delineates Wheatley's publication history. Additional information came from archival sources, namely the *Accessible Archives Database* and the *English Short Title Catalog* (ESTC). I accessed these databases from the New York Public Library and the Schomburg Center for Research in Black Culture (SC) during a Hope College–sponsored summer research fellowship. I remain grateful for that support and the mentorship and funding provided by my doctoral-granting institution, Howard University.

2. In "The Tongues of the Learned Are Insufficient," Christopher Felker names Susannah Wheatley and Selina Hastings as two of the "six principal figures" who were responsible for the 1773 volume of *Poems*. The others named were Lord Dartmouth, John Thornton, booksellers Cox & Berry, and London printer Archibald Bell.

3. See the first stanza of Wheatley's poem "On Imagination" (1773) in *Complete Writings*. Lines 9–12 read: "Now here, now there, the roving *Fancy* flies / Till some lov'd objects strikes her wand'ring eyes / Whose silken *fetters* all the senses bind / And soft *captivity* involves the mind." All subsequent quotations are taken from Carretta's *Phillis Wheatley: The Complete Writings*.

4. Similar to Richard Nisbet, Thomas Jefferson argued that the existence of educated indentured servants was not reason enough to abolish slavery. First published in London in 1782, Jefferson's *Notes on the State of Virginia* underwent at least five editions before the end of the eighteenth century. According to the *English Short Title Catalogue* (ESTC), Jefferson's *Notes* was published in London (1782, 1787), Paris (1784), Philadelphia (1788, 1794), and Baltimore (1800).

5. As an American patriot, Isaiah Thomas supported Wheatley by printing her poems in his magazine. The *Massachusetts Spy* eventually became a part of Thomas's printing company. Thomas (1749–1831) sold books in Worcester and Boston, Massachusetts. He advertised *The Massachusetts Spy* as "free and uninfluenced." As described in his 1791 proposals for an authorized American English Bible, Isaiah Thomas wanted "[to appeal] to Christians of Every Denomination" (ESTC micro 35mm). For Thomas, Wheatley qualified as Christian with something valuable to say. Aware of the slave system, Thomas did not use those barriers to exclude Wheatley's

voice. As Hugh Amory explains in "Reinventing the Colonial Book," Isaiah Thomas was one of the early printers to try to combine printing, binding, ink printing, and bookselling into one publishing business (54).

6. The book *Poems on Comic, Serious, and Moral Subjects* was marketed as the second edition to Wheatley's original 1773 volume, although textual evidence in the advertisements showed the actual year of publication as January 1, 1787 (SC Micro R-961.C). In some ways, this second edition's title undermines Wheatley's original intentions for discourse on religion, patriotism, and human rights.

7. The author of *Grub Street,* Pat Rogers referred to J. French's edition *Poems on Comic* as part of a "milieu of dunce hood" (277).

8. Predominately published in Philadelphia and New York, Freneau (1752–1832) was considered the most famous patriot poet of his time. Freneau's newspaper reported on issues concerning the development of the country. See Freneau's numerous publications in the *English Short Title Catalog* (ESTC).

9. See William Robinson's detailed account of Wheatley's volume publications and published poems in periodicals in *Bio-Bibliography.*

10. Publisher and editor George W. Light writes, "the author of this Memoir is a collateral descendant of Mrs. Wheatley" (29). Odell is said to have gathered information from her grandmother who supposedly knew Wheatley (Light 28). Identifying the *Memoir* author as Margaretta Odell, scholars like Julian Mason and William Robinson discuss the lasting effects of Wheatley's incorrect biographers (Mason xi; Robinson, "Quandry" xii). See Mason's *Poems of Phillis Wheatley* and Robinson's "Phillis Wheatley: Colonial Quandary."

11. While *Uncle Tom's Cabin* sold approximately three hundred thousand copies in its first year (1852), Eastman's *Aunt Phillis's Cabin* only sold between twenty thousand and thirty thousand copies. *Uncle Tom's Cabin* sold ten thousand copies within a week, one hundred thousand in ten weeks, and three hundred thousand by the end of the year. The text underwent many British editions in the 1850s; it was also translated into every European language, doubling the total sales (Mayer 420). For more statistics, see Henry Mayer's *All on Fire* (New York: St. Martin's Press, 1998).

12. *Douglass' Paper* does include Wheatley in other articles. In particular, Wheatley is included in "Our Literature" on September 23, 1853, and

"Origin, History and Hopes of the Negro Race," which was published on January 27, 1854. Another response to *Uncle Tom's Cabin* is discussed in *Douglass' Paper.* The text, *Uncle Tom's Cabin as it is,* is given a poor review. Published on October 15, 1852, the editors called the book "miserably bad" and filled with "'nigger talk,' pointless and prosy" (Douglass 1990).

13. Known for closely following the John Brown case, the editors of this publication once remarked, "State-breaking is a new species of crime. A burglar breaks into your house to steal your goods, but John Brown broke into Virginia 'to bring stolen goods out of the state'" (Mayer 495).

14. Although Wheatley does not appear in all of the black abolition newspapers, Donald Jacobs's *Antebellum Black Newspapers* is a resourceful guide for finding where and when black authors are published.

15. It is unclear whether this letter to Rev. Samuel Cornish in *Freedom's Journal* came from John Brown Russwurm. Russwurm did leave the newspaper around 1830. Changing his mind about the principles behind colonization, Russwurm decided to immigrate to Liberia, where he became an active leader in Monrovia's government. See also Mary Sagarin's *John Brown Russwurm: The Story of Freedom's Journal, Freedom's Journey.*

16. Ignatius Sancho, who lived and died in England, served as a high-ranking butler to one of England's dignitaries, and he later ran a grocery store that catered to an elite clientele. As a letter writer, Sancho corresponded with servants, gentry, and aristocrats in England, America, and India. Though he and Wheatley did not meet, Sancho was aware of her work, as evident in the *Letters of the Late Ignatius Sancho,* which was printed in London in 1782, 1783, and 1784. Because Sancho was popular in his own right, his comments about Wheatley continued to circulate after she died. Sancho's praise for Wheatley was in accordance with others in abolitionist presses.

Sancho's letter LVII to Fisher also discussed his concern for Wheatley as a slave. He called Wheatley's master, John Wheatley, hypocritical for publishing the works of the poet, but for not emancipating her. Wheatley had been free for almost five years by the time Sancho wrote the letter in 1778, but reprints of Wheatley's volume did not indicate her emancipation. Supporters like Sancho did not see Wheatley as simply Boston's adopted protégé, but was looked to by abolitionists as proof of the ends of slavery and by fellow blacks—such as Sancho and Jupiter Hammon—as a flag bearer for their race. See Sancho, *Letters.*

17. Grégoire dedicated a chapter in his text to fifteen African intellects from ancient and contemporary Colonial times. See his chapter on black literature and the arts in *An enquiry concerning the intellectual and moral faculties.*

18. On June 8, 1839, and October 2, 1841, Wheatley's poems appeared in the black newspaper, *The Coloured American.* Published in New York like *Freedom's Journal,* they are not reprinted in these issues, but she is mentioned as an example of black skin not having a "destructive affinity with the mind" (*American,* October 2, 1841). Her letter to Joshua Coffin was printed in John Greenleaf Whittier's *Pennsylvania Freeman* before it appeared in *The Coloured American* on June 8, 1839. See *Accessible Archives Database.*

19. For further discussion on the cultural developments of literature, see John Guillory's *Cultural Capital* or David Hall's *Cultures of Print.*

20. *The African Repository* (started in 1825) was the official magazine of the American Colonization Society (started in 1816). The American Constitution banned the international slave trade in 1808. British antislavery forces sought parallel action and established the British colony, Sierra Leone, while Americans established the colony of Liberia.

21. Originally a supporter of colonization, Garrison eventually rejected the notion of African reparation by relocating blacks in Liberia. His newspaper printed comments from the American Colonization Society (ACS), but once Garrison learned of the hardships it caused, he did not continue to support ACS practices. Nonetheless, Garrison reported the details of colonization in his pages. In *Of One Blood: Abolitionism and the Origins of Racial Equality,* Paul Goodman explains the solution devised for the growing "free black" citizenship in Europe and America. With federally mandated military patrols off the African coast, Great Britain and America attempted to stop the international slave trade by "bringing West Africa under Anglo-American influence" (Goodman 15). In the decades to follow this establishment, the ACS worked with the federal government toward purifying America. In response to the domestic threat that free blacks posed to the slave system, federal laws continued to make living very difficult for free blacks in America. Once Garrison was educated on the politics of antislavery—particularly by the education of blacks who supplied him with the arguments and back issues of the *African Repository,* a monthly magazine released by the New York Antislavery Society—Garrison used the pages of the *Liberator* to unmask the evils of colonization.

To borrow Paul Goodman's terms, Garrison used his publication to convert whites from "gradualism to immediatism" and from "colonization to emancipation" (Goodman 54). Garrison's 1832 *Thoughts on African Colonization* argued that "colonization strengthened slavery while defaming and degrading free blacks" (Goodman 56). Gradualism was the belief that blacks could eventually become free after a term of service. Immediatism was the belief in total abolition, free of any servant obligation. The *Liberator* had articles and letters that argued for emancipation without the "[removal] of tens of thousands of free blacks to an undeveloped region in Africa thousands of miles away" (Goodman 16). Phillis Wheatley's poetry appeared in the press during a time when free states were trying to expand and slave states attempted to extend their power and wealth structure, which was largely maintained by slave labor and the cotton industry.

22. Bryant's poem was published in the *Liberator* in vol. 1, no. 3, p. 11; Whittier was published in vol. 1, no. 4, p. 16. Poems by Garrison and Ann Maria Wells appeared in many issues. The one I refer to is from vol. 1, no 6, p. 24. In his 1846 *Voices of Freedom,* John Greenleaf Whittier reportedly dedicated a poem to Garrison's relentless pursuit for slave emancipation. See Mayer, 349. Other writers included in the *Liberator* are Henry Wadsworth Longfellow, Alonzo Lewis, J. J. Snelling, Lord Byron, Shakespeare, Hannah F. Gould, and Ettrick Shephard. Lewis, who was the second vice president of the Anti-Slavery Society, was also a schoolmaster and mapmaker. Snelling wrote an article on Wheatley later in his career. As contemporaries of Garrison, Lewis's and Snelling's poems also appear in vol. 2 of the *Liberator.*

23. Maria Stewart (1803–1879) was a journalist, essayist, and orator. Author of *Meditations,* Stewart often wrote of African female liberation within the confines of temperance. She wrote for the *Liberator* from 1831 to 1833 under the heading "Ladies' Department." The graphic for the column showed a lady in chains with a caption above her head: "Am I not a woman and a sister?" Like the abolitionist slogan, Stewart encouraged women to strengthen their communities by starting their own businesses. As one of the first female public speakers, Stewart is known for giving a public speech in Boston in 1831. She acknowledged one of her mentors as journalist David Walker, writer of *Appeal in Four Articles.* See *Maria W. Stewart: Essays and Speeches,* edited by Marilyn Richardson (Indiana UP, 1987).

24. Other black writers besides Maria Stewart and Wheatley may have been published in 1832, but initials or pseudonyms masked their names.

Though Wheatley's poetry is not in the 1833 volume of the *Liberator* (vol. 3), several poems by George Horton are reprinted in those issues. *Aesop's Fables* were sometimes published in the "Moral" section of the *Liberator,* and the *Narrative of Chloe Spears,* writer unknown, was published throughout vol. 3 in the "Juvenile Department."

25. Joan Sherman explains Horton's beneficial relationship with Captain William H. S. Banks and the Ninth Michigan Cavalry Volunteers. See Sherman's biography in the introduction of *Black Bard of North Carolina.*

26. George Duyckinck was the brother of Evert Augustus Duyckinck Sr., who led a publishing firm, Duyckinck and Company, from 1785 to 1833.

27. The Duyckinck *Cyclopaedia* was arranged chronologically, and Wheatley appeared in the second of three time periods: the Colonial Era, the Revolutionary Period, and the Present Century.

28. Wheatley's letter and poem to Washington were printed in the *Pennsylvania Magazine* or *American Monthly Museum,* April 1776. It can also be found in *Phillis Wheatley: Complete Writings,* edited by Vincent Carretta (New York: Penguin, 2001).

WORKS CITED

Armory, Hugh. "Reinventing the Colonial Book." *A History of the Book in America, Volume One: The Colonial Book in the Atlantic World.* Hugh Armory and David Hall, eds. New York: Cambridge UP, 2000. 26–54.

Bel, Phillip A. *The Coloured American.* "African American Newspapers: The Nineteenth Century." 1990. *Accessible Archives Database.* 20 Jan. 2003. www.accessible.com

Bly, Antonio T. "Wheatley's On the Affray in King Street." *Explicator* 56.4 (Summer 1998): 177–80.

Cadbury, Henry J. "Negro Membership in the Society of Friends." *Journal of Negro History* 21.2 (April 1936): 151–213.

Carretta, Vincent, ed. "Introduction." *Phillis Wheatley Complete Writings.* New York: Penguin, 2001. xiii–xlvii.

Clarkson, Thomas. " . . . an African girl, who made no contemptible appearance in this species of composition." *Critical Essays on Phillis Wheatley.* Ed. William H. Robinson. Boston: G. K. Hall, 1982. 43–44.

Douglass, Frederick. "African American Newspapers: The Nineteenth Century." 1990. *Accessible Archives Database.* 20 Jan. 2003. www.accessible. com

Duyckinck, George L., and Evert A. Duyckinck. "Introduction and Preface." *Cyclopedia of American Literature: Embracing Personal and Critical Notices of Authors, and Selections from their Writings, from the Earliest Period to the Present Day, with Portraits, Autographs, and other Illustrations.* Ed. M. Laird Simons. Philadelphia: William Rutter & Company, 1965. v–xii; 381–85.

Eastman, Mary Henderson. *Aunt Phillis's Cabin; or, Southern Life as it is.* Upper Saddle River: Gregg, 1968.

Felker, Christopher. "'The Tongues of the Learned Are Insufficient': Phillis Wheatley, Publishing Objectives, and Personal Liberty." *Resources for American Literary Study* 20.2 (1994): 149–79.

Garrison, William Lloyd. *The Liberator,* vol. 1, no. 1–vol. 2, no. 52 (1 January 1831–29 December 1832), pp. 1–208; vol. 4, no. 12 (March 22, 1834) p. 47; vol. 33, no. 49 (December 4, 1863) p. 196. *Kraus-Thompson Organization Limited Microform Division:* Box 7696-001 (1 January 1831–27 December 1834), Box 7696-002 (3 January 1835–29 June 1838).

Goodman, Paul. *Of One Blood: Abolitionism and the Origins of Racial Equality.* Berkeley: U of California P, 1998.

Grégoire, Henri. *An enquiry concerning the intellectual and moral faculties, and literature of Negroes followed with an account of the life and works of fifteen Negroes & mulattoes, distinguished in science, literature and the arts.* Brooklyn: T. Kirk, 1810. 155–241. *Library of American Civilization:* fiche LAC 12839.

Guillory, John. *Cultural Capital: The Problem of Literary Canon Formation.* U of Chicago P, 1993. 3–84.

Hachey, Thomas, and Ralph Weber, eds. *Voices of Revolution: Rebels and Rhetoric.* Illinois: Dryden Press, 1972. 209–17, 231–47.

Hall, David D. *Cultures of Print.* Amherst: U of Massachusetts P, 1996.

Hammon, Jupiter. "An Address to Miss Phillis Wheatly [*sic*] Ethiopian Poetess, in Boston, Who Came from Africa at Eight Years of Age, and Soon Became Acquainted with the Gospel of Jesus Christ." *Phillis Wheatley: The Complete Writings.* Ed. Vincent Carretta. New York: Penguin, 2001. 204–7.

Horton, George Moses. *The Black Bard of North Carolina: George Moses Horton.* Ed. Joan R. Sherman. Chapel Hill: U of North Carolina P, 1997.

Jacobs, Donald M., ed. *Antebellum Black Newspapers: Indices to New York Freedom's Journal (1827–29), The Rights of All (1829), The Weekly Advocate (1837), and The Colored American (1837–41).* Westport: Greenwood, 1976. 3–160.

Jefferson, Thomas. "Query XIV. Laws." *Notes on the State of Virginia.* Ed. William Peden. Chapel Hill: U of North Carolina P, 1955. 130–49.

Knapp, Isaac., ed. "Notes." *Memoir and Poems of Phillis Wheatley, a Native African and a Slave. Also, Poems by a Slave.* Boston: Isaac Knapp, 1838. Schomburg Center Microfiche R-961, pt. 1, section F.

Levernier, James A. "Style as Protest in the Poetry of Phillis Wheatley." *Style* 27.2 (Summer 1993): 172–93.

Light, George W., ed. "Notes." *Memoir and Poems of Phillis Wheatley.* Boston: George W. Light, 1834.

Mayer, Henry. *All on Fire: William Lloyd Garrison and the Abolition of Slavery.* New York: St. Martin's, 1998.

Mason, Julian, ed. "Introduction and Notes." *The Poems of Phillis Wheatley.* Chapel Hill: U of North Carolina P, 1966.

Mott, Abigail. "A Short Account of Phillis Wheatley." *The Liberator* 2.7 (1832): 28. Ed. William L. Garrison. Kraus-Thompson Organization Limited Microfilm Division: Box 7696-001.

———. *Biographical Sketches and Interesting Anecdotes of Person of Colour. To Which Is Added a Selection of Pieces in Poetry. Compiled by A. Mott.* New York: Printed by order of the trustees of the residuary estate of Lindley Murray, 1839.

———. *Narratives of Colored Americans.* New York: William Wood & Co., 1875. Database: Documenting the South. <http://docsouth.unc.edu/neh/mott/menu.html>

Nisbet, Richard. *Slavery Not Forbidden by Scripture: Or, a Defence of the West-Indian Planters from the Aspersions thrown out against them, by the Author of a Pamphlet Entitled "An Address to the Inhabitants of the British Settlements in America, upon slave-keeping" By a West Indian.* Philadelphia: Printed [for John Sparhawk?] 1773.

Odell, Margaretta Matilda. "Memoir." *Memoir and Poems of Phillis Wheatley, a Native and African Slave.* Boston: George W. Light, 1834. Schomberg Center Microfiche R-96, pt. 1, section E.

Robinson, William H. *Phillis Wheatley: A Bio-Bibliography.* Boston: G. K. Hall, 1981.

———. "Phillis Wheatley: Colonial Quandary." *CLA Journal* 9.1 (1965): 25–38.

Rogers, Pat. *Grub Street: Students in a Subculture.* London: Methuen & Co. Ltd., 1972: 18–94, 175–217, 276–349.

Romans, Bernard. *A Concise Natural History of East and West Florida.* New York: Printed for the author, 1775.

Russwurm, John B., and Samuel Cornish. *Freedom's Journal.* 1990. "African American Newspapers: The Nineteenth Century." *Accessible Archives Database.* 20 Jan. 2003. www.accessible.com

Sagarin, Mary. *John Brown Russwurm: The Story of Freedom's Journal, Freedom's Journey.* New York: Lothrop, Lee, & Shepard, 1970. 11–126.

Sancho, Ignatius. *Letters of the Late Ignatius Sancho, An African.* Ed. Vincent Carretta. New York: Penguin, 1998. ix–xxxix.

Stewart, Maria W. *Maria W. Stewart, America's First Black Woman Political Writer: Essays and Speeches.* Ed. Marilyn Richardson. Bloomington: Indiana UP, 1987. 1–35.

Thatcher, Benjamin. "Introduction." *Memoir and Poems of Phillis Wheatley.* Boston: George W. Light, 1835.

Thomas, Isaiah. *To the Customers for Thomas's Massachusetts Spy.* Worchester, Massachusetts: Printed by Isaiah Thomas, 1786. ESTC Microfilm 35mm.

Wheatley, Phillis. *Letters of Phillis Wheatley.* Ed. Charles Deane. Boston: Massachusetts Historical Society, 1864. Schomburg Center Microfiche R-961, pt. 1, section G.

———. *Phillis Wheatley: The Complete Writings.* Ed. Vincent Carretta. New York: Penguin, 2001.

Willard, Carla. "Wheatley's Turns of Praise: Heroic Entrapment and the Paradox of Revolution." *American Literature: A Journal of Literary History, Criticism, and Bibliography* 67.2 (June 1995): 233–56.

Phillis Wheatley: The Consensual Blackness of Early African American Writing

Phillip M. Richards

It is no accident that early black writing is an Enlightenment phenomenon. The first African writers of the Anglo-Atlantic world turned their appropriated Europeanized consciousness back upon the West itself. Through them, the West saw itself mirrored in African eyes. Eighteenth-century travel narratives often featured an exotic traveler whose reports represented Western culture from a foreign vantage. From this perspective, the taken-for-granted realities of early modern society revealed their nature as the creation of a particular society in a certain time and place. This convention points to an important enlightenment "truth" elaborated by eighteenth-century French and Anglo-Atlantic thinkers such as Montesquieu in *The Persian Letters,* Swift in *Gulliver's Travels,* and Tom Paine in *Common Sense.* Not only are our society's most basic truths social fictions, but we acquire self-consciousness by stepping out of our accustomed social position and viewing ourselves from the standpoint of the other. Through his or her strangeness, the other becomes a vehicle by which we know and define ourselves. As eighteenth-century explorers and travelers mapped new territories, they discovered not only new worlds, but themselves. Given this situation, black writers would have been invented had they not eventually appeared. In British North America, this act of invention took place and shaped the art that African Americans eventually produced.

Historically speaking, black writing in the Anglo-Atlantic world emerges as literate blacks turn their attention to poetry, preaching, and oratory in late-eighteenth-century New England. Soon after mid-century, the religious tracts of Lemuel Haynes, the poetry of Phillis Wheatley, and the sermons and verses of Jupiter Hammon join a burgeoning New England pamphlet literature promoting revivalist enthusiasm, responding to the horrors of the Revolution as it had to the French and Indian War, as well as commenting on the eventual separation between Great Britain and her colonies. Black literary personae set forth the social structures, values, and rituals that created order amidst American and African American society in the tumult of Revolutionary and post-Revolutionary life. Black writing emerged as black writers undertook the sustained task of setting forth the consensual worldview by which their culture lived. In doing so, the first African American writers measured members of the white Anglo-Atlantic world by its own standards, and extended the implications of its central ideologies.

At the heart of early-eighteenth-century black expression was a preconceived language of sentiment, which had emerged first among white writers—often in execution sermons and narratives in the seventeenth and eighteenth centuries (Howard). This language appropriated the modes of feeling drawn from Puritan theology and piety setting forth what Clifford Geertz has called the "moods and motivations" of religion (Geertz 94–98). A shared language of sentiment allowed black writers such as Phillis Wheatley, Jupiter Hammon, and Olaudah Equiano to communicate with a white audience, in a consensual language, framing showed values. These black personae that appeared in public discourses such as execution narratives and sermons became the basis by which the first African American writers communicated with the larger world.[1] Within the context of this world, white Western audiences grasped the possibility of a "black" voice whose psychology mirrored their own, and black writers formulated their own place within a white Anglo-Atlantic world.

This black voice grew more important as whites had increasing reason to define themselves vis à vis a growing black population. During the first three-quarters of the eighteenth century, the numbers of the black population increased rapidly. The moral and social control of blacks as well as whites became an important goal of New England life in a white society that increasingly feared crime, independence, and anger.[2] In this context, the black persona easily became a mirror image for those socially disruptive emotions and intellectual attitudes within the white public consciousness. Through such a reflection, whites observed those psychological impulses, which they wished to control in themselves. The unintended consequences of this development, however, was that blacks became humanized as emotionally, intellectually, and psychologically complex human beings. Before the actual advent of black writers, plausibly "human" rhetorical stances for blacks had existed. In this respect, black writing largely emerged from the ideological dynamics of Puritanism.

Dickson Bruce has persuasively argued that Anglo-American literary languages provided the rhetoric and substance of early black expression (65). An

Phillip M. Richards

examination of Phillis Wheatley's appropriation of Puritan piety into a sentimental discourse illustrates this development. The poet's characteristic verse often addressed itself to the new nation's traumatic experiences through a discourse of feeling. She and her work were not exceptional in this regard. As I argue elsewhere, this language of sentiment also dominates the writing of Hammon, Equiano, many of the slave narrators, as well as other texts produced by African American writers. Sentimental language addressed to trauma appears vividly in the first recorded poem by a black writer, Lucy Terry's "Bars Fight" (August 28, 1748). These verses directly address the crisis of order in mid-eighteenth-century British North America. Terry's doggerel commemorated the response of a western Massachusetts town to a Native American attack during the French and Indian War. The crude popular ballad speaks to the trauma created by death, disruption of family, and communal destruction. In recounting this disaster, Terry's poem implicitly celebrates the courage and tenacity, needed by a mid-eighteenth-century frontier community in western Massachusetts. Adopting the traditional stance of a poet facing social collapse, the black writer sets forth a civic ideal, drawing upon shared sentiment in war-ravaged Westfield.

> August, 'twas the twenty-fifth
> Seventeen hundred forty-six,
> The Indians did in ambush lay,
> Some very valiant men to slay,
>
> The names of whom I'll not leave out:
> Samuel Allen like a hero fout [fought],
> And though he was so brave and bold,
> His face no more shall we behold.
>
> Eleazar Hawks was killed outright,
> Before he had time to fight—
> Before he did the Indians see,
> Was shot and killed immediately.
>
> Oliver Armsden he was slain,
> Which caused his friends much grief
>   and pain.
> Simeon Arsden they found dead
> Not many rods distant from his head.

Adonijah Gillet, we do hear,
Did lose his life which was so dear.
John Sadler fled across the water
And thus escaped the dreadful slaughter.

Eunice Allen sees the Indians coming
And hopes to save herself by running;
And had not her petticoats stopped her,
The awful creatures had not catched her,

Nor tommy hawked her on the head,
And left her on the ground for dead.
Young Samuel Allen, Oh, lack-a-day!
Was taken and carried to Canada.
(Carretta 199–200)

Terry's role as an exponent of her community's values lay in her silences as well as in her statements. Essential to the poem's rhetoric is its assumption of an interracially shared geographical, cultural, and social world whose communal familiarity makes explicit description unnecessary. A battle has taken place, and the poem's persona-voice simply assumes that the audience will identify the event's site, time, participants, and climactic conditions with little prompting. The speaker slights these preliminaries in order to address the poem's real subject: the trauma of unexpected attack generating a chaotic scene of anger, brute force, confused response, unsettling fear, and fight. The most fundamental human instincts and bodily responses to the external world have taken over this intimate community's experience. And the poet offers as consolation, the memory of their names, sometimes heroic postures, and suffering in order to imply the stoicism and civic virtues required for survival on the western New England frontier during the French and Indian War. The poem reminds the audience of the emotional and cultural qualities that define it as a people.

The text's reliance on the features of oral communication—reference to shared understandings about the poem's setting, its spontaneous rather than an ascending, plotted string of explosive events, and an ethos of confrontation (here between the community and the Indian attackers)—creates a rhetorical situation in which the poet's authority depends on vivid, speechlike expression rather than calculated design of imagery, plot, characterization, and figurative language. The speaker's authority comes not from a cultivated writer's skill but

Phillip M. Richards

from the evocation of strongly felt emotions of a forceful talker manipulating the fellow feeling of her audience.

The speaker's rhetorical strategy lies in her ability to assuage her audience's grief, fright, and horror with the solemnity and dignity of public memorial. In this world of feeling, Terry's race does not represent a barrier between her and her white listeners. Indeed, her status as a black may lead to the attribution of a special sensitivity to sentiment sometimes associated with marginal people. In all of these aspects, the poem reproduces the rhetorical, intellectual, and social world of early black writing. The verse demonstrates the rhetorical possibilities open to an articulate black spokesperson in a residually oral, late-eighteenth-century culture inhabiting a fluid, unpredictable environment. This poem shows a black poet who—whatever her crudeness of expression—appears aware of the public literary dimension of her role as community spokesperson. Terry's consciousness of her public importance in this poem is corroborated by her place in her community's traditions. Like the slave narrator Venture Smith and the preacher Lemuel Haynes, she became a local folk legend by virtue of her status as a black writer.[3]

Terry's poem is a rough example of a sentimental language that Puritan thinkers and writers formulated into an ideological system of ideas and feelings. Within texts embodying this discourse, modes of feeling associated with religious conversion and the Christian life provided the content and personae of an imagined black's discourse before a white audience. Underlying the interior intellectual and emotional attitudes of this example of "black personae and voices" was the conversion process itself: the shock of the sinner's awakening to her or his sin, the agonized soul's wrestling with her or his sinfulness, the sinner's frustrated attempts to will her or his spiritual transformation, the joy of discovering grace, the saint's benevolent love of the other saints, and the converted woman or man's persisting conflict between sinful and godly motives. As Philip Greven and Murray Murphey have argued, these attitudes constituted a temperament or sensibility that included internalization of authority, hatred of the self, displaced aggression, and rerouted affections to others. This temperament included self-restraint and forcefulness, dictatorial attitudes, and resistance to authority (Murphey; Greven). Drawing on these conventions, white Anglo American writers interpreted the psychology and actions of black criminals in sermons and criminal narratives. In all cases, whites as well as blacks were invited to identify the black criminal as possessing autonomous faculties of intellect and will. Although blacks were routinely considered intellectually and morally inferior to whites, this discourse put forward blacks as the moral and psychological equals of whites. The egalitarian force of this discourse made explanation and rationalization necessary to sustain the fiction of black inferiority.

From the perspective of a saint undergoing the process of preparation for salvation and conversion, the black voice could not only become a mirror for sinful attitudes but also an exemplary figure for the white audience. As such an exemplary figure, the black voice defined its identity in terms of a central religious and psychological ritual that provided the most important emotional and intellectual bonds among the saints in the Christian community. These methods not only helped create social order, but represented the sentiment that bound an organic Christian community, transcending even its hierarchies of race. Similarly, because the biblical text provided the subject for the sermon, the criminal and her or his spiritual plight implicitly became a typical figuration of Old or New Testament figures such as David, Cain and Abel, or the redeemed thief crucified with Christ. Within this context, the black figure was not only a moral being but also an actor in the Protestant history of redemption. Both of these features made the execution sermon a ritual that defined consensus and cosmic order in a community that perceived itself threatened.

Cotton Mather's work vividly illustrates the way that a minister might draw upon Puritan sentimentalism for a universally accepted psychology of sin. Mather was exceptional in seizing upon topical occasions to expound theological doctrine. And his sermon collection, *Pillars of Salt*, dramatizes the sinful (what he calls a "reprobate") mind as the concomitant of God's continued permission of sin.[4] The sinner's malevolent will, according to Mather, is inherited from the fallen Adam. Mather goes on to append a series of execution narratives to the sermon, most of which display the perpetrator's capital crime as the consequence of his unregenerate will. Mather extended this notion in an execution sermon, *Tremenda: The Dreadful Sound with which the Wicked are to be Thunderstruck*, wherein he describes a sinner's spiritual awakening. Within the sermon, the notion of spiritual awakening resonates in variously. On the one hand, awakening stirs the sinner's horror; on the other, the call to repentance may be the preliminary to a Christian's repentance, an act announced by God's "joyful sound" (Mather *Tremenda*). The event of the subject's execution becomes God's terrifying call to the sinful and her or his eventual hope of redemption.

The exemplary situation of the sinner Joseph Hanno, the prisoner and subject of the appended execution sermon, serves as an appropriate example. He has been religiously educated, well treated, and freed from slavery. As such, he is the embodiment of a privileged white sinner. At the same time, repeated sinful activity has led him to murder and all that it implies: the flaunting of Puritan norms of self-control, family order, and moral scrupulosity. This sensationalistic preaching also portrays the attractiveness of crime (that otherwise might be thought heinous) through a depiction of wrongdoing which yielded the pleasures of antisocial rebellion. In Mather's sermon, blackness is a metaphor for entrenched wickedness, stemming from original sin: an ingrained evil that leads the sinner actively to choose rather than oppose evil. The convict's evil is embodied in his blackened character: a will infused with evil. And Hanno's conversion significantly comes only after he realizes that his redemption must come from a hope for divine grace. This knowledge appears in Hanno's self-abnegating acts of will, his self-condemnation. This self-abnegation represents a breaking of the will that contrasts vividly with his earlier pride in his knowledge of Puritan doctrine (Greven 32–43, 87–99).

The extent of Hanno's authorship in the dialogue between minister and convict appended to the sermon is not clear. What is important about the execution confession is the way in which it draws its rhetoric from a conversion-based Puritan piety. The narrative creates a black persona who becomes a model for the moral introspection necessary for the Christian life, particularly for assurance of grace. Hanno's conversion depicts a black version of anticipated saintliness that transcends even a will habituated to evil. At the same time, Hanno's immoral actions objectify similar impulses on the part of his white audiences. (Hanno's murder of his wife is typical of a number of crimes by whites who kill relatives.) Mather's characterization of the black figure gains its rhetorical force from its capacity to dramatize and provide a catharsis for his audience's guilt. And Hanno himself gains a human complexity as he becomes identified as sinful (but attractive in sin's beckoning way), proud, and finally broken when he acquires a hope of grace.

Hanno's execution sermon and dialogue is typical of other homilies and narratives concerning black criminals from the late seventeenth to the mid-eighteenth centuries. (Afterward the criminal narratives would change, influenced by the literary conventions of the picaresque [Cohen 499–500].) However, earlier execution sermons and narratives suggest the breadth of rhetorical strategies, literary devices, and points of view that a black individual might use in addressing a white society. Blacks could be moral exemplars. If they were associated with evil, the evils they represented were also the evils of whites. Indeed, the observations of black criminals by whites—as it was enforced by many sermons—allowed whites to examine their own moral state in a distanced, objective way. Such observations implied, on the part of blacks, a knowledge of human sinfulness about which whites often deluded themselves. This stance implicitly gave blacks leeway to assume the role of moral exemplars whose religious experience led them to understandi their white audience. The popular cultural form of the execution sermon itself implied the possibility of human sympathies between blacks and whites, not to mention a subtle promotion of the intellectual capacities of African Americans.[5] And the often-confident rhetoric of a Wheatley, a Hammon, or a Lemuel Haynes emerges from the assumption of the existence of such sentimental and emotional capacities that made interracial moral sympathy possible.

Phillis Wheatley is the preeminent example of an African American writer whose work emerged from an appropriation of "black" personae available from the religious discourse of late-eighteenth-century New England culture. Wheatley's verse frequently advanced interracial acts of consensus, animated by the religious sentimentality of a "black voice." Significantly, she acquired the literary background needed to shape an evangelical religious language into cultivated expression. Raised like many New England slaves in the homes of wealthy masters, Wheatley embodied the commercial wealth that allowed Boston to become a provincial center of Anglophone culture in the late eighteenth century. The leisure with which she learned to read, study the classics, and compose verse was an extension of the cultivated wealth of the prosperous colonial American family that she "served." At the same time, Phillis, through Mrs. Wheatley, had extensive contacts to the missionary circle around the Countess of Huntington. And Phillis Wheatley grew up in communication not only with figures such as the missionary-promoter, John Thornton, but also with the New Divinity evangelist Samuel Hopkins, who had a pulpit in nearby Newport, Rhode Island, the location of Obour Tanner, whom Wheatley visited. Wheatley's experience represented the evangelical context in which American republicanism developed as a political ideology complemented by Protestant piety.

In "Phillis Wheatley and the Sentimental Tradition," Annie Finch writes, "Sentimental art seems to presuppose a public community of viewers who will feel what the artist has intended them to feel" (5). And what Wheatley intended her largely Christian audience to perceive was the range of emotions, attitudes, and ideas associated with Protestant conversion, particularly benevolence as Christian social love.

This language appears throughout her poetry, but most straightforwardly in her various letters to friends and co-religionists. Wheatley's "sentimentality" was, I argue, deeply grounded in both the language of feeling associated with conversion-based Puritan piety and late-eighteenth-century Edwardsean conceptions of benevolence as central to the saint's holiness and his relation with other Christians (Conforti 109–24). This link between Wheatley's "sentimentality" and New Divinity discourse may well have had a more concrete historical basis. Samuel Hopkins, a late-eighteenth-century Edwardsean minister (a theological disciple of Jonathan Edwards), settled in Newport, Rhode Island in 1769. His coming and his ministerial tenure were supported by a group of pious Newport women that included a memoirist, biblical commentators, and the intensely religionist Sarah Osborn.[6] Hopkins reprinted Osborn's memoirs, and the two shared an intensely sentimental piety much like that expressed by Wheatley. In a published tract, "The nature, certainty and evidence of true Christianity," Osborn describes a conversion and experience of religious assurance that anticipates Wheatley's writing in several ways.

Among Wheatley's most important productions were letters to her fellow evangelicals John Thornton, the Countess of Huntingdon, Obour Tanner, and Samuel Hopkins. In this connection, it is significant that Osborn as well as Samuel Hopkins ministered to black groups in Newport. Equally important is the fact that Wheatley's friend Obour Tanner, whom the poet mentions to Hopkins, also lived in Newport. Osborn's sentimental discourse—which well may have affected Wheatley directly—joined Edwards's religious aesthetics with the language of the devout soul's voluntary choice and "broken will." Her piety is grounded in the aesthetic sentiment which constitutes the believer's pleasure.

> Well, upon *this discovery* of the amiable and lovely Jesus, if
> I know that I have a being. I do know that God compelled or
> *sweetly constrained* me to throw down the weapons of my rebel-
> lion, and to *submit* to HIM as *Prince* and *Saviour,* and consent
> to be saved by him in His own way, and upon his own terms.
> . . . Yea, *God caused my Heart to go out after him* in strong and
> vehement desires, and to choose him in all his offices, with all
> his benefits, to be my portion for ever. Yea, he appeared to me to
> be in himself the most lovely and desirable object, the fairest of
> ten thousand fairs. (Osborn 5–6)

Wheatley deploys this sentimental and aesthetic language vividly in her letters, which embody and enact a form of Christian friendship with her correspondents, moving in much the same way as does Osborn's writing. She thus writes her evangelical mentor, the British missionary John Thornton, referring to the Puritan convention of awakening on a sickbed:

> O that my eyes were more open'd to see the real worth, and true excellence of the word of truth, my flinty heart Soften'd with the grateful dews of divine grace and the stubborn will, and affections, bent on God alone their proper object, and the vitiated palate may be corrected to relish heav'nly things. It has pleasd God to lay me on a bed of Sickness, and I knew not but my deathbed, but he has been graciously pleas'd to restore me in great measures. I beg your prayers, that I may be made thankful for his paternal corrections, and that I may make proper use of them to the glory of his grace. (140–41)

Wheatley's observations not only describe her spiritual state but signal her shared sensibility of broken will, ambivalence toward the self, internalized authority, and benevolent love of God—all of which establish her membership in the company of saints constituted by Thornton's missionary group. Her display of this Christian sensibility identifies her to her mentor, Thornton, as a fellow saint with authority to address him as an equal. In the context of her writing, this spiritual provides the rhetoric by which she gains a prophetic status.

From her earliest poetry, Wheatley fashioned a literary persona based upon the language of evangelical conversion. In the poem "On Virtue," she depicts a common scenario in Puritan religious practice: the striving for grace that results not from effort but from the infusion of holiness into the human soul.

> O Thou bright jewel in my aim I strive
> To comprehend thee. Thine own words declare
> Wisdom is higher than a fool can reach.
> I cease to wonder and no more attempt
> Thine Height t'explore, or fathom thy profound.
> But O my soul, sink not into despair.
> Virtue is near thee, and with gentle hand
> Would now embrace thee, hovers o'er thine head.
> Fain would the heav'n-born soul with her converse,
> Then seek, then court her for her promis'd bliss. (11)

Phillip M. Richards

The "heav'n-born soul" is the soul regenerated by divine grace, now empowered to grasp piety. Although the prospective convert must seek grace, she or he must realize her or his total inadequacy to deserve or even ask for it. As a saint, Wheatley depicted herself in the process of an internal war—a psychomachia or conflict of the soul—between her holy motivations and her sinful ones. Memory in her poem "On Recollection" functions as a vehicle for introspection that reveals past offenses against God's laws, fomenting an internal spiritual conflict.

> Now eighteen years their destin'd course have run,
> In fast succession round the central sun.
> How did the follies of that period pass
> Unnotic'd, but behold them writ in brass!
> In Recollection see them fresh return,
> And sure 'tis mine to be asham'd, and mourn.
>   O *Virtue*, smiling in immortal green
> Do thou exert thy pow'r, and change the scene,
> Be thine employ to guide my future days,
> And mine to pay the tribute of my praise. (35)

Similarly in Wheatley's letters to Obour Tanner, she reminds her fellow slave that the two must strive to live a life of piety.

An important function of Wheatley's deployed religious feeling is the resolution of trauma in the late-eighteenth-century Anglo-Atlantic world. In much of her occasional writing, Wheatley was a sentimental poet who addressed her white audience's emotional crises of separation, illness, and death.[7] The elegies, for example, present the mourners found in the poem with a traumatic image of death—a shock that Wheatley describes not only within the surviving relatives or friends but also in herself. However, in verse such as "A Funeral Poem on the Death of C.E. an Infant of Twelve Months," the poet fashions a consolation for death in a shared appreciation of the difficulties of the Christian life. The departed has evaded these deep internal conflicts and won heaven in a state of joyous purity.

> . . . The raptur'd babe replies,
> "Thanks to my God, who snatch'd me to the skies,
> E'er vice triumphant had possess'd my heart,
> E'er yet the tempter had beguil'd my heart,
> E'er yet on sin's base actions I was bent,

E'er yet I knew temptation's dire intent;
E'er yet the lash for horrid crimes I felt
E'er vanity had led my way to guilt,
But, soon arriv'd at my celestial goal,
Full glories rush on my expanding soul."
Joyful he spoke: exulting cherubs round
Clapt their glad wings, the heav'nly vaults resound. (38)

Beyond the poet's rationalization of her subject's crisis of separation is her capacity to return the parents to the joy they felt with the living child. The poem fulfills the parent's desire for the now-dead infant's well-being, and their narcissistic wish for their own heavenly comfort. Wheatley's response to the crisis of death contains a shrewd psychological understanding of the parents' deepest motivations, and Wheatley resolves their sense of trauma through an appeal to these impulses.

Drawing upon her culture's capacity to accept a sentimental black voice as its psychological mirror, Wheatley self-consciously wrote as a poet of religious consensus, a symbol of shared feelings of piety. Her occasional sentimental poetry sought to provide cohesion within Puritan New England society. In many ways her poetry looked back to white "black voices" of the execution sermon which dramatized theological themes warning the youth against sin and examined proper relations between masters and servants. Written during the 1770s and 1780s, Wheatley's sentimental poetry of trauma spoke to the political tensions implicit in a socially stratified nation's commitment to Puritanism's piety and republican political ideology. Wheatley is quite properly known as a poet of religion who fashioned such immensely popular cultural poems as the internationally known elegy on George Whitefield. The topical success of this power came from her understanding of Whitefield's immense popularity as a reflection of the potential interracial tension in Revolutionary America. Whitefield's life as it is depicted in the poem embodies the conventional Puritan sentiments of conversion:

Thy sermons in unequall'd accents flow'd
And ev'ry bosom with devotion glow'd
Thou didst in strains of eloquence refin'd
Inflame the heart, and captivate the mind.
Unhappy we the setting sun deplore,
So glorious once, but ah! It shines no more. (15–16)

Phillip M. Richards

The neoclassical structures (its rhyming couplets) of this poem suggest an upper-class spokesman addressing a polite public in the language of a clerical, legal, and political elite. However, Whitefield also emerges here as an evangelical in the style of post-Awakening revivalist clergy who increasingly challenged that elite. The large crowds who came to see him in open areas—rather than in congregational sanctuaries—represented an egalitarian movement that fueled the symbolism and the practical politics of the American Revolution. In these two opposing aspects, Wheatley's poem captures the social and cultural bearing of a nervous late-eighteenth-century elite as well as her period's intense egalitarianism: its fear of social, moral, and cultural disruption. Whitefield becomes her symbol of a new American prophet able to negotiate the often-contending claims of a diverse society.

This negotiation was a generic task of some late-eighteenth-century American poetry. Similar tensions appear in a 1774 newspaper poem titled "Epitaph of a Faithful Servant," which confronts the period's deep conflict between egalitarian impulse of virtue and the reality of social hierarchy.

> Should full-blown pride in tawdry accent say.
> What mighty deeds have dignify'd this day;
> Or was he rich is fortune or in blood?"
> Ah, he was more, much more, for he was good!
> His life in science and obedience spent
> He gain'd not riches, but he gain'd content,
> Whilst o'er himself he kept a strict control,
> And heap'd up treasures that enrich'd the soul.
> Of temp'rance try'd, an every-ready hand,
> A yielding nature, pliant to command:
> Yet firm in morals resolutely just,
> Of softest manners, but a rock in trial
> His sense was plain, nor yet his converse rude,
> A feeling heart that teem'd with gratitude.
> In this kindred mourn thy early dawn.
> Thy master lov'd thee and inscribes thy tomb
> O take thy workes, by heavens decree,
> Where service is eternal liberty. (Anon. 4)

This poem predictably invokes a conventional sentimental sphere that acknowledges the slave's moral nature but also his social inferiority to the master.

The crisis of the bondsman's death raises the issue of the servant's just desert, echoing a conventional tension within master-servant relations. In the sermon *Tremenda*, Cotton Mather stresses the duty of servants to exercise self-control as they stayed within their social place, hence living in Christian harmony with masters who were their moral equals. The anonymous topical poem above also celebrates the slave's virtues in the codes of contemporary republican, and largely classical virtue: "temp'rance" (or Greek *sophrosyne*), a self-control in all matters, cultivation in sentiment and feeling, social love and "amiability" that tolerated the prima facie injustice of temporal slavery. By 1774, however, this tension within New England slavery had itself become compelling in republican terms, and this poem seeks to reconcile the traditional world of hierarchy with those frequently egalitarian impulses. The poem negotiates the task of resolving social contradiction by understating the slave's inferiority and the deference she or he owes the master; yet the political implications of the slave's inferiority are clearly bothersome to the verse's poetic voice.

Thus, the speaker early on characterizes as "tawdry" the verse's critical question of the slave's reward for his virtue. Significantly, however, the end of the poem honors the "tawdry" voice's question, assuring the audience at the very end that the slave's works will be honored with liberty in heaven. This poem performs the task of consensus building by deferring the slave's reward to a redemptive future. This deferral, however, leaves the present racial contradictions of Whig Christian rhetoric unresolved. The black is a slave, and implicitly the master is a tyrant. The Whig slaveowner is an example of the very corruption that undermines liberty.

These poems show how the institution of slavery destabilized republican and Whig ideologies in late-eighteenth-century America. An inability to balance the various imperatives of the sentimental sphere in a slave society only pointed to the way in which human bondage might upset the imperatives of power, virtue, and moral self-consciousness upon which the republic was coming to rest. Wheatley's poetic success should be understood in terms of her appropriation of her culture's means of resolving class and cultural conflicts. The distinctiveness and memorable aspect of Wheatley's poetry emerges in the black poet's capacity to fashion a moral voice that by which the poet established those delicate balances of feeling on which her culture depended.

Significantly, many of Wheatley's topical poems speak directly to the theme of an imbalance of power between the black speaker and her white audience. Among these are "To Maecenas," "To the University of Cambridge in

Phillip M. Richards

New England," and "To the Right Honourable William, Earl of Dartmouth, His Majesty's Principal Secretary of State for North-America, &c." Within these poems a shared sentimental sphere of piety becomes the ground of republican virtue shared by both the black author and her white alleged superior, and this image of shared Puritan sentiment becomes the basis for consensus between social unequals. Indeed, this rhetorical situation is an important part of both her poetry and the authenticating documents that establish them. For example, Wheatley's "On Messrs. Hussey and Coffin" serves as an authenticating document that reproduces the domestic spheres wherein the poetic voice confronts her betters. Here, the domestic sphere is translated to an idealized realm of Christian community. And in the verse itself, the paternalistic world of Wheatley's speaker—that of the Negro serving girl who in the course of her domestic work improves upon what she hears for moral effect—suddenly becomes a community of shared piety, in which the servant assumes momentarily moral and religious equality before her betters.

> Did Fear and Danger so perplex your Mind,
> As made you fearful of the Whistling Wind?
> Was it not Boreas knit his angry Brow
> Against you? or did Consideration bow?
> To lend you Aid, did not his Winds combine?
> To stop your Passage with a churlish Line,
> Did haughty Eolus with Contempt look down
> With Aspect windy, and a study'd Frown?
> Regard them now;—the Great Supreme, the Wise,
> Intends for something hidden from our Eyes.
> Suppose the groundless Gulph had snatch'd away
> Hussey and Coffin to the raging Sea;
> Where wou'd they go? where wou'd be their Abode?
> With the supreme and independent God,
> Or made their Beds down in the Shades below,
> Where neither Pleasure nor Content can stow.
> To Heaven their Souls with eager Raptures soar,
> Enjoy the Bliss of him they wou'd adore.
> Had the soft gliding Streams of Grace been near,
> Some favourite Hope their fainting hearts to cheer,
> Doubtless the Fear of danger far had fled:

No more repeated Victory crown their Heads.

Had I the Tongue of a Seraphim, how would I exalt thy
Praise; thy Name as Incense to the Heavens should fly, and the
Remembrance of thy Goodness to the shoreless Ocean of Beatitude!—
Then should the Earth glow with seraphick Ardour.

'Blest Soul, which sees the Day while Light doth shine,
To guide his Steps to trace the Mark divine. (74)

By the poem's end, the head note's world of a patronizing slave-master, one in which Wheatley is referred to as a "Negro Girl," has become an image of intraracial and spiritual unity—the goal of both Wheatley's worldwide missionary movement and of the Whig revolution. This unity emerges, as the tensions of many of Wheatley's occasional poems do, amidst the poet's and her audience's response to trauma. As in Terry's "Bar's Fight," crisis opens up a perspective of the way to the stock of shared feelings of fear, implicit in the political visions of the missionary movement and the American Revolution. This union is, importantly, the projection of a wish implicit in the subjunctives of the poem's second part. What would have happened, the speaker wonders, had the men been killed? Having made this imaginative leap, Wheatley can project their salvation in heaven; indeed, the speaker can imagine herself a heavenly angel, praising God. And in this moment, transformed servant and master enjoy a sense of religious community as they praise God together, consolidating and extending the poem's pious interracial consensus into day-to-day, face-to-face reality.

Wheatley's literary accomplishment emerged from her ability to do what the 1774 poet of the "Epitaph of a Faithful Servant" could not do nearly so well. She defined the worth of the serving person not merely as an object of piety but as a useful exponent of social and spiritual values that provided social explanation for those periods of recollected trauma—death, illness, and separation which emerge in every household—even the household of the *Courant* poem quoted above. This establishment of the worth of the "servant" happens again in poems such as "To a Lady on Her Coming to North America with Her Son, for the Recovery of Her Health," "To a Lady on Her Remarkable Preservation in an Hurricane in North-Carolina," "A Farewel to America. To Mrs. S.W.," and even in other poems which console whites for their grief. Wheatley's elegy to Whitefield suggests the process by which a primarily religious poet becomes a writer of sentimental literature addressing the political contradiction of social hierarchy in an era of democratization. Indeed his death is a moment of

Phillip M. Richards

Anglo-American consensus, a consensus including the Anglo-Atlantic missionary movement, "youth," "blacks," and New England itself.

> "Take him, ye *Africans,* he longs for you,
> "*Impartial Saviour* is his title due:
> "Wash'd in the fountain of redeeming blood,
> "You shall be sons, and kings, and priests to God."
> Great *Countess,* we *Americans* revere
> Thy name, and mingle in thy grief sincere;
> *New England* deeply feels, the *Orphans* mourn,
> Their more than father will no more return. (16)

Extending her religious understandings to a schematized understanding of the republican state, she represents that the life of a republic depends upon an elite's virtue: her or his capacity to imagine and pursue strategies for the good of the society as a whole. The possible collapse of virtue through the "corruption" of selfishness, luxury, or tyrannical power threatened not only the governing class but also the governed. A republic's survival depended upon political structures that encouraged virtue, checked corruption, and thus prevented tyranny.[8] Within the context of Wheatley's discourse, sentimental piety became an antidote against corruption. Her religious poems establish a moment of stability that portrays the tensions between a hierarchical republican world and a democratizing public.

The logic of this Protestant response to corruption pushed Wheatley toward millenarian, antislavery politics. From Wheatley's religious perspective, the creation of a democratic culture meant the immediate abandonment of the social hierarchy (and implicit corruption) of slavery as well as the establishment of a kingdom of God. Wheatley's antislavery statements not only came from her call for a renewed millennial covenant with God, the purification of Protestant America, but also for the creation of a national civic virtue. The immediate call appears in the speech she gives the subject of her elegy "On the Death of General Wooster."

> ["]Permit me yet to paint fair freedom's charms
> For her the Continent shines bright in arms
> By thy high will, celestial prize she came—
> For her we combat on the field of fame
> Without her presence vice maintains full sway
> And social love and virtue wing their way

O still propitious be thy guardian care
And lead *Columbia* thro' the toils of war.
With thine own hand conduct them and defend
And bring the dreadful contest to an end—
For ever grateful let them live to thee
And keep them ever virtuous, brave, and free—
But how, presumptuous shall we hope to find
Divine acceptance with th'Almighty mind—
While yet (O deed ungenerous!) they disgrace
And hold in bondage Afric's blameless race?
Let virtue reign—And thou accord our prayer
Be victory our's, and generous freedom theirs." (93)

As General Wooster's expiring spirit indicates, the purpose of the revolution was the establishment of "social love" which binds organic community and the "virtue" necessary for the establishment of the republic. At the heart of the establishment of these sentiments is the creation of the new nation's covenant, "acceptance" with God.

The establishment of the new nation therefore depends on an immediate abandonment of slavery, itself a form of tyranny. The connection between virtue, social love, and natural rights is made more explicitly in Wheatley's published excerpt of a letter written by the poet to the Native American missionary Samson Occom.

Those that invade them [our natural rights] cannot be insensible
that the divine Light is chasing away the thick Darkness which
broods over the Land of Africa; and the Chaos which has reign'd
so long, is converting into beautiful Order, and [r]eveals more
and more clearly, the glorious Dispensation of civil and religious
Liberty, which are so inseparably united, that there is little or no
Enjoyment of one without the other: Otherwise, perhaps, the Israelites had been less solicitous for their Freedom from Egyptian
Slavery; I do not say they would have been contented without
it, by no Means, for in every human Breast, God has implanted
a Principle, which We call Love of Freedom; it is impatient of
Oppression, and pants for Deliverance; and by the Leave of our
Modern Egyptians I will assert, that the same Principle lives in
us. (152–53)

Phillip M. Richards

Through another set of tropes, white Americans become the tyrannical slave-holding Egyptians, and the deliverance of blacks becomes central to a redemptive history that will create the "beautiful order" of the millennium.

Peter Coviello has shown that Thomas Jefferson, an intellectual skeptic also of sorts, and Wheatley shared a common language of trauma. Wheatley shared with Jefferson a political language of evangelical republicanism that saw slavery as tyrannical corruption, and linked freedom with the fulfillment of the new nation's covenant status. This political discourse itself depended on a language of religious feeling. "The whole commerce," Jefferson writes in *Notes on the State of Virginia*, between master and slave, is "a perpetual exercise of the most boisterous passions, the most unremitting despotism on the one part, and degrading submissions on the other" (Jefferson 162). Drawing upon the language of the covenant and Wheatley's "infused natural liberties," Jefferson also observes in the same text that slavery must nullify God's approbation of the new nation.

> And can the liberties of a nation be thought secure when we have removed their only firm basis, a conviction in the minds of the people that these liberties are of the gift of God? That they are not to be violated but with his wrath? Indeed I tremble for my country when I reflect that God is just. . . . (Jefferson 163)

The point here and throughout this essay is not that blacks merely used a Puritan theology and sociology as well as a republican discourse. Black writers inherited their oppositional stance toward society from the identical oppositional discourses of Whig and Puritan political languages. Indeed, black writers were "oppositional" only to the extent that Whig and Puritan political languages created opposition voices in the broader American polity. In the same way that the American revolutionaries made "oppositional" republican and Protestant languages into a discourse of consensus, so did the first black writers. In making such a language of unity, the blacks were indeed only exploiting ambiguities that the white writers such as Mather and Jefferson encountered themselves.[9]

Wheatley's task of creating social consensus inevitably made her aware of the political implications of her religious language—an awareness also shared by Samuel Hopkins. Black writers did not need to subvert American values: indeed they were the monitors of a "corruption" that threatened to subvert the republic itself. As late-eighteenth-century American culture came to democratize itself, it created a space for pamphleteers such as Thomas Paine, erudite languages of "country" ideology, and Puritan theology, this idea of culture sifted down to the demotic level of black life. From these political languages, black writers were able to construct African American voices that claimed legitimacy in the public sphere. These political stances deployed resistance to slavery and egalitarian racial relations as the basis of a national consensus. Against the backdrop of the Revolution's frequent trauma, Wheatley offered the consolation of interracial community. In doing so, she translated the meanings of Whig evangelical politics across ethnic lines, seizing on her era's literary identities to politicize the nation's taken for grantedblack "moral" voice.

NOTES

1. For my understanding of execution sermons, I have drawn on Ronald A. Bosco's "Lectures at the Pillory: The Early American Execution Sermon" and Daniel E. Williams's "'Behold a Tragic Scene Strangely Changed into a Theater of Mercy': The Structure and Significance of Criminal Conversion Narratives in Early New England."

2. For the standard social historical narrative of black life in early New England, see Lorenzo Greene's *The Negro in Colonial New England* and Ira Berlin's "Time, Space, and the Evolution of Afro-American Society on British Mainland North America."

3. On Lucy Terry's popular reputation, see Frances Foster, *Written by Herself: Literary Production by African American Women, 1746–1892.* On the reputation of Venture Smith, see Arna Bontemps, ed. "The Traditions of Venture," *Five Black Lives.* On the reputation of Lemuel Haynes, see Richard Newman, ed. *Black Preacher to White America: The Collected Writings of Lemuel Haynes, 1774–1833.*

4. My interpretation of these texts, though developed separately, runs parallel to Richard Slotkin, "Narratives of Negro Crime in New England, 1675–1800."

5. I refer to such execution sermons as Byles, *The prayer and plea of David;* Thaddeus Maccarty, *The Power and grace of Christ display'd to a dying malefactor.* (Boston: Printed and sold by Kneeland and Adams, next to the treasurer's office, in Milk-Street, MDCCLXVIII. [1768]); and, Conant, *Blood of Abel.*

6. On the relationship between the women's society (of which Osborn as a part) and Samuel Hopkins, see Conforti, 102–6. On Osborn's life and her relation to Hopkins in particular, see Hambrick-Stowe, "Spiritual Pilgrimage of Sarah Osborn."

7. In an important discussion of the sentimental language of trauma in Wheatley and Thomas Jefferson, Coviello has discussed Wheatley's secular languages of dislocation in "Agonizing Affection."

8. On classical republicanism, see Pocock, *Machiavellian Moment;* Wood, *Creation of the American Republic,* 114–18; and Bailyn, *Ideological Origins of the American Revolution.*

9. Dana D. Williams gives a linguistic account of these difficulties in *Word in Black and White,* 18–19, 28–29.

WORKS CITED

Anon. "Epitaph on a Faithful Servant." *Connecticut Courant,* October 24, 1774, 4.

Bailyn, Bernard. *The Ideological Origins of the American Revolution.* Cambridge: Harvard UP, 1967.

———. "Time Space, and the Evolution of Afro-American Society on British Mainland North America." *American Historical Review* 85.1 (February 1980): 44–78.

Bontemps, Arna, ed. "The Traditions of Venture." *Five Black Lives.* Middletown: Wesleyan UP, 2–34.

Bosco, Ronald A. "Lectures at the Pillory: The Early American Execution Sermon." *American Quarterly* 30.2 (Summer 1978): 156–76.

Bruce, Dickson D. *The Origins of African American Literature, 1680–1865.* Charlottesville: U of Virginia P, 2001.

Byles, Mather. *The prayer and plea of David, to be delivered from blood-guiltiness, improved in a sermon at the ancient Thursday-lecture in Boston, May 16th 1751 Before the execution of a young Negro servant for poisoning an infant. By Mr. Byles.* Boston: Printed and sold by Samuel Kneeland, opposite the prison in Queen Street, 1751.

Cohen, Daniel A. "Social Injustice, Sexual Violence, Spiritual Transcendence: Construction of the Interracial Rape in Early American Crime

Literature, 1767–1817." *William and Mary Quarterly*. 3rd ser., 56.3 (July 1999): 481–526.

Conant, Sylvanus. *The Blood of Abel, and the blood of Jesus considered and improved, in a sermon delivered at Taunton, December the first, 1763. Upon the day of the execution of Bristol, a Negro boy of about sixteen years old, for the murder of Miss Elizabeth McKinstry.* By Sylvanus Conant, A.M. Pastor of the First Church in Middleborough. Boston: Printed and sold by Edes and Gill, in Queen-Street, M,DCC,LXIV. [1764].

Conforti, Joseph A. *Samuel Hopkins and the New Divinity Movement: Calvinism, the Congregational Ministry, and Reform in New England Between the Great Awakenings.* Grand Rapids: Wm. B. Eerdmans, 1981.

Coviello, Peter. "Agonizing Affection: Affect and Nation in Early America." *Early American Literature* 3.3 (2002–3): 439–68.

Finch, Annie. "Phillis Wheatley and the Sentimental Tradition." *Romanticism on the Net*. Issues 29–31. February–May 2003. http//www.erudit.org/revue/ron2003/n.29/00723ar.html

Foster, Frances Smith. *Written by Herself: Literary Production by African American Women, 1746–1892.* Bloomington: Indiana UP, 1993.

Geertz, Clifford. "Religion as a Cultural System." *The Interpretation of Cultures*. New York: Basic, 1773.

Gilroy, Paul. *The Black Atlantic: Modernity and Double-Consciousness.* Cambridge: Harvard UP, 1993.

Greene, Lorenzo. *The Negro in Colonial New England*. 1942. New York: Athenaeum, 1971.

Greven, Philip. *The Protestant Temperament: Patterns of Child-Rearing, Religious Experience, and the Self in Early America.* New York: Knopf, 1977.

Hambrick-Stowe, Charles E. "The Spiritual Pilgrimage of Sarah Osborn (1714–1796)." *Church History* 61.4 (December 1992): 408–21.

Howard, June. "What Is Sentimentality?" *American Literary History* 11.1 (Spring 1999): 63–81.

Jefferson, Thomas. *Notes on the State of Virginia.* Ed. William Peden. 1787. Williamsburg: Omohundro Institute of Early American History and Culture at Williamsburg, Virginia, 1982.

Mather, Cotton. *Pillars of salt. An history of some criminals executed in this land, for capital crimes. With some of their dying speeches; collected and published for the warning of such as live in destructive courses if ungodliness. Whereto is added, for the better improvement of this history, a brief discourse about the dreadful justice of God, in punishing of sin, with sin.* Boston: Printed by B. Green, and J. Allen, for Samuel Phillips at the Brick Shop near the old meeting-house, 1699.

———. *Tremenda. The dreadful sound with which the wicked are to be thunderstruck. In a sermon delivered unto a great assembly, in which was present a miserable African, just going to be executed for a most inhumane and uncommon murder At Boston May 25th. 1721. To which is added a conference between a minister and the prisoner, on the day before his execution.* Boston: Printed by B. Green, for B. Gray & J. Edwards, & sold at their sips, 1721.

Murphey, Murray G. "The Psychodynamics of Puritan Conversion." *American Quarterly* 31.2 (Summer 1979): 135–47.

Newman, Richard, ed. *Black Preacher to White America: The Collected Writings of Lemuel Haynes, 1774–1833.* Brooklyn: Carlson Publishing, 1990.

Osborn, Sarah. "The nature, certainty and evidence of true Christianity; in a letter from a gentlewoman in Rhode-Island, to another, her dear friend, in great darkness, doubt and concern of a religious nature." Providence: J. Carter, 1793.

Pocock, J. G. A. *The Machiavellian Moment: Florentine Political Thought and the Atlantic Republican Tradition.* Princeton: Princeton UP, 1975.

Slotkin, Richard. "Narratives of Negro Crime in New England, 1675–1800." *American Quarterly* 25.1 (1973): 3–31.

Wheatley, Phillis. *Phillis Wheatley: Complete Writings.* Ed. Vincent Carretta. New York: Penguin, 2001.

Williams, Dana D. *The Word in Black and White: Reading "Race" in American Literature, 1638–1867.* 1992. New York: Oxford UP, 1993.

Williams, Daniel E. "'Behold a Tragic Scene Strangely Changed into a Theater of Mercy': The Structure and Significance of Criminal conversion Narratives in Early New England." *American Quarterly,* vol. 38, no. 5 (Winter, 1986): 827–47.

Wood, Gordon. *The Creation of the American Republic, 1776–1787.* New York: Norton, 1967.

The Pan-African and Puritan Dimensions of Phillis Wheatley's Poems and Letters

Babacar M'Baye

Phillis Wheatley was an eighteenth-century African American writer who strongly identified with Africa's suffering from the Atlantic slave trade and developed sustained criticisms against slavery, racism, and other injustices against blacks in America and Africa. In her poems and her extant letters, Wheatley makes strong Pan-Africanist and other nationalist references that allowed her to offset the occasional ambivalence that she expressed toward Africa. She was part of a small, elite group of Western-educated black intellectuals such as Olaudah Equiano and Ottobah Cugoano whose views on Africa did not represent those of all other black populations in the West. She received an education and eventually acquired freedom, experiences, and opportunities that were not available to most blacks in the West. Yet she utilized her elite status and individuality by linking her suffering to blacks in Africa and to the African diaspora, thereby becoming a pioneer figure of Pan-Africanism.

Wheatley drew upon African oral narratives and worldviews that resonated with key ideas and rhetorics of Puritanism. She used these narratives, worldviews, ideas, and figures of speech in order to gain admissibility and recognition in America and fight for the freedom of blacks. The purpose of this comparison of Puritan and Wolof Islamic cosmogonies is not to force European values on African ones, but to give a specific African theological and cultural context to the writings of Wheatley, which have so far been examined, for the most part, in their Christian and Western contexts.

Here Pan-Africanism refers to the relationships that black populations from the United States, the Caribbean, and England drew among themselves from the 1770s through the end of the twentieth century in order to resist, collectively or individually, European slavery, imperialism, colonization, and racism. My conception of Pan-Africanism is indebted to Iris Schmeisser's interpretation of the adjective "Pan-African" as a word that "signifies a specific construction of black otherness and how ideas about black otherness functioned within the actual cultural, historical, and political contexts of their times, as they [Africans] were embedded in the specific dialogues and significations of the contemporaneous discursive order that characterized the cultural landscape of Paris in the interwar years" (117). Schmeisser's definition of Pan-Africanism allows us to stress both continuities and transformations in the development of the movement as well as the specific contexts in which it evolved. Yet Schmeisser's representation of Pan-Africanism as a movement that developed only in the cultural landscape of Paris during the interwar years is somewhat reductive, since it ignores the constructions of "black otherness" during the eighteenth and nineteenth centuries.

Sterling Stuckey's major study of eighteenth-century Pan-Africanism, *Slave Culture: Nationalist Theory and the Foundations of Black America* (1987), argues that the Pan-African struggle in the diaspora started between 1800 and 1807 when a Pan-African consciousness was being formed in the culture of the African slaves in the Americas. Slaves in South Carolina and in the West Indies, "who had experienced the Middle Passage and had retained memories of the complexities of African culture," were able to draw from shared experiences and cultures that influenced their political visions, religious outlook, and resistance against slavery (44). One example of a diasporan African community given by Stuckey is the ceremony of "election day" in eighteenth-century New England in which slaves chose a king who "carried himself as ruler and treated his [black] followers like subjects" and "controlled [their affairs] on behalf of others." For Stuckey, the behavior of the black ruler and subjects during the parades of kings and governors in eighteenth-century New England reveals "the existence of elements of a Pan-African culture in New World slavery," especially since "substantial numbers of slaves in Cuba and North America came from essentially the same areas of Africa" (79).

Stuckey's arguments demonstrate the strong and pervasive impact of African culture on the traditions that the enslaved Africans invented in the diaspora. Discussing a Senegambian tale entitled "The Hare Seeks Endowments from Allah," the collector Emil Magel writes, "The presence of the elephant in many Wolof stories attests to its former existence in the Senegambian savannah regions. In the early years of European trade with the Senegambian people, ivory was an important cash crop. Today, Wolof people know about elephants only through oral narratives" (181). The Senegambians, a displaced African community, who were brought to the Atlantic world through this trade carried these oral narratives or learned them from other African slaves during or shortly after the Middle Passage. This transplantation of African oral narratives allows us to make intertextual and comparative analyses between these tales and African American slave narratives.

The concept of the black Atlantic refers to the historical experiences and cultures of blacks in the West and to a promising field of scholarship that explores the connections between Africa and its diaspora. The term "black Atlantic" became popular in academia when Paul Gilroy coined it in *The Black Atlantic: Modernity and Double Consciousness* (1993) to refer to the ambivalent representation of race and nationalism in African American and African British literary and intellectual history. In Gilroy's *Black Atlantic,* Africa is theorized in terms of dualities that reveal the diversity of modern black cultures (4). The concept of black Atlantic literature is used herein to identify the literature produced by blacks living in the Western world since the mid-eighteenth century.

The term "diaspora" comes from the Greek word *Diaspeirein* (to spread about) (Bonnett 2). Originally referring to the dispersion of the Jews outside Israel in the twentieth century, the term "diaspora" has been enlarged to include the dispersal of Africans in New World societies by historical forces such as slavery, colonization, wars, and migrations (Segal xiii). The notion of "African diaspora," which I will use interchangeably with the term "black diaspora," is indebted to Michael L. Blakey's definition of the term "diaspora." As Blakey suggests, the idea of diaspora "assumes the character of a dynamic, continuous and complex phenomenon stretching across time, geography, class, and gender" (388).

Constructing a coherent biography of Phillis Wheatley is problematic because certain key experiences such as the events that led to her enslavement from the Senegambian coast of Africa and the predicaments that she faced as a child during the Middle Passage remain unknown. Another difficulty in tracing the early details of her life is the lack of information regarding the interactions that she had in her early career with her white critics. In *The Trials of Phillis Wheatley: America's First Black Poet and Her Encounters with the Founding Fathers* (2003), Henry Louis Gates Jr. writes: "We have no transcript of the exchanges that occurred between Miss Wheatley and her eighteen examiners" (29). The only document available is the "Letter of Attestation," which serves as prefatory matter in her 1773 *Poems on Various Subjects, Religious and Moral.*

While there have been extensive studies about Wheatley's life, experiences, religious beliefs, and social connections, they have not been African-centered, since they do not show how Wheatley's networking through letters, poems, and other forms of communications in the Atlantic world were Pan-Africanist. In other words, most studies about Wheatley do not show how her writings project a humane image of Africa and blacks that seeks to dismantle the yoke of slavery and misrepresentation. Interpreting Wheatley's writings only in terms of individuality and hybridity fails to show the strong relationships she developed with Africa despite her sporadic ambivalence toward the continent.

In spite of the scant data about her biography, moreover, much can be known about Wheatley's relationship with Africa by analyzing representations of this country in her poems and letters. Speaking to this effort, James A. Rawley has observed, "These letters add important details to our meager knowledge of Phillis, such as her relations with the major influence upon her life, Susanna Wheatley; her religious outlook; her attitude toward returning to her native Africa, as well as a negative clue to her African origin" (665).

John C. Shields's essay, "Phillis Wheatley" (2001), argues that Wheatley was born "in or around 1753, probably along the Gambia River in West Africa" (774). In the Introduction to *The Poems of Phillis Wheatley* (2002), Julian D. Mason Jr. contends that, on July 11, 1761, Wheatley arrived in Boston as a slave on the schooner called *Phillis.* In late July 1761, Susanna Wheatley, the wife of John Wheatley, a prominent merchant from King Street, Boston, purchased her and took her to their home (48). Wheatley grew up with her owner's twins Mary and Nathaniel. Through the help of Mary, she learned to speak and write English. Sixteen months after her arrival in America, she read passages from the Bible and Western classics, and was able to write letters and poems to her friends (Salisbury 29–30).

By the time she was fourteen, Wheatley wrote her first extant poem (Estell 234). Dated 1765, the poem was entitled "On Messrs. Hussey and Coffin," which was published in December 1767 in Newport, Rhode Island (Mason 50). The poem deals with how God's grace saves two sailors from a storm on the coast of Cape Cod. Wheatley praises God as "the Great Supreme, the Wise, / [who] Intends for something hidden from our Eyes" (133), suggesting the fervent religious and spiritual essence seen in her early poems. In that same year, she also wrote an elegy that was published some three years later under the title, "A Poem by Phillis Wheatley, A Negro Girl, On the Death of Reverend Whitefield" (Estell 812). When she was eighteen, she composed a volume of thirty-eight verses entitled *Poems on Various Subjects, Religious and Moral,* which was published in England in 1773. In "The Day When America Decided that Blacks Were of a Species that Could Create Literature" (1994), Gates emphasizes how this phenomenal work brought Wheatley fame, recognition, freedom, and the title of first African American poet to publish a book in English (50–51). As Mason points out in his "Introduction to *The Poems of Phillis Wheatley*" (1989), in spite of her notoriety, Wheatley suffered from frail health that was aggravated by the harsh, damp climate of New England, perhaps leading to her premature death in Boston on December 5, 1784 (55).

Wheatley's career was not easy. As Gates and Maria Wolf suggest in "An Overview of Sources on the Life of Juan Latino, the 'Ethiopian Humanist'" (1998), she had great difficulty finding a publisher for her *Poems:*

> When her master, John Wheatley, [sent] her manuscript to printers in Boston, they expressed profound doubts about the very capacity of an African to write a poem in a Western language, especially the sort of verse to be found in Wheatley's manuscript, replete with classical, canonical allusions to figures and themes of Graeco-Roman mythology, and Latin phrasing found here and there. (14)

According to Gates, sometime in October 8, 1772, eighteen men, including Thomas Hutchinson, the governor of Massachusetts, met with Wheatley in Boston's Town Hall "to verify the authorship of her poems and to answer a much larger question: was a Negro capable of producing literature?" (*Trials* 5). The interaction between the elite white men and Wheatley was tainted by the subtle racism that prevented whites in colonial America from acknowledging the intelligence and humanity of blacks. Given these so-called Enlightenment conditions, Early American whites took part in the racist tradition in which philosophers from Francis Bacon and David Hume to Immanuel Kant misrepresented blacks as people who possessed no arts, sciences, or feeling.

Thomas Jefferson, who was the leading intellectual spokesperson of the elite white men in America, extended this demeaning attitude toward Wheatley's *Poems* and the entire black race. In *Notes on the State of Virginia* (1781), he asserts,

Among the blacks is misery enough, God knows, but no poetry. Love is the peculiar cestrum of the poet. Their love is ardent, but it kindles the senses only, not the imagination. Religion indeed has produced a Phyllis Whately [sic]; but it could not produce a poet. The compositions published under her name are below the dignity of criticism. (140)

Jefferson's assessment reflects his deep-seated racism against blacks, as well as his anxieties about a potential wave of liberation from injustice that Wheatley and other literate blacks represented in America. Jefferson's denigration of Wheatley may stem from his discomfort about her potential role as instigator of black protest against slavery in America. Prior to insulting Wheatley, Jefferson expresses profound trepidation about the possible retaliation of enslaved Africans against their white masters. He writes, "Deep rooted prejudices entertained by the whites; ten thousand recollections, by the blacks, of the injuries they have sustained; new provocations; the real distinctions which nature has made; and many other circumstances, will divide us into parties, and produce convulsions . . ." (138). Thus, Jefferson was well aware of the significance of Wheatley's work since the injustices against blacks in America, that he represents in his writings, were central issues in Wheatley's poetry.

Wheatley, as we have observed, possessed a number of privileges that few blacks in the Atlantic world had. She used these privileges to crisscross the Atlantic and develop subversive ways of fighting for equality. Her privileges derived principally from the ways she utilized the support she received from the Wheatleys, their connections in England, and from the support she gained in America to develop her own rebellion against slavery and its misrepresentation and exploitation of Africans.

Susanna Wheatley was a prime figure among Wheatley's supporters, since she allowed the African American poet to make the acquaintance of Reverend George Whitefield, the pioneer Methodist about whom Wheatley wrote in "A Poem by Phillis Wheatley, A Negro Girl, On the Death of Reverend Whitefield." Susanna knew Whitefield and often entertained his sympathizers, called "the connection," in her home (Rawley 668).

In certain letters written to her benefactors, Wheatley reflects a hybridlike influence of Calvinistic Methodism, Puritan faith, and Senegambian religious traditions. In her letter, "To the Rt. Hon'ble the Countess of Huntingdon," written in Boston on October 25, 1770, in which she expresses her sympathies to the countess on the passing of Reverend Whitefield, Wheatley intersperses comments about her African identity. She represents herself as an "untotor'd African" whose poetry cannot suffice to depict the fascinating qualities of Reverend Whitefield, who is "this Citizen of Zion!" (162).

Within this same letter, Wheatley infuses into her Calvinistic religious poetics elements that derive from both European and African cultures. Her representation of Reverend Whitefield as a "worthy chaplain" to the Countess of Huntingdon, whose passing is a "Greater gain" for himself, reflects a world-view that some whites and blacks in America shared. This "Greater gain" signals that the death of a saint should be rejoiced since the passing emanates from divine will and brings peace to both the deceased and the living while simultaneously maintaining harmonious relationships between the two parties. This Puritan concept of death is evident in Wheatley's Calvinist representation of the countess as a person whose actions of kindness, faith, and fairness toward Whitefield mirror those of the Divine Benefactor (God) that the reverend has rejoined in heaven.

In "Phillis Wheatley's Struggle for Freedom in Her Poetry and Prose" (1988), Shields suggests that the poet's elegies

> . . . resemble the Puritan funeral elegy. This poetic form con-
> tains first a portrait or biography of the deceased, whose life is
> divided into three stages: vocation or conversion, sanctification
> or evidence of good works, and glorification or treatment of the
> deceased's joyous reception into heavenly reward. The second
> section of the Puritan funeral elegy, called exhortation, urges
> the living to put off mourning and to concentrate on earning for
> themselves a reward similar to that of the deceased. (246)

This ideology about death is consistent with the African conception of life and death as two related parts of a cycle that join the living and the deceased eternally through continual worship. The many elements of the Puritan funeral elegy are similar to those found in the Senegambian Islamic and Wolof funeral elegies in which, upon news of the deceased person, the community gathers to perform three major rites: testify to the good deeds and the moral character of the individual before the burial; mourn the individual for only a limited length of time, usually during the first hours or days after the passing; and, finally, urge the closest family and friends of the departed to please the person who has passed into heaven by ceasing to cry and by performing good deeds during their lifetime which will please the individual who has passed into heaven.

The representation of heaven in the Senegambian-Islamic worldview as a place of tranquility may be perceived by noting how, in the 1770s, the Almamy (Head Cleric) Abdul Kadir of the empire of Futa Toro, in northern Senegal, attempted to convert many inhabitants from the empires of Waalo and Jolof, in northwest and central Senegal, into the Islamic faith by assuring them that they would secure their place in paradise through holy war. According to Lucie Gallistel Colvin, "The Almamy issued the call to jihād, bringing in men, women, and children, old, lame, and blind, each anxious to secure his place in heaven through this religious military service [jihād]" (601). This quotation suggests that the Senegambian-Islamic representation of heaven stands as a place of eternal reward and quiescence.

Though, in his *The Wolof of Senegambia* (1967), David P. Gamble describes the mourning period in Wolof Senegambian society to last for months, and the author identifies the following elements of Wolof funeral traditions that are consistent with the patterns of Puritan elegy. These aspects include the announcement of the deceased's name, the testimony of relatives and friends regarding what they know about the departed, and a mourning period that can last up to four months (69). The elements found in the Wolof mourning traditions parallel those in the Puritan elegy, as seen in Wheatley's writings. Both customs, for instance, attach a primary importance to public witnessing and testimony of the deeds that the departed performed during his or her lifetime. Also, both traditions attach a major significance to the spoken word as a means for strengthening the faith and the wisdom of a community in the process of mourning the deceased.

Another good example that shows the retention of the Senegambian folkloric elements in her writings occur in the letter Wheatley wrote to Miss Obour Tanner on March 21, 1774. As Benjamin Quarles argues, Miss Tanner, whose first name is also spelled as Abour, was, like Wheatley, born in Africa and was "of a deeply religious bent" (463). In her correspondence to Miss Obour, Wheatley thanks Susannah for adopting her when she was "a poor little outcast & a stranger" and treating her "more like her child than her servant." Revealing her respect for commitment, knowledge, and faith, Wheatley shows her appreciation for the invaluable teachings she received from Susannah's dedication to alleviating the sorrows of the outcast and to fortifying "the upper courts of the Lord" (178).

Wheatley's letter to Miss Tanner intertwines Puritan and African religious beliefs and poetics by making a public testimony about the departed while

Babacar M'Baye

praying for the sanctification of the living. This letter conveys the value of spirituality and family that one also finds in Senegambian oral narratives. For instance, like Wheatley, the character in the Wolof tale, "Kumba the Orphan Girl," exhibits a fervent belief in a Divine Benefactor who is similar to the Calvinist God found in Wheatley's missive. The Wolof tale suggests that the African conception of freedom is achieved through trials, resilience, and the ability to negotiate with strangers and receive kind treatment from them.

In the Wolof tale, a young woman named Kumba is forced by her step-mother to go to the Sea of Denyal to wash a cup that has indelible stains. After long walks, unsuccessful attempts, and hunger, Kumba met a woman "whose children were lions, tigers, and hyenas." Kumba did whatever the woman asked her to do, such as putting an old bone and a grain of rice in an empty pot and cooking it. The next day, the woman gave Kumba three eggs and told her to break them on her way home. (Magel, "Kumba" 193) When she broke the eggs, a herd of cattle, a flock of goats, and numerous servants began to follow her. Kumba remained free and victorious from that day on (Magel, "Kumba" 92–93).

Kumba's faith and the support of the old woman figure allow her to avoid being eaten by the lions, tigers, and hyenas, in the same way Wheatley's religious conviction and network of female supporters permit her to achieve success and gain her freedom. Like Wheatley, Kumba survives hardships with a strong spirit of resilience and a belief in the possibility of divine intervention and social justice. Both Wheatley and Kumba achieve spiritual strength, freedom, and success, thanks to the kindness of a stranger who adopts them in spite of their status as outsiders. Wheatley's former status as "a poor little outcast & a stranger" who was added to Susanna's family correlates with Kumba's early position as an outsider who was tied to the family of "lions, tigers, and hyenas."

Both Wheatley and Kumba exemplify humility toward the mother figures that nurture them so that they can turn an oceanic journey into an experience of glory, freedom, and recognition. The primary mother figure of Wheatley was Susanna herself, who opened the doors of international success to her. Rawley asserts, "Susanna directly influenced the girl's religious life, and was responsible for the poet's dedication of her book to the Countess of Huntingdon, and Phillis' poems about Whitefield and the Earl of Dartmouth. It was Susanna who planned for the publications of the *Poems,* and in England enabled the poet to meet distinguished personages, and ultimately secured the slave's freedom" (668). Susanna, like the Countess of Huntingdon, plays a role that is parallel to that of the woman figure in the Senegambian tale, which is to provide material and spiritual support to a black orphan girl.

Drawing from the Puritan worldview, Wheatley uses a rhetoric that admonishes slaveowners for their sins against God. Her rhetoric is inspired by the Jeremiad, which, as Sacvan Bercovitch argues, is a political sermon that warns people against divine revenge against sins such as "false dealing with God, betrayal of covenant promises, the degeneracy of the young, [and] the lure of profits and pleasures" (4). Wheatley utilizes this worldview in her rhetoric in which she tactfully substitutes the meaning of blackness from the racial innuendo that was traditionally attached to it with a nonracial one in which the color "black" signifies the spiritual perdition that awaits whites who have sinned against God by selling their fellow human beings. Wheatley's concept of sin derives from the Puritan and Christian Protestant philosophy in which the world is represented as a stable cosmos regulated by Divine will and good until it was corrupted with the original sins of Adam and Eve. In "Types of Puritan Piety" (1987), Gerald C. Brauer states as follows:

> They [Puritans] asserted that human beings were created by
> God, in the very image of God in a state of innocence, but that
> in Adam and Eve they fell from this state into sin and so were cut
> off, estranged at enmity with God their creator, and with their
> fellow human beings. Puritans believed that only God could
> bridge that gulf that stood between human beings and the
> divine. (43)

This Puritan cosmology that informs Wheatley's poetry is comparable to the worldview of the Murid of Senegal in which the holy city of *Tuba,* identified in the figure of "The Lote Tree," stands as the link between the divine, human beings, and the underworld. In "Touba: A Spiritual Metropolis in the Modern World" (1995), Eric Ross describes *Tuba* as "a cosmological symbol—the *axis mundi,* transcending the earthly and heavenly spheres" and represents "The Lote Tree," which identifies the city, as a medium that assures "proper passage through judgment and into paradise" (223). Ross's semiotic construct indicates the duality in the African conception of the world as a cosmos that is composed of two antithetical forces (the earth and the heavens), which are mediated by individuals who are sanctified by the divine.

A minor theme in Wheatley's poetry is that of atheism. This theme, which revisits Wheatley's rhetoric of sin, resonates in a 1767 poem appropriately entitled "Atheism." Here Wheatley begins a spiritual representation of blackness

Babacar M'Baye

when she confronts atheist philosophers of her time by asking, "Where now shall I begin this Spacious Field / To tell what curses unbelief doth yield?" (129). These lines follow the traditional African storyteller's way of introducing an oral narrative with questions and moral parables to both himself/herself and the listeners. As Ayi Kwei Armah shows, the African storyteller initiates a tale by asking philosophical questions such as: of what time, age, and context are the story about? Is the story about that marvelous black time before the desert was turned into desert? Or is it about the time when the bards sang praises to the spirit holding people together (2)? Wheatley follows this narrative process by letting the reader know that her story focuses on the Judeo-Christian conception of time, and the chaos that will prevail in the world if individuals do not believe in a higher power. She asks the reader, "If there's no heaven whither wilt thou go?" (129).

In the rest of "Atheism," Wheatley uses metaphors for darkness such as "the Shades below" and "the deepest hell" in order to represent hell as the abode of those who use secular or ancient philosophical learning to oppose the divine knowledge and wisdom of "the Book of praise" (the Judeo-Christian Bible) (130). It is therefore evident that Wheatley's concept of darkness identifies the moral and spiritual "perdition" that she associates with slave ownership.

Yet, more importantly, this darkness signifies on the moral chaos that Wheatley views as resulting from a break with God's divine plan. For her, this plan is "That covenant [which] was made for to ensure / Made to establish lasting to endure" (130). Though she does not define the idea of "covenant" in clear terms, Wheatley alludes to it in the way she stresses not only the belief in "essence of God" but also in the sustenance of this "essence" through love. In this sense, she places human equality at the center of her theology in order to show her critics that slaves, who have been mistreated inhumanly against the principle of the "covenant," have earned the right to be rehabilitated spiritually and intellectually.

In "An Address to the Deist," also written in 1767, Wheatley continues her quest in exploring the dangers of moral corruption that white slavers faced by specifically pointing at the "black despair" that awaits those who question the existence of "th' Almighty monarch." Addressing these "moral" sinners, Wheatley implores them to "Attend to Reason whispering in thine ear / Seek the Eternal while he is so near" (132).

Moreover, using the jeremiad, Wheatley invokes the theme of Christ's sacrifice in order to suggest the unequaled suffering that blacks have paid for shielding their fellow human beings from utter destruction. She writes:

"Father forgive them," thus the Saviour pray'd
Nail'd was king Jesus on the cross for us
For our transgressions he sustain'd the Curse. (132)

The Jesus in this poem serves as a metaphor for the slaves who endured in-commensurate pain that paid for the salvation of whites, but who, in return, have never been paid for the suffering incurred by them. In the poem "An Address to the Deist," Wheatley attempts to resolve this contradiction by de-manding black admissibility and freedom and stressing the immense social, political, and economic work that must be done on both sides of the Atlantic before whites can benefit from the sacrifices of both Jesus and the African slaves who gave their lives in martyrdom. Conscious of the urgency of this collective human action, she asks white America a straightforward question: "Must Ethiopians be employ'd for you?" (131), emphasizing the urgency of African equality to Europeans and African inclusiveness in American society.

"America," written in 1768, while critical of Britain's tyrannical stronghold over New England, walks the fine line between satire and praise while stress-ing the right of the colony to prosper like its mother. Wheatley's statement, "O Britain See / By this New England will increase like thee" (135), indirectly alludes to the unspoken right that African Americans had to be as free and independent from American slavery as the whites who subjugated them had wanted to be from English colonization.

Furthermore, other poems condemn slavery's suppression of the right of African Americans to achieve freedom. In "To The Right Honourable William [Legge], Earl of Dartmouth, His Majesty's Principal Secretary of State for North America" (1772), the poet describes slavery as a system that was inimical to the ideals of justice and freedom that America represented. She asserts:

No more, *America,* in mournful strain
Of wrongs, and grievance unredress'd complain,
No longer shall thou dread the iron chain,
Which wanton *Tyranny* with lawless hand
Had made, and with it meant t' enslave the land. (74)

The imagery of "the iron chain," the reference to the "grievance unredress'd" that complains, and the allusion to the "*Tyranny* with lawless hand" which is "meant t' enslave the land" suggest Wheatley's portrayal of the horrors of slav-ery. For Wheatley, ending slavery would have allowed America to become a free nation where justice and law would prevail. In making America's freedom contingent upon the remedy of the unresolved injustices within its "lawless land," Wheatley calls for the emancipation of the enslaved Africans. As James Levernier points out, this rhetoric appealed to clergymen and abolitionists in both England and America (24).

Wheatley also discusses her origins in Africa. These representations of Africa are, however, ambiguous. Wheatley was reluctant physically to go to Africa while she was spiritually willing to reconnect with the continent. On the one hand, she was disinclined to go to Africa because she occasionally regarded African societies and cultures as strange and unfamiliar. On the other hand, she was probably disposed to travel to Africa, because she often represented Africa and African-descended people, including herself, in remarkably positive terms. The ambiguity in Wheatley's relations with Africa reveals her unresolved desire both to weaken and to strengthen her ties to the continent.

In a letter to John Thornton dated October 30, 1774, she declined an invitation to serve as a missionary in the village of the Anamaboe. In the letter, she references her anxiety about going to Africa in order to work as a *servant of Christ*" (84). In the same correspondence, she also expresses a sense of humility toward the Anamaboe that reveals some unwillingness to go to Africa. She asks:

> . . . but why do you hon'd sir, wish those poor men so much
> trouble as to carry me so long a voyage? Upon my arrival, how
> like a Barbarian shou'd I look to the Natives; I can promise that
> my tongue shall be quiet/for a strong reason indeed/being an
> utter stranger to the language of Anamaboe. (184)

Wheatley's statement suggests her respect for the culture of the Anamaboe. Her fear of being unable to speak the language of the Anamaboe reflects her deference for their civilization and her eagerness to assume a position of innocence and blissful ignorance toward their culture and language. This humble posture must be taken into account even if it does not offset the degree of implicit condescension that Wheatley projects toward the Anamaboe. Wheatley's concern about the time and the distance that it would take her to travel to the village of the Anamaboe indicates her reluctance to go to Africa. Her fear of being looked on as a "Barbarian" who is unfamiliar with the language of the Anamaboe evidences serious hesitancy and doubt in her desire to go to Africa.

In certain poems in which Wheatley mentions Africa, she reflects this aloofness toward Africa and, occasionally, depicts African peoples and cultures through Eurocentric and primitivistic eyes. One example is the poem "On Being Brought from Africa to America" (1773), in which Wheatley represents Africans as *"Pagans."* She represents herself as a person who was brought from the *"Pagan land"* by "mercy" and was taught about God and redemption. Yet she also depicts herself as an individual who "May be refin'd, and join th' angelic train" (18).

This poem reveals paradoxes in Wheatley's relations with Africa. When she calls Africa her *"Pagan* land" with people who "May be refin'd, and join th' angelic train," she may be saying that the conditions of continental Africans could be improved by the same Christianity that allowed European Americans and African Americans to gain spiritual freedom. As Sondra O'Neale argues in "A Slave's Subtle War: Phillis Wheatley's Use of Biblical Myth and Symbol" (1986), Wheatley uses the image of the "angelic train" to symbolize "the purity that evangelicals assumed for themselves both in time and in eternity" (147). Wheatley wanted blacks to be given the same opportunity to enter the threshold of Christian purity to which whites aspired by faith.

The way in which she uses the endearing possessive pronoun "my" to identify Africa as her *"Pagan* land" may suggest her nationalist and resolute attempt to claim Africa and appropriate the distorted images that Europeans created about the continent in order to correct them on her own. In this sense, Wheatley sought to create a new form of "black otherness" by accepting the African identity Europe rejected and transforming it into an identity that allows blacks to be liberated from European oppression and primitivistic representations of Africa.

Yet there is a serious problem in Wheatley's representation of Africa in the poem, which is its repetition of European stereotypes about Africa. The Christianity that Wheatley praises is the Christianity that white missionaries brought to slaves in the United States and later wanted blacks of Africa to embrace unquestionably. While Christianity was a strong and legitimate spiritual resource and tool of resistance for Wheatley and many blacks, the missionaries that spread the Judeo-Christian tradition in Africa assumed that traditional African religions were "dark," "pagan," and "heathen." While she does not clearly express this bias, Wheatley somewhat conveys it in her depiction of Africa as a *"Pagan* land" and her idea that Africans will be "refin'd" by Christianity. This dimension contradicts the pride that Wheatley expresses when she describes herself as a descendant of a "sable race," revealing her unresolved double consciousness toward Africa. In *Kinship: A Family's Journey in Africa and America* (1999), Philippe Wamba analyzes this dilemma as follows:

For Wheatley, reconciling her historical ties to Africa with her adoptive American culture became an effort to *transcend* her African identity; she acknowledged the inferiority of her background, but reminded her readers that it was a circumstantial, not innate, condition and had not prevented her from finding religious salvation and rising in civilized American society, and would not prevent others like her from doing the same. (84; emphasis in original)

By giving more value to her Christian heritage and her American identity than to her African background, Wheatley showed, in this instance, that she was negatively impacted by Western misrepresentation of Africa as backward.

Yet, despite her disruptive relations with Africa in "On Being Brought," Wheatley continued to identify herself as an African. In "To Maecenas" (1773), she describes herself as a person from *"Afric's* sable race":

> The happier *Terence* all the choir inspir'd,
> His soul replenish'd, and his bosom fir'd;
> But say, ye *Muses,* why this partial grace,
> To one alone of *Afric's* sable race;
> From age to age transmitting thus his name
> With the first glory in the rolls of fame? (11)

The passage reflects Wheatley's admiration and pride in how Terence, a Roman poet of African descent, was able to use his oratorical skills in order to inspire the world and achieve his freedom. Terence (c. 195 or 185–159 B.C.), whose full name was Publius Terentius Āfer, was a successful writer of Roman comedies who was brought to Rome as a slave. His owner, Terentus Lūcānus, later educated him and freed him in Rome on account of his literary talents (Harvey 416).

Wheatley's description of Terence as a product of *"Afric's sable* race" attributes Terence's choiring abilities and "grace" to his African origins, thus letting it be known that she was proud of her African heritage and of the fact that both she and Terence were poets of African descent who had demonstrated, through their literary work, an uncontested power of imagination and love for mankind. Wheatley's attempt to know why the *"Muses"* favored Terence alone by giving him glory shows that she perceived herself as one of the talented African artists. As critic Betsy Erkkila describes, in "Phillis Wheatley and the Black American Revolution," "Self-consciously placing herself and her poems within a specifically African tradition, Wheatley registers her own ambitious desire to share—or perhaps transcend—the 'first glory' of her African forbears in a poetics of ascent" (231–32).

In other poems, Wheatley appropriates the African identity that she prided in Terence in order to promote her own poetic self. In "Hymn to Humanity. To S.P.G. Esq," she calls herself *"Afric's* muse" who honors her friends and works to move their "tender human heart" (97). Wheatley's act of calling herself *"Afric's* muse" attests her desire to identify herself as an African. In *The Heath Anthology of American Literature* (1990), William H. Robinson and Phillip M. Richards interpret Wheatley's representation of herself as an African as an expression of her racial self-consciousness (1048–49).

Yet, given the elusive nature of Wheatley's rhetoric, one wonders if her imagery of *"Afric's muse"* derived from a genuine sense of African consciousness or from deceptive strategy. As Houston Baker rightly points out in *The Journey Back: Issues in Black Literature and Criticism* (1980), "One pauses to ask if her reference to nationality was calculated merely to win added admiration from or to shock a white public that sometimes argued that the human heartbeat is not a property of the black world, or whether it is actually an indication of an extended African consciousness" (11). The inconsistency that Baker identifies in Wheatley's poetry is, however, put to rest, since there are instances in which Wheatley's identification with Africa is sometimes reliably genuine and sincere. One example occurs in the poem "To The University of Cambridge, New-England" (1773), in which she expresses a strong desire to be seen as an *"Ethiop"* (African). She views herself as *"An Ethiop"* whose mission is to tell the students of Cambridge that slavery, or the "sable monster" which prevails in the "sable Land," is the greatest sin of all (196–97).

Wheatley's reference to herself as *"An Ethiop"* conveys her desire to be regarded as an African who emphasizes her blackness to denounce the barbaric institution that oppressed blacks of both sides of the Atlantic Ocean. Her self-depiction as an "Ethiop" deserves recognition, even if it might have been driven by her attempt to differentiate herself from Europeans and making it seem that she, the African, could write good poetry. Even if a strategic quest for literary notoriety and fame may have led Wheatley to represent herself as an *"Ethiop"* or an *"Afric,"* the simple fact that she called herself an African registers her strong degree of black racial consciousness and African identity.

Ultimately, the question as to whether Wheatley viewed herself as wholly African or not does not undermine the fact that she utilized African discursive

Babacar M'Baye

and rhetorical practices even when she might have done so for self-promotion. For example, in "To His Honour," she mourns the loss of a departed friend's wife and calls herself "the *Afric* muse" who brings "heavenly tidings" to a grieving husband. In order to bring solace to the bereaved husband, Wheatley assures that his wife is waiting in paradise. Wheatley tells the husband:

> There sits, illustrious Sir, thy beauteous spouse;
> A gem-blaz'd circle beaming on her brows.
> Hail'd with acclaim among the heav'nly choirs,
> Her soul new-kindling with seraphic fires,
> To notes divine she tunes the vocal strings,
> . . .
> Nor canst thou, *Oliver,* assent refuse
> To heav'nly tidings from the *Afric* muse. (117)

The way in which Wheatley describes Oliver's deceased wife as a spirit that is being welcomed in heaven with music and praise shows that she mastered the traditional African poet's art of actualizing the past in mythical, vivid, theatrical, and lifelike images. This device is similar to the narrative strategy that Anthony Graham-White described as the storyteller's impersonation of the character of the epic "as dramatically as possible" (27). Wheatley employs this type of impersonation, as she adorns the prophetic role of an *"Afric"* muse whose status as emissary of deities allows her to crisscross the worlds of the living and dead and bring the solace of music, artistry, and "heav'nly tidings" to a bereaved spouse. In this sense, Wheatley was an early African oracle and *griotte,* the latter being an African francophone term for "female African-centered historian, storyteller, and diviner."

Moreover, Wheatley was a Pan-Africanist because she frequently and assertively represented Africa as a place where peace and freedom needed to be restored. In response to the poem "The Answer [By the Gentleman of the Navy]," in which the author had called her "The lovely daughter of the Affric shore" (141), Wheatley wrote "Phillis's Reply" in which she proudly portrayed Africa in romanticized terms as her land of origin. She depicts the Gambia as the pleasing land where her soul wishes to return "with native grace in spring's luxuriant reign." Later, she gives a picture of the scenic view of "Afric's blissful plain" and "the warm limits of the land and main" (144).

In this poem, written on December 5, 1774, Wheatley remembers the Gambia region where she came from. Wheatley's reference to "Gambia" and

"*Afric*" reveals her willingness to identify the Senegambian coast as her place of birth. She equates the splendor and beauty of this coast with that of Britain's shores, illustrating her promotion of a positive image of Africa in the Western world and her desire to return to her homeland in spiritual or physical ways. Wheatley did, then, present a positive image of Africa, even while she often contradicted this portrayal in some parts of her writings.

By representing Africa in positive terms, she compensates for her previous positions toward Africa. Alternatively, she might have wanted to gain the same type of recognition that Milton (or "British Homer") and Isaac Newton, whom she describes as "Those bards whose fame in deathless strain arise" (143–44), received for presenting beautiful images of European society. From this perspective, she wanted to create a poetic tradition that was equal or superior to those of European authors. Therefore, Wheatley's writings are both African and American since they had a larger goal of ascertaining her rights as not just a gifted American author but also her respect for and consciousness about Africa and her African cultural identity.

Yet Wheatley's reminiscence of Africa was more than just a search for cultural authenticity; it was a strategy that prepared her for addressing the contradictions of American slavery. In numerous poems, she attempted to convince white American dignitaries such as General Washington of the injustice of holding Africans in bondage. In "To His Excellency General [George] Washington," written on October 26, 1775, she mixes praise for Washington with a critique of his involvement in the slave institution that she viewed as being contradictory to the ideals of liberty and democracy that America supposedly embodied. In the first portion of the poem, Wheatley, a skilled literary *griotte,* sings a ravishing praise-song for Washington by describing his successful actions in patriotic battles. Wheatley depicts herself as the "Muse" who bows while her pen tells the stories of Washington's triumphs in battles (145). She writes:

> Shall I to Washington their praise recite?
> Enough thou know'st them in the fields of fight.
> Thee, first in peace and honours,—we demand
> The grace and glory of thy martial band.
> Fam'd for thy valour, for thy virtues more,
> Hear every tongue thy guardian aid implore!
> (145–46)

This passage suggests the strong influence of traditional African narrative techniques on Wheatley's poetry. The impact is visible in the recurrence of exclamatory and interrogative lines, the gradual and sequential order of the narrator's description of events, and the direct and emotionally driven praise of a larger-than-human hero (or heroine). These rhetorical strategies are common in the traditional African poetics of ethnic groups such as those of the *Mandingo* of Mali, the *Wolof* of Senegambia, or the *Zulu* of South Africa. Samba Diop has shown that African *griots* and *griottes* who narrate the epics of Sunjata Keita, Chaka Zulu, and Njajaan Njaaye in order to praise royalties and other famed individuals use similar narrative strategies (107–8). In this sense, Wheatley could be considered as one of the first black American writers to infuse *griotte* poetics within African American literature.

In a similar vein, Wheatley's poem indicates African consciousness in its centeredness on black freedom. This consciousness manifests in the first stanza where she suggests the dilemma she faced as an elite black poet who expressed admiration for a white leader who nonetheless was tied to the system of slavery. Wheatley expresses the paradox she felt toward an American Declaration of Independence that tolerated the capture and exploitation of human beings. She writes:

> Celestial choir! enthron'd in realms of light,
> Columbia's scenes of glorious toils I write.
> While freedom's cause her anxious breast alarms,
> She flashes dreadful in refulgent arms.
> See mother earth her offspring's fate bemoan,
> And nations gaze at scenes before unknown!
> See the bright beams of heaven's revolving light
> Involved in sorrows and veil of night! (145)

This passage personifies Columbia, a name for America, as a goddess who epitomizes freedom, motherhood, and life sustenance for all Americans that Wheatley perceived as "nations" gazing "at scenes before unknown!" (145). The narrator's reference to the divine light that is "involved in sorrows and veil of night" may be read as a foregrounding of the moral darkness in which slavery put the American people, revealing a dilemma that could have been overcome only through acceptance of and surrender to the freedom from "Britannia" for which Columbia stands.

Later, Wheatley describes how the "eyes of nations" remain fixed on Columbia's Revolutionary War while "round increase the rising hills of dead" (146). This example shows that one of Wheatley's major goals in writing about General Washington may have been to help him see the contradiction of the American patriots' fight to defeat the British at a time when blacks and other groups in America were taken away from their homeland(s). By critiquing this tyranny, national silence, and passivity toward injustice through her reference to the peoples' "cruel blindness to Columbia's state" (146), Wheatley was able to intersperse into her poetry a subtle denunciation of the political leadership that Washington represented without alienating the man behind the general, whom she continued to admire and support personally. Wheatley uses the clause, "cruel blindness to Columbia's state," which describes Britain's disgraceful role of oppressor during the Revolutionary War, and to signify America's sightlessness toward the predicament of blacks within "Columbia's state."

In the final section of "To His Excellency General [George] Washington," Wheatley tells Washington that he should continue his war for freedom and expect, as rewards, "a crown, a mansion, and a throne that shine" (146). This passage reveals the strong and continuous esteem that Wheatley held for Washington despite her disapproval of his complicity in the treatment of enslaved blacks that she conveyed in the subtext of her eulogy. Here Wheatley gives evidence that she was a conscious and tactful black intellectual who used her somewhat privileged literary and social status in order to criticize, though implicitly, the oppression of slavery to an elite white audience that could identify with her on several levels—intellectual, emotional, and patriotic.

Wheatley used literature, moreover, as a strategic means of resistance. For example, in her poem "On the Death of General Wooster," written in July 1778, she takes advantage of her privileged status as a renowned poet in order to defend the cause of the enslaved African people. Recounting General Wooster's "warlike deeds" in terms that recall her depiction of Washington, she directly attacks the institution of slavery and demands African American freedom. In this poem on Wooster, she writes,

> But how, presumptious shall we hope to find
> Divine acceptance with th' Almighty mind—
> While yet (O deed Ungenerous!) they disgrace
> And hold in bondage Afric's blameless race?
> (149–50)

Babacar M'Baye

This passage reflects a spirit of explicit and unflinching resistance that Wheatley affirms by suggesting the paradox that African Americans experience living in a freedom-seeking American nation in which they are denied the respect, equality, and freedom that are given to whites. Wheatley was, despite her privileged status, strongly committed to the improvement of the conditions of African Americans.

Through her poems and letters, Wheatley identified with Africa in complex and ambivalent terms that reflect doubt and uncertainty about the continent. Her identification with Africa is both indefinite and supportive since it might have derived from either a heartfelt bond with Africa or a superficial attachment to the continent. This uncertainty stands as evidence of her ambiguous relationships with Africa. Yet this ambivalence did not prevent her from denouncing the oppressions whites perpetrated against the enslaved Africans. By vehemently criticizing the impact of slavery on the enslaved Africans, Wheatley used her poetic skills as weapons of resistance against slavery. In so doing, she developed a tremendously strong tradition of Pan-Africanist analysis of the predicament of people of African descent during slavery that deserves more attention than it has so far received.

WORKS CITED

Armah, Ayi Kwei. *The Healers*. Portsmouth: Heinemann, 1979.

Baker, Houston, Jr., *The Journey Back: Issues in Black Literature and Criticism*. Chicago: University of Chicago P, 1980.

Bercovitch, Sacvan. *The American Jeremiad*. Madison: U of Wisconsin P, 1978.

Blakey, Michael L. "Bioarchaelogy of the African Diaspora in the Americas: Its Origins and Scope." *Annual Review of Anthropology* 30 (2001): 387–422.

Bonnett, Aubrey W., and G. Llewellyn Watson. *Emerging Perspectives on the Black Diaspora*. Lanham: UP of America, 1990.

Brauer, Gerald C. "Types of Puritan Piety" *Church History* 56.1 (March 1987): 39–58.

Colvin, Lucie Gallistel. "Islam and the State of Kajoor: A Case of Successful Resistance to Jihad." *Journal of African History* 15.4 (1974): 587–606.

Diop, Samba. *The Oral History and Literature of the Wolof People of Waalo, Northern Senegal: The Master of the Word (Griot) in the Wolof Tradition.* Ontario: Edwin Mellen, 1995.

Erkkila, Betsy. "Phillis Wheatley and the Black American Revolution." *A Mixed Race: Ethnicity in Early America.* Ed. Frank Shuffleton. New York: Oxford UP, 1993. 225–40.

Estell, Kenneth. "Phillis Wheatley Folio." *The African-American Almanac.* Ed. Kenneth Estell et al. Detroit: Gale Research, 1994. 812.

Gamble, David P. *The Wolof of Senegambia: Together with Notes on the Lebu and the Serer.* London: International African Institute, 1967.

Gates, Henry Louis, Jr. "The Day When America Decided that Blacks Were of a Species That Could Create Literature." *Journal of Blacks in Higher Education* 5 (Autumn 1994): 50–51.

———. *The Trials of Phillis Wheatley: America's First Black Poet and Her Encounters with the Founding Fathers.* New York: Basic Civitas, 2003.

———, and Maria Wolf. "An Overview of Sources on the Life of Juan Latino, the 'Ethiopian Humanist.'" *Research in African Literatures* 29 (Winter 1998): 14–51.

Gilroy, Paul. *The Black Atlantic: Modernity and Double Consciousness.* Cambridge: Harvard UP, 1993.

Graham-White, Anthony. *The Drama of Black Africa.* New York: Samuel French, 1974.

Harvey, Paul, ed. *The Oxford Companion to Classical Literature.* Oxford: Clarendon, 1969.

Jefferson, Thomas. *Notes on the State of Virginia.* Ed. William Peden. Chapel Hill: U of North Carolina P, 1982.

Levernier, James A. "Phillis Wheatley and the New England Clergy." *Early American Literature* 26.1 (March 1991): 21–38.

Magel, Emil A. "The Hare Seeks Endowments from Allah." *Folktales from the Gambia: Wolof Fictional Narratives.* Ed. Emil Magel. Washington, D.C.: Three Continents, 1984. 179–81.

———. "Kumba the Orphan Girl." *Folktales from the Gambia: Wolof Fictional Narratives.* Ed. Emil Magel. Washington, D.C.: Three Continents, 1984. 90–95.

Mason, Julian D., Jr. "Introduction to *The Poems of Phillis Wheatley.*"
In *Modern Critical Views: African-American Poets: Phillis Wheatley
through Melvin B. Tolson.* Ed. Harold Bloom. Philadelphia: Chelsea
House, 2003. 47–68.

O'Neale, Sondra. "A Slave's Subtle War: Phillis Wheatley's Use of Biblical
Myth and Symbol." *Early American Literature* 21.2 (September 1986):
144–65.

Quarles, Benjamin. "A Phillis Wheatley Letter." *Journal of Negro History*
34.4 (October 1949): 462–64.

Rawley, James A. "The World of Phillis Wheatley." *New England Quarterly*
50.4 (December 1977): 666–77.

Robinson, William H., and Phillip M. Richards, eds. "Phillis Wheatley."
The Heath Anthology of American Literature. Ed. Paul Lauter. Vol. 1.
Lexington: D. C. Heath, 1994. 1048–49.

Ross, Eric. "Touba: A Spiritual Metropolis in the Modern World." *Canadian
Journal of African Studies* 29.2 (1995): 222–59.

Salisbury, Cynthia. *Phillis Wheatley: Legendary African-American Poet.*
Berkeley Heights: Enslow, 2001.

Schmeisser, Iris. "Vive L'Union de tous les Noirs, et Vive l'Afrique: Paris
and the Black Diaspora in the Interwar Years." *Source: Revue d'études
Anglophones* 17 (Automne 2004): 114–43.

Segal, Ronald. *The Black Diaspora: Five Centuries of the Black Experience
Outside Africa.* New York: Noonday, 1995.

Shields, John C. "Phillis Wheatley." *African American Writers.* Ed. Valerie
Smith et al. 2nd ed. New York: Scribner, 2001. 773–92.

———. "Phillis Wheatley's Struggle for Freedom in Her Poetry and Prose."
The Collected Works of Phillis Wheatley. Ed. John C. Shields. New York:
Oxford UP, 1988. 229–70.

Stuckey, Sterling. *Slave Culture: Nationalist Theory and the Foundations of
Black America.* New York: Oxford UP, 1987.

Wamba, Philippe. *Kinship: A Family's Journey in Africa and America.* New
York: Dutton, 1999.

Wheatley, Phillis. *The Collected Works of Phillis Wheatley.* Ed. John C.
Shields. New York: Oxford UP, 1988.

An Untangled Web: Mapping Phillis Wheatley's Network of Support in America and Great Britain

Zach Petrea

The immense public popularity of Phillis Wheatley, which cannot be doubted, was unfortunately as brief as her life: a short thirty-one years. Yet her influence as "the first truly American poet in our literary history" and "the first black, the first slave, and the second woman to publish a book of poems in the United States" (Kaplan 150) continues to reverberate today. Amazingly, Wheatley was not only the "first American woman poet in 120 years to speak poetically of politics or other such 'men's work'" (Watts 37), she was also a slave. That she was "precondemned on three counts: she was a woman, she was an African, and she was a slave" (O'Neale 501), and yet was still able to garner such distinction, seems to warrant her a significant place in literary history, both because of her situation and her achievement; unfortunately, widespread reclamation of her substantial influence has only just begun. Sadly, a significant reason for Wheatley's marginal stature can be attributed to one of America's greatest intellects and most revered minds: Thomas Jefferson.

Of all that has been said about Wheatley since her first publication in 1767, possibly the most publicly influential, and damaging, has been Jefferson's remark in his 1785 *Notes on the State of Virginia*, that "[R]eligion, indeed, has produced a Phyllis Whately [*sic*]; but it could not produce a poet. The compositions published under her name are below the dignity of criticism. The heroes of the Dunciad are to her, as Hercules to the author of that poem" (147). Regrettably, because of Jefferson's considerable reputation, his derogatory comments about Wheatley's ability have overshadowed, by far, the compliments paid to her by other contemporary and noted intellects, including Benjamin Rush (1746–1813), who said in 1773 that her "singular genius and accomplishments are such as not only do honor to her sex, but to human nature" (Mason, "Introduction" xlii–xliii). And yet, despite numerous efforts to dispute Jefferson's judgment, it seems that his estimations have proven far more durable, and remain seemingly impervious to refute. Even the famed French philosopher Voltaire (1694–1778) stated in 1774 that "Fontenelle avait tort de dire qu'il n'y aurait jamais de poetes chez les Negres: 1y a actuellement une Negresse qui fait de tres-bons vers anglais" (Fontenelle was wrong to say that there would never be any poets among the Negroes: there is currently a Negress who makes some very good English verse) (Mason, "Introduction" xliii), yet it is Jefferson's negative opinion that still continues to weigh down an otherwise deserving reputation.

Other well-known refutations to Jefferson's critique are those from Gilbert Imlay (1754–1828) and Samuel Stanhope Smith (1751–1819). Interestingly, Smith took issue with Jefferson's denial by comparing the poet to plantation owners when he queried, "I will demand of Mr. Jefferson, or any other man who is acquainted with American planters, how many of those masters would have written poems equal to those of Phillis Whately [*sic*]" (Mason, "Introduction" xliv). Imlay, on the other hand, resorted to a more personal attack on Jefferson's judgment, when he declared that in "estimating her genius and Mr. Jefferson's judgment; and I think, without any disparagement to him, that, by comparison, Phyllis [*sic*] appears much the superior" (229). However, perhaps most unfortunate of all is that despite Johann Friedrich Blumenbach's (1752–1840) assertion that, "scarcely anyone who has any taste for poetry could read [Wheatley's poems] without pleasure" (Grimsted 428), those who are supposed to have a love for literature have been content to echo Jefferson and ignore Wheatley's considerable poetic ability. Seemingly, the teachers of literary history have been content to lament, like Henri Gregoire (1750–1831), that it must be "very much regretted that such an esteemed man as Jefferson had made such remarks" (Mason, "Introduction" xliv). Surely, such noted and notable discourse among the eighteenth century's most distinguished minds warrants a more comprehensive rejoinder, something considerably more than a passing "regret."

While it is not my intention to engage in any sort of vindication, or textual examination, of Wheatley's literary prowess, it is my hope that a preliminary discovery of her personal relationships will contribute to such future investigations. My work then can be seen as an initial attempt to map Wheatley's particular literary circles, the groups of people with and on whom she had contact and influence. Whether contact was direct or indirect, an essential framework of those principally involved with Wheatley's life and poetry is necessary for

Zach Petrea

any sustained attack on the belief that this amazing poet was merely, or only, an interesting footnote best known because of her pigmentation. Such a literary archaeology will help to lay the groundwork for continued research into literary points of intersection and comparative studies. Ultimately, this work reveals that the groups that provided Wheatley with essential support during her life were disparate and varied, yet they were all joined through their desire to see Wheatley, and many others like her, enjoy success.

MANUSCRIPT COMMUNICATION

In order fully to understand the nature and scope of Wheatley's network of support, it is necessary to recognize the reality of print culture during this time period. As Mukhtar Ali Isani has noted, the scarcity of resources and massive expense it took to produce a newspaper or magazine made space for information extremely limited: "the colonial newspaper was almost universally only four pages long, with little more than a page devoted to news that was not political or commercial" ("Contemporaneous Reception" 267). As such, Isani concludes, the fact that Wheatley won "recurring attention in these pages is impressive" (261). On Wheatley's publication record alone (some forty-two newspapers and magazines), Julian Mason's assertion that "Wheatley's poems were indeed known among the prominent families of Charleston . . . as well as among those of Boston, elsewhere in New England, New York and Philadelphia" (54), is safe in its underestimation, for her work also appeared in Ireland, Scotland, Sweden, Germany, England, and even France.

The forty-plus papers Wheatley appeared in makes a general tracking of the dispersal of her work relatively easy, but the informal nature of private correspondence makes interpersonal contact much more difficult and tentative. Until the turn of the nineteenth century and the advent of mass printing and cheap distribution, an elaborate and extensive manuscript culture of written letters and notebooks sent from friend to friend constituted everyday communication for the literate class. Indeed, Moses Coit Tyler's understanding that "the correspondence of our Revolution, both official and unofficial, constitutes a vast, a fascinating, and a significant branch of its literature" (12) was far ahead of even most contemporary scholarship concerning private/public sphere circulation in Early America.

This vast private, manuscript culture was reinforced by a specifically American version of the French club culture. Called "salons," these gatherings consisted of family and friends who met to discuss news, pleasure, and entertainment. While the most notable American salons originated at the Graeme Park and Morven estates (Elizabeth Graeme Ferguson [ca. 1737–1801] and Annis Boudinot Stockton [1736–1801], respectively), these intellectual meetings and social gatherings precipitated discussion far removed from their elite, urban location. As stated by Philip F. Gura,

> eighteenth-century America had an elaborate "club" culture
> derived from and comparable in sophistication to that which
> thrived contemporaneously in England and on the Continent—
> miniature, self-contained worlds in which gentlemen, and their
> ladies, shared each other's company for conversation, wit, music,
> and *literature*. (169; emphasis in original)

That these salons were "self-contained worlds" does not, however, insinuate that they were isolated from the rest of the culture. In fact, it is precisely because these gatherings were individuated from popular culture that men and women were able to share "each other's company for conversation, wit, music, and *literature*," and were free from the constraints of the norms of mainstream society, which would otherwise have prevented such open and frank discussions. From these literary salons, the republican courts and levees of Martha Custis Washington (1731–1802) would spring and eventually point to the new century's public spectacle of Congress. The acclaim and renown of the women involved in the salons would eventually loosen social codes of conduct so much that, according to Margaret Bayard Smith (1778–1844), the House of Representatives would become "the lounging place of both sexes, where acquaintance is as easily made as at public amusements" (95). While a feminine presence in such a purely political sphere did not guarantee any direct access to political power, it was nonetheless an important step and a hard-earned victory. What is more, this crucial step would have been impossible without the literary/social club of half a century before.

Karin A. Wulf notes that, prior to the Revolution, the salons were gatherings often "held in the home of a wealthy female member of the literati," and that they "welcomed and promoted aspiring writers as well as more established authors" (*"Milcah"* 24; emphasis in original). Such an acceptance of both known and unknown authors into the same circle affected an atmosphere similar in function to the more famous Bluestocking Club in England. These American salons, then, created and perpetuated a mode of discourse respon-

Zach Petrea

sible for contributing to the dissemination of literature and knowledge in the era before mass-market printing. It would be difficult to overestimate the importance of these clubs for women of the time; the salons provided a place where women were able to share their ideas on literature and art with men, a hitherto unheard-of phenomenon. And for a woman such as Wheatley, who was triply oppressed, her dependence upon others, specifically other women, was even more acute. Given the aforementioned tendencies of the salon, it would be hard to imagine then, that someone as unique as Wheatley would not have been discussed at gatherings such as these. In order not to depend on conjecture, however, it is certain that, whether due to these types of festivities or not, Wheatley's popularity was such that Jefferson *had* to discuss her in his *Notes,* even if it was only to denigrate her abilities. Certainly one would not attract the attention, no matter how negative, of one of the country's most important minds, unless she or he was already a significant subject.

The importance of Jefferson's need to disparage a poet he considered so poetically challenged is seen not only in the fact that his comments were racially motivated, but because they were also political in force. That a woman poet, and more specifically a slave woman, could achieve so much is evidence in the growing power of women writers at this time and can partially be attributed to the success of the salons and to Wheatley's public presence. That women had a private place to air their thoughts and feelings in mixed company allowed for the dispersal of ideas deemed threatening by and to the masculine hegemony. As such, Wulf notes that these gatherings eventually became imbued with "political significance" and were attacked "as emblematic of society run amok" by the more conservative and nervous populace ("*Milcah*" 25). It needs, therefore, to be understood that at this time, men were popularly (and egoistically) considered the only "able bodies" for politics and public discourse. Socially, women were thought to be confined to the domestic sphere of housework and child rearing (Mulford 4). The construction of the salon, then, granted women a place within their own "world" in which to speak and act like men. Ann Willing Bingham (1764–1800), whose drawing room at her Mansion House in Philadelphia "may have done more to foster communication between Federalists and Democratic-Republicans than any other site outside the floor of Congress" (qtd. in Rust 287), would become a prime example of the promise offered by the salons, and the exemplar of masculine apprehension.

Though it is politically and historically significant that Bingham "used her influence to argue for women's significance in public life" (Rust 287), it is more important to the present study that she fostered such a dialogue through the use of the written word. Bingham not only argued publicly, via print, with Jefferson's view on feminine domesticity, but so highly regarded Susanna Rowson's novel, *Trials of the Human Heart,* so much for its empowering message, that she "ordered 26 copies . . . presumably for distribution among her acquaintances" (Rust 287). Her use of literature as a deliberate provocateur was a public attempt in the 1790s to "disrupt any easy opposition between a rarified home life and a bustling civic one" (Grimsted 12). The eventual success of the salons in changing attitudes and cultural assumptions is partly due to women like Bingham, and those who came before, like Wheatley. Tangible effects wrought by the salon culture, moreover, can easily be seen in the proliferation of women's seminaries, and the general encouragement of female education based upon the new understanding of republican motherhood.[1]

As Bingham's example illustrates, it should be readily evident that the club culture was heavily dependent on the printed word for discussion topics. These groups did not, nevertheless, rely solely on published works, or novels for that matter, because they also utilized miscellanies, commonplace books, and regular correspondence. In fact, it is for the salon's ready use of various letters and personal work that Wulf termed these clubs "epistolary salons." Similarly, Mulford has called these circles "friendship networks," for their reliance on poetry, prose, and general information from many different writers from different parts of the country to stimulate and encourage debate. Mulford, like Wulf, labels these exchanges as a type of "circulating library" whereby, through the exchange of literature and letters, these networks heightened the "sense of community" felt by women in a "world that left them largely isolated . . . a world in which their actions outside the home, would almost always be called into question" (5). The emotional segregation of men and women during this time made such communication, to those involved in these communities of correspondence, significantly more important than idle entertainment.

Indeed, these epistolary associations became lifelines in connecting sometimes vastly separated friends and family. In order to "preserve their networks, women would write frequent letters and notes, if conveyance was regular, and they would write long letter journals to far off friends if conveyance was infrequent" (Mulford 8). A notable example is that of Esther Edwards Burr (1732–1758) and Sarah Prince, who wrote multiple types of letters to each other; if the information was time sensitive, they wrote brief missives sent through the mail or carried by third parties. If the correspondence was of the general variety, the longer letter-journals would be used. These long journals were sometimes

Zach Petrea

called "paquets," and were essentially "a kind of literary diary." It would be a mistake, however, to perceive that these journals were used solely for personal reflection because they were in fact "also a documentary testament to the significance of women's literacy for forming relationships and expressing sentiments on subjects ranging from politics and war to marriage and housework" (Wulf, *"Milcah"* 1). The importance of these packets cannot be overstated; Prince's packets to Burr ran upward of some 320 pages each, thereby testifying to both the dedication and the care taken to send and read such voluminous communiqués.

It would also be a mistake to assume a limit on the number of acquaintances or friends being addressed in each paquet; Burr refers to several unnamed individuals, as seen in the entry for February 15, 1757, where she states "Tuesday-Writing to Stockbridge so must beg an excuse—Wednesday writing yet to one friend and another" (*Esther* 244). While Stockbridge is identified as the home of her parents, the vague reference "yet to one friend and another" stands to illustrate the number of conversations that occurred simultaneously. Similarly, Milcah Martha Moore's (1740–1829) commonplace book comprises some sixteen authors, while Ann Eliza Bleecker's (1752–1783) "Memoir" contains at least a dozen separate correspondences. In fact, Bleecker's book provides additional evidence as to the number of readers and the precarious nature of these circles for any given piece. Specifically, Bleecker mentions some sort of missive or newspaper that she whimsically named the *"Albany Gazette,"* which "being handed about from one company to another, is entirely lost" (xvi). The same letter goes on to make light of "(S)everal political and satirical pieces [that] shared the same fate" (xvi), which not only illustrates the precarious expanse of readers but also the involvement of women in public discussions and the dispersal of such discussions among their reading community.

Esther Burr's journal further reveals the depth of investment in writing for women of this time, when she notes at only nine years old, that "all this family keep journals" (*Esther* 11). Admittedly, born to the colonies' most famous minister, Jonathon Edwards, Esther led an elite life; nonetheless, other members of the elite, and even some of the less fortunate, would have duplicated her journaling experience. At one point, only three years later, Burr comments offhandedly of a friend "with whom, I sometimes exchange letters" (30). At only twelve years of age, then, Burr was already a member of a writing community that extended well beyond her immediate physical locale.

The deeply personal relationship shared between obviously intellectual women can also be seen through their writing as illustrated in Burr's adult correspondence when she addresses Prince directly. Several times throughout her journal, Burr states that "I have a few moments stolen from company to talk with *you*" (Burr, *Esther* 252; emphasis added), or excuses her brevity or absence of an entry by exclaiming that "I could not get one minutes [rest] to say one word to *you*" (57; emphasis added). Bleecker also understands writing as direct and personal communication rather than indirect message transmission, when she begs excuse for the length of her letter explaining, "but I am fond of talking to *you*" (132; emphasis added). This kind of association, where writing is intimate and verbal, not mechanical or impersonal, marks a unique understanding of correspondence, one altogether lost in today's visual society.[2] Letters were not, however, merely an unnoticed substitution for physical presence, for Bleecker acknowledges in a letter to her half-sister that she "is condemned to moon-light, as I see your [face] only by reflection; that is, by your letters" (132). Despite the obvious yearning for a physical body in close proximity, the exchange of letters connected women to a group, a network of support, a literal sisterhood, and most important, this practice provided a public forum in which to air highly personal grief, joy, and frustration.

The journal of Esther Burr reflects the depth of attachment these women established in their communities and to the assumption of indirect readers, given that "[R]ecipients of letters and manuscripts would frequently read missives while in company as entertainment" (Mulford 8). A not uncommon example, then, would be the situation described by R. L. Edgeworth in a letter to British friend Anna Letitia Barbauld (1743–1825), wherein Edgeworth mentions "the eight readers around our table" (Le Breton 95). This kind of public event would establish situations where multiple people (new friends of one of the correspondents) could become intimate with the original author, such as with the famous case of Susanna Wright (1697–1784) and Hannah Griffits (1727–1817). At one point, Burr even specifically addresses the public reading of her texts when she directs Sara Prince to send "Love to all and everybody that loves you" (*Journal* 217). The unidentified "everybody that loves you" has been referred to several times throughout the correspondence as "the Sisterhood," a group Prince even satirically labeled the "Freemason Club" (Burr, *Journal* 167). At one point, Burr bluntly directs Prince to send "Love to . . . all the Sisterhood for whom I feel a great friendship altho' some of 'em are unknown to me by sight" (Burr, *Journal* 209). Rather than expressing a superficial formality, Burr is genuinely concerned with people she has never met but was probably acquainted with them through reading paquets and letters that were copied or transferred to her.

Zach Petrea

The indirect transferal of letters is intimately tied to the relaxed manner of manuscript transmission itself. Several times throughout the paquet, Burr refers to letters she is sending to third parties by way of Prince, and vice versa, as if this type of transferal was a normal routine. Further, the two women possessed such a close bond that it seems as if each was allowed to read these third-party letters before passing them on to their intended recipients.

This type of third-party transmission was in no way unique to the Burr/ Prince instance. In a letter from Joseph Reed to his wife Esther Reed, Joseph mentions that he "found two large packets from England containing a very long letter from your Brother, one from Govr. Johnston & several for you & your mamma" (Reed). These paquets are noteworthy for the circuitous route the letters took; first from Esther's brother to her husband and then into her own hands, before ultimately reaching her mother. Interestingly, Joseph also refers several times to Esther's private correspondence, as if he had read it, while Esther is addressed in letters written to Joseph, from her brother, as if she were meant to read those as well. Similarly, Esther Burr's husband, Aaron Burr (ca. 1716–1757), is addressed several times in Prince's letters to Esther, and he responds in Esther's letters to Prince, which gives the feeling that families were open to such an extent that anything of a "private" nature was only private to the outside world, while everything was public within the family.

Understanding that the notion of a family was not exclusively tied to blood relations, but also encompassed the members of these writing communities, one could easily understand why the sending of third-party manuscripts to those outside the immediate reading circles was also not unusual. Wulf records how in a letter to a cousin, Hannah Harrison, she had "by Accident" obtained a "journal without [the author's] consent" and that "she would pass it along as soon as she received permission to do so, for it contained 'Most surprising, and Entertaining Anecdotes'" ("*Milcah*" 26). The fact that a journal was obtained "accidentally" implies the relaxed manner in which manuscripts might frequently exchange hands and the wide trajectory with which they might travel. Harrison's tone also sounds certain of the affirmation, leading to the assumption that, although this type of third-party sharing usually necessitated a formal consent, it was probably rarely denied.

Additionally, given the popularity of a particular piece among a community, the original author might even be encouraged to seek publication, as was the case of Gilbert Imlay, whose correspondent (Mary Wollstonecraft [1759–1797]) so enjoyed his letters she thought he should collect them:

> I requested my friend to send me, at his leisure, a complete description of the western country of America. . . . All this he has done in so ample a manner. . . . I thought that the letters which had imparted to me and a small circle of friends so much information and entertainment, would prove acceptable to the public. (Imlay v)

The result of the letters to Wollstonecraft was Imlay's *A Topographical Description of the Western Territory of North America* (1797), which was so popular that it went through three editions in four years. Similarly, the eventual publication of *The Posthumous Works of Ann Eliza Bleecker, in Prose and Verse* (1793), is prefaced by an address entitled "To the Public," which states that "we think it necessary merely to note, that having been frequently solicited to publish, in a separate volume, a part of those writings of Mrs. Bleecker which had appeared in the *New York Magazine*." In reviewing Bleecker's publications, which total some half dozen poems, it becomes immediately obvious that the call for a more complete dissemination of her work must be partly based on those who knew other unpublished work of the author. Bleecker's fame must, therefore, be partly based on the salon culture in which manuscripts were circulated that prevailed at the time. Consequently, it should not be assumed that this culture was confined to urban centers, for according to her "Memoir," even in Bleecker's countryseat, she frequently "wrote while with company, at the desire of someone present without premeditation, and at the same time bearing a part in the conversation" (xvii). It was also not uncommon for extemporaneous works written "without premeditation," and personal correspondence in general, to be published when the subject proved to be sufficiently interesting and noteworthy.

No stranger to this intricate world of print, Phillis Wheatley's letter discussing slavery with Reverend Samson Occom was printed "in at least eleven New England newspapers in the spring of 1774" (Grimsted 443n163), and has been often printed since, for her account of human freedom is eloquent. As such, it deserves one more recurrence:

> for in every human Brest, God has implanted a Principle, which we call Love of Freedom; it is impatient of Oppression, and pants for Deliverance. . . . How well the Cry for Liberty, and the reverse Disposition for the Exercise of oppressive Power over others agree,—I humbly think it does not require the Penetration of a Philosopher to determine. (Wheatley, *Collected Works* 177)

Zach Petrea

Similarly, Selina Hastings, the Countess of Huntingdon (1707–1791), wrote a letter to Ann Hyam that related the death of the Queen, and was found in Milcah Martha Moore's commonplace book (220). This instance is another such case where a personal letter would be passed among a group of friends and eventually would find its way into mass circulation. Assuredly, these particular, though not uncommon instances, show that popularity and poetic renown during the eighteenth century was based not on modern concepts of publicness but on a decidedly more fluid, and, in some cases, an even more "public" model than print culture proper would allow.

It needs to be emphasized that Phillis Wheatley, a slave in the merchant family of John Wheatley, was made famous because of her propensity for language and her ability to master linguistic conventions. However, because of her circumstance, Wheatley would not have been able to accomplish anything without the support of a vast network of friends and like-minded individuals, joined through writing circles and epistolary salons. That Wheatley was able in 1773 to publish a collection of poems titled *Poems on Various Subjects, Religious and Moral* testifies both to her genius and to her mistress's faith in the young slave, but also to their inability to publish on their own. The extant book of poetry was published in London and is actually the result of a second proposal, after the first attempt made in Boston did not meet subscription totals. It has been proposed that the lack of interest in the colonies was due to racial bias, but for whatever reason, the fact was that the Wheatleys could not secure publication without the aid of a substantial transatlantic connection. A connection headed and made possible primarily through Selina Hastings, the Countess of Huntingdon, luckily facilitated the publication of *Poems*.

CONNECTIONS

Any account of Wheatley's connection begins at her home in Boston, with Susanna Wheatley, who can be praised for allowing Phillis Wheatley to write and for exposing the slave girl to the cultural elite of America and England. Only through Susanna and her relentless promotion was Wheatley introduced to the countess, and from her, to the literati. It must be acknowledged, then, that "any account of Phillis Wheatley's poetic achievement is also an account of the clergymen, merchants, political figures, gentry, and nobility in both Britain and America who helped to bring her poetry to prominence" (Wilcox 9). Such patronage, no matter how prestigious, it must be remembered, cannot take away from this young women's pure genius. And yet, even those who helped in her promotion and advancement can, and must, still be held accountable for maintaining her in bondage, no matter how "nominally a slave" (Mason, "Introduction" 64) she might have been.

Similarly, Wheatley's fame can be "the result of the efforts of a white trans-atlantic circle of supporters who became adept at marketing Wheatley to suit both contemporary expectations and their own ends" (Wilcox 2). This circle (or, more specifically, groups of concentric circles) included some of the most prestigious people of the century, and no matter how flattering to Wheatley these people were, they supported and promoted her work, not solely out of Christian piety (although this cannot be totally denied), but also because the "privileged white Americans, members of the cultural elite . . . had a stake from the beginning in Wheatley's ability to publish" (Wilcox 2). Primarily, her success, with the proper guidance and litigation, could, and would, help the abolition cause. As such, Wheatley has also been a target for men like Jefferson and countless others since who deny her ability based not on her work but on her sex and on the color of her skin. However, Wheatley was, in the words of Isani, "an ambitious and worldly-wise woman, acquainted with notables of her time, and capable of unabashedly representing her own interests" ("Phillis" 255). Despite the efforts of those who sought to use her for their own interests, either positively or negatively, Wheatley was, after all, a strong and intelligent woman who fought for her own rights.

It has been noted that because of her sex and her status as a slave, Wheatley would have had initial trouble being published. Yet Wheatley's position as a slave for whom the "very act(s) of writing tested social attitudes" (Foster 17) and her sex, which contributed to her supposed "(S)arcastic superiority," created a situation wherein Wheatley was "quintupally barred from public display" (Grimsted 347). Ironically, these very significant obstacles helped her cause, specifically in that "the fact that this enslaved black women wrote at all took precedence in the public mind over anything that she said" (Wilcox 1). In a case of misdirection, where a feint hides reality, Wheatley's "race assured continuing attention to her work, [and] perhaps also circumvented the inter-pretive rigor with which it has been treated" (Grimsted 344). Simultaneously, while her race overshadowed her message, Wheatley's status as a slave "pro-vided her with a freedom that many New England women did not feel, for she had not been educated to believe herself limited to the domestic and religious" (Hornstein 250). Wheatley's status thus allowed her a certain leeway, often but not always, to disseminate a subversive message, while her abduction from a different culture at an intellectually conscious age (seven or eight) also allowed her some freedom from the moral and ideological constraints of her captors. In sum, her doubly marginal status and consequent novelty would have helped her circulation in a society where, much like today, "readers had an enormous appetite for the work of unusual literary prodigies" (Wilcox 12). In a seeming twist of fate, it was ultimately Wheatley's status as a black woman that both caused her enslavement and, eventually, her release.

CONNECTIONS IN AMERICA

It is sadly ironic that in 1761, the same year Wheatley was bought off the block, James Otis (1725–1783) gave a speech supporting the Revolutionary struggle and denouncing slavery saying that the "Colonists are by the law of nature free born, as indeed all men are, white or black" (Grimsted 397). For the rest of Wheatley's short life, she faced the harsh consequences of being black, being a woman, and being a slave. Virtually alone, Wheatley fought racist and sexist ideologies, eventually dying alone and destitute. Her fight, however, was not ineffectual, for she influenced many through her struggle, including James Otis's sister, Mercy Otis Warren (1728–1814). Warren, the Revolutionary historian and satirist, famous for her friendship with Abigail Adams, was known for writing poems and plays critical about both men and politics. Considering Warren's abiding interest in current events and Wheatley's penchant for addressing those events, Jacqueline Hornstein cautiously asserts that, "Mercy Otis Warren might have read Wheatley's popular verse," and that if perchance she did, "Wheatley's works would have encouraged her literary ambitions for they showed that women could write successfully about vital current issues" (253–54). While it cannot be shown how much of an influence was exerted, Jeffrey H. Richards has shown through Warren's correspondence that she did, in fact, know of and appreciate Wheatley.

According to Richards, Warren's sister-in-law, Sarah Walter, lived for a time in Boston before moving to England and marrying an English baronet, Robert Hesilrige. It is unknown whether Sarah knew of Wheatley before her move, but in 1773 she sent two books to Warren, one by a "Mrs. C.," who Richards believes is probably Hester Chapone (1727–1801), member of the Bluestockings, and one by Wheatley. While I disagree with Richards's identification of Mrs. C., who I believe is probably Elizabeth Carter (1717–1806), both women were nonetheless members of the Bluestocking circle.[3] In stating a preference, Warren admits that while at face value, she favors the English woman, when considering the background of the two, she states unequivocally, "I think that the last [Wheatley] must bear the palm of superior applause as best entitled to the claim of original genius" (Richards 42). Here, then, Warren serves as a prime example of the effect that these circulating libraries could have in exposing one of the preeminent female literary figures of the day to Wheatley's verse.

Later that same year, Warren would write to Catherine Sawbridge Macaulay (1731–1791), the "celebrated female historian" and Bluestocking, hence striking up a correspondence that would last the rest of their lives. In fact, Macaulay would stay at Mount Vernon for ten days with George and Martha Washington (Ferguson, *First Feminists* 399), and then at Milton Hill with the Warrens in 1785 (Richards 44). It has even been asserted that Warren's *History of the Rise, Progress and Termination of the American Revolution, Interspersed with Biographical and Moral Observations* (1808) was inspired by Macaulay's own *History* (Mazzucco-Than 97). It cannot be ascertained whether or not these two very knowledgeable and politically active women actually discussed poetry or current events, but how fascinating it would be to have listened to their conversations, for Wheatley's name would have likely come up.

Warren's correspondence, which "has long been recognized as a significant documentary source for historians of the revolutionary period" (Mazzucco-Than 26), because of her intimate connections with such luminaries as Martha Washington, Hannah Winthrop, and Abigail Adams, shows her appreciation for another woman poet. Of the previously mentioned women, Warren's friendship with Abigail Adams is the most famous, beginning sometime in 1754. When considering the extent and duration of the friendship, it is difficult to imagine how the two would not discuss Wheatley, or at the very least, forward her book for perusal. As of yet, however, I have found no mention or notice of Wheatley in correspondence between the two.

Likewise, there is no concrete or circumstantial evidence of Warren's discussing Wheatley with Martha Washington, but considering the impact and import of Wheatley's work for abolitionist and feminist ends, it is not inconceivable. Warren first met George and Martha Washington in 1775, while accompanying her husband on one of his political trips. Warren would eventually dedicate her book of poems, *Poems, Dramatic and Miscellaneous* (1790), to Washington. Warren, who was already well known for her poem about the Boston Tea Party, "The Squabble of the Sea Nymphs; or the Sacrifice of the

Tuscararoes" (Mazzucco-Than 53), which was requested by John Adams, might easily and without difficulty have discussed other poetry and literature with Washington.

That Mercy would converse with Washington about verse is not inconceivable. In the same year as Mercy's own introduction to Washington, Wheatley wrote a letter to Washington from Rhode Island and included a poem dedicated to him. As well, the fact that George Washington had a copy of Wheatley's 1773 *Poems* in his library also increases the probability that Warren and Martha Washington discussed the African American artist. Upon reception, Washington invited Wheatley to come visit him at Cambridge, which she did in 1776. In fact, both letter and poem were printed in the *Pennsylvania Magazine*, "whose editor, Thomas Paine, presented them to the public as '*written by the famous* Phillis Wheatley, *The African Poetess*'" (Kaplan 163; emphasis in original). Thomas Paine is further linked to Wheatley in that it was Benjamin Rush who helped Paine edit, publish, and title Paine's most famous tract, Common Sense (1776) (Stozier 419), and Rush has already been shown not only to know of Wheatley, but also to appreciate her work.

The same year that Mercy and Wheatley were seeking Washington's patronage, significant events were then occurring in Philadelphia. The first antislavery society in America, the Society for the Relief of Free Negroes Unlawfully Held in Bondage, was formed. Among notables associated with the society, Benjamin Franklin served as president with James Pemberton and Jonathan Penrose as vice presidents, and Benjamin Rush as secretary (Poole 42–45). Although a detailed list has yet to be compiled of the other members, the society proves interesting in another connection. The society would continue after the war, holding regular meetings until 1787 when the Pennsylvania constitution was revised to include the "Abolition of Slavery" and the "Relief of Free Negroes." These two amendments were passed in no small part because of the efforts of the society, but also because of pressure brought by Anthony Benezet (1713–1784), who "held private interviews with every member of the government on the subject" (Poole 42). Benezet was himself a staunch abolitionist and voluminous correspondent and author. Many, if not all, of the leading abolitionists can be traced directly to Benezet.

Pertinent to the present discussion, however, is the fact that Benezet wrote to the Countess of Huntingdon "representing the horrors of the slave traffic, which her managers were encouraging" in America. It seems that upon Reverend George Whitefield's (1714–1770) death, the evangelist bequeathed an

Orphan House to the countess and that after reading Benezet's complaints against the property, which was trafficking in slaves, "she expressed her determination no longer to countenance it, but to use every means to prevent it" (New 353). Unfortunately, it will never be known what would have happened had the countess's determination not been interrupted by the war. After cessation of hostilities, all of the countess's land was confiscated by the American government. Despite the efforts of Benjamin Franklin, who agreed to be a trustee of the estate (Stevens 170), neither his nor anyone else's influence was able to return her property to her.

In other interesting Wheatley connections, Benezet began a correspondence with Granville Sharp (1735–1813) in 1772, after each man had unknowingly republished the others' work in their respective countries. As a portent of the friendship to come, Benezet's letter of introduction reached Sharp on the day that Lord Mansfield gave his decision on the Somerset trial, which, in effect, freed all slaves who set foot on English soil (Armistead 32). The correspondence of these two men benefited not just their own interests but had a profound effect on others as well. It was through Benezet's influence that Sharp began a correspondence with Benjamin Franklin in April 1773 (Armistead 36), and then, just the next month, in May of that same year, Benezet would also connect Sharp with Benjamin Rush. Of the two connections, Rush and Sharp developed an intimate bond that produced a friendship that would last for some thirty-six years (Woods 1).

At this point in time, Rush had been under the tutelage of Benezet and active in the abolition movement for a number of years. In fact, it was Benezet who requested that Rush write his 1773 address on slavery, which specifically mentions Wheatley (D'Elia 44). While there is no record of either Rush or Benezet personally meeting Wheatley, Rush's knowledge of her has already been discussed. When combined with the fact that Wheatley met both Sharp and Franklin in London, during her stay in the summer of 1773, and Benezet's known correspondence with the Countess of Huntington and George Whitefield (Armistead 51–52), it is nearly impossible that Benezet would not be aware of her. Even if the two never corresponded directly, a man of such ambition, who dedicated his life to ending slavery, would definitely have known about Wheatley's life and work.

The connection of Rush and Wheatley is far more interesting and complicated than even this tangled web implies. By the time of his 1773 essay, Rush had known and corresponded with Whitefield for nearly twenty years, ever since their first meeting in 1754. The two men were so amiable that they would actually stay at each other's houses when traveling abroad (D'Elia 37). Further, Rush also possessed an "unusual talent for poetry composition" (Stozier 418), and contemplated writing a memoir or elegy upon his friend's death in 1770 (D'Elia 37n11). When considering the popularity of Wheatley's own elegy on Whitefield, it is conceivable that its publication allowed Rush to become acquainted with her work. Whether through association or merely through Rush's 1773 essay, Wheatley was also aware of Rush, and it is documented that she corresponded with him, for she includes a letter "To Dr. B. Rush, Phila" in her 1779 proposal for a second volume of work (191). Unfortunately, the manuscript has not yet been found.

Additional connections to Rush can be asserted since it is possible that Wheatley's "poems drew Rush's wife to her patronage, which, in turn, spurred Rush to use Wheatley's achievements as evidence in the rights debate" (Cima, "Black and Unmarked" 474). The assertion is based at least partly on the word of the nineteenth-century editor and poetaster Rufus Griswold, who states that upon Wheatley's death, her husband, John Peters, took her manuscripts and "subsequently went to the south, carrying with him these papers which were never afterward heard of. The manuscripts, however, are still in existence: they are owned by an accomplished citizen of Philadelphia, whose mother was one of the patrons of the author" (31). According to William H. Robinson, this "accomplished citizen" was Dr. James Rush (1786–1869), son of Benjamin Rush and Julia Stockton Rush (1759–1848) (Robinson, *Phillis Wheatley in the Black* 66). Given the donation of four unpublished manuscripts to the Library Company in Philadelphia upon James Rush's death, the view that either Julia or Rush himself were Wheatley's patrons seems veritable (Robinson, *Phillis Wheatley in the Black* 67). Even if this evidence is circumstantial, it would be reasonable to assume that Peters would attempt to sell his wife's manuscripts to a known abolitionist, and to a man whose well-known philanthropic tendencies would later culminate in the donation of some fifty-two hundred acres of his own land to the Abolition Society (D'Elia 95).

The possession of Wheatley's manuscripts by either of the Rushes would also concretely connect Wheatley to Julia's famed mother, Annis Boudinot Stockton. The connection between Rush and the Stocktons was no ordinary formality or social bond. Although the marriage of Rush to Julia was quite a spectacle (it was actually the only wedding to ever have three signers of the Declaration of Independence present: Richard Stockton, Rev. Witherspoon, and Rush himself), Rush was also a lifelong and intimate friend of the Stocktons (Booth 299). At one point, during Rush's Edinburgh stay, Richard Stockton specifically instructed Rush to act on his behalf in order to convince Rev. Dr. Witherspoon to leave Edinburgh and become the president of New Jersey College (Booth 16). Rush was not only trusted with business matters but very personal ones as well. In an unusual twist, Rush was entrusted to transport his future wife, when she was only four years old, from the college hall to her father's house at their Morven estate (Goodman 40). It should be obvious that the connection between Rush and the Stocktons was considerable—and with his tendencies and contacts, to assume that he would not have discussed the phenomenon that was Phillis Wheatley is quite unacceptable.

Similarly, the connection between mother and daughter was substantial. As a poet and hostess of one of the most famous literary salons in the colonies, Annis Boudinot Stockton clearly had many similar interests that would have made Wheatley interesting to her. However, even had she not approved of or liked Wheatley, Stockton, as an educated woman, still would have been familiar with the current literary field. In one instance, Stockton writes to her daughter, in March 1793, concerning Mary Wollstonecraft's *A Vindication of the Rights of Women* (1792). In this letter, Juliet, though too radical for her mother's taste, gives vent to her limited admiration for Wollstonecraft as a "great genius." Stockton's letter continues to use Wollstonecraft's treatise to discuss many other social issues as well. Stockton's topics range from the preferable difference in treatment of American versus European women (in that American women "have their equal right of everything, Latin and Greek excepted") to her detestation for those who confuse the exercise of "the virtues of moderation and forbearance [in] avoiding disputes" with "Slavish fear" and thence to her somewhat contradictory position "that there is no sex in Soul," while proclaiming adherence to the equality of the separate spheres (Mulford 305–7). Interestingly, though Stockton admonishes the sexes to remain in their place, she goes on to mention a general disgust for Rousseau, whom she labels "a refined Idiot, rather than an enlightened philosopher" (Mulford 305). Apparently, though women should stay in their place, they were free to comment on the other sex.

As important as her cultural critiques are, however, Stockton's query at the beginning of a letter addressing Julia states, "I wonder you never Sent me your Critique" (Mulford 305). such a query exemplifies the norm of familiar exchange and discussion between the two women. It is not too far a leap,

Zach Petrea

then, to assume that the two discussed other current and controversial figures. Even if the Rushes had not been patrons of Wheatley, the chance that the two women would have discussed Wheatley is beyond doubt. Similarly, Stockton exchanged material with Esther Edwards Burr, who, in turn, exchanged books and poems with Sarah Prince. Just as Stockton had debated contemporary issues with her daughter, Burr and Prince discussed their perspectives on Samuel Richardson's novel, *Pamela, or, Virtue Rewarded* (1741) in light of their religious preferences. Specifically the two women condemned the value placed on money and the licentious behavior of the characters within the novel and its accurate reflection of the world at large (Burr, *Journal* 107–8). Though the specific instance is somewhat older, Burr shows the same desire to critique literature and society at large that Stockton evinced. That the two analytical minds were friends should come as no surprise, and neither should be the possibility that Wheatley may have been a topic of debate.

Both the Stockton and Rush families were intimate with the Graeme family as well. In particular, Elizabeth Graeme Ferguson was best friends with Annis Stockton and her daughter, Julia. Ferguson, like Stockton, was a well-known lady of literary repute, who wrote poems and plays. In fact, David Shields says that Elizabeth Graeme Ferguson "presided over the most brilliant literary salon in colonial America," which, when considered with Stockton's salon, can indirectly connect "a network of female literary communication that would include Hannah Griffits, Esther Edwards Burr, Mary Read, Anna Young Smith, Rebecca Moore Smith, Elizabeth Norris and Susana Wright," along with a host of male figures such as Francis Hopkinson, Nathaniel Evans, and Joseph Green (339). Surrounded by some of the most intelligent and artistic people in the colonies, it is impossible that Wheatley's work or situation would not come up in such literary circles.

Of the men mentioned in connection with the salons, Joseph Green is the same individual who testified for the attestation notice preceding Wheatley's poems. His public affirmation of Wheatley's abilities and presence among a highly motivated and intellectual group assures a lively discussion of Wheatley and her work. Incidentally, of all the men mentioned in the preceding paragraph, Ferguson's friendship with Benjamin Rush was quite possibly the most influential on her work. At the end of the war, Rush risked his reputation and livelihood for Ferguson when he offered to intercede on her behalf and help retain her estate. Because of a poor choice in marriage, Ferguson was left to fight against Congress in its attempt to confiscate her property after her Tory husband repatriated to England. After several people refused Ferguson's pleas for help, Rush intervened and was able to save her house, though he was unable to retain all of her property (Booth 148–52).

As impressive as the social network between the two salons appears, conspicuously missing from the correspondence list is reference to Milcah Martha Moore. Moore, in whose commonplace book appear works by her friends Susannah Wright, Elizabeth Graeme Ferguson, and cousin Hannah Griffits, was a prolific compiler; to date she is known to have composed at least three commonplace books. The third compilation, recently published as *Milcah Martha Moore's Book: A Commonplace Book from Revolutionary America* (1997), serves as an intentional provocateur when taken holistically. Her book demands discussion through provoking argument by its very layout. Moore positions letters and poems by people from many sides of the debate over the Revolution, including the grouping of revolutionary and loyalist tracts. That some of the entries are not original to Moore's book, "but come from material that was widely circulated in hand-written manuscript and in print [serves to] reflect Moore's interest in public, especially political issues" (Moore xiii). It should be emphasized, however, that as a public document, something written by and for a group of women, the book reflects her *group's* interest in public and political issues. Wheatley, in her peculiar situation, would most likely have been a major talking point.

The inclusion in Moore's book of pieces by such various individuals such as Benjamin Franklin, Patrick Henry, Queen Caroline, and the Countess of Huntingdon underscores the existence of a manuscript culture. That Susannah Wright maintained long-lasting friendships with Benjamin Franklin and Benjamin Rush explains the appearance of letters by Franklin and Patrick Henry. While letters by the Queen and countess do not necessarily denote a meaningful connection, as they could be passed circuitously for their content, the countess's letter to Ann Hyam provides interesting possibilities of a connection to Moore. Unfortunately, nothing has yet been found. Further, when considering that Benezet tutored Moore's brothers-in-law (Moore xii–xviii, 191), and Rush's connection to numerous individuals aforementioned, it appears highly likely, given the nature of the manuscript culture, that Milcah Martha Moore as well as the others associated with the two salons, would have been familiar with Phillis Wheatley.

The celebrity of Wheatley was such that even the renowned naval captain John Paul Jones exchanged poetry with her in 1777 (through fellow captain and Boston native Hector McNeill). According to Daniel Ennis, Jones initiated contact with Wheatley in hopes that the association of his name with hers would have a positive impact on his social position. The son of immigrants, Jones "suffered from lack of roots in the country," and he desperately wanted to raise his "cultural capital" (Morison 91). In Jones's position, a poetic exchange with a person of prestige would definitely contribute to this goal (Ennis 89). Jones's aim was not to use Wheatley in any pejorative way, however, but rather to credit Wheatley on her substantial accomplishments and thereby rise in rank himself. Further, according to Ennis, whether Wheatley was aware of Jones's intentions or not, she was attempting a similar social venture: "Jones and Wheatley were actually engaged in similar projects. They were both trying to overcome and/or erase given identities by fashioning new, specifically American identities" (88). Wheatley's manipulation of social perception for her own gain should not come as a surprise considering what she was fighting against. In the words of Isani, Wheatley was "an ambitious and worldly-wise woman, acquainted with notables of her time, and capable of unabashedly representing her own interests" ("Phillis Wheatley" 255). Wheatley's contact with Jones would have, therefore, helped both aspiring writers; just as Jones collected letters from Adams, Jefferson, and Franklin, so too did Wheatley correspond with many people of repute.

As a matter of fact, the attestation at the beginning of her *Poems* is a veritable list of the Boston elite. Gay Gisbon Cima has asserted that many "of the signatories had already met Phillis at one time or another, either in the Wheatley home on a social visit, or at religious services or in the marketplace" (*Early American* 90). Undoubtedly Wheatley met many prominent men as Cima describes, sometimes socially and sometimes propitiously in the street, but there should be no reason to limit her access to Boston alone. Specifically, M. A. Richmond maintains that "the Wheatleys, sufficiently affluent to vacation in Newport . . . would have brought their prize intellectual possession with them and would have mingled with such resident families as were sufficiently wealthy to own slaves" (44). One such slave was Obour Tanner, a lifelong friend and correspondent to Wheatley. James A. Levernier goes even further in his estimation of the importance of these vacations, and points out that the Wheatleys' preacher, Samuel Hopkins (1721–1803), was stationed at Newport for some time, and as a result "Wheatley spent a great deal of time in Newport" (33). Her time in Rhode Island was not idle either; according to Levernier, these trips were the foundation of Wheatley's connection with the New England clergy, some of whom signed Wheatley's attestation. Wheatley's book served, then, not just to fuel the debate about African intelligence or feminine ability, but also to reflect how a "lowly slave" could mingle in prestigious company. Further evidence of prominent personages associated with Wheatley may be found in her poems. To be sure, her work reveals much more than her simple and self-effacing claim that they were merely "Products of leisure Moments" (Shields, in *Collected Works,* "Preface").

Of the many reasons that Wheatley no doubt had for publishing, one of the foremost in her mind must have been the possibility of freedom. It is even likely that Wheatley had this goal in mind when she wrote "To a Gentlemen on His Voyage to Great-Britain for the Recovery of His Health" (1767). The gentleman has been identified by Julian Mason as "Joseph Rotch, a brother of William Rotch Sr., both members of the prominent merchant family of the same name of New Bedford and Nantucket" (qtd. in Robinson, *Phillis Wheatley in the Black* 51). While this poem may appear simply to express her desire for the return of the "Gentlemen's" health, Robinson points out that Rotch's sister, Elizabeth Rotch Rodman (1757–1856), "was a friend of the slave, and interested in every case of humanity" (Robinson, *Phillis Wheatley in the Black* 51). Thus, this additional contextual hint implies that there might have been ulterior motives for Wheatley's verse.

Possibly even more directly related to Wheatley's reason for writing the poem, however, was the fact that the house of William Rotch Sr. (1734–1828) himself was "constantly tenanted by runaway slaves" (Grover 6). That Wheatley was aware of the presence of a sympathetic family there can be no doubt, and even though the assumption may be speculative, their reputation can be sure to have traveled far and wide among the black population. Grover supplies further evidence of the Rotches' sympathies in that the entire Rotch family was active in aiding runaway slaves. In fact, William Rotch's son, Thomas (1767–1823), housed "the first documented fugitive in New Bedford . . . for more than a year" (6). Although the man referenced dated from 1792, several years after Wheatley died, the incident reveals an attitude that must have been active long before. Thomas was not the only Rotch to be concerned about slavery; even his brother, William Rotch Jr. (1759–1850), wrote about being "almost daily concerned in protecting the injured Africans and promising their liberation where any pretence can be found to avoid the law" (Grover 7). That there was a family abhorrence to slavery is further illustrated by the story of Thomas Jr.'s son, Thomas, who is reported to have pursued a slave catcher some sixty miles in order to put him in jail for striking the escaped slave the catcher was sent to apprehend (Grover 9). Although these instances occurred well after Wheatley's death, the reputation of the Rotch family had likely reached Wheatley's ears. Her poem, then, could be seen as a medium to initiate or maintain contact with a family that was known for aiding escaped slaves. Whether Wheatley had any plans to escape at this time cannot be known, but the act of preserving contacts sympathetic to her situation illustrates her subversive abilities.

The particular manner in which Wheatley knew, or knew of, the Rotches, is less than clear. However, William Sr.'s uncle Benjamin (ca. 1702–1758) and his family lived in Boston. Of Benjamin's descendants, his son, Captain Joseph Rotch (1733–1809), moved to New Bedford in 1767 (Bullard 15), and is, therefore, a possible connection between Wheatley and the Bedford Rotches. While all the Rotches were Patriots and not likely to have been intimate with the Tory Wheatleys, it is possible that the Wheatleys and Rotches were formal acquaintances in the shipping business. With respect to the Rotches' shipping business, there is an interesting side note: two of the three ships associated with the Boston Tea Party, the Beaver and the Dartmouth, were owned by members of the Rotch family; William Sr. and his brother, Francis Rotch (1750–1822), respectfully (Stackpole, "Whose" 5). Further, according to accounts of that night, it was Francis Rotch who was made intermediary between the Patriot instigators (Sam Adams, John Hancock, Dr. Warren, John Bradford, etc.) and Governor Hutchinson.

Over the course of the entire ordeal, which lasted nearly three weeks, Francis was called from meeting to meeting, and asked repeatedly by the Patriots to force his ships to depart without unloading their shipment of tea (Stackpole, "Francis" 23). Although he could not comply with their request, it has been said that his "shrewd and sincere handling of the situation at least saved the tea ships from damage despite the fact their cargoes were dumped into the harbor" (Stackpole, "Whose" 5). It is a testament to the social standing of the Rotch family in general and Francis in particular that he was able to appease both sides, and save himself the undue loss of life or property. Surely, the Rotch family's prestige and propensity for helping slaves was well known, such that Wheatley knew of them and desired contact. Even if she proved unaware of their leanings, their social position was such that Wheatley could have used their standing to attain some measure of respect for herself, just as John Paul Jones would later attempt to do with her.

Of other notables, there is less definite, but considerable circumstantial evidence of contact. According to Arthur A. Schomburg, an admittedly less than reliable source, Wheatley was once invited to spend the afternoon with Colonel Fitch's wife (Heartman 11). Even if the story itself, which involves taking tea with the lady and her daughters, is fictitious, that Wheatley was entertained by a family of note is not surprising. Schomburg's story bears no identification of time or place, merely that he included the story after discussing Wheatley's return from England, which would place the dinner encounter sometime in late 1773 or early 1774. Left equally vague is the specific Colonel Fitch being referenced. Genealogies show two Colonel Fitches; Thomas V. (1725–1795) and his brother Jonathon (1727–1793), but both men were residents of Norwalk, Connecticut. The fact that these two men were Patriots makes the encounter with Wheatley less likely. Thomas was, in fact, the namesake of the epithet "Yankee Doodle," and was "one of the chief American military commanders at Norwalk" (R. Fitch 136, 140). While the title "Yankee Doodle" was bestowed upon him during the French and Indian War, the possibility that the Wheatley family was on visiting terms with this Colonel Fitch, so close to the outbreak of major hostilities, remains highly doubtful.

Rather, a more logical and probable Fitch is Samuel Fitch (ca. 1724–1799), who not only had Tory sympathies, but lived in Boston for four years in the late 1760s (J. Fitch 84). While Samuel Fitch was never a colonel, he did become advocate-general in the Admiralty Court, which might explain the confusion between these three distinguished Fitches. Further, Samuel and his wife, Betsie Lloyd, owned Pew 60 at the King's Chapel (J. Fitch 85), the same church frequented by the Wheatley family. While Phillis Wheatley did not attend King's, but rather the Old South, the possibility that her master or mistress arranged such a meeting with Samuel Fitch is likely. Interestingly, Samuel, before permanently moving to London in 1776, enlisted as a sergeant in the Associated Loyalists and served as a loyalist volunteer at the battle of Bunker Hill in 1775 (J. Fitch 85).

The relationship between the Fitch and Wheatley families helps to explain one of Wheatley's first published poems, "On Messrs. Hussey and Coffin" (1767). According to Charles W. Akers, in 1767 the Wheatleys "entertained at his dinner table two gentlemen from Nantucket who had just narrowly escaped shipwreck in a fierce storm off Cape Cod" (397). Wheatley was so impressed with their story of survival that she wrote a poem in their honor. However, neither Akers nor the accompanying submission letter sent with the poem to the printer explains who either of these men were or their relationship to the Wheatleys. Although I have been unable to find out precisely who these men were, or why they dined with the Wheatleys, there are several interesting connections between the Fitch family and the Coffin family. Jedediah Fitch (1681–1756), a grand-uncle of Samuel Fitch, married an Abigail Coffin of Nantucket.

Zach Petrea

Similarly, two of Jedediah's grandsons, Jonathon Gorham Fitch (1740–1814) and younger brother Jedediah Fitch (1763–1836), also married into the Coffin family when they married Elizabeth and Lydia Coffin, respectively. That the Fitch and Coffin families were close there can be no doubt. Given, then, that Samuel Fitch was on social terms with the Wheatleys, it would be conceivable that he would look out for his family relations, and be sure that they were accorded comforts with friends or other interested Christian associates from church. Of course, while it is also possible that the two men spoken of in the poem were merely employed by the Wheatley family, or only invited over to provide interesting conversation, the Nantucket connection between the Coffin and Fitch families is strong enough to warrant the assertion of interaction.[4]

As has been identified before, many of the more prominent personages known to Wheatley on both sides of the Atlantic were clergy or otherwise church-related. Levernier has written a thorough article on Wheatley's connection to the New England church network, in which he states that she "maintained an extensive network of connections with several prominent members of the New England clerical establishment" (23). Among her patrons and correspondents were her own ministers, Dr. Joseph Sewell and Dr. Samuel Cooper, and eventually through marriage to the Wheatleys' daughter, Dr. John Lathrop. The Wheatleys proved propitious to Phillis Wheatley's advancement as well, in that their house served as a staging ground for many British preachers and several of the Countess of Huntingdon's emissaries, including Timothy Pitkin (1766–1847), Samuel Hopkins, Ebenezer Pemberton, Eleazer Wheelock, Nathaniel Whitaker (1730–1795), Charles Chauncy (1705–1787), and George Whitefield. This observation does not suggest, however, that Wheatley only met those who came through Boston. In 1773, under the guidance of the Wheatleys' eldest son, Nathaniel, Phillis Wheatley personally delivered her manuscript to the London printers and toured with luminaries.

CONNECTIONS IN GREAT BRITAIN

Upon Wheatley's return to America, she wrote to General David Wooster (1711–1777), giving him a brief description of her stay in London, that she

> Was introduced to Lord Dartmouth and had near half an hour's conversation with his Lordship . . . Then to Lady Cavendish, and Lady Carteret Webb, Mrs. Palmer, a Poetess, an accomplished Lady. [To] Dr. Thos. Gibbons . . . Benjamin Franklin

Esqr. F.R.S., Greenville [*sic*] Sharp Esqr. who attended me to the Tower & show'd the Lions, Panthers, Tigers, &c. . . . Mr. Brook Watson Mercht. (Shields, in Wheatley, *Collected Works* 169–70)

While Benjamin Franklin's visit to Wheatley's lodgings is well known, as is the conversation with Lord Dartmouth (1731–1801), the lesser-known Thomas Gibbons (1720–1785) was a poet and minister. Wheatley most likely met Gibbons at the request of the Countess of Huntingdon whose connection to Gibbons had by 1773 been some decades old. In fact, just as Wheatley was in London to dedicate a book of poetry to the countess, Gibbons had previously dedicated his only book of poetry, *Juvenilia: Poems on Various Subjects of Devotion and Virtue* (1750), to her.

Though these first names are easy to account for, the last two names mentioned in Wheatley's brief account, "Greenville" (for Granville) Sharp and Brook Watson, have been somewhat confused. In Sally Smith Booth's otherwise very insightful book, *The Women of '76*, she states, "Watson, Lord Mayor of London, had made a gift of the epic [*Paradise Lost*] to the young poet during her festive European tour" (42), when in all actuality, Brook Watson was not lord mayor of London until 1774. In 1773, at the time of Wheatley's London trip, Frederick Bull was the lord mayor, and there is no mention of his having entertained Wheatley. Such an event would not be surprising, however, considering that the poet was scheduled to appear before the King.

It is interesting to note, moreover, that in 1787 Brook Watson joined the committee of the Society for Enforcing the King's Proclamation against Vice and Immorality, among whose thirty members included the Duke of Montagu, Lord Dartmouth, Samuel Thornton, and William Wilberforce (1753–1833) (Wilberforce and Wilberforce 394). It is unclear how or why Wheatley met Watson, but that he was able to join a society that included such prestigious figures, and eventually become Lord Mayor, testifies to his above-average social standing. Of the other members of the society, Dartmouth and Wilberforce also knew of Wheatley, and it can be deduced that Samuel Thornton most certainly knew of Wheatley, as his brother was John Thornton (1720–1790), one of the Countess of Huntingdon's most important emissaries and the addressee of three of Wheatley's extant letters.

Beyond the countess, John Thornton personally knew Wheatley through his contact with the Wheatley family, as they were entrusted to supply money, care, and housing for many of the countess's benefactors who passed through Boston. In one instance, Thornton instructed the Wheatleys to give money to

Zach Petrea

the Reverend Occom (the same minister to whom Wheatley's published essay about slavery is addressed), who had just been to England to raise money for Eleazer Wheelock's school for Native Americans (see Klein). At some point during Wheatley's London trip, she was even able to stay for some time at Thornton's house in Clapham (Robinson, "Phillis Wheatley in London" 188). This visit enabled Wheatley to become somewhat close to his female relations (Grimsted 390). Thornton is also important for his association with the Clapham Sect, a part of Wheatley's "Methodist Connection," and his two protégés, Bluestocking Hannah More, and Reverend John Newton (1725–1807), writer of "Amazing Grace" and coauthor of *The Olney Hymns* (1779).

The story of "Amazing Grace" is well known, and even if it were not for Newton's connection with Thornton, one could expect that a reformed captain of a slave ship would be conscious of current issues dealing with slavery. As it stands, however, Newton quit the business and dedicated himself to the Lord's service, eventually coming under the influence of George Whitefield and John Wesley. After being ordained, Newton moved to Olney, Surrey, where together with intimate friend and fellow poet William Cowper (1731–1800), he would eventually write the *Olney Hymns* (Martin and Spurrell xiii). Thornton's connection with Newton should not be underrated in that "it was only by John Thornton's personal efforts that the Bishop of Norwich was persuaded to ordain" Newton, and that Thornton was also solely responsible for getting Newton his living at Olney (*Clapham* 106). The two men corresponded often, and they so frequently discussed Wheatley that they dropped all formality and began to simply refer to her as "Phillis." Though Newton does not mention Wheatley in his *Thoughts upon the African Slave Trade* (1787), he would leave a lasting mark on the slavery debate due to his later involvement with Wilberforce. It was to Newton that Wilberforce turned when in need, and it was Newton who would be the cause of Wilberforce's spiritual conversion and eventual involvement in the abolition movement.

In the latter half of the eighteenth century, the abolition movement consisted almost entirely of the Clapham sect, which was, perhaps, the most historically influential in slavery issues. The men most often associated with this group were Zachary Macaulay (1768–1838), John Thornton, Granville Sharp, and William Wilberforce. While the connection between Benezet, Rush, and Sharp has already been noted, there is much left to say about the importance of Sharp's meeting with Wheatley. Granville Sharp had, in the previous year, represented James Somerset in the trial heard by Lord Mansfield, whose decision set free all slaves who set foot on English soil (Klingberg 38–41). Wheatley's earlier-than-scheduled departure was not, as some scholars have asserted, that "Wheatley *had* to return to Boston" (Wilcox 10–11; emphasis added), or that she was "summoned," or "called" back. Instead, considering that Wheatley spent a day with Sharp, it can be assumed that he offered her the same freedom granted to Somerset. That Wheatley *did* return at all is a testament to the devotion and genuine affection she held for her mistress. This act of devotion was so forceful that Cima claims a direct link between this choice and her eventual freedom, in that Wheatley's return "so powerfully proved her moral superiority that the Wheatleys were forced to manumit her" (*Early American* 92). Whatever her reason for returning, however, Wheatley rationally decided that to return to America was more important than being free in England (and being introduced to the King); her action was definitely not the subservient obeisance of a mindless slave.

Sharp, not content with his part in this historic trial, was later elected president of the Abolition Society, an organization formed in 1787 with the help of Thomas Clarkson (1760–1846) and William Wilberforce (Klingberg 73). Sharp even helped Clarkson publish his *Essay on the Slavery and Commerce of the Human Species,*[5] which specifically discusses Phillis Wheatley as evidence for the intellectual capabilities of Africans, and quotes many lines of her poetry (Klingberg 76). Though Wheatley was dead by the time of its publication, Clarkson's knowledge of Wheatley would have been a probable topic for conversation when he met both William Wordsworth (1770–1850) and Samuel Taylor Coleridge (1772–1834) sometime in 1798–99. Although the first documented meeting of the three was in November 1799 when they spent the day vacationing and walking in the Lake District (Wilson 99), they were sure to have met at some point earlier. And though there may be no concrete connections between the founders of Romanticism and the poetry of Wheatley, the possibility of Wordsworth and Coleridge discussing Wheatley is too tantalizing not to mention.[6]

Of the Methodist connection, Samuel J. Rogal has discussed several ways in which Wheatley was introduced into the circle, most notably through the Countess of Huntingdon, but also through the aforementioned John Thornton, Lord Dartmouth, and John Wesley. Wesley liked Wheatley for her verse as well as her religious message, and though he sometimes exercised rather extreme authorial control of her poems, he nonetheless published several of Wheatley's pieces in his *Armenian Magazine* (Rogal 85). In total, over three years from 1778 to 1791, Wesley published four of Wheatley's poems. Though Wesley pub-

Zach Petrea

lished and edited her for his own purposes, the printing of her work in his magazine "emphatically represents the extent to which Phillis Wheatley's poetry focused attention upon the prominent issues of her lifetime" (Rogal 94), and thus provides another source of her popularity beyond her skin and sex.

While Rogal cautiously asserts that Wesley "perhaps came to know of the Black poet's work from friends and acquaintances who had passed copies of the 1773 edition of her *Poems* on to him" (90), Muktar Ali Isani more definitely suggests "that the editor of the *Armenian* had access to a range of Wheatley Poetry" in manuscript form ("Methodist Connection" 109). Wesley, one of the principal proponents of Methodism, was intimate with nearly all of Wheatley's known associates; and, as such, he could have gotten her work fairly directly and easily. Although there was an initial split between what would become the Methodist sects, the principals maintained lasting relationships; as Stevens states, a "difference of opinion, relating to the Calvinistic controversy, produced a divergence on their practical plans, which, with some temporary asperities, soon became cordial and obviously providential" (145). Stevens continues to delineate the "quadruple alliance" of the two Wesley brothers, Whitefield, and the countess, holding that they all "agreed to meet as often as convenient and co-operate in their common work" (161). Such close working relationships ensured that, even if Wheatley did not personally meet Wesley, he received notice of her through the countess.

Of the many other contacts Wheatley made through the countess, none was possibly more important than the two sisters mentioned in Wheatley's letter to General Wooster: Carteret and Cavendish. Of the two, the more immediately significant is Lady Margaret Cavendish (1714–1785), who after her first marriage became the Duchess of Portland. According to the countess's biography, Lady Cavendish was of like mind and "distinguished for her love of the fine arts, and patronage of literature" (New 50). These two women took care to preserve their "intimate" friendship through frequent visits to each other, and supported each others' activities, as can be seen through Lady Cavendish's meeting with Wheatley while in London. Patronage of the arts among elite women at this time was somewhat common, especially among this group of highly active and intellectual women.

Such an instance of literary patronage can be seen in the mutual friend of Cavendish and the countess, Elizabeth Robinson Montagu (1720–1800). A significant amount is known about the countess's relationship with Montagu from the fact that that the countess first became acquainted with Montagu through Montagu's cousin, Lady Mary Wortley Montagu, with whom the countess was a good friend (Knight 11). The eventual friendship that formed between Elizabeth Montagu and the countess was such that the countess was present at Montagu's wedding (New 51). On the other hand, while it is not known how the two met, it is sufficient that Lady Cavendish had a "warm friendship and long correspondence with" Lady Montagu (Blunt 2). Montagu, referred to alternately as the "Queen of the Blues" and "the female Maecenas," together with her sister, ran what would become arguably the world's most famous literary salon, the Bluestocking Club (Tinker 173).

Montagu's interest "in the adversity of women of all ranks, from their own, to servants, to those somewhere in between," was precipitated by Elizabeth Montagu's stated fear, that if "the rich people do not check their wanton extravagance to enable them to assist the poor I know not what must become of the laboring people" (Larson 206–7). Given her "concern to promote female learning," which was the foundation for the Bluestockings, it would be expected that a club which facilitated "intellectual conversation about literature, history, and politics" (Eger 123) would take interest in such a case as Wheatley. One telling example of Montagu's active interest in poets of talent occurs when she contacted Anna Laetitia Barbauld (1743–1825) after reading Barbauld's 1773 *Poems.* In her letters, Montagu states that she was ultimately urged to make contact because "I always wish to find great virtues where there are great talents, and to love what I admire" (Le Breton 39). It should be natural, then, that Montagu would be interested in Wheatley, who was not only a great talent, but also in a highly unusual position. As a result of Montagu's letter of introduction, Barbauld would eventually become included in the group of women, and though she would exchange letters with many of the Bluestockings, she would correspond most with Elizabeth Montagu and Hannah More.

Montagu concludes her letter to Barbauld by offering her services: "if any work appears in the Literary World which you would wish to have convey'd to you, favour me at any time with your commands" (Le Breton 40). While such an assertion of access to "any work . . . in the literary world," may seem like a grandiose claim, during this time period, with Montagu's wealth and resources, it would not have been far from the truth. The possibility of Montagu's interest in Wheatley is important to establish, not only for the multitude of people associated with the Bluestockings (Horace Walpole, Dr. Johnson, Garrick, Sir Joshua Reynolds, etc.), but also for her probable introduction of Wheatley to Lord Thomas Lyttleton (1744–1779).

While Wheatley does not mention meeting Lyttleton, there is a London advertisement that states she met with him for some time (Wilcox 12); such

Zach Petrea

a meeting would seem to be the result of not one connection, but several. Similarly, though the mentioning of Wheatley does not seem to appear in Lyttleton's work, he was Montagu's dear friend, mentor, and one of her "favorite correspondents" (Larson 207). As a testament both to Lyttleton's positive assessment of Montagu and her philanthropic tendencies in general, Lyttleton calls her "an highly-instructed, accomplished woman, possessed of great affluence, who . . . makes her drawing room the *Lycaeum* of the day [and] patronizes the learning which she has herself adorned" (Lyttleton 192). I highlight Montagu's connection with Lyttleton, because although the countess knew Lord Lyttleton since before he was granted his lordship (Lyttleton 63), the countess was not in London at the time of Wheatley's trip. It is, of course, possible that the countess had asked Lyttleton to see Wheatley, but I submit that since Montagu's salon was in London and Lyttleton was intimate with several Bluestockings, it was their circle that more directly influenced his decision.

That Lyttleton met Wheatley at all is of special significance due to Lord Lyttleton's confession that "except in some few instances, I am not very partial to *literary ladies:* they are, generally, of an impertinent, encroaching disposition" (193; emphasis in original). As such, any meeting with a "literary lady" of repute can be expected to have been made under a modicum of duress. As a man of stature, it is improbable that Lyttleton would be thus influenced by only one person, so his connection with others in Montagu's circle is equally important. In the same letter that Lyttleton describes Montagu, he refers to "Miss Carter," that is, the Elizabeth Carter (1717–1806) who "enjoyed a preeminent reputation as the intellectual paragon of the Bluestockings." What is more, many of the Bluestockings "opposed slavery, including Elizabeth Carter, who was an original subscriber to the committee to abolish the slave trade" (Ferguson, *First Feminists* 327). The established antislavery sentiment of the members combined with the Bluestocking dedication to develop "their intellectual capacities" (Meyers 262), makes frank discussion about literature, especially literature written by a slave, more than likely. That the Bluestockings also desired the establishment of a permanent "discourse of culture and civility" (Kelly 165) strongly suggests that discussion of current political and social events, such as Phillis Wheatley, was probable.

Further, explicit knowledge of Wheatley by a Bluestocking is found in the correspondence of Hannah More (1745–1833), of whom Lyttleton states, "No one takes more pains than Mrs. M——to be surrounded with men of wit" (65). And surround herself she did, for More kept company with the likes of Edmund Burke, Samuel Johnson, David Garrick, Horace Walpole, William

Wilberforce, and the Thorntons. Although it took the encouragement of Bristol friends, and her sister (the housekeeper of Sir Joshua Reynolds), to move More to London in 1774, More instantly became friends with the literati of the time. More's knowledge of literature surely aided in her acclimation to the new environment, since, in fact, one of her favorite pastimes since childhood was "riding to London to see bishops and booksellers" (Murch 14). The speed with which More befriended the elite group of writers speaks well of her use of the early incursions into the city, while her knowledge and tastes ensured their continued friendship.

Of the subsequent friends that More made, the most important to the Wheatley connection are Frances Reynolds (1729–1807), Thornton, and Wilberforce. In fact, it was in correspondence with Frances Reynolds, the sister of Joshua Reynolds (1723–1792), in which More spoke positively of Wheatley.[7] In this letter, dated September 10, 1774, More asks Frances whether she had seen a poem called "The Female Advocate" (1774). This poem was apparently sent anonymously since More does not mention the author's name (this instance further testifies to the pervasiveness of correspondence, in that anybody could send a well-known figure a letter and be assured that it would at least be read, if not responded to). In More's letter to Reynolds, More states that "Mrs. Chapone and I are under infinite obligations" to the unidentified author for acquainting them with "Phillis Wheatley the *black girl*" (1; emphasis in original). More then continues to postulate as to the reason the author would send her such a poem; "I have a notion the comparison of Phillis and I occurred to her from the similarity of our complexions as well as talents" (1–2). The positive reception by More of a linkage between her own talents and "complexion" to Wheatley's is definitely a significant and noteworthy admission.

Additionally, More's disclosure that Chapone and she only learned of Wheatley from the poem indicates that More must have passed the poem on to her friend Chapone. It is interesting to note that More had not met Chapone in person since she states in the letter that "the complexion of Mrs. Chapone's person I have not the honour to know, that of her mind, I well know and greatly venerate" (2). Here again is evidence of third-party transmission, an example of the path a letter of interest might take, and the intimacy that was possible through these letters. It is also possible that the author of the poem was attempting to initiate such a correspondence with More herself since the attempt to earn a patron at this time was in no way unique or uncommon. Charles Scruggs has already described the socially benevolent atmosphere where "bards from the lower classes . . . were patronized by people of position" (282), and provides

Zach Petrea

a list that includes a virtual who's who of London society. Particularly telling are the names of Lyttleton and More.

The poem, "The Female Advocate; a Poem. Occasioned by Reading Mr. Duncombe's Feminead" (1774), was written by Mary Scott (ca. 1751–1793), and "celebrated historical and contemporary female 'worthies'" (Ferguson, *Subject to Others* 127). That Scott would enroll Wheatley in their number, when her treatise was based on the assumption that "if men can be brought to recognize that women can write as well as men, they must in time admit women to the sciences and to equal education" (Todd 280), is both highly confrontational and revolutionary. Although it is not known what came of Scott's contact with More, More's dispersal of Scott's poem to her own correspondents seems to have helped raise Scott's prestige.

Of More's other connections, her friendship with John Thornton was possibly her most important, at least financially speaking. More, like the other Bluestockings, was highly ambitious and very involved in charity organizations and school building. To help in this regard, More received some six hundred pounds annually from Thornton for her various enterprises, no small fortune at the time (Klingberg 107). Thornton's influence can also be felt in John Newton's correspondence with More (Bull 347), as was her acquaintance with another member of the Clapham Sect, Zachary Macaulay. For Macaulay, his friendship with More was propitious, for he would eventually meet "the young lady who was to be his wife, while on a visit to Hannah More" (*Clapham* 116). The intimacy of these two circles, and their corresponding interests, is revealed by the personal connections of the members. In fact, More was so comfortable with the Clapham Sect that she even referred to the group as "Mr. Wilberforce and his Myrmidons" (Wilson 50). Such an epithet is both jocular and flattering, with the equation of Wilberforce to Achilles and the rest of his famed army, the Myrmidons. At the same time, however, the reference is also sincere with respect to the scope of the war against slavery that the group was mounting.

Though to some just a "lowly slave girl," Wheatley's impact on the war against slavery should not be underestimated, for within one year of its London publication, Mary Scott would compose her poem, "The Female Advocate" (1774), and enroll Wheatley in the number of female dignitaries. As ironic as it may seem, the scourge of slavery ultimately helped Wheatley free not only herself, but others as well. The literary productions of her pen and the subsequent evidences of her intellect would ultimately help fan the flames of debate that surrounded slavery. As eloquently stated in Grimsted, Wheatley's art and craft secured forever her name in "the rolls of fame" as "a Phoenix of her race" from whose "ashes . . . she helped kindle [the] flame in subsequent generations of Americans" (444). It needs to be reemphasized that mere months after the publication of Wheatley's first and only book, she was already considered among the elite of historical figures. In Scott's words,

> Daughter of Shenstone hail! Hail charming maid,
> Well hath thy pen fair nature's charm display'd!
> The hill, the grove, the flow'r enamell'd lawn,
> Shine in thy lays in brightest colours drawn:
> Nor be thy praise confin'd to rural themes,
> Or idly-musing Fancy's pleasing dreams;
> But still may contemplation (guest divine)
> Expand thy breast, and prompt the flowing line.
> (Ferguson, *First Feminists* 361–62)

This present work attempts to heed Scott's poetic appeal: to expand Wheatley's praise, to fuel further contemplation, and to reposition a poet in her rightful place in American literary history. Though unequal in eloquence to Scott's verse, the purpose of this present work was also to recognize the enormous influence that a "lowly Boston slave" had on both American and British society. Through a preliminary archaeology of Wheatley's support network, this vast web of personal relations reveals her extensive influence on the intellectual climate of the late eighteenth century, and exposes a number of potentially fruitful later comparative treatments.

NOTES

1. See Kerber's *Women of the Republic.*

2. Although I am forced to acknowledge the pervasiveness of certain modern modes of communication, especially e-mails and instant messages, I would argue that these forms of communication still possess a certain aura of immediacy and instant gratification that separates them from letters proper. Rapid real-time conversation via instant message definitely elicits a fast-paced interaction, one altogether different from more traditional journals and the extensive manuscripts written during the time here discussed. Even emails are more imbued to modern speed expectations: although they

Zach Petrea

too may take time to be replied to, the sender still knows that the message has been sent and received. The generic pejorative term used today in reference to the Post Office, "snail-mail," easily identifies a thought process unused to the delay required by a society dependent upon letters and journals for communication.

3. As I endeavor to explain below, Hannah More credits a poem by Mary Scott, "The Female Advocate," with introducing both Chapone and herself to Wheatley in 1774, obviously sometime after the 1773 letter here discussed.

4. Interestingly, there was also a Coffin involved in the Tea Party; the captain of the *Beaver,* the ship owned by William Rotch Sr., was Hezekiah Coffin of Nantucket (Stackpole, "Whose" 6).

5. This tract was actually only made possible by Clarkson's accidental discovery of Anthony Benezet's *Historical Account of Guinea* (Klingberg 76).

6. In a similarly intriguing case, Dr. Akenside, author of *Pleasures of Imagination* (1744), was patronized by the Huntingdon family (Seymour, *Life and Times* 195).

7. Here then is a third connection to Sir Joshua Reynolds. Isani previously stated that the Mrs. Palmer mentioned in Wheatley's account of her trip is Joshua Reynolds's older sister, Mary Reynolds Palmer (1716–1794) ("Phillis Wheatley in London" 256n3).

WORKS CITED

Akers, Charles W. "'Our Modern Egyptians': Phillis Wheatley and the Whig Campaign Against Slavery in Revolutionary Boston." *Journal of Negro History* 60.3 (1975): 397–410.

Armistead, Wilson. *Anthony Benezet. From the Original Memoir: Revised with Additions.* 1859. Freeport: Books for Libraries, 1971.

Bleecker, Ann. *The Posthumous Works of Ann Eliza Bleecker, in Prose and Verse. To which is added, A collection of Essays, Prose and Poetical By Margaretta V. Faugeres.* New York: T. and J. Swords, 1793.

Blunt, Reginald, ed. *Mrs. Montagu: "Queen of the Blues": Her Letters and Friendships from 1762 to 1800.* Vol. 1. London: Constable, 1924.

Booth, Sally Smith. *The Women of '76.* New York: Hastings House, 1973.

Bull, Josiah. *Letters of the Rev. John Newton of Olney and St. Mary Woolnoth.* London: Religious Tract Society, 1869.

Bullard, John M. *The Rotches.* New Bedford: Cabinet, 1947.

Burr, Esther Edwards. *Esther Burr's Journal.* Ed. Jeremiah Eames Rankin. 3rd ed. Washington, D.C.: Woodward & Lathrop, 1903.

———. *The Journal of Esther Edwards Burr, 1754–1757.* Ed. Carol F. Karlsen and Laurie Crumpacker. New Haven: Yale UP, 1984.

Cima, Gay Gibson. "Black and Unmarked: Phillis Wheatley, Mercy Otis Warren, and the Limits of Strategic Anonymity." *Theatre Journal* 52.4 (2000): 465–95.

———. *Early American Women Critics: Performance, Religion, Race.* New York: Cambridge UP, 2006.

Clapham and the Clapham Sect. London: Edmund Baldwin, 1927.

D'Elia, Donald J. "Benjamin Rush: Philosopher of the American Revolution." *Transactions of the American Philosophical Society.* New Series 64.5 (1974). 1–113.

Eger, Elizabeth. "Representing Culture: 'The Nine Living Muses of Great Britain' (1779)." *Women, Writing and the Public Sphere, 1700–1830.* Ed. Elizabeth Eger, Charlotte Grant, Cliona O. Gallchoir, and Penny Warburton. Cambridge: Cambridge UP, 2001. 104–62.

Ennis, Daniel J. "Poetry and American Revolutionary Identity: The Case of Phyllis Wheatley and John Paul Jones." *Studies in Eighteenth-Century Culture* 31 (2002): 85–98.

Ferguson, Moira, ed. *First Feminists: British Women Writers, 1578–1799.* Bloomington: Indiana UP, 1985.

———. *Subject to Others: British Women Writers and Colonial Slavery, 1670–1834.* New York: Routledge, 1992.

Fitch, John T. *Descendants of the Reverend James Fitch: 1622–1702.* Vol. 1. Camden: Picton, 1996.

Fitch, Roscoe Conkling. *History of the Fitch Family A.D. 1400–1930.* Vol. 1. Haverhill: Record, 1930.

Foster, Frances Smith. *Written by Herself: Literary Production by African American Women, 1746–1892.* Bloomington: Indiana UP, 1993.

Goodman, Nathan G. *Benjamin Rush: Physician and Citizen 1746–1813.* Philadelphia: U of Pennsylvania P, 1934.

Grimsted, David. "Anglo-American Racism and Phillis Wheatley's 'Sable Veil,' 'Length'ned Chain,' and 'Knitted Heart.'" *Women in the Age of the American Revolution.* Ed. Robert Hoffman and Peter J. Albert. Charlottesville: UP of Virginia, 1989. 338–444.

Griswold, Rufus Wilmot. *The Female Poets of America.* 1873. New York: Garrett, 1969.

Grover, Katherine. *Fugitive Slave Traffic and the Maritime World of New Bedford.* New Bedford Whaling National Historic Park, 1998.

Gura, Philip F. "Writing the Literary History of Eighteenth-Century America: A Prospect." *The World Turned Upside-Down: The State of Eighteenth-Century American Studies at the Beginning of the Twenty-First Century.* Ed. Michael V. Kennedy and William G. Shade. Bethlehem: Lehigh UP, 2001. 164–85.

Heartman, Chas. Fred. Introduction. *Phillis Wheatley: Poems and Letters.* New York, 1915.

Hornstein, Jacqueline. "Literary History of New England Women Writers: 1630–1800." Thesis New York U, 1978.

Imlay, Gilbert. *A Topographical Description of the Western Territory of North America: Containing a Succinct Account of Its Soil, Climate, Natural History, Population, Agriculture, Manners & Customs.* 3rd ed. 1797. New York: Augustus M. Kelley, 1969.

Isani, Mukhtar Ali. "The Contemporaneous Reception of Phillis Wheatley: Newspaper and Magazine Notices during the Years of Fame, 1765–1774." *Journal of Negro History* 85.4 (2000): 260–73.

———. "The Methodist Connection: New Variants of some Phillis Wheatley Poems." *Early American Literature* 22 (1987): 108–13.

———. "Phillis Wheatley in London: An Unpublished Letter to David Wooster." *American Literature* 51.2 (1979): 255–60.

Jefferson, Thomas. *Notes on the State of Virginia.* Ed. Frank Shuffleton. New York: Penguin, 1999.

Kaplan, Sidney. *The Black Presence in the Era of the American Revolution: 1770–1800.* Washington: New York Graphic Society, 1973.

Kelly, Gary. "Bluestocking Feminism." *Women, Writing and the Public Sphere, 1700–1830.* Ed. Elizabeth Eger, Charlotte Grant, Cliona O. Gallchoir, and Penny Warburton. Cambridge: Cambridge UP, 2001. 163–80.

Kerber, Linda K. *Women of the Republic: Intellect and Ideology in Revolutionary America.* New York: Norton, 1986.

Klein, Milton M. *An Amazing Grace: John Thornton and the Clapham Sect.* New Orleans: UP of the South, 2004.

Klingberg, Frank J. *The Anti-Slavery Movement in England: A Study in English Humanitarianism.* 1926. Hamden: Archon, 1968.

Knight, Helen C., comp. *Lady Huntingdon and Her Friends; or, The Revival of the Work of God in the Days of Wesley, Whitefield, Romaine, Venn and Others in the Last Century.* New York: American Tract Society, 1853.

Larson, Edith Sedgwick. "A Measure of Power: The Personal Charity of Elizabeth Montagu." *Studies in Eighteenth-Century Culture* 16 (1986): 197–211.

Le Breton, Anna Letitia. *Memoir of Mrs. Barbauld, Including Letters and Notices of Her Family and Friends.* London: George Bell and Sons, 1874.

Levernier, James A. "Phillis Wheatley and the New England Clergy." *Early American Literature* 26 (1991): 21–38.

Seymour, Aaron C. H. *Life and Times of Selina, Countess of Huntingdon. By a member of the House of Shirley and Hastings.* 4th ed. Vol. 1. London: W.E. Painter, 1844.

Lyttleton, Thomas. *Letters of the Late Lord Lyttleton: Complete in One Volume.* A New Edition. London, 1792.

Martin, Bernard, and Mark Spurrell. *The Journal of a Slave Trader (John Newton): 1750–1754.* London: Epworth, 1962.

Mason, Julian D., Jr. Introduction. *The Poems of Phillis Wheatley.* Ed. Julian D. Mason Jr. 2nd ed. Chapel Hill: U of North Carolina P, 1989.

Mazzucco-Than, Cecile. "'As Easy as a Chimney Pot to Blacken': Catherine Macaulay 'the Celebrated Female Historian.'" *Prose Studies: History, Theory and Criticism* 18.3 (1995): 78–104.

Meyers, Sylvia Harcstark. *The Bluestocking Circle: Women, Friendship, and the Life of the Mind in Eighteenth-Century England.* Oxford: Clarendon, 1990.

Moore, Milcah Martha. *Milcah Martha Moore's Book: A Commonplace Book from Revolutionary America.* Ed. Catherine La Courreye Blecki and Karin A. Wulf. University Park: Penn State UP, 1997.

More, Hannah. "Letter to Frances Reynolds." 10 September 1774. Ms Hyde 25(3). Courtesy of the Houghton Library, Harvard College Library.

Morison, Samuel Eliot. *John Paul Jones: A Sailor's Biography.* Boston: Little Brown, 1959.

Mulford, Carla. Introduction. *Only for the Eyes of a Friend: The Poems of Annis Boudinot Stockton.* Ed. Carla Mulford. Charlottesville: UP of Virginia, 1995.

Murch, Jerom. *Mrs. Barbauld and Her Contemporaries; Sketches of Some Eminent Literary and Scientific Englishwomen.* London: Longmans, Green, 1877.

New, Alfred H. *Memoir of Selina, Countess of Huntingdon.* Rev. ed. New York: Protestant Episcopal Society for the Promotion of Evangelical Knowledge, 1859.

O'Neale, Sondra A. "Challenge to Wheatley's Critics: There Was No Other Game in Town." *Journal of Negro Education* 54.4 (1985): 500–511.

Poole, William Frederick. *Anti-Slavery Opinions before the Year 1800.* Cincinnati: R. Clarke, 1873.

Reed, Joseph. Letter to Esther Reed. June 11, 1778. *Letters of Delegates to Congress, 1774–1789:* Vol. 10: June 1, 1778–September 30, 1778. Ed. Paul H. Smith et al. Washington, D.C.: Library of Congress, 1976–2000. 1 Feb. 2007. http://memory.loc.gov/ammem/amlaw/lwdg.html

Richards, Jeffrey H. *Mercy Otis Warren.* New York: Twayne, 1995.

Richmond, M. A. *Bid the Vassal Soar.* Washington, DC: Howard UP, 1974.

Robinson, William H. *Phillis Wheatley in the Black American Beginnings.* Detroit: Broadside, 1975.

———. *Phillis Wheatley and Her Writings.* New York: Garland, 1984.

———. "Phyllis Wheatley in London." *College Literature Association Journal* 21 (Dec. 1977): 187–201.

Rogal, Samuel. "Phillis Wheatley's Methodist Connection." *Black American Literature Forum* 21.1–2 (Spring–Summer 1987): 85–95.

Rust, Marion. "'Into the House of an Entire Stranger': Why Sentimental Doesn't Equal Domestic in Early American Fiction." *Early American Literature* 37.2 (2002): 281–309.

Scruggs, Charles. "Phillis Wheatley and the Poetical Legacy of Eighteenth-Century England." *Studies in Eighteenth-Century Culture* 10 (1981): 279–95.

Smith, Margaret Bayard. *The First Forty Years of Washington Society, Portrayed by the Family Letters of Mrs. Samuel Harrison Smith (Margaret Bayard) from the Collection of her Grandson, J. Henley Smith.* Ed. Gaillard Hunt. London: Unwin, 1906.

Stackpole, Edouard Alexandre. "Francis Rotch's Account of the Boston Tea Party." *Historic Nantucket* 23.3 (1976): 20–23.

———. "Whose Tea Party? An Editorial." *Historic Nantucket* 21.2 (1973): 5–6.

Stevens, Abel. *The Women of Methodism: Its Three Foundresses, Susanna Wesley, the Countess of Huntingdon, and Barbara Heck; with Sketches of Their Female Associates and Successors in the Early History of the Denomination.* 4th ed. New York: Carlton & Porter, 1866.

Stozier, Charles B. "Benjamin Rush: Revolutionary Doctor." *American Scholar* 64.3 (1995): 415–22.

Tinker, Chauncey Brewster. *The Salon and English Letters: Chapters on the Interrelations of Literature and Society in the Age of Johnson.* New York: Macmillan, 1915.

Todd, Janet, ed. "Scott, Mary." *A Dictionary of British and American Women Writers 1660–1800.* London: Methuen, 1987.

Tyler, Moses Coit. *The Literary History of the American Revolution 1763–1783.* 1897. Vol. 1 of 2. New York: Frederick Ungar, 1957.

Watts, Emily Stipes. *The Poetry of American Women from 1632 to 1945.* Austin: U of Texas P, 1977.

Wheatley, Phillis. *The Collected Works of Phillis Wheatley.* Ed. John C. Shields. New York: Oxford UP, 1988.

Wilberforce, Robert Isaac, and Samuel Wilberforce. *The Life of William Wilberforce.* Vol. 1 of 5. London: John Murray, 1838.

Wilcox, Kristin. "The Body into Print: Marketing Phillis Wheatley." *American Literature* 71.1 (1999): 1–29.

Wilson, Ellen Gibson. *Thomas Clarkson, A Biography.* New York: St. Martins, 1990.

Woods, John A., ed. "The Correspondence of Benjamin Rush and Granville Sharp, 1773–1809." *Journal of American Studies* 1.1 (1967): 1–38.

Wulf, Karin A. *"Milcah Martha Moore's Book:* Documenting Culture and
Connection in the Revolutionary Era." Introduction. *Milcah Martha
Moore's Book: A Commonplace Book from Revolutionary America.* Ed.
Catherine La Courreye Blecki and Karin A. Wulf. University Park:
Penn State UP, 1997.

Phillis Wheatley's Theoretics of the Imagination: An Untold Chapter in the History of Early American Literary Aesthetics

John C. Shields

Two studies that allegedly do the work of tracing the development of literary aesthetics in Early America are Max I. Baym's *A History of Literary Aesthetics in America* and James Engell's *The Creative Imagination: Enlightenment to Romanticism.* Baym's helpful volume opens, interestingly, with Jonathan Edwards (I would have started with Anne Bradstreet and Edward Taylor) and closes its eighteenth-century treatment with Philip Freneau. Yet we find no mention of Phillis Wheatley. James Engell's more comprehensive examination of the creative imagination (Baym concentrates on beauty) in Great Britain and the Continent hazards a brief detour into Early America, but disappointedly he focuses on Philip Freneau alone. So once again we encounter no mention of Wheatley.

Given Wheatley's brilliant and revolutionary analysis of the imaginative faculty, this stubborn refusal to recognize her elaborate theoretics of imagination urges this essay. While it is certainly true that the journey of Wheatley's "On Imagination" amid the principal proponents of British and Continental romanticism is fascinating, what we concentrate on here is the thought, both European and Early American, that preceded and came to frame her own stunning performances. The tracing of the possible role of Wheatley's "On Imagination" in late-eighteenth and early-nineteenth-century Europe will form the subject of a later study.

In this present essay, first we explore the literary aesthetic background that embraced Wheatley's theory of imagination, this background including the insightful (positive and negative) conceptions of imagination among Europeans and Early Americans. Then we interrogate Wheatley's pursuit of her unique, for the time, theoretics of this important creative faculty in "On Recollection," "Thoughts on the Works of Providence," and "On Imagination," these three poems constituting her "Long Poem." This study does not emphasize a Burkean notion of imagination as promulgator of a false consciousness. Such a philosophical/aesthetic position grows largely out of a perceived suspicion of the imaginative faculty as a habit of mind which, if relied upon, can bring about false and/or unreliable opinion. This conservative perception may be easily located in aesthetic philosophy, for example, in Hobbes's *Leviathan* (1651) and Locke's *Essay Concerning Human Understanding* (1704; especially in his condemnation of imagination in his brief, appended diatribe against enthusiasm).

Because Wheatley is often erroneously believed to have borrowed slavishly from the work of Alexander Pope, we would do well to consider briefly the weight of the actual evidence regarding this alleged influence. Almost certainly, Wheatley would have become familiar with Pope's *Works* by way of Mather Byles, Wheatley's principal literary mentor who lived across the street from the Wheatley mansion. This same Byles, named for his uncle, Cotton Mather, inherited his uncle's extensive library upon his death in 1728. According to Peter T. Kyper, Byles's library contained "over two thousand volumes" and "was considered one of the best in the colonies." Kyper is careful to add that, because of Byles's strong literary leanings, his library housed "a great number of literary works (as opposed to theological works)" (Kyper 3). As Kyper claims that Byles very likely owned a copy of Pope's *Works* by the late 1730s, Wheatley would have had easy access to Pope's printed poems and "Prefaces."

In his *The Creative Imagination*, James Engell records that Pope refers to imagination only once in the early *Essay on Criticism* (1711) but notes in the "Preface" to his translation of Homer's *Iliad* (1715) that Homer projects a peculiar "Force of the poet's Imagination" (Engell 40). While this early description strikes an almost enthusiastic chord, reflecting, so Engell holds, exposure to Addison's positive evaluation of imagination, in his 1713 *Spectator* series of essays devoted to explanation of "the pleasures of the imagination," clearly by publication of the second epistle of *An Essay on Man*, appearing in March 1753, Pope has rethought his earlier, positive position toward the imaginative faculty. Indeed, here "Imagination plies her dang'rous art / And pours it [what fills the head] all upon the peccant part" (Pope 134). Significantly Engell fails to point out this shift in Pope's judgment, albeit, given the availability of Pope's texts to her, Phillis Wheatley surely did not fail to come across this shift.

If Wheatley is supposed to have placed so much store on Pope's works and thought, then why does she, in her crucial "On Imagination," celebrate imagination, particularly the operation of her own, with undeniable vim and verve?

John C. Shields

For a response to this query we must, perhaps surprisingly, travel no further than the writers of Wheatley's eighteenth-century New England. It is ironic that the orthodox Joseph Sewall, grandson of the diarist Samuel Sewall and Wheatley's religious "monitor," according to her own testimony, served as a conduit to the early-sixteenth-century skeptic Pierre Charron, friend and disciple of Michel de Montaigne.

The connection to Charron that Joseph Sewall enabled for Phillis Wheatley was bridged by Joseph Seccombe, who has the distinction of authoring the first tract on sport published in America, this effort a sermon extolling the value of fishing, especially on the sabbath. Sewall had delivered Seccombe's ordination sermon, in which Seccombe and two other young clergy were commissioned to minister to Native Americans. After three years of service, which clergy in New England and Britain judged to be distinguished, Seccombe accepted a call to the church at Kingston, New Hampshire. He assumed the duties of minister in October 1737, after which Seccombe settled down (having married in January 1738) to the relatively quiet life of a prosperous parson.

Seccombe was not always well fixed, however; having humble origins, Joseph found himself, because of his evident intelligence and genteel disposition, well supported in his grammar school days and throughout his college tenure at Harvard (A.B. 1731). This financial support came from the generosity of Old South Church, which he had joined, following his mother, in 1723. As his ties with Old South Church were, then, almost from the beginning quite strong, and all his publications appeared first in Boston, it is reasonably certain that this thinking man's works were available to the young and eager student Phillis Wheatley, in the large book repository within Old South Church. Seccombe died in 1760, just a year before Wheatley arrived in Boston. Given Sewall's role as spiritual counselor to Wheatley and his association with Seccombe, it is likely that Sewall directed Wheatley's attention to this man's well-known works.

Perhaps the most substantial link between Wheatley and Seccombe occurs in the several textual connections between Wheatley's last extant poem, "Elegy on Leaving—," wherein she bides adieu her poetic pursuits, and Seccombe's "Ye Happy Fields," in which he expresses great reluctance upon leaving behind pristine nature's "sweet Composers of the pensive soul." Seccombe's eight-line poem which appends his homily, *Business and Diversion . . . in the Fishing Season,* and which, as we have observed, serves as an apology for the sport of fishing, reads as follows:

Ye happy Fields, unknown to noise and strife,
The kind Rewarders of industrious Life;
Ye shady Woods where once I us'd to rove,
To think for Man, and praise the God above;
Ye murmuring Streams that in Meander roll,
The sweet Composer of the pensive soul,
Farewell.—The city calls me from your Bowers;
Farwell amusing Tho'ts and peaceful Hours. (22)

Seccombe's 1734 homily, which was published in Boston and would have been readily available to Wheatley, had in his closing "prayer" on the page preceding "Ye Happy Fields" extolled the "Fields and Groves," "the flowry Beauties" of the warmer seasons (spring, summer, and fall) and the other "Delights" of nature, all redolent of Vergillian pastoral.

The minister is studious to explain, in the sermon nonetheless, that all these "rich Provision[s] of Nature" can not finally "satisfy . . . the Soul of a Christian." Note, nevertheless, that "Ye Happy Fields" surprisingly contains little Christianity; rather Seccombe's poem, unlike the sermon, represents a largely secular vision, as does Wheatley's "Elegy on Leaving—."

Just as Wheatley describes in her poem, "ye friendly bow'rs," wherein she "pensively . . . stray'd," and a "pebbl'd brook" that contributes to the ambience of "simple Nature's various charms," all these captivating enchantments of an escape from the "crowds and noise" of an urban setting (156), Seccombe has "shady Woods," "happy Fields," and "murmuring Streams" within which the poet/minister "us'd to rove" to compose his "pensive soul," these enticements resembling Wheatley's while depicting refuge from the city's "Noise and Strife." Whereas Wheatley's use of nature bespeaks that of a poet seeking to create poetry, "Rapt with the melody of Cynthio's [the Sun's] strain / There first my bosom felt poetic flame" (156), Seccombe appears disposed to discover the pleasures of nature "To think for Men, and praise the God above," or perhaps to concentrate upon the composition, not of poetry, but of a minister's sermon.

In any event, both Wheatley and Seccombe clearly enjoin a nostalgic world of pastoral and then express definite regret for what each perceives to be a necessary abandonment of this happy, preferred realm. While Seccombe bids "Farewell to amusing Tho'ts [imagination] and peaceful Hours," perhaps so that he can more concentratedly embrace the onus of his ministry, Wheatley, with more at stake, surrenders the writing of poetry, her life's work. She does so, very likely because of failing health. The thought and images advanced in each writers' poems, nevertheless, indicate more than casual literary parallels.

When we examine another of his sermons, however, we discover that Seccombe may not have been as "safe" a writer as Sewall probably thought him to be. In his homiletic, treatiselike *Some Occasional Thoughts* (1742), for example, we encounter the name of the famous skeptic, Pierre Charron, and a quote in a footnote from his *de la Sagesse* (*Concerning Wisdom*). According to Eugene F. Rice Jr. in his *The Renaissance Idea of Wisdom*, Charron's *de la Sagesse* (1601) marks "the triumph of wisdom as a naturally acquired moral virtue"—not a gift of God's grace. In other words, in this widely circulated renaissance work, Charron constructed "a purely human wisdom" (179), re-calling the ancient, classical understanding of the term. Seccombe's subject in *Some Occasional Thoughts* is the recent spate of enthusiasm brought on by George Whitefield's emotional preaching; Whitefield, about whom Wheatley would later write an internationally published and famous elegy, was chaplain to Selina Hastings, Countess of Huntingdon, but was also much hailed as the dramatic "Voice" of the Great Awakening. Even Jonathan Edwards, spear-head of the Great Awakening, had lamented that Whitefield's provocation of trances, visions, and such enthusiastic responses had too often become mani-festations of hypocrisy.

As Seccombe opens *Some Occasional Thoughts* with a quote from Edwards, one would expect these two to be in accord. Such is certainly *not* the case. Whereas Edwards in his *Treatise on the Religious Affections* holds firmly that the imagination is the means through which Satan invades the human soul, Seccombe argues that "The Divine Spirit, striving with Man, would operate on the *Imagination.*" Even though Seccombe acknowledges that the imagina-tion is "a lower Power of human Nature" (Wheatley later elevates imagina-tion to the highest level of the mind), he declares that, "Yet under Conduct of Understanding, it's a very useful and powerful Faculty" (9).

What provokes further interest here is that, in a footnote to this same passage, Seccombe quotes the following from Charron's *de la Sagesse:* "Imagination . . . is a loud, a blustering and restless Faculty [which] seems perfectly bound up in the profoundest Sleep, but is continually buzzing at the brain, like a boiling Pot" (9). What we notice here is that, although Seccombe appears to cite Charron as an authority on imagination, what he has actually done amounts to an extension of Charron's thought in which he somewhat el-evates imagination by giving it more "favorable press" than even Charron had

ventured. We find here that Seccombe is assuredly opposed to Edwards's vili-
fication of imagination. Seccombe concludes his discussion of imagination by
maintaining that, "Though the Divine Spirit makes Use of the Imagination, it
can never be serviceable without the Understanding" (9).

So although we have not moved to the position to which Wheatley later
came, we have certainly departed from Edwards's Calvinistic point of view.
It is worth noting that Seccombe quotes Charron from George Stanhope's
1707 translation of Charron's French *Sagesse,* not from the much earlier 1625
Samson Leonard translation, thereby ascertaining that Charron was alive and
well in Massachusetts Bay; as well, when Seccombe died, he left a library of
five hundred volumes. So the copy of *Concerning Wisdom* Seccombe used
could well have been his own and thereby have come into the hands of Phillis
Wheatley. Seccombe's attitude toward imagination, then, becomes a suit-
able "theoretical" framework for Samuel Cooper's 1761 positive assertion that
"Imagination! [is a] heav'n-born maid" (*Pietas* 45).

Charron, in the Stanhope translation, makes several additional and provocative observations regarding the imaginative faculty, which move beyond
Seccombe's interest but which accord provocatively with Wheatley's later
theoretics. According to Charron, the imagination is an essential and highly
charged faculty which "keeps all [the other parts of the mind] about it awake
and sets the other Faculties on *work*" (Charron, Stanhope trans., 119; all
quotes from this translation). Gendering imagination as female, which, given
Wheatley's preoccupation with the Muses and with female deities, would
have appealed to her, the French skeptic imparts to the feminine faculty great
power and responsibility: " . . . the Acts of Recollection, representing to the
Intellectual Faculty, laying up in the Memory, and drawing out those Stores
again for Use, are all of them Operations of the Imaginative Faculty" (119).
Wheatley's own "On Recollection" speaks of the memory in similar terms
as that mental power whose "secret stores . . . to the high-raptur'd poet gives
her aid" (62).

Most significantly, moreover, Charron maintains further that memory and
"Fancy, come within the compass of This [imagination], and are not (as some
pretend) Powers of the Mind, distinct and separate from it" (119–20). So we
observe that, to this important aesthetic theorist, both fancy and memory serve
the imagination and are therefore subordinate to it. I have been unable to discover another theorist who insists upon this actually quite specific description
of the operation of imagination, until of course we come to Phillis Wheatley. It

John C. Shields

may be then that this authoritative theorist may well have served Wheatley in a pivotal capacity.

Charron exuberantly holds that the imagination "is *Hot*," which causes poets to indulge "in bold and lofty Flights of Fancy" (116). Here we see a powerful, influential theorist assert that imagination is clearly associated, as in Wheatley, with the condition of high rapture or intense enthusiasm and with the notion of apparently boundless flight. No less a figure than Francis Bacon in 1605 appears to have taken instruction from Charron when the British philosopher describes imagination as an "extremely licensed" mental power which can "make unlawful matches and divorses of things" (Spingarn 1: 5). Both these thinkers point directly to Wheatley's "Thoughts" wherein she speaks of a realm residing in the dreaming mind where "ideas range / Licentious and unbounded" and "Where *Fancy's* queen in giddy triumph reigns" (47).

To suggest that the New England intelligentsia were unaware of aesthetic thought in Great Britain during the eighteenth century would indeed be preposterous. So, as promised above, we will, in attempting to establish an adequate context for Wheatley's maturing aesthetic theoretics as touches the imagination, journey for a time, among several British thinkers, all of whom would surely have been aware of Charron's *de la Sagesse.*

Virtually none of the eighteenth-century British aestheticists, nevertheless, pick up on Charron's effort to distinguish imagination and fancy, although they appear to agree with Charron—and many others from Plato and Aristotle to thinkers of the Renaissance—that the imagination is the poet's faculty. Beyond his somewhat disparaging remarks in *Leviathan,* however, Hobbes, in his 1650 "Answer to Davenant's Preface to *Gondibert,*" makes no distinction between fancy and imagination, genders fancy as a feminine principle, identifies fancy as a faculty of flight which can "fly from one Indies to the other, and from Heaven to Earth" (59), and notes that "Poets are Painters" (61—this last observation echoing Horace). John Dryden, just fourteen years later, puts on the breaks regarding the imagination when he admonishes that "imagination in a poet is a faculty so wild and lawless, that like a high-ranging spaniel, it must have clogs tied to it, lest it outrun judgement" (Engell 35).

Mather Byles, one of Wheatley's mentors who wrote in America almost eighty years later, appears for a time to indulge his "wild imagination" with impunity, as Wheatley would do over a hundred years after Dryden. To return to Britain, John Dennis, called by some the greatest critic of his age, in remarkable disagreement with Locke, celebrates the enthusiastic passions. In the fourth chapter of *The Grounds of Criticism* (1704), titled "What the Greate Poetry Is, What Enthusiasm Is," Dennis identifies the "Enthusiastick Passions" as "those emotions which excite great poetry. Contemplation and meditation give rise to these emotions" (Dennis 1: 338), the strongest of which "must be rais'd by religious Ideas; that is, by Ideas which either shew the Attributes of the Divinity, or relate to his worship" (1: 339). In his *Religious Sublime,* David Morris interprets Dennis's perspective as having moved a significant step beyond Longinus. In Morris's words: "For Longinus, the interaction of passion and imagination contributed to the sublime; for Dennis it created the sublime" (Morris 66).

Anthony Ashley Cooper, Third Earl of Shaftsbury, who, according to Douglas Den Uyl, author of the contemporary "Foreword" to Shaftsbury's *Characteristics,* "wrote one of the most important and influential books of the eighteenth century" (A. Cooper 1: vii), remarks in a 1708 "Letter Concerning Enthusiasm" that, regarding poetic affatus, *"Inspiration* may be justly call'd *Divine* ENTHUSIASM: For the Word it-self signifies *Divine Presence,* and was made use of . . . to express whatever was sublime in human Passions" (A. Cooper 1: 34). Perhaps Wheatley actually saw this tract; it is certain that her enthusiastic pursuit of poetic afflatus constitutes a dominant pattern in her poetry.

Sounding much like a paraphrase of Charron, Shaftsbury holds that appetites and desires reside in the imagination, that the imaginative faculty is "a Business which can never stand still" (A. Cooper 1: 199), and that this faculty becomes manifested in *"Giddiness* and *Dream"* (A. Cooper 1: 201). Shaftsbury even goes so far as to recommend writing as an invaluable *"self-examining* Practice and Method of *inward* Colloquy" (A. Cooper 1: 202). To be sure, here Shaftsbury draws on the introspective tradition of meditation, a tradition that Wheatley clearly inherited. But like Dryden, Shaftsbury strongly advises that fancy (not here made distinct from imagination) and enthusiasm require "some Controuler or Manager" (A. Cooper 1: 198); in order to guard against "mere Imagination or the Exorbitancy of Fancy" (A. Cooper 2: 90), one must acknowledge that what he insists on here is a healthy moderation, summoning up the classical Greek cultural ideal of *sophrosyne*—nothing in excess, sanity in all things, the golden mean.

While Shaftsbury's sentiments on inspiration could have provided Wheatley useful instruction, Dennis's welding of imagination and the feeling of the sublime of course predicts Wheatley's combination of these two aesthetic categories in "On Imagination." Her work, nevertheless, demonstrates

John C. Shields

that, once again, she did not agree with Shaftsbury's notion of a manager for imagination, or for that matter for the sublime. Indeed, the principle of order in her liberated poetics was the imagination itself. Joseph Addison, Edmund Burke, and Henry Home, Lord Kames proved to be more favorable, more compatible theorists regarding imagination, and therefore more in line with Wheatley's interpretation than Shaftsbury, albeit these later British thinkers indicate contiguities of thought no more remarkable than the parallels between the African American poet and the French Charron or the British Dennis.

Joseph Addison, who was one of the most enthusiastic early advocates for imagination and whose *Spectator* was the most widely read of the gentleman's magazines of eighteenth-century England, expressed in language designed to edify English gentlemen some of the most lofty but clearly stated ideas about the sublime working in concert with the imagination. In *Spectator* 412, for example, Addison writes: "Our imagination loves to be filled with an Object, or to grasp at anything that is too big for its Capacity. We are flung into a pleasing Astonishment at such unbounded Views, and feel a delightful Stillness and Amazement in the Soul at the Apprehension of them" (3: 540).

This passage identifies the imagination as the faculty of one who desires intensely to grasp the infinite and the ineffable. Samuel Holt Monk, author of the authoritative *The Sublime,* holds that what Addison describes here is "essentially the sublime experience from Addison to Kant" (Monk 58). Wheatley's "On Imagination" articulates the power Addison extols, but with a significant difference:

> From star to star the mental optics rove,
> Measure the skies, and range the realms above,
> There in one view we grasp the mighty whole,
> Or with new worlds amaze the unbounded soul. (66)

Wheatley's words, "view," "grasp," "amaze," "unbounded," and "soul," echo Addison. Like Addison, Wheatley specifies a limitless vision, but she adds the idea of "new worlds." While Addison's description speaks of views in created nature, Wheatley's "new worlds" introduces the poet's conception of myth-making. Indeed, Wheatley proceeds to build not one but two heterocosmic worlds in remarkable anticipation of the apocalyptic Romantics.

In his extremely popular *Philosophical Enquiry into the Origin of Our Ideas of the Sublime and Beautiful* (1757), Edmund Burke concentrates on a sensationalist view (which holds that all knowledge originates in sensation) regarding the psychology of the imagination/sublime. Sounding a perception of divine wisdom which parallels Wheatley's, Burke declares:

> Whenever the wisdom of our Creator intended that we should be affected with anything, he did not confide the execution of his design to the languid and precarious operation of our reason; but he endued it with powers and properties that prevent [precede] the understanding, and even the will, which seizing upon the senses and imagination, captivate the soul before the understanding is ready either to join with them or to oppose them. (107)

As expected from a psychology of sensation, Burke's center of interest here is directed not toward God and devotion but toward an analysis of response. In Wheatley's work she, too, is driven to an analysis of how the power of imagination and its attendants—memory, fancy, the senses, and the appetites—interplay in her construction of a poetic world. To be sure, such an undertaking, the creation of a new world, flies fully in the face of Burke's position that "the imagination is incapable of producing anything absolutely new" (17).

In Wheatley's analysis, however, these powers usurp reason at that moment that she, in remarkable contrast to the Burkean notion of false consciousness, elevates the imagination, having finally absorbed all its attendant parts, to the position of reason as "leader of the mental train" or, indeed, as the poet's "reason." In "On Imagination," then, the poet pictures the mind's eye—that is, the fancy—as seizing upon "some lov'd object" which "all the senses bind, / And soft captivity involves the mind" (65). But in her determination to carve out an idea of infinite space, she opts to ascribe to the unbounded and even at selected moments "licentious" imagination the power(s) of enabling her to launch offensives into the infinite realm of freedom, thereby bypassing the less free, less licensed, understanding or reason.

As Phillis Wheatley was certainly, if regrettably, no stranger to pain and this world's vicissitudes, she may well have found Burke's aesthetic analysis of pain in the *Enquiry* to be useful to her own management of pain, especially in her poetry. Burke affirms, for perhaps the first time, that terror and imagined pain leading to astonishment serve as sources for the idea of the sublime. In anticipation of Kant's "Analytic of the Sublime," as well as Keats's oxymoronic figures of "sad joy," Burke bases his theory of the sublime upon "Whatever is fitted in any sort to excite the ideas of pain, and danger, that is to say, whatever is in any sort terrible, or is conversant about terrible objects, or operates in a

John C. Shields

manner analogous to terror" (39). Monk states that " . . . in introducing pain as the basis of sublimity, he [Burke] opens the way for the inclusion of ideas and images in art that had hitherto been considered as lying outside the sphere of aesthetic pleasure" (91). Wheatley derives the emotions of pain and danger which evoke the sublime from three sources within her own experience: first, from the desire to escape temporal "woes, a painful endless train" (152); second, from depicting the wrath of an angry god as in "Goliath of Gath," "Isaiah lxiii," and "Niobe in Distress . . ."; and third, from an aching reluctance to surrender her poetic world.

Henry Home, Lord Kames, in his *Elements of Criticism* (1762), focuses, not on pain, but on the pleasure obtainable from imaginative literature. Having settled on Addison's earlier description of grandeur or greatness as the sublime, Kames asserts that the enthusiastic passions "commonly signify the quality or circumstance in objects by which the emotions of grandeur and sublimity are produced; sometimes the emotions themselves" (Kames 1: 211). In this last phrase Kames foreshadows Kant, who will later insist that the sublime does not reside "in any of the things of nature, but only in our own mind" (114). To Kant, the feeling of the sublime never occurs "in objects" but always results from a mental response to their contemplation. Like Kant, Wheatley, as we have seen, considers the sublime to be a mental response and thereby avoids Lord Kames's tendency to confuse object and response.

In his examination of the sublime, Kames emphasizes height, but he studiously avoids identifying the sublime as an elevated distance above the contemplating person. He does, nevertheless, maintain that "Ascent is pleasant because it elevates us" (1: 220) and that "an expression or sentiment that raises the mind" is "great or elevated" (1: 223). "The effect of motion and force *in conjunction* [emphasis mine] provokes the most sublime response, which," continues Kames, "the image of the planetary system most successfully stimulates." In close anticipation of Wheatley's descriptions, Kames even goes so far as to declare: "But if we could comprehend the whole system at one view, the activity and irresistible force of these immediate bodies would fill us with amazement: nature cannot furnish another scene so grand" (1: 256). Three lines from Wheatley's "Thoughts on the Works of Providence" amply display Kames's motion combined with force:

> Ador'd the God that whirls surrounding spheres,
> Which first ordain'd that mighty Sol should reign
> The peerless monarch of th' ethereal train. (43)

As we have observed of "On Imagination," the poet and her readers "comprehend the whole system at one view." The mind's eye takes in this view while at the same time enjoying the celestial motion in these lines:

> From star to star the mental optics rove,
> Measure the skies, and range the realms above,
> There in one view we grasp the mighty whole. (66)

The similarities here are striking. Clearly Wheatley registers contiguities of thought with the Brits. At the same time, however, she departs from them when she elevates imagination to the poet's reason and when she constructs new worlds.

Just at a moment when British aesthetic theory would appear to have been warming to Wheatley's use of imagination and the sublime, a reactionary response is levied. In *The Creative Imagination*, James Engell misses this reactionary response when he remarks of William Duff's 1767 *Essay on Original Genius* that Duff "attains a view of the imagination as a broad and natural power whose scope in poetry is 'absolute and unconfined'" (84). Three years after the *Essay*, however, Duff countermands his earlier position. Indeed, in the 1770 *Critical Observations on the Writings of the Most Celebrated Original Geniuses in Poetry*, which Engell does not mention, Duff, toward the end of this later work, finds in the poetry of the Italian Ludovico Ariosto, especially in his *Orlando Furioso*, abundant evidence that, characteristic of original genius, is "an irregular greatness, wildness, and enthusiasm of imagination" (296–97). So Duff's radical shift to a decidedly negative position toward the imagination assuredly comes as a surprise in the last pages of *Critical Observations* when he admonishes that "There is indeed at the same time great danger of being betrayed into error, from the unrestrained indulgence of imagination on religious subjects" (353).

If it is true that all great geniuses of letters pursue a nondenominational theology in their work—a process that Wheatley, somewhat following the example of Charron, most assuredly does embrace—then all literary geniuses must err, according to Duff, with stubborn alarm. As for Wheatley's experimentation with heterocosms, Duff maintains that "This tendency to contrive visionary schemes, it is obvious, arises from imagination irregular and unchastised." Such a dangerous imagination must be tamed "by the chastening power of the reasoning faculty" (*Critical Observations* 356). So Duff's final pronouncement against imagination has moved, most disappointingly, not a dust mote away from the position of Jonathan Edwards.

While the British aesthetes at several points appear to be providing Wheatley useful instruction in her intellectual shaping of her own poetics, they finally give her less than courageous and/or liberal assistance. For the most formative sources of what we may now call Wheatley's rebellious spirit within the realm of literary aesthetics, an aesthetics that clearly points toward romanticism, we must turn, perhaps surprisingly, to Colonial Americans. All these potential teachers resided in Wheatley's own Boston, among whom numbered Joseph Seccombe, Charles Chauncy, some of the poets of the 1761 *Pietas et Gratulatio* (including Samuel Cooper), William Billings, and her principal literary model, Mather Byles.

In his attempt to construct an intellectual history of the imagination in his *Creative Imagination,* James Engell not only neglects to investigate the contribution of Charron's *de la Sagesse* or of William Duff's *Critical Observations,* he fails to give any attention to Seccombe, Cooper, Chauncy, Billings, or Byles. While he suggests that Philip Freneau initiates an analytical examination of the fancy in "The Power of Fancy" (1770; it is unlikely that Wheatley knew this poem, at least not before her 1773 *Poems*), he finds that no really penetrating pursuit of the imaginative faculty occurred in America before Poe and Emerson (Engell 188–96).

Joseph Seccombe, Wheatley's fellow traveler on the path toward wisdom who cited Charron in the Stanhope translation of *de la Sagesse,* and Charles Chauncy, who signed Wheatley's "To the Public," her letter of attestation regarding the authenticity of her authorship—each commented on the imagination and enthusiasm prompted by the Voice of the Great Awakening, George Whitefield. We have already examined Seccombe's endorsement of the imagination. Chauncy, however, despite his identity as an Old Light liberal minister, expressed an opposing attitude toward imagination. For in the same year (1742) as Seccombe's endorsement, Chauncy, in *Enthusiasm Described and Caution'd Against,* declares in rhetoric predicting the hostility Edwards would show in the later *Affections,* that his purpose in this published sermon is to admonish the people "against the wilds of a heated imagination" (Chauncy i).

Equating the terms "enthusiasm" and "imagination" throughout this sermon, Chauncy claims with an exaggeration betraying the passion of his own imagination: *"Enthusiastic wildness has slain its thousands"* (iii; italics in original). At one point Chauncy even calls imagination "meer pretense" (2). Despite the fact that he acknowledges that the etymology of imagination "carries in it a good meaning, as signifying inspiration from God" (3), he stubbornly insists, "But the word is more commonly used in a bad sense, as intending an *imaginary,* not a *real* inspiration" (3). Toward the sermon's end, Chauncy holds "Next to the Scripture, there is no greater enemy to *enthusiasm,* than *reason*" (18).

Here this minister displays the conservative position of a New Light Calvinist, a contradictory posture for one whose career has been judged to have been that of a liberal. Chauncy's assertions are, nevertheless, the more interesting for two reasons. First, if he is to be believed, that imagination is "more commonly used in a bad sense," then Seccombe's position toward this faculty assumes the character of rebellion. And second, Chauncy's equation of imagination and the enthusiastic passions or the feeling of the sublime only reinforces the argument that, by 1742 in Wheatley's Boston, these two aesthetic categories were thought to blend or to operate inseparably. Although Chauncy viewed that the operation of these two faculties in concert could only lead to perdition (in accord with Edwards's *Affections*), Seccombe assuredly did not; in his opinion the path from imagination to the divine is direct and unobstructed. As well, of course, all this attention given to the imagination/sublime attests irrefutably that this faculty enjoyed considerable public impact, hence underscoring Engell's unfortunate ignorance regarding Early Americans' growing aesthetic sophistication. This contextualization of Wheatley's own experimentation with imagination can only raise our expectations that it was not only credible but may well have been, given her obvious predilection for aesthetics, inevitable.

Samuel Cooper (1725–1783), who was old enough to have read these tracts by Seccombe and Chauncy when published, demonstrates in the thirteenth poem of the 1761 *Pietas et Gratulatio* that he has not merely agreed with Seccombe, but that he has extended the earlier minister's analysis of imagination. In the first of the two English poems, the thirteenth and the twenty-eighth, thought by the most reliable authorities to be by Cooper (Akers, *Divine* 376–77n40), the poet repeats his intense desire for liberty so evident in the "dedicatory" essay. For example, Cooper disperses throughout this elegy on George II's death such phrases as "liberty, bright goddess," "every patriot [with] virtue crown'd" and a "grand design . . . Sacred to liberty and law" (S. Cooper, *Pietas* 46, 47). Cooper closes the poem with an image of the new young monarch, George III, "Stretching each nerve to freedom's goal. . . . For Heaven and Earth delight in Patriot Kings" (S. Cooper, *Pietas* 51–52). The language here closely resembles that of Wheatley, especially in "To George Washington" and "Liberty and Peace."

It is in the following stanza lamenting the death of George II, however, that Cooper states his grasp of imagination as an aesthetic category:

John C. Shields

Imagination! Heaven-born maid!
Descend and dissipate the cloud,
The black'ning cloud, which soils the mind
Too deeply tinctur'd with its grief:
Oh! Speak the virtues of the god like man.
(S. Cooper, *Pietas* 45)

Without qualification (no necessary manager), Cooper identifies imagination as the divine maiden, Minerva or Athena, personification of wisdom. In this stanza, imagination does not merely work in association with the divine; she is herself divine and is asked to descend from her sublime abode to "dissipate" Cooper's "black'ning cloud" of grief by speaking or narrating the deceased's accomplishment.

With this poem, Phillis Wheatley, as a student of poésis, may well have been guided by her "Friend sincere . . . [who] Encourag'd oft, and oft approv'd her lays" (153), to consider imagination to be the *unqualified* poet's understanding or reason, the principle of order, the arranger, organizer, and/or creator. At the same time, Cooper here portrays imagination as a possible mediator between the divine and man. It is very likely this last function, and the association of that function with the act of poésis, which most appealed to the young black slave woman become poet.

The poem that immediately follows "On Imagination" in *Poems*, "A Funeral Poem on the Death of C.E. an Infant of Twelve Months," displays unmistakable ties to Wheatley's preceding analysis in "Imagination" of the poet's reason. In her elegy, for example, the departed "wings his instant flight" through "airy roads" "To purer regions of celestial light" (69), much like imagination's swift course through the cosmos to discover "Th' empyreal palace of the thund'ring God" (66). As well, Wheatley's deceased subject, echoing Kames's most profound expression of the sublime, takes in "the universal whole" wherein "Planets on planets run their destin'd round" (69). Just three pages earlier, "On Imagination" describes a parallel moment in which we as empathic readers may "in one view . . . grasp the mighty whole" (66). The thought in Cooper's elegy in *Pietas*, then, bespeaks strong contiguities to Wheatley's own poetic praxis.

Several other links between Wheatley's oeuvre and the *Pietas* volume should be pointed out. In the twenty-eighth poem of the volume, also by Samuel Cooper, for example, appear the statements "fan the sacred fire" (86) and "fan the sacred flame" (89). These declarations of poetic afflatus do not occur in Pope, Milton, or Shakespeare, but do closely resemble Wheatley's line in "Hymn to the Morning" about the Muses: Calliope's "fair sisters fan the pleasing fire" (56). Cooper's celebration in this poem of the accession of George III is punctuated throughout with elements of pastoral as he narrates this new opportunity for "The Graces and the Virtues [to] join / T'adorn the Royal Train." Here we find "sequester'd bowers" which echo Philomela's (the nightingale's) "thrilling musick," causing "each soft passion of the grove / To charm the royal ear" (87, 88, and 89).

As well, the *Pietas* volume in general makes much of "patriot—virtue[s]" (35, etc.), "silken thought[s]" (16), pointing to Wheatley's "silken fetters" (65), and occasions when "glorious liberty her pinions spread" (23). Throughout the collection, the attributive "celestial" recurs with frequency, perhaps encouraging Wheatley's frequent use of this modifier.

William Billings, Wheatley's next close mentor in the evolution of her poetics of the imagination, was America's first native-born composer. His *New-England Psalm-Singer* (1770), a collection of church anthems and songs, enjoyed considerable fame well into the nineteenth century. It has been observed by a mid-nineteenth-century American historian of music that Billings's "Chester," a hymn of intense patriotism, "did more to inspire a spirit of freedom than any one thing that occurred at this critical moment [the American Revolution]" (Gould 44). This hymn's lyric stanza reads:

> Let Tyrants shake their iron Rod,
> And Slav'ry clank her galling Chains;
> We fear them not, we trust in God,
> New England's God forever reigns!
> (Billings 321)

With its rhetoric concerning "Tyrants" who enslave, and its clanking, "galling Chains," along with its declaration of strong belief in the Deity, this hymn cannot but have exercised an influence on the young Wheatley.

These two, William Billings and Phillis Wheatley, definitely knew one another. Indeed, Billings collaborated with Wheatley in their shared effort to commemorate the death of Samuel Cooper. Cooper died on December 29, 1783. On January 2, 1784, an eight-page pamphlet appeared that was prepared for the occasion of Cooper's well-attended funeral. This pamphlet included Wheatley's elegy on Cooper, which we have examined; Wheatley's "Elegy . . . [on the] Learned Dr. Samuel Cooper" was followed by a two-page "Anthem" by Billings. Wheatley and Billings probably met as early as 1769. In October of that year, Billings entered a notice in the *Boston Gazette:*

> John Barry [then Billings's associate] and William Billings Begs [*sic*] Leave to inform the Publick, that they propose to open a Singing School THIS NIGHT, near the Old South Meeting-House, where any Person inclining to learn to Sing may be attended upon at said School with Fidelity and Dispatch. (McKay and Crawford 36)

These Singing Schools were ordinarily attended, "for the duration of three months . . . mostly [by] young adults and teenagers" (McKay and Crawford 37). Wheatley, about sixteen at the time and given the assurance that *"any Person* inclining to learn to sing [emphasis mine]" would be welcome to attend would have been an ideal candidate for Billings's Singing School. As the "Old South Meeting-House" was the church that the Wheatley family attended and was under the ministry of Wheatley's "monitor," Joseph Sewall (who had died on June 27 of the same year), it is most likely that Susannah Wheatley, along with her daughter, Mary, and Phillis herself would have taken an interest in this notice. The fact that Billings includes in *The New-England Psalm-Singer* an anthem entitled "Africa," which speaks of "Fears, / Suspicions and complaints," evoking the possibility that Billings herein delivers Wheatley an embedded message regarding her difficulty with Boston's racial prejudice, when combined with the other factors above, multiplies the probability that Wheatley attended Billings's Singing School.

Certainly, the patriotic rhetoric of Billings's anthem, "America," with its sentiments that the American colonies are a land bereft of "Persecution's Iron claws"—indeed, a country where "Liberty erects her Throne" and "Freedom lift[s] her cheerful Head"—would have greatly appealed to Wheatley's identical sentiments that she expresses in her numerous political, but always patriotic, poems. Given all these indications just enumerated, the probability that Wheatley knew Billings's *New-England Psalm-Singer,* which he used as a tool of instruction in his singing schools, is all but irrefutable. Particularly of interest to this ambitious young poet would have been Billings's brief, prefatory essay, "To all Musical Practitioners," wherein Billings makes several provocative observations regarding the "Rules for Composition" (32).

Billings prescribes, for example, that *"Nature is the best Dictator"* (italics in original). Nature must lay the Foundation" for the air or song (or poem in reference to Phillis Wheatley), so Billings continues. Indeed, "Nature must inspire the Thought. . . . the more Art is display'd, the more Nature is decorated." Billings interestingly exacts no qualifying intervention of judgment or reason, no "manager." When Wheatley remarks in "On Imagination" that "*Fancy* dresses to delight the Muse" (68), she appears to be in agreement with Billings's position that "Art," the artificial creator of the anthem or of a poem, decorates nature herself.

Billings further refines his analytical understanding of the creative process by declaring, "Fancy goes first, and strikes out the Work roughly, and Art comes after, and polishes it over." We have here an inchoate grasp of how the piece of music, or the poem, comes into being, except that in Wheatley, "Art" has become the "imperial queen," imagination. I do not mean to suggest that Billings here draws a clear distinction between fancy and imagination. What he does describe, however, is a line of thought that begins to separate elements of the poetic process into identifiable compartments of responsibility, a responsibility that owes little or nothing to reason or judgment per se, but which somewhat echoes Charron's delineation of memory and fancy as subordinate to imagination.

Billings moves on to state daringly that " . . . if I am not allow'd to transgress the Rules of Composition, I shall certainly spoil the Air, and Cross the Strain, that fancy dictated" (32). To a young but maturing poet, such a liberalizing of the creative process could only have encouraged Wheatley in her personal, interior quest for liberation. Billings expands upon the creative process for poets when he says that he has "felt the disagreeable and slavish Effects" of exterior restraints imposed upon the artist; such restraints have been felt, so Billings holds, by "every composer of Poetry, as well as Musick." Billings reinforces what he sees as a close alliance between poetry and music when he declares that "Poetry and Music are in close connection, and nearly allied, besides they are often assistants to each other and like true friends often hide each others [*sic*] failings" (32).

One additional pronouncement of Billings that Wheatley would have found compelling is as follows: "I don't think myself confin'd to any Rules for composition laid down by any that went before me" (32). Taking Billings as an authority for composition, whether of music or poetry (and, after all, Billings did compose most of his own lyrics), Wheatley could have, taking up Billings's lead, found herself liberated all the more, if not in her actual adaptation of form, definitely in her internal choice and handling of poetic subject. When we add to what we have already pulled together about Billings and Wheatley—first that the text of Billings's "America" is actually that of Mather Byles's famous "New-England Hymn" and that Billings eventually became a communicant of Byles's Hollis Street Congregational Church—the relationship between Wheatley and Billings becomes solidified.

Although Wheatley did not regularly attend Byles's Hollis Street Church, that she knew Byles well is virtually donnèe. Both poets deal, in "Eternity" by Byles and in "Thoughts on the Works of Providence" by Wheatley, with subjects of lofty grandeur or sublimity. In these same pieces, Byles and Wheatley both speak of the overwhelmingly sublime image which is, according to Boileau, the pioneer translator of Longinus' *On the Sublime,* the first light of creation as presented in Genesis 1:3: "And God said, Let there be light, and there was light." Byles renders this sublime image in the following manner: "Anon Creation rose in instant Bloom, / And smiling Light dispel'd the horrid Gloom" (*Poems on Several Occasions* 107). Wheatley's persona is even more dazzled by this sublime moment:

> "Let there be light," he said: From his profound
> Old Chaos heard, and trembled at the sound;
> Swift as the word, inspir'd by pow'r divine,
> Behold the light around its maker shine,
> The first fair product of the omnific God,
> And now through all his works diffus'd abroad. (47)

In Wheatley's conception the experience of first light becomes synaesthetic; that is, both the senses of sight and sound are evoked, not the sense of sight alone, as in Byles.

Wheatley's construction of a more dramatic and intense image suggests an expansive awareness of the possibilities of the sublime as a manifestation of the enthusiastic powers—not merely as an image of grandeur. Byles uses the word "sublime" seven times in his volume; Wheatley uses the word four times in a body of poems that is far more extensive than that of Byles. But each time Byles uses this word, he always does so as a reference either to the sublime style or to height. He speaks of the language of Milton's *Paradise Lost* as an example of "the true Sublime" (*Poems on Several Occasions* 25), and he describes the new home of the deceased Daniel Oliver as "your sublime Abode" (42). Wheatley, however, uses the word "sublime" first to indicate height or loftiness and second to suggest majesty or awe. In "Isaiah LXIII" she characterizes God-like motion as sublime: "Say, heav'nly muse, what king, or mighty God, / That moves sublime from Idumea's road?" (60). Here "sublime" is used not simply as an adverb of place or height but also as an adjective describing the manner of majesty.

Other vocabulary parallels include Byles's "Fancy rove perpetual" (*Poems on Several Occasions* 33) and Wheatley's "the roving Fancy flies" (65); the rendering by both poets of the eyes of celestial beings flashing preternatural light (such light imagery ultimately derives in each case most likely from Dante's *Paradiso*); and Byles's "the frozen Floods" and Wheatley's "The frozen deeps" (66). Echoes of Byles's vocabulary in Wheatley are too numerous to be accidental. But if they do indicate that Wheatley found Byles's choice of language appealing, they also illustrate that she was an inventive student—one who was generally capable of improving upon her mentor.

Both poets as well build in their works a poetics in which an enthusiastic persona desires ardently to soar, by means of poesy, toward God. In the poem, "To an Ingenious Young Gentleman on His Dedicating a Poem to the Author," which appeared first in the *New England Weekly Journal* in 1727 and later in his 1744 volume, Byles employs a rhetoric of ecstasy in which his persona appears to want to unite with God above. The poem's speaker first dares to "Soar sublime" (*Poems on Several Occasions* 52); then Byles states:

> Ravish'd my Ear receives the heav'nly Guest,
> My heart high-leaping, beats my panting Brest:
> Thro' all my Mind incessant Rapture reigns,
> And joys immortal revel in my Veins. (53)

Later in the poem, the thinly veiled persona becomes "Convinc'd, I own Eternity a NOW" (56). Byles concludes this finally abortive attempt at ecstatic unity with God by offering the following, somewhat pompous advice to the "ingenious" young man:

> Thus let your Poesy refine, improve,
> And match the Musick of the Choirs above;
> Still from your Lips let such soft Notes arise,
> And songs of Seraphs sound beneath the Skies,
> Till as your Muse, your Soul expands her Wings,
> And to their bright Abodes, exulting, springs. (56–57)

Byles's prescription of a poetics that matches "the Musick of the Choirs above" suggested to Wheatley an approach to the composition of poetry that offered her temporary relief from a hostile world where she found herself confined as a slave. At an early point in his *Occasions,* Byles has a "Hymn to Christ" that speaks of "ev'ry Sense" (*Poems on Several Occasions* 17) and subsequently cites Pascal's triad of memory, reason and Love: "To Thee my Reason I submit, / My Love, my Mem'ry, Lord" (18). As we have observed, Wheatley too treats memory, understanding, and love as will in "Thoughts on the Works of Providence."

In Wheatley's hands her poetics becomes adapted to her personal predicament and serves her as a source of freedom, a momentary means of escape from harsh reality into the imaginary, happy world of the poem. "On Imagination" demonstrates the power Wheatley attributes to the world of the poem in words that echo Byles:

> Soaring through the air to find the bright abode,
> Th' empyreal palace of thund'ring God,
> We on thy pinions can surpass the wind,
> And leave the rolling universe behind. (66)

Like Byles's, Wheatley's objective is to reach God, but the younger poet strikes a different note in this picture. She maintains that the poem permits the imagination full range; so powerful is the imagination in her poem that it can permit the mind to absent itself from "the rolling universe."

While the older Byles had in his poetry extolled "my wild imagination" (*Poems on Several Occasions* 26), the same author, in one of his prose ventures into literary criticism, "Bombastic and Grubstreet Style: A Satire" (appeared first in the *New England Weekly Journal,* April 17, 1727) complained of an "Extravagance of Imagination" (Miller and Johnson 2: 691), predicting Dr. Johnson's exact phrasing later in the century. As well in the same poem in which he had conjured his "wild imagination," he insists in this poem's conclusion that what his imagination has summoned is merely a congeries of "ideal Dreams, / Imaginary Trances! vain Illusions!" (*Poems on Several Occasions* 34). Byles, then, like most before him, demanded that imagination be restrained or managed. At another point, the poet soon to become minister remarks the "busy Fancy" (42), once again calling up Pierre Charron. Finally, to Wheatley, however, the power of imagination can even "with new worlds amaze th' unbounded soul" (66). Byles too claimed in "To Pictorio" that "at our Word, new Worlds arise" (93). But he does *not,* as Wheatley *does,* move on to construct new worlds. Wheatley's poetics, then, moves into a realm distinct from that of Byles. He had advanced the aspiration that human poetry could strive toward imitation of angelic song (the music of the spheres).

As Wheatley emphasizes the capacity of poetry to build new, reified worlds, she sees poetry, then, not merely as an imitative activity, but as a potentially mythic, re-creative one. The remainder of "On Imagination" constitutes an attempt to create not one but two new worlds in the face of an unsatisfactory one:

> Though *Winter* frowns to *Fancy's* raptur'd eyes
> The fields may flourish, and gay scenes arise;
> The frozen deeps may break their iron bands,
> And bid their waters murmur o'er the sands. (66)

In the midst of "*Winter* austere" (66), the power of imagination enables the poet to construct an opposing world of warm spring and, a bit later, another world celebrating the warm sun. But these imaginary worlds can only bring temporary escape; for "northern tempests damp the rising fire; / They chill the tides of *Fancy's* flowing sea" (68). Wheatley's recognition of the power of the imagination to conjure up a new world and of its inevitable failure to sustain this new world anticipates Keats's "Ode to a Nightingale" where the English poet discovers, like she already has, that the wings of poesy provide an escape which is all too brief.

Surely Wheatley's bondage urged upon her this essentially romantic approach to the writing of poetry; certainly her use of "iron bands" as a metaphor for ice cannot be construed as accidental. Here as in every other instance cited in this examination, Wheatley demonstrates that she surpasses Byles in forcefulness and in imagination. Unlike Byles who had bade "adieu to the airy Muse," Wheatley pursued the art of poetry as a serious commitment throughout her short adult life.

We come to understand, then, that Wheatley carries with her a far graver burden than Byles, who, a free white man, would never be forced to bear. As a woman and a slave, she can not follow Byles into productions of "the airy Muse"; indeed the pleasure she seeks is hardly "airy" but is rather of the highest order—the pleasure, the absolute joy, of liberation. Simply speaking, much more is at stake for this young genius whose regrettable circumstances have thrust her into slavery. Wheatley's intense desire to write comes from within; as she puts it so well, "an intrinsic ardor prompts [me] to write" (15). But it is not this intrinsic ardor alone that motivates her to acquire knowledge and to yearn for wisdom and then to articulate in words what life has taught her. For she, unlike Byles, is not free.

John C. Shields

When we consider how these two express their concerns about imagination, we encounter a radical difference. While Byles at times *appears* to be pro-imagination, he finally characterizes an enthusiastic imagination as delusional. Here Byles actually carries his negative attitude a step or two beyond the many who, as we have observed, required a manager for imagination. To charge imagination with providing the source for trances and "idle Dreams" amounts to one of the most hostile attitudes we have come across, resembling the fanaticism of Jonathan Edwards. Wheatley, of course, chose a diametrically opposed path, one that elevated imagination to the poet's reason.

British authors and the French Charron were of importance to her, especially Charron's distinction between fancy and imagination. Her American mentors, Joseph Seccombe (by way of reputation), Samuel Cooper, William Billings, and Mather Byles, nevertheless, played far more consequential roles in helping to shape her poetics of imagination.

While we have often touched upon the poems that make up Wheatley's "Long Poem," now we examine "On Recollection," "Thoughts on the Works of Providence," and "On Imagination" as a unit. Wheatley adroitly attests that she is thoroughly engaged with the poetic process—that is, with the act of creating a poem, in "On Recollection," a poem wherein she demonstrates her subtle turn toward interiorization, signaling the first period of her poetic maturity.

In order to accomplish the five-stress iambic line of heroic verse, Wheatley opts to open "Recollection" with the older form of memory's name, "Mneme," rather than choosing the four-syllable, less ancient "Mnemosyne." Hence Wheatley suggests her sophistication as a classicist. This faculty, of course, gendered female, is, according to Wheatley, one of power. Recognizing Mneme as an "immortal pow'r," Wheatley calls up "Thy pow'r" (line 7), "thy pow'r" (line 38) again, and "her pow'r" in order finally to assert her own power in application of this faculty, for it is after all the power of her own memory that summons "from night" "the long-forgotten" (line 7). Upon first encounter, this powerful faculty "sweetly plays before the *fancy's* sight" (line 8). To Wheatley this play becomes most manifest as "nocturnal visions" that Mneme "pours" into the mind wherein an "ample treasure" of separate memories registers as "secret stores." Mneme's "stores" arrange themselves as a "pomp of images display'd" which give "to the high-raptur'd poet" assistance in the construction of her poems.

It is of great significance to observe that Wheatley insists that this treasure trove of images occupies "the unbounded regions of the mind." This insistence establishes that this poet's memory, which knows no bounds, is free to explore without restraint—that is, bereft of the chains of slavery. Such a perspective here points directly to Wheatley's liberation poetics. Interestingly, Charron had earlier held that "Memory acts not at all but is purely Passive" (Charron, Stanforne trans. 19). To the skeptic it is imagination which "collects together the Ideas and Figures of Things"; at this early point in Wheatley's evolving poetics, her enthusiasm for memory's "immortal pow'r" leads her to ascribe to Mneme what she would soon hold to be the responsibility of fancy. Later she would invest memory with less "pow'r."

In "Recollection," nevertheless, the poet names memory "The heaven'ly *phantom* [who] paints the actions done / By ev'ry tribe beneath the rolling sun" (lines 17–18). So Wheatley is going to present, then, a sweeping panorama that will condemn vice and praise virtue. "Virtue" brings to her mind sounds "Sweeter than music to the ravish'd ear" which recall to her the "entertaining strains" of Virgil's eclogues "Resounding through the groves, and hills, and plains" (lines 22–24). From this representation of idyllic pastoral, the poet shifts quickly, but *apparently* innocuously to the realm of vice in which memory unveils "each horrid crime" attended by "Days, years misspent" conjuring "a hell of woe!" This woeful hell brings up "the worst tortures that our souls can know" (lines 27–30).

After a casual reading one is inclined to think, because the poet declares that her memory causes these horrid crimes to return, hence provoking her "to be asham'd, and mourn," that the crimes are probably her own. Closer inspection, however, "paints" quite a different picture. Indeed, what would an asthmatic, benign teenager closely supervised by her white owners know of "the worst tortures"? Recall that Phillis, gallingly and unimaginatively named for the slaver that brought her, was seven or eight years old when she was sold on the block, July 11, 1761, with nothing but a piece of dirty carpet to conceal her nakedness. So she was certainly old enough to have recorded implacably on her memory the horrors of the terrible Middle Passage. Acknowledging that the mores governing the behavior of young African girls would have universally demanded these female children exercise modesty, one can readily grasp why the young girl's piece of dirty carpet would have forced shame upon her.

As for her mourning, this innocent victim of slavery no doubt possessed a plethora of occasions for her grief, such as the loss of her parents, siblings, and other family members, not to forget the loss or possible deaths of those Africans who befriended her on the wretched journey from Africa to Boston. Viewed from this perspective, Wheatley's ostensibly sweeping prospect ac-

John C. Shields

tually bespeaks an intensely personal experience, virtually unmatchable by any whites in her "adoptive" Boston. Using the pastoral world of Virgil's eclogues, which always hold the possibility of subversion, Wheatley, while looking harmless, has accomplished the construction of a powerful indictment of slavery. The poet's experience of the follies (which in Joshua 7:15 and Judges 20:6 of the KJV referred to evil[s], sin[s], or crime[s]) of "eighteen years" have passed, to the white folks, "Unnotic'd." But, so she continues, now we "behold them writ in brass!" In Shakespeare's *Henry VIII*, the English bard has the lines, "Mens evil manners live in brass, their virtues / We write in water" (4.2.45–46). (The writing in water brings to mind Keats's requested epitaph, "Here lies one whose life was writ in water.") We may, then, readily conclude that this most clever and well-read poet has, in "On Recollection," written anything but an innocuous tract, for as Wheatley so pointedly admonishes: "The wretch [a white enslaver], who dar'd the vengeance for the skies, / At last awakes in horror and surprise" (lines 43–44).

"Thoughts on the Works of Providence," which advances Wheatley's quest for a poetics of imagination a few steps further, arguably falls into the realm of the *meditatio* or meditation emphasizing that, from the days of ancient classicism, the major faculties of the mind have consisted of memory, understanding, and will. The ancients traditionally divided memory into the senses, the appetites, and the imagination. Hence once again the poet is concerned to treat "unbounded space" (line 22), "misspent time" resulting in a need to mourn folly or evil/sin (lines 67–68) and a condition of creativity in which the poet soars in a state of "rapture" (line 45). Opening the poem with a ten-line invocation, her longest single invocation, hence suggesting the significance of this exercise of the mind, Wheatley establishes that the "monarch of the earth and skies" will serve as her locus or necessary location on which to focus her attention; this process of establishing a locus is, according to classical rhetoric (whence the meditative process originates), the first step governing the *meditatio*. This focus upon the sun (with a possible pun on Son, though Wheatley here makes no mention of Jesus or Christ) enables Wheatley to treat two attendant, though merely apparent, concerns, the vastness of space and the importance of wisdom (recall Charron's *de la Sagesse* or *Concerning Wisdom*).

Another connection between Joseph Seccombe and our poet that arises at this point is evident in his own quest for wisdom, which would without doubt have piqued Wheatley's curiosity. Indeed one of Seccombe's published sermons was *A Specimen of the Harmony of Wisdom and Felicity* (1743). In this homily, which as we have observed of Seccombe before, resembles a treatise more than a sermon, Seccombe states in his preface that "By Wisdom Man knows himself and is humble, acquaints himself with Men and pays Deference to every one according Desert." Reflecting gentlemanly desire to achieve wisdom and happiness in a secular world, Seccombe's disposition would have served the maturing poet most constructively as a guide toward the adoption of a well-functioning, even diplomatic demeanor.

Surely Wheatley's poetic persona in "Thoughts" bespeaks, at least on the surface, a preoccupation with appearing to be humble and diplomatic as the poet pursues the burden of providing her readers, white and black, instruction in the quest for a wise disposition. As in the earlier "On Recollection," Wheatley again takes up consideration of the force of "nocturnal visions." In "Thoughts," however, the poet displays progress in her thinking. "As reason's pow'rs by day our God disclose," writes the poet, "So we may trace him in the night's repose." Notice that Wheatley has not yet concluded that imagination is the poet's reason, as she would do in the later "On Imagination."

Her movement into the seemingly harmless world of sleep/dream, however, suggests an advance in her theoretics, for in a state of sleep/dream, daily, quotidian "action ceases" but "ideas range / Licentious and unbounded o'er the plains." In other words, the "unbounded space" of the exterior universe, which provokes an awestruck response to the God of nature, becomes a kind of mirror for her focus on redirecting her attention to the interiorization which points toward the limitless realm of the human mind, particularly the poet's mind. While the exterior world of Boston, for example, would confine her in the shackles of slavery, Wheatley claims ownership of her own interior, limitless mind. In this interior world, which also knows no bounds, we discover that "Fancy's queen in giddy triumph reigns" (lines 83–88). Here Wheatley predicts the "imperial queen" of "On Imagination," just as she sets up a relationship between the mental functions of fancy and imagination, wherein fancy becomes subordinate to the superior, imperial imagination.

Hence, in "Thoughts," Wheatley has turned an ostensible search for wisdom into an exercise in self-discovery. The ultimate objective of the meditative process is, indeed, to bring about precisely such an interior discovery of self. "Thoughts" then has provided Wheatley the opportunity to explore the faculties of the mind as she engages the "powers" of memory, wherein she finds her focus on the exterior God of nature; the understanding, which enables her to refocus her attention on individual "power" to discover her own limitless mind; and finally her will (memory, understanding, and will identify the tripartite

John C. Shields

structure of the *meditatio*) which she comes to realize constitutes her central means of internal empowerment.

"On Imagination," the last portion of her "Long Poem," thoroughly enacts Wheatley's discovery of her individual empowerment over her own poetic creations. As pertains to her entire, extant poetry, "On Imagination" surely exemplifies her pièce de résistance. This complicated poem was certainly touted as her best work in the years following her premature death on December 5, 1784. Here her debt to Charron and others comes to an abrupt end. For despite Charron's division of the mind into understanding, memory, and imagination, in significant contradistinction to the ancients, despite his hedging separations of fancy and imagination wherein fancy serves imagination, and despite British and American eighteenth-century aesthetic theorists who precede, and probably were examined by, Wheatley, regarding her use of imagination, this excellent and original poet follows a course plotted by her own, individual needs and aspirations.

In the first three stanzas of "On Imagination," Wheatley establishes a tension between imagination, whom she names the "imperial queen" in the first line, and the "roving Fancy." Whereas imagination produces multiple "works" (poems) and bright forms which stand "in beauteous order," all demonstrating the overriding power of this faculty, the fancy flits here and there, as if on a mission to affix upon "some lov'd object" to bring into focus the mind's eye of the poet. It would appear that it is the province of the fancy to bind all the senses, thereby captivating the mind by means of "silken fetters."

While Wheatley may have appropriated the phrase "silken fetters" from Mark Akenside's 1744 *Pleasures of the Imagination* wherein he has the line, "The silken fetters of delicious ease" (book 2, line 562), this phrase in Wheatley's hands bears at least double meaning. For to a slave fetters are, perhaps, just chains; yet *these* chains are indeed silken, and more importantly they are imposed by choice of the poet on the operation of her own mind in the act of creation. Thereby they become manifestations of her own intellectual property. So the bow toward white enslavement registers on a minimal level, if at all. Most cleverly, Wheatley has accomplished in her application of this phrase a metaphor of liberating empowerment, not one of debilitating restriction.

The next line, *"Imagination! who can sing thy force?"* makes a radical break away from the notion of a "roving *Fancy*." This powerful faculty can soar through the air, emphasizing the cosmic possibilities for this faculty, and even discover "the bright abode . . . of the thundering God." Perhaps this God of thunder is the Old Testament Jehovah; perhaps he is Jupiter, god of thunderbolts. The reference, probably deliberately, remains ambiguous. Wheatley is next careful to propose that "We," she and her readers, can, on wings of poesy, "surpass the wind / And leave the rolling universe behind." From this immense expanse, we can each grasp in a single view "the mighty whole."

Then the poet collapses this cosmic perspective, as we have seen in "Thoughts," in order to capture a completely interior moment of discovery. As she puts it so well, "Or with new worlds amaze th' unbounded soul" (lines 13–21). What is particularly stunning here is that next Wheatley proceeds to construct a completely secular heterocosm, an alternative world. From a dynamic description of the feeling of the sublime, she rapidly descends into the interior realm of her own mind; this great rapidity of movement from the cosmic to the mind's interior predicts Kant's description in his "Analytic of the Sublime" of a pattern of vibrations between the object or expanse contemplated and the mind in the act of contemplation. The poet has here attempted, by use of her imagination, to bridge the gap between a vision of the divine, the "imperial abodes," and the secular world of warm pastoral.

Wheatley, in seizing this moment of interiorization as an opportunity to build a new world, has taken the poet's license to exceed vibratory movement and to linger for a time in a delightful realm of happy, earthlike images, all of which are assuredly absent of any hint of slavery. As she has it, "Though Winter frowns to Fancy's raptur'd eye," she will use her poet's mind, her "mental optics," to shape a world of flourishing fields and "gay scenes," sounding much like Vergil's pastoral or perhaps even a nostalgic recollection of her native Gambia. In "On Recollection," fancy is a faculty (sub-faculty) of sight, which focuses on a memory that "plays" before and thereby assists "the high-raptur'd poet" in fashioning her poem. Here, however, the fancy is itself the agent that intensifies the poet's vision of the new world; this functioning as an intensifier is consistent with fancy as a captivator who binds "all the senses" in stanza three. As in "Recollection," then, we view the poet as having achieved an ecstatic state of creativity. But it is the imperial queen who, with the fancy's aid, supervises the "wond'rous acts" of the poet—that is, her poems—and finally produces a "beauteous order."

The frowning winter evocative of forbidding cold conjures a perhaps inevitable parallel to the Boston white folks, especially those who hold slaves; the necessity to search for and find a warm realm bereft of slavery, therefore, becomes acute. For in Wheatley's secular heterocosm, "The frozen deeps may break their iron bands, / And bid their waters murmur o'er the sands." In this alternate world, cold, inhospitable winter warms to a temperate summer wherein fields may bear new life; release from the white folks' cold bondage produces a fecund fertility wholly free of stultifying, disabling shackles. Just so Wheatley has now pointedly applied her creative mind to the task of achieving liberation, first and foremost, of course, for herself but excluding no one.

Albeit forbidding *"Winter"* may look with scorn on the ecstatic, wondrous production of the poet, Wheatley's heterocosm exhibits warm waters that "murmur o'er the sands," perhaps echoing the strand along Wheatley's native Gambia. Significantly, the innocuous sounding "Fair *Flora"* vaunts "her fragrant reign" and decks the plain with "her flow'ry riches," evoking the "Licentious and unbounded" ideas ranged "o'er the plains" in "Thoughts," though the earlier abstract ideas here enact concrete expression. In this poet's alternative world, *"Sylvanus,"* another harmless-looking figure from ancient classicism, joins Flora as he crowns the forest trees with leaves.

When we discover, however, that, according to William King's immensely popular *Heathen Gods and Heroes,* which appeared in 1710 and was readily available to Wheatley, "Flora was a Courtezan, who got a great sum of Money by her immodest Practices" but willed her fortune to the people of Rome "upon condition that the Games called Floralia might be celebrated annually on her Birth-day" (193). Sylvanus, who was, again according to King, "always in the company of Pan" was god of "the Woods and Shepherds, and the Boundaries of Land" (186). His office actually was to rule over wild, uncultivated lands. So Flora as a prostitute connotes profligacy or, as in "Thoughts," licentiousness and Sylvanus as the god in charge of that realm outside urban confines—that is, the wild, unregulated forests and uncultivated fields beyond the limits of civilization—conjures a world of disorder, certainly not given, nevertheless, to the sadly calculated practice of slavery. What may appear on the surface to be harmless proves to be the precise opposite. And Sylvanus' association with Pan, well known for his sexual exploits, also serves as a link to Flora's sexual abandon.

We should add, nevertheless, that, on the one hand, Flora did represent the beauty of flowers and therefore of pastoral warmth and, on the other, that Sylvanus was clearly associated with wisdom, sometimes called the wise old man of the forest, and through Pan was a supporter of music. Wheatley has, then, depicted in the first of her two heterocosms a strikingly complex vision, one of course with no hint of slavery. Her poetics of liberation is surely alive and quite well in this ostensibly trouble-free arena, which promises both beauty and pleasure and an unlimited space wherein the poet can pursue the unbounded limits of her individual imagination—all constituting a kind of poetic paradise.

In the next stanza, the poet moves, one believes with reluctance, from gems of dew and sparkling nectar on blooming roses, to celebration of the powerful imagination as unchallenged "leader of the mental train." So powerful, recall the power of memory, has imagination now become to Wheatley that imagination, without qualification (no manager) casts reifications of her abstract thoughts into "full perfection." Indeed in this perfect world, even the "subject-passions bow," for "Of subject-passions sov'reign ruler Thou." This somewhat puzzling assertion becomes clear when we discover that, in Pope's "Epistel to Bathurst" (1733), passion connotes, in the eighteenth century, "the Motives of Avaricious men" (176); surely to this female slave, the most compelling manifestation of avarice was embodied in the institution of slavery, as is the case in Pope's "Epistle." In Wheatley's perfect world, then, even despised slavery disappears; for as she most affectively puts it, at the command of her imagination, "joy rushes on the heart." The intensity of Wheatley's moral vision in these lines must not go unremarked. Indeed as she calls her *Poems . . . Moral,* here as in the earlier "On Recollection," Wheatley summarily condemns the practice of slavery. In *Imagination under Pressure, 1789–1832: Aesthetics, Politics, and Utility,* John Whale emphatically asserts of his revisionist evaluation of British romanticism that the imagination "inhabits a particular moral and ethical space" (195). Certainly we can now declare that Wheatley's sensibility resides firmly within just such a "moral and ethical space." If Wheatley's British and Continental audiences could grasp her condemnation of her hated institution, their enthusiasm for reading her often-reprinted texts far exceeded mere curiosity, for her texts may well have helped to promote the later Romantics' great moral preoccupation, particularly regarding freedom for all human beings.

To return to "On Imagination," not yet fully satisfied with the power of her imagination, the poet proceeds next to construct still another heterocosm, this second depiction probably kindled by the preceding "joy" that darts through her "glowing veins." Now fancy as an agent of mental involvement sweeps "th' expanse on high" and fastens on Aurora, always in Wheatley evocative of her memory of her beloved mother. (If the reader finds my "always" extreme, know I should be pleased to be proven wrong.) This particular citation of Aurora (Wheatley calls up the dawn on numerous occasions, even writing "An Hymn

John C. Shields

to the Morning") is accompanied by Tithonus, perhaps the dawn's most beloved paramour. As Aurora leaves "Tithon's bed," her "cheeks all glowing with celestial dies," her light produces "a pure stream." These images of her mother's dawn occupy the space of a triplet, the only one in the poem, thereby bringing special importance to its content. Why? When we discover that the union of Tithonus and Aurora produced Memnon, a prince of Ethiopia, and that Wheatley was fond of calling herself "an Ethiop," this heterocosm assumes personal significance. For if Aurora represents her mother, then Wheatley figuratively becomes Memnon's sister, hence her proudly naming herself an Ethiop.

This second heterocosm allows the poet next to behold the ".monarch of the day," recalling the "monarch of th' etereal train" (43) in "Thoughts," who tips "all the mountains . . . with radiant gold." The ecstasy of this second reified, mythical world is short lived, however, as the poet acknowledges, now with unmistakable reluctance, that she cannot indefinitely sustain her mythical worlds. But note that Wheatley carefully tells us in this poem's concluding lines that the *"Fancy"* has dressed these worlds "to delight the *Muse."* Most regretfully now, "Winter austere forbids me to aspire." The white folks who earlier frowned on her enraptured vision now demand that her adventure "Cease." Note, nevertheless, that it is finally only by her own edict that she brings the poem to a close: "Cease, then, my song, cease the unequal lay."

This somewhat troubling last line does not leave the reader with a perfectly clear motive for her conclusion. Indeed, what is "unequal" about her song? Does this comment, "unequal lay," serve as a subversive complaint regarding her social status? Is her poem unequal to the task of long sustaining a mythical world? Even the Keats of "Ode to a Nightingale" finally has to abandon his beloved bird's song. In any event, Wheatley has in "On Imagination" accomplished the composition of a powerful explication regarding the operation of her own imagination. Her identification of imagination as "leader of the mental train" enacts a revolutionary moment in the evolution of literary aesthetics. While the Early Americans, Samuel Cooper and William Billings, levy enthusiastic observations about imagination, it is time that we all give Phillis Wheatley the credit due her for being the first to recognize imagination as occupying the highest rank among a poet's faculties, hence serving as the poet's reason.

Unquestionably this revolutionary elevation of imagination points directly to the several romanticisms of the Continent and of Great Britain. Equally without doubt, we may conclude that the narration of Wheatley's construction of a poetics of imagination attests a chapter in American literary aesthetics of major importance, a significance that cannot be exaggerated.

WORKS CITED

Addison, Joseph. *The Spectator.* Ed. Donald F. Bond. 4 vols. London: Oxford UP, 1965.

Akenside, Mark. *The Poetical Works of Mark Akenside.* London: George Bell, 1894.

Akers, Charles W. *Divine Politician: Samuel Cooper and the American Revolution in Boston.* Boston: Northeastern UP, 1982.

Bacon, Francis. "Advancement of Learning." *Critical Essays of the Seventeenth-Century.* 1908. Ed. J. E. Spingarn. Vol. 1. Honolulu: UP of the Pacific, 2005.

Baym, Max I. *A History of Literary Aesthetics in America.* New York: Ungar, 1973.

Billings, William. *The New England Psalm Singer* (1770). Ed. Karl Kroeger. Vol. 1 of *The Complete Works of William Billings.* Boston: American Musicological Society and Colonial Society of Massachusetts, 1981.

Burke, Edmund. *Philosophical Enquiry into the Origin of Our Ideas of the Sublime and Beautiful.* Ed. J. T. Boulton. New York: Columbia UP, 1958.

Byles, Mather. *God Glorious in the Scenes of the Winter.* Boston: Green for Gookin, 1744.

———. *Poems on Several Occasions.* Boston: 1744.

———. *Poems on Several Occasions.* Introduction by C. Lennart Carlson. New York: Columbia UP, 1942.

Charron, Pierre. *Of Wisdom: Three Books Written in French.* Trans. Samson Lennard. London: Blount and Aspley, 1625.

———. *Of Wisdom: Three Books Written Originally in French by the Sieur de Charron.* Trans. George Stanhope. 2nd ed. London: R. Bonwick, 1707.

Chauncy, Charles. *Enthusiasm Described and Caution'd Against.* Boston, 1742.

Cooper, Anthony Ashley, Third Earl of Shaftsbury. *Characteristics of Men, Manners, Opinions, Times.* 6th ed. 3 vols. London: J. Purser, 1737–38.

John C. Shields

Cooper, Samuel. "XIII" and "XXVIII" in *Pietas et Gratulatio*. Boston: J. Green and J. Russell, 1761. 43–52, 86–90.

Dennis, John. *The Critical Works of John Dennis*. Ed. Edward N. Hooper. Vol. I. Baltimore: John Hopkins UP, 1939.

Duff, William. *Critical Observations on the Writings of the Most Celebrated Geniuses in Poetry*. London, 1770.

———. *An Essay on Original Genius and Its Various Modes of Exertion in Philosophy and the Fine Arts, Particularly Poetry*. London, 1767.

Engell, James. *The Creative Imagination: Enlightenment to Romanticism*. Cambridge: Harvard UP, 1981.

Gould, Nathaniel D. *Church Music in America*. 1853. New York: AMSP, 1972.

Hobbes, Thomas. "Answer to Davenant's Preface to Gondibert." *Critical Essays of the Seventeenth Century*. 1908. Ed. J. E. Spingarn. Vol. 2. UP of the Pacific, 2005.

———. *Leviathan*. 1651. Indianapolis: Hackett, 1994.

Kames, Lord, Henry Home. *Elements of Criticism*. 2 vols. 6th ed. 1785. New York: Garland, 1972.

Kant, Immanuel. *Critique of Aesthetic Judgment*. Trans. James C. Meredith. Oxford: Clarendon, 1911.

King, William. *An Historical Account of the Heathen Gods and Heroes*. London, 1710.

Kyper, Peter Thomas. "The Significance of Mather Byles in the Literary Tradition of America: A Study of His 'Poems on Several Occasions' and His Literary Criticism." Auburn University, 1974.

Locke, John. *An Essay Concerning Human Understanding*. 4th ed. 2 vols. 1704. Ed. Alexander C. Fraser. New York: Dover, 1959.

McKay, David, and Richard Crawford. *William Billings of Boston: Eighteenth-Century Composer*. Princeton: Princeton UP, 1975.

Miller, Perry, and Thomas H. Johnson, eds. *The Puritans: A Source Book of Their Writings*. Rev. ed. 2 vols. New York: Harper and Row, 1963.

Monk, Samuel Holt. *The Sublime: A Study of Critical Theories in XVIII-Century England*. 2nd ed. Ann Arbor: U of Michigan P, 1960.

Morris, David B. *the Religious Sublime: Christian Poetry and Critical Traditions in Eighteenth-Century England*. Lexington: U of Kentucky P, 1972.

Pietas et Gratulatio (anonymous). Boston: J. Green and J. Russell, 1761.

Pope, Alexander. *The Poetry and Prose of Alexander Pope*. Ed. Aubrey Williams. New York: Houghton Mifflin, 1969.

Rice, Eugene F., Jr. *The Renaissance Idea of Wisdom*. Cambridge: Harvard UP, 1958.

Seccombe, Joseph. *Business and Diversion Inoffensive to God, and Necessary for the Comfort and Support of Human Society . . . in the Fishing Season*. Boston: Kneeland, 1743.

———. *Some Occasional Thoughts on the Influence of the Spirit with Seasonable Cautions against Mistakes and Abuses*. Boston, 1742.

———. *A Specimen of the Harmony of Wisdom and Felicity*. Boston, 1743.

Shakespeare, William. *Henry VIII. The Riverside Shakespeare*. Ed. G. Blakemore Evans et al. 2nd ed. Boston: Houghton Mifflin, 1997. 1026–64.

Whale, John. *Imagination under Pressure, 1789–1832: Aesthetics, Politics, and Utility*. Cambridge: Cambridge UP, 2000.

Wheatley, Phillis. *The Collected Works of Phillis Wheatley*. Ed. John C. Shields. New York: Oxford UP, 1988.

John C. Shields

To "pursue th' unbodied mind": Phillis Wheatley and the Raced Body in Early America

Mary McAleer Balkun

> *Restrain the sorrow streaming from thine eye,*
> *Be all they future moments crowned with joy!*
> *Nor let thy wishes be to earth confin'd,*
> *But soaring high pursue th'unbodied mind.*
>
> —"To His Honour the Lieutenant-Governor,
> on the Death of His Lady. March 24, 1773"

Phillis Wheatley lived and wrote in an interesting and complex moment in the history of the body, one that was informed by a variety of philosophical, theological, scientific, and even social movements. The influence of Enlightenment philosophic thought—the work of Descartes, Locke, and Berkeley, to name a few—was felt throughout the eighteenth century, especially in debates about the relationship of the mind/soul to the body; the relationship of the individual to society; questions about natural law, free will, and autonomy; and theories about race. The latter part of the century also saw an increased—and some would argue concomitant—interest in scientific theories that were intended to explain racial differences, along with the emergence of pseudo-sciences, such as phrenology, which could be used toward the same end. Finally, this near-obsession with the body had its antithesis as well: bodily disgust and repulsion, the response to which was an interest in refinement and gentility and efforts to deny, mask, or eliminate, if possible, those functions of the body that were seen as offensive and crude. Taken together, these three interrelated movements provided a useful set of ideas and discourses for a young, black, female slave who inclined toward the public realm and authorship.

As an African American slave, Wheatley would have had her own reasons for minimizing the body she inhabited, one that was both black and female, and for refocusing the reader of her poems on the content instead of the mind inhabiting that body. The convergence of various strains of thought at the end of the eighteenth century simply provided her with a vocabulary and a set of reference points that had not been available previously. Wheatley builds on these strains, enlisting several strategies in her poems to shift the attention of the reader away from the fact of her physical self in order to emphasize the message she is trying to convey, whether it is the equality of all people, the capacity of blacks to be saved, or the evils of slavery. These strategies are also reflected in her letters and in the portrait used as the frontispiece to her only published book of poetry. They include a repeated emphasis on the soul/spirit/ mind as opposed to the physical self and the adoption of voices, usually of the deceased, that allow her to project her message through another/another's self. In addition, Wheatley rarely refers to her own physical presence in the world; and when she does so, it is in abstract and idealized ways, such as when she calls herself an "African" or "Ethiop." The result is an amorphous and even ungendered body, one not bounded by time or space in the conventional sense.

Critical approaches to the raced body can vary widely, which seems to be even more the case when the subject is Phillis Wheatley. For years, scholars argued that Wheatley ignored or underplayed the problems of race in eighteenth-century America, and in particular the fact of slavery. That perception has been modified in recent years by those who have argued for Wheatley's subversive tactics in drawing attention both to her race and slavery.[1] By the same token, there are critics who believe that, contrary to the argument being made here, Wheatley in fact emphasizes the body in her verse. In "Other Questions: Phillis Wheatley and the Ethics of Interpretation," Robert Kendrick contends that while Wheatley wants to be seen as equal, "[s]he does not simply want abstract recognition, equality as a matter of discourse, but equality as a matter of physical, lived contact with her audience. She must be *seen* equally; this emphasis on the body, and her body, continues throughout her poetry" (47). He cites "To Maecenas" and "On the Death of the Reverend Mr. George Whitefield" and the references in these poems to "Afric's sable race" and being an "Ethiop" as evidence of this emphasis on Wheatley's raced body (48).

According to Kendrick, "As the performance of her elegies suggests that the only recognition of death and mourning comes from the reception and recognition of another living, embodied subject, Wheatley's position throughout her work demands that readers recognize the living body which produced this text" (48). However, such a reading does not take into account eighteenth-century attitudes toward the body, and especially the black and female body. Also, given the evidence of Wheatley's pragmatism and resourcefulness (for example, her subtle co-opting of the rhetoric of revolution in her verse), it does not seem likely that she would have undermined that work by emphasizing the fact of her physical self in the face of potential public hostility and skepticism.

As it was, the truth of her authorship was only resolved by such means as public performances (Flanzbaum 71) and the attestation of eighteen of Boston's finest citizens. As John Wood Sweet points out, "black and Indian Christians who became celebrities were constantly reminded of—and prompted to promote—their racial roots and their cultural origins" (127). Thus, the impetus to advertise her race seems to have come consistently from others, not Wheatley herself (this extends to the inclusion of her portrait in the published manuscript, discussed below). In fact, when John Thornton suggests that, having won her manumission, she should marry either Bristol Yama or John Quamine and return with them to Africa to work as a missionary, she gently rebuffs his suggestion, arguing (among other points), "Upon my arrival, how like a Barbarian Should I look to the Natives" (Wheatley 159). Wheatley perceives herself to be an American, and one who is not only civilized but refined as well, a position inculcated in her by her mistress, Susannah Wheatley. An anecdote related by Helen M. Burke, who credits it to a nineteenth-century biographer of the Wheatley family, suggests the genteel circumstances in which Wheatley was raised. It seems that a young black male slave, Prince, sent to fetch Wheatley home in a carriage due to inclement weather and her fragile health, was seen by Mrs. Wheatley sitting on the same seat as "my Phillis," a transgression for which he was "severely reprimanded" (Burke 40).

Katherine Fishburn makes a similar case for black embodiment, albeit in slave narratives, in *The Problem of Embodiment in Early African American Narrative*. She maintains that writers of these narratives (and slaves in general), rather than embracing the duality of Western metaphysics and disowning their bodies, privileged what she describes as the "body-self" (xii), "an antimetaphysical critique that was premised on recalling the body and honoring its recollection of Being" (xiii). While Fishburn's argument is provocative in terms of the slave narratives she discusses, it does not account for someone like Wheatley, who was completely immersed in Western culture and its literary tradition as a result of her education and associations. She was also separated from her parents at a young age, had little memory of them, and was isolated from other slaves, with few exceptions, limiting her accessibility to the "West African world view" (3) on which Fishburn bases her argument (at least in part). Wheatley's poetry actually models the very privileging of mind and negation of the body that Fishburn describes, but her engagement with these ideas is in the service of a larger project, one that is designed to increase the awareness of her reader and gain sympathy and understanding for the position of blacks, whether free or enslaved. Owned by someone else, with the limitations of her "self" already proscribed by ideas about the black body in the eighteenth century, and working within a poetic tradition that has consistently worked to control the bodies of women,[2] Wheatley's best strategy was to minimize the body she inhabited in order to move beyond the otherwise narrow constructions available to her.

Much has been written about the body—its construction, its gendered/raced/classed aspects—in the last thirty years, enough to have become something of a cottage industry in literary studies. Most critics identify the work of Michel Foucault as the starting point for this relatively recent interest in the material nature of the self, especially his now classic histories of the body, *Discipline and Punish* and his three-volume *History of Sexuality*. In addition, studies such as those by Peter Stallybrass and Allon White (*The Politics and Poetics of Transgression*), Thomas Laquer and Catherine Gallagher (*The Making of the Modern Body*), and Elaine Scarry (*The Body in Pain: The Making and Unmaking of the World*) have provided new ways to think about bodies.[3] As Janet Moore Lindeman and Michele Lise Tarter explain in their introduction to *A Centre of Wonders: The Body in Early America:*

> Bodies are not only physical phenomena but also surfaces of
> inscription, loci of control, and transmitters of culture. They
> are never unmediated; they are related but not reducible to cul-
> tural concepts of differentiation, identity, status, and power. As
> Stallybrass and White assert, "The body cannot be thought
> separately from the social formation, the symbolic typography,
> and the constitution of the subject. The body is neither a purely
> natural given nor is it merely a textual metaphor, it is a privi-
> leged operator for the transcoding of these other areas." Encom-
> passing both the physical and the symbolic, it is, therefore, fully
> enmeshed in the social relations of power. Bodies are always
> in the process of becoming; as open-ended categories, they are

Mary McAleer Balkun

amendable to codes that restrict, contain, open, or expand them and the cultural and contextual interpretations of their corpo-reality. (2)

For Phillis Wheatley, raised and educated in the Western literary tradition, favored servant of a liberal mistress, and, by all accounts, well aware of the political and philosophical discussions of the day, the physical body was indeed both expansive and restricted, subject—perhaps more than most (if we think of her examination by the eighteen illustrious male citizens of Boston that Henry Louis Gates describes in his "Foreword" to the *Collected Works*)—to the "cultural and contextual interpretations" to which Lindeman and Tarter refer. Being able to manipulate those interpretations was not only crucial, it was also a strategy she had learned from her favorite poet, Alexander Pope.

According to Charles Scruggs, what Wheatley took from Pope "was an ability to transform her real self into an imagined self, a persona which functioned as a means to a precise end, rhetorical persuasion. Instead of being a liability, this imagined self became a poetic asset" (284–85). Scruggs argues that Wheatley used this persona as "the cornerstone of an argument which she was building in a poem, and since the imagined self was based upon assumptions about race and 'natural genius' which she and her age understood, the poem was convincing to the people who read it" (285). However, while there is a distinct "Wheatley" persona that appears in the poems, the poet is also able to adopt others' selves, literally speaking for them at times. Her ability to manipulate her own identity, to slide into the "skin" of another, so to speak, and to control the boundaries of her authorial self (as much as any woman of her time) is due in large part to the prevailing attitudes toward bodies in the eighteenth century.

The mind-body relationship has long been a vexed one in Western thought, and this problematic relationship was no less true during the Enlightenment. For Descartes, who is credited with our modern conception of the body, along with Locke, Hume, Berkeley, and others, determining the right relationship of mind to the body—the way the one influenced the other and how that happened—was a fundamental philosophical problem to be addressed. What these thinkers have in common, to greater or lesser degrees, is the belief that while integrated and dependent upon one another, the mind and body are separate entities, and the mind is or should be the more privileged of the two. Emmanuel Chukwudi Eze also credits the Enlightenment philosophers with "codifying and institutionalizing both the scientific and popular European perceptions of the human race." He claims that the writings on race of Hume,

Kant, and Hegel "played a strong role in articulating Europe's sense not only of its cultural but also *racial* superiority" (5).[4] Although there are no specific references to Enlightenment philosophy in Wheatley's poems or letters, these ideas permeated the eighteenth century, influencing such contemporary thinkers as Jonathan Edwards, George Whitefield (to whom she wrote an elegy), Thomas Paine, and Benjamin Franklin, informing the rhetoric of revolution and religious revivalism that Wheatley used in her poetry.[5] Dualism provided her with a rationale for minimizing the reality of her physical self while privileging the mind/soul/spirit. Once the supremacy of the mind over the body has been established, the speaker in a Wheatley poem often returns to the matter of race, but usually in order to make the case that it is meaningless, that the same God has made all of us and all in God's image and likeness. While there are variations, of course, this pattern can be seen, for example, in poems such as "To Maecenas," "On Being Brought from Africa to America," "To the University of Cambridge, in New-England," "Thoughts on the Works of Providence," and "To the Rev. Dr. Thomas Amory."

The pattern—as well as several other body-related tropes—is introduced in the first poem in Wheatley's published collection, *Poems on Various Subjects, Religious and Moral* (1773). Traditionally read as a tribute to her patroness, the Countess of Huntingdon, "To Maecenas" introduces a number of important rhetorical "moves" Wheatley will make again and again in her verse; it is also one of the few poems that makes direct reference to her physical or "mortal" self. The poem begins with an address to Maecenas (the wealthy and influential patron of Virgil and Horace), but immediately in the third line Wheatley posits an emotional connection (emotions being aligned with the physical) between poets and this particular patron ("What felt those poets but you feel the same") (3) that suggests a similar bond of sentiment between Wheatley and her patroness. In the next line, Wheatley immediately turns to matters of the "soul," and this dichotomy continues throughout the poem. The poet (Homer) can make the gods (spirits otherwise) appear "in mortal form" (8), while the "deep-felt horror" that "thrills through all [her] veins" (14) and the tears that flow from her eyes in the second stanza are replaced by her claim that, with the influence of the Muses, "the same beauties should my mind adorn / And the same ardors in my soul should burn" (25–26).

The mind-body split is captured fully in the final two lines of the stanza, where she despairs, "But here I sit, and mourn a grov'ling mind / That fain would mount, and ride upon the wind" (29–30). Even her description of

Mary McAleer Balkun

Terence, her model of an African artist, is described in terms of body and soul: "His soul replenish'd, and his bosom fir'd" (38). Here she also uses another strategy designed to alter perceptions of the black body, the reference to Terence as "one alone of Afric's sable race" (40). The elevated diction of the word "sable" and the reference to Africa—a term that can be traced back to the Middle Ages (Lacey 151–52)—are designed to evoke a far different picture of the black body than most of her readers would have had in mind. Portrayals of the body may also be seen in references to her physical self, which depict her either as exhibiting traits associated with sensibility (horror, tears), as a child either attempting to emulate those she admires, or as a major poet "snatch[ing] a laurel from thine honour'd head / While you indulgent smile upon the deed" (46–47).

In the figure of Terence, Wheatley raises questions about the viability of poetic production for an African if his is the only one whose name is remembered down through the ages. More importantly, it is with this figure that Wheatley introduces yet another motif: her loose figuration of personal, and especially gendered, identity in her poetry. Wheatley not only aligns herself with Terence, a male poet (as were Homer and Virgil, who are also referenced in the poem), but she also aligns Maecenas with her female patroness. Vincent Carretta has suggested that "[a]s an aristocratic widow, Huntingdon had virtually all the authority and power of a male. Wheatley's decision to address the Countess in the guise of a male would be understandable" (xx). However, it is also possible that Wheatley's ability to conceive of identity in flexible ways may have been one she was forced to develop in order to overcome perceptions about her own limitations as an African. Rather than being limited by Western philosophical ideas of duality, Wheatley seems to have adapted for her uses the very "privileging of mind" and separation of "embodiment from reason" that Lindeman and Tarter claim the European *philosophes* instigated (4).[6]

Thus, "To Maecenas" sets the stage for a number of tropes that reappear throughout the volume, as well as in Wheatley's letters; the most common of these is the speaker's desire to move beyond the boundaries of the physical world and the limitations of the body and, as she says here, "ride upon the wind" (30). This sentiment also appears in poems such as "On Being Brought from Africa to America," wherein the speaker manages to place emphasis on the inner self, even though this poem is one of the few in which she refers directly to her skin color. As with Terence, black skin becomes "sable" and part of a larger whole—"our sable race" (5)—while her "benighted soul" can be taught "to understand" (2), and her own "diabolic die" will not stand in the way of her salvation and admittance to heaven (6). It is in "To the University of Cambridge, in New-England," however, where we find Wheatley's tour de force in the use of these various tropes. The third poem in the book, it begins with references to the mind and the soul, but by the end she has very firmly set her "audience"—the young men of Harvard University—back on earth. This poem also contains the first direct reference to Wheatley's skin color in the collection, although she refers to herself as an "Ethiop" (28), one of the personae she traditionally adopts. In this poem, the emphasis for these young men is very much on their work on earth and their actions as the future generation. The poem ends on an unusually negative note regarding the wages of sin, one that recalls the tone of the jeremiad: "Its transient sweetness turns to endless pain / And in immense perdition sinks the soul" (29–30). There is no suggestion here that heaven is inevitable; in fact, it seems almost out of reach, which is especially ironic given prevailing attitudes toward black redemption. However, in this poem Wheatley's color-blind vision means that "the whole human race by sin had fall'n," and not just the children of Cain.

Yet, this poem is not about Wheatley or her body. Instead, she turns the tables on these white sons of the elite class, focusing her gaze on them, refusing to allow them to ignore the corporeality of their existence, especially in her allusions to pain and suffering, and setting an agenda for their activities both at school and in the world. They are "blooming plants" (27) while she is an "Ethiop"; they are corporeal while she is an abstract concept representing an entire race of people, in fact, all Christians. Because the speaker of the poem is addressing young men at an institution of higher learning, the premise is that she must be of either equal or even greater intelligence, and perhaps even superior in experience. This position is actually enhanced by Wheatley's negation of her physical self. The "unbodied mind" that she alludes to in these poems (and a phrase that also appears in her poem, "To His Honour the Lieutenant-Governor on the Death of His Lady, March 24, 1773") is used by Samuel Johnson in his dictionary as one definition of "intelligency" and "intelligential" (Johnson). It appears in other works from the period as well, including the Thomas Tickell poem, "To the Earl of Warwick, On the Death of Mr. Addison" (1721).

The pattern established in "To Maecenas," "On Being Brought from Africa to America," and "To the University of Cambridge" continues with some modifications in "Thoughts on the Works of Providence." Here,

Wheatley immediately aligns herself with soul and mind, commanding in the opening line that her soul "Arise . . . on wings enraptur'd" (1), and then asking that her soul be guided and that the muse "raise [her] mind to a seraphic strain" (10). In addition, Wheatley engages in this poem the matter of her race more overtly than in much of her other work. Having established herself as a mind and a soul, she can later refer easily to "our race" and have its meaning remain completely ambiguous. In fact, there are a series of allusions here that might well be double entendres: "So rich, so various are thy beauteous dies" (43), while this line is ostensibly about the rising sun, it could also refer to the various colors of the people on whom that sun shines, while "The sable veil, that Night in silence draws" resonates with the black skin that, like the darkness of night, "Conceals effects, but shews th' Almighty Cause" (54). These readings seem even more likely when one considers the final stanza of the poem, in which Wheatley directly addresses differences of race:

> All-wise Almighty providence we trace
> In trees, and plants, and all the flow'ry race;
> As clear as in the nobler frame of man,
> All lovely copies of the Maker's plan. (71–74)

Here, not only does man mirror the workings of providence as seen in the natural world but all men and women are copies made by the same hand.

There is evidence to suggest that Wheatley's writing was both informed by and a response to ideas about the relationship between black bodies and intellect prevalent during the period. These attitudes toward race and the ways they were manifested in the late eighteenth century have been addressed by a variety of critics. According to Lindeman and Tarter, for example, in early America, "[r]ace became a 'natural' category based on the visual evidence of African and Indian bodies marked as 'black' and 'red,' and, in the process, the body became what Robyn Wiegman calls 'the origin of race truth.'" The result was so-called scientific theories, such as "polygenesis," which maintained that "phenotypic variance was due to the separate origins of the races" (3). Sweet also observes that attitudes linking race and behavior in the late eighteenth century "were part of a much broader set of intellectual concerns that involved the nature of human reproduction, the inheritance of physical and mental traits, the potential of education to shape character, and the extent to which physical bodies manifest inner qualities of mind" (7). Richard H. Popkin points out that racists in the period believed skin color was just one of "a fundamental, unchangeable set of defects that made blacks inferior to whites. The human body, they maintained, limited or determined what mental development was possible. The body fixed the space the brain could occupy, and presumably brain size related to mental capacity" (421). Thus, the body itself determined the limits of development that were possible for the person of color. It was against such limits that Wheatley struggled, to which her repeated references to flight and escape in the poems attest.

The fourteen elegies that constitute a large portion of Wheatley's book may thus be read not only as an attempt to forge a sense of community with a set of like mourners, as Kendrick maintains (44), but also as a way to insist on the essential unimportance of the body. Because an emphasis on the soul or the self that lives on after death reflects both traditions of the elegy and Christian theology, Wheatley's use of these ideas is completely fitting in this context; however, as Shields points out, "Wheatley's elegies generally concentrate more on exhortation of the living than on portraiture of the deceased" (246). Her tone verges on outright admonishment at times, as she charges the subject of the elegy—the living relative(s) left behind—not to wish for the deceased's return, while she simultaneously celebrates the now bodiless state of the departed. A look at just a few of the elegies bears this out.

In "On the Death of a Young Lady of Five Years of Age," the poet addresses the parents of the child, describing her flight to a "fair ethereal light" (1) where she "finds unknown beautitude" (4). It is a place where she "feels the iron hand of pain no more" (6), is "No more distress'd in our dark vale below" (10) and is "Freed from a world of sin, and snares of pain" (25). Thus, the speaker is moved to ask the grieving parents, "Why would you wish your daughter back again?" (27). Instead, she charges them to "check the rising tumult of the soul" (28) and look forward to that day when they will again see their daughter in heaven: "Yourselves, safe landed on the blissful shore, / Shall join your happy babe to part no more" (35–36). The child is even pictured as gesturing to her parents to join her in heavenly bliss, a conceit that recurs in many of the elegies. However, in order to get there, the parents (and readers) must first do several things:

> Adore the God who gives and takes away;
> Eye him in all, his holy name revere,
> Upright your actions, and your hearts
> sincere (30–32).

Mary McAleer Balkun

Following the reference to the "snares and pain" of life on earth, Wheatley's suggestion that God appears in all, the speaker included, can be read as an allusion to her own state as a slave, regardless of how well she may be treated. Life on earth is associated in the elegies with being bound, fettered, and confined. It is a "dark vale" ("On the Death of a Young Lady" 10), a "dusky shore" ("To the Honourable T.H., Esq." 16), and a place where the "pow'rs of night" must be fought ("On the Death of a Young Gentleman" 1). References to the actual body are few and far between, but when they do occur they are consistently negative, focusing on the body in pain or as the source of temptation, and in "To a Lady on the Death of her Husband" the poet refers to the husband's body as "the cold shell of his great soul" (25). In the same poem, death is described as a state wherein "heavy fetters" keep one's "senses bound in never-waking sleep" (13–14).

The heavenly realm, on the other hand, is a place for "th'immortal mind" ("To a Lady on the Death of her Husband" 34) and the "heav'n ascended mind" ("To a Clergyman" 10); a place where the mind is "free from scornful pride" ("To the Honourable T.H., Esq." 11) and where one can "pursue th'unbodied mind" ("To His Honour the Lieutenant-Governor" 42). "To a Lady on the Death of Three Relations" is a poem that contains several references to the mind, the spirit, and ideas, especially in the second half. At the moment of death, it is the mind that rises to heaven. Furthermore, the poet suggests that the mind can overcome grief, and that the latter is inconsequential if the mind has but the will to move beyond it: "Weep not for them, who wish thine happy mind / To rise with them, and leave the world behind" (17–18), and again a few lines later, "Ascend the sacred mount, in thought arise" (27). And although neither the negative images of earth/the physical state nor allusions to the preeminence of mind appear in every poem, they occur often enough to suggest an ongoing preoccupation.

As Jeffrey Hammond writes in *The American Puritan Elegy; A Literary and Cultural Study*, "All elegies honored the dead, but the manner in which they did so revealed the living for who they were and where they stood" (Hammond 19). While Wheatley's elegies insist on the pleasures of a bodiless/incorporeal existence, there is more to her position than a belief in the afterlife and salvation. In fact, references to God or being with God are rare (see "On the Death of a Young Lady of Five Years of Age" and "On the Death of a Young Gentleman"), although she does allude to other heavenly beings, such as "raptur'd seraphs" ("To a Lady on the Death of Three Relations" 30),

To "pursue th' unbodied mind"

"saints and angels" ("On the Death of a Young Lady of Five years of Age 20), and "choirs angelic" ("To a Clergyman on the Death of his Lady" 7). While there is certainly glory and peace, Wheatley's vision of heaven emphasizes the lack of pain, earthly troubles, and cares.

Given her own lifelong ill health, it should not be surprising that Wheatley would champion an existence where she was not only no longer ill but also no longer enslaved. Her letters make repeated references to sickness and recovery, both her own and that of others. In an April 21, 1772, letter to John Thornton, for example, she writes, "It has pleased God to lay me on a bed of Sickness, and I knew not but my deathbed, but he has been graciously pleas'd to restore me in a great measure" (163). Several of her references to illness come in letters to Obour Tanner, such as the one written on July 19, 1772: "While my outward man languishes under weakness and pa[in], may the inward be refresh'd and Strengthened more abundantly by him who declar'd from heaven that his strength was made perfect in weakness!" (165–66). Consolation for the grieving, because it takes the form of celebrating the benefits of a bodiless state, may provide Wheatley with consolation as well. Shifting the reader's attention to otherworldly things then becomes a strategy for dealing with her own physical limitations.

It is also in the elegies that Wheatley regularly co-opts others' voices, enlisting the deceased—and their absent bodies—in her project to raise awareness of the condition of blacks in general and herself in particular. Kendrick considers what he calls "supplemental voices" in Wheatley's poetry, although he believes she uses these voices "to lead the reader into an intersubjective and reflexive process of (re)membering his or her own position relative to another's." The truth about Sewell's death—which in this case is spoken by Fame—cannot come from "[t]he positionless voice of empirical 'fact,' it can only come from an 'embodied *person's* reply to Wheatley'" (44). Kendrick continues, "Performatively, as she closes the elegy she also assumes his position, finishing Sewell's words of life by signing for him in his absence. The positions of poet and minister, mourner and mourned, thus fold into each other, but this folding does not lead to closure or an interiorization of the other party" (45). Wheatley thereby participates in the exercise of mourning "in the hope that this party [the reader] will join in the process" (Kendrick 46). However, while Kendrick's theory is intriguing, it fails to account for the fact that Wheatley, on a number of occasions, literally puts words into the mouths of the deceased. In the poem for Sewell, the epitaph she writes could be her own, whether in the role of "minister," or in her roles as poet and Christian.

Mary McAleer Balkun

The performance of others' selves is most apparent in a poem like "On the Death of the Rev. Mr. George Whitefield" (15), where Wheatley has Whitefield himself enjoin those he leaves behind to "Take him [Christ], ye wretched, for your only good, / Take him ye starving sinners, for your food" (28–29). Even more dramatically, in the same stanza she has Whitefield speak directly to the matter of black salvation: "Take him, ye *Africans*, he longs for you, / *Impartial Savior* is his title due" (34–35). This is followed in the next stanza by the line "Great Countess, we *Americans* revere / Thy name" (38–39), which merges the speaker, this time Wheatley herself, with the mass of her countrymen.[7] It is a merging that happens more easily now that "Whitefield" (at least in theory) has "spoken" on behalf of Africans, including them in a future where he sees both them and Americans as "sons, and kings, and priests of God" (37).

Wheatley's adopting of another's self also appears in "To a Clergyman on the Death of his Lady," where she again has the dead speak to the living. The lady, "to flesh no more confin'd" (9), leans down from heaven to communicate with her spouse, urging him to "share with me the raptures of the skies" (8). Once she has finished her plea—which includes references to their children joining them one day as well—Wheatley returns to the poem as herself, urging the grieving husband to "no more with grief retire" (33), but to "rise sublime, to equal bliss aspire" (35). Just as the clergyman's task has been "t'unfold the oracles divine" (38) and "soothe our woes" (39) so the poet now steps in "a cordial to impart" (41) to ease his grief and dry his tears. Having erased her own physical self, and because she generally uses this rhetorical ploy in the elegies, Wheatley is more able to adopt another persona, speaking with her or his voice. It is a strategy she uses sparingly, and for maximum effect, pairing it with a form of omniscient narration that allows her to see and hear the deceased and express their wishes in her own "voice" as well.

One of the sentiments Wheatley often has the deceased express, whether in their voice or her own, is a request for a moderation of grief in those left behind. From one elegy to the next, the motif is repeated: "Let hope your grief control" in "On the Death of a young Lady of Five Years of Age" (27); "The raging tempest of their grief control" in "On the Death of a young Gentleman" (21); "Then, mourner, cease; let hope thy tears restrain" in "To a Lady on the Death of Three Relations" (23); "No more complain, but be to heav'n resign'd" in "To a Clergyman on the Death of his Lady" (37); and the list goes on. Aside from the traditional Christian belief that excess grief is unwarranted and even sinful, these calls for restraint also signal the eighteenth-century interest in refinement, much of which was directed toward the body.

In these calls for a cessation of mourning, Wheatley typically uses words like "restraint," "control," and "noble," terms that any devotee of refinement would have recognized. In the poem "On the Death of a Young Lady" (the term "lady" also suggests refinement), Wheatley admonishes the parents to "Restrain [their] tears, and cease [their] plaintive moans" (24) and to "check the rising tumult of the soul" (8)," urging on them "Calm, in the prosperous, and adverse day" (9). Heaven itself is a place of refinement, largely because the wants and cares of everyday life, especially those involving the body, have been eliminated. When Wheatley has an infant speak (through her) about the benefits of having died young in "A Funeral Poem on the Death of C.E. an Infant of Twelve Months," s/he enumerates the sins thereby avoided: vice, temptation, bad behavior, vanity, and so on. Wheatley's repeated injunctions to mourners to curb their emotions, like the overly formal and ornate prose of her letters, and even the portrait that served as the frontispiece to her book of poems, signal her co-optation into the culture of refinement.

Raised and educated by the proper Susannah Wheatley, Phillis Wheatley was indoctrinated into ways of thinking and behaving that embraced the refined and proper. In *The Refinement of America,* Richard L. Bushman traces the interest in gentility in America from 1690, when the first evidence of it emerged, to the mid-nineteenth century, when many in the middle class were reasonably able to imitate the refined behavior and possessions of the gentry. Some of the important aspects of refined behavior included control of one's emotions, control of one's body, and even letter writing. While "Being overcome with feeling in consequence of delicate sensibilities was a pleasurable indulgence of the genteel life, all the more pleasurable because the surge of strong emotion attested to the possession of genteel virtues" (Bushman 82), one was also supposed to exhibit self-control and moderation of those emotions, and this is what Wheatley endorses in the elegies. This is one way to understand her measured response to slavery: as a performance of gentility rather than as a true indication of her feelings.[8]

Even the *philosophes* weighed in on this matter, maintaining that "only those who could control their physical and emotional passions could achieve self-mastery" (Lindeman and Tarter 4). It is telling—and especially interesting given Wheatley's poem and later attempts to gain his favor—that George Washington himself produced a conduct manual, "Rules of Civility and Decent Behavior In Company and Conversation," that was a copy of a seventeenth-century "English courtesy book" (Bushman 31). The emphasis on self-control

Mary McAleer Balkun

was at the heart of ideas about both race and refinement in the late eighteenth century. The delicacy with which she generally treated matters of race and the subject of slavery may well have been the result of her indoctrination into a code of genteel behavior.[9]

There are indications, however, especially in her letters, that Wheatley was not quite as pliant or as accepting of her condition as she may have seemed. Of course, her well-known letter to Samson Occom is her most direct response to the injustices of slavery, with statements such as this: "for in every human Breast, God has implanted a Principle, which we call Love of Freedom; it is impatient of Oppression, and pants for Deliverance; and by the Leave of our Modern Egyptians I will assert, that the same Principle lives in us" (177). Even the letters to her friend Obour Tanner contain statements that seem coded, with lines that are reminiscent of the double entendres Wheatley was so fond of in her poetry. These often take the form of a desire for patience and/or acceptance, or resistance to temptations of various sorts.

For example, in a letter dated May 19, 1772, Wheatley asks that "this goodness & long Suffering of God lead us to unfeign'd repentance" (142), while in another letter dated July 19, 1772, she writes, "Let us be mindful of our high calling, continually on our guard, lest our treacherous hearts Should give the adversary the advantage over us" (166). As Sweet explains:

> The experience of enslavement in eighteenth-century New England fostered simultaneous and conflicting identities. Onstage, before masters or the public, slaves had good reason to act deferential and contented; offstage, that is, among their peers, they could express resentment and question the legitimacy of colonial authority. Slavery, as it was negotiated in practice, informally with masters, depended on slaves making bargains in the context of unequal power and without recourse to public authority. (98)

For Wheatley, despite her role as an "almost-daughter" rather than a servant, life as a slave was clearly troubling. It could be that because she knew her own apparently acquiescent exterior was hiding a self that was more frustrated and dissatisfied, she was less inclined to privilege the physical self. She knew from firsthand experience that it could not necessarily be trusted.

While gentility in this period was about the control of one's emotions and actions, it was also about the body, both its presentation and its behavior, with the ultimate goal being that "there were to be no reminders of the existence of base parts of the body. . . . In company, the body was to be presented and conceived of as immaculate, devoid of every form of filth and baseness" (Bushman 42). Therefore, true gentility deemphasized the body and emphasized the inner self, which was then reflected through the body. Refinement was also a response to the very real problems of the flesh in the eighteenth century. As Roy Porter observes:

> To a degree that is hard to imagine nowadays, visible, tangible flesh was all too often experienced as ugly, nasty and decaying, bitten by bugs and beset by sores; it was rank, foul and dysfunctional; for all of medicine's best efforts, it was frequently racked with pain, disability and disease; and death might well be nigh. Letters and diaries—to say nothing of Swift's satires or the cartoons of Hogarth and Gillray—document at length and with passion the intense repugnance people so frequently felt towards their own noisesome flesh and that of others. (25)

"Negros" may be "black as *Cain*" (7), in Wheatley's words, but they "May be refin'd" as well, and not simply to "join th'angelic train" (8), although that was certainly one goal.

Another characteristic of the refinement movement, and one evident in Wheatley's writing, was its resonance with Christianity. According to Bushman, the literature of gentility took for granted that the refined person was also a Christian, although this refinement did not include "the emotional excesses of evangelical religion. Instead, the gentleman embodied the Christian moral values of compassion, kindness, and humility. Good manners expressed a Christian regard for the happiness of others" (80–81). Thus, "In its true and most refined form, gentility was meant to be a spiritual condition" (Bushman 80). Wheatley's poem "To the Rev. Dr. Thomas Amory," written to honor the English Presbyterian minister and author of *Daily Devotion Assisted and Recommended, in Four Sermons* (Carretta 180), embodies these very characteristics, and also demonstrates her awareness of the hallmarks of gentility. The poem begins by enumerating what she perceives as Amory's goals in his sermons—"To cultivate in ev'ry noble mind, / Habitual grace, and sentiments refin'd" (1–2). In addition, he possesses virtue and wisdom, and his sermons give the lie to the boasts of the atheist. Finally, when he dies, he will be remembered as all gentlemen should be, as a man of "A noble title, and a superior name!" (27–28).

Mary McAleer Balkun

There is additional—and poignant—evidence of Wheatley's recognition of the ephemeral nature of public opinion when it came to gentility in an October 30, 1770, letter she wrote to John Thornton. Here she acknowledges that, just as he seems to have suggested, she was no longer held in the same regard or treated in the same way once Susannah Wheatley had passed away. She writes, and her tone is surprised but also somewhat bemused, "The world is a severe Schoolmaster, for its frowns are less dang'rous than its Smiles and flatteries, and it is a difficult task to keeping the path of wisdom. I attended, and find exactly true your thoughts on the behavior of those who seem'd to respect me while under my mistress patronage; you said right, for Some of those have already put on a reserve" (183). Without the protective veneer of Susannah's presence, Wheatley is no longer accepted, bearing out—in reverse—Bushman's theory that "The ultimate test of one's position and culture was admission to the public activities of polite society" (185).

Despite this apparent lack of acceptance, letter writing remained Wheatley's primary contact with those outside her immediate circle, and it provided another avenue for advertising her gentility. Her discourse in the letters is elevated and formal, the kind of performances Bushman indicates was common of letters in the genteel tradition, where " . . . even in the most casual exchanges between close friend, the formal note remains, reminding us that the writers never completely forgot that their writings were a performance" (91). In addition, "letters presented a refined spirit in the act of revealing its sensibility, its vivacity, and its delicacy" (92). Letter writing was one way for Wheatley to convey the perception to others that she was a lady. (After she obtains her freedom, nevertheless, this perception is undercut by the economics of her situation; in several letters she alludes to books sold and not sold, and in one case, she appends to an elegy on the death of General Wooster a request for his wife, Mary Wooster, to return copies of any unsold books.) It was a version of her that was also conveyed by another kind of "text" associated with her physical self, the portrait done of her by Scipio Moorhead, the African American painter and poet.

The painting was specified by the Countess of Huntingdon for inclusion as the frontispiece in Wheatley's volume of poetry; this specification is according to Wheatley's letter to the countess of October 10, 1772, in which she writes, "if you was So desirous of the Image of the Author as to propose it for a Frontispiece I flatter myself that you would accept the Reality" (167). However, if one of Wheatley's intentions in the poetry is to avert the gaze of the reader from her physical self, then she would also have understood that the painting had the potential to undermine this project. The portrait has been described and discussed by a number of critics:[10] it shows the young Wheatley sitting at a table, pen in hand, dressed neatly, with her hand at her chin and her eyes raised upward. The oval framing of the picture contains the words "Phillis Wheatley, Negro Servant to Mr. John Wheatley, of Boston." Barbara E. Lacey considers this portrait, in conjunction with other images, in "Visual Images of Blacks in Early American Imprints," describing Wheatley's appearance as "inwardly directed, reading her thoughts" (172). Lacey also points out that "Portraits usually were undertaken after sitter and artist had determined how the individual wished to be represented in respect to expression, pose, and accompanying goods. Thus, when analyzed, frontispieces can reveal important elements of black self-construction" (169). If Wheatley did indeed have a say in how she was portrayed in the painting, it would provide additional evidence of her interest in refinement and her concomitant interest in regulating the body.

Posture and the way the body was held were important elements of the refined self and signaled control as well. As Bushman explains, "To achieve artistic control of one's physical being, a primary rule was to remain erect, to keep the line from the base of the spine through the neck to the back of the head as straight as possible. While sitting for portraits, people turned their heads and even inclined them but without allowing their chins to fall" (64). This is certainly an apt description of Wheatley in her portrait. Additionally, in keeping with the female modesty also required of the genteel, she does not look directly at the viewer but rather seems to be looking beyond herself.[11] If Wheatley's book is the "body of work" standing in for her actual body, with her image included, the image is one adapted to align her more closely with her readers: in clothing they would have recognized as neat and of good quality, labeled as a "servant" rather than a slave, and with the accoutrements of literacy before her. It is the working of her mind that has placed her in this privileged, refined position, but this position has also (as with Frederick Douglass in the nineteenth century) led her to understand fully her condition and its limitations. The result must surely have been galling. Given this, it is not hard to imagine that the frequent invocations not to grieve—the reminders that future rewards await one in heaven—are intended to console herself as much as the mourners to whom the elegies are addressed.

Mary McAleer Balkun

By moving beyond the body, Wheatley is suggesting another way to manage the material fact of race, and not only hers but that of all "Africans." This rhetorical ploy is in direct opposition—and possibly in response—to the body consciousness of the period. Wheatley's response seems to have been to eliminate as much as possible the corporeal body, focusing the reader first on the mind or soul that inhabits that body and then on greater truths, such as the equality of all in God's eyes and the rewards of virtuous behavior.

In a discussion of both Wheatley and Samson Occom and their ways of negotiating race, Sweet maintains that both of them came to realize that "the more completely they mastered English culture, the more successfully they displayed their *refined sensibilities,* and the more public recognition they won, the more they found themselves defined racially, as prodigies, examples, or exceptions" (127; emphasis added).[12] Wheatley's may have been an ideal and even daring project, but their possession of refined sensibilities may also point to a hallmark of American culture, as Bruce Kuklick notes: "From the middle of the eighteenth century American thinkers have been attracted to idealism, that speculative view that existence is essentially mental" (xii). It is her poems that best speak to Wheatley's idealizing project, and there are two in particular that seem a fitting way to end a discussion of her use of various discourses to create a space for herself that privileged what she thought rather than what she looked like. "On Recollection" and "On Imagination" appear at almost the exact center of her published manuscript, and they both celebrate her intellectual ability and refinement and work against racist notions of circumscription. These are also poems in which all the various strategies discussed come into play: the emphasis on the mind, the invocation of another voice or persona, and the language of refinement.

"On Recollection" is a double-edged sword, a poem that suggests the torments imposed by the memory of bad behavior and alludes to the evils of slavery. It opens with a two-word statement—"*Mneme* begin" (1) (*Mneme* is "memory")—that can be read as a request for the workings of memory to commence, but also as an invocation in the strictest sense: for memory to speak through the poet. While the second line contains a reference to her race—asking the Muses to inspire "Your vent'rous Afric"—Wheatley refers to her project in the poem as a "great design" (2). As opposed to other poems, where she seems to wonder whether her poetic skills are up to the task at hand, in this case Wheatley is merely asking for assistance as she "thy glories sing" (4) and celebrates "Mneme" (memory). There is a feeling of confidence exhibited in this poem that is startling. Again, in the second stanza, Wheatley becomes "the high-raptur'd poet" (14) whom memory aids "Through the unbounded regions of the mind" (15), a direct contrast to the bound body she inhabits.

This allusion, while not unusual in Wheatley's work, in this poem signals the start of a series of statements that are highly suggestive given her enslaved status. Having asserted herself as favored by the Muses, and in particular by Mneme, Wheatley describes a force of memory "Diffusing light celestial and refin'd" (16) and highlighting the "actions done / By ev'ry tribe beneath the rolling sun" (17–18). She begins the third stanza by asserting that memory is "enthron'd within the human breast" (19), not just the white one, and then proceeds to a warning about those who ignore the workings of memory (anticipating by well over one hundred years Santayana's famous injunction about history):

> But how is *Mneme* dreaded by the race
> Who scorn her warnings and despise her grace?
> By her unveil'd each horrid crime appears,
> Her awful hand a cup of wormwood bears.
> Days, years misspent, O what a hell of woe!
> Hers the worst torture that our souls can know.
> (25–30)

The language here—and it is powerful and stark—is reminiscent of that in a Shakespeare tragedy, invoking the evils of slavery and its impact on the enslavers. The fourth stanza starts with a reference to Wheatley's age (although this must only be approximate, given her lack of birth records or family history). Now eighteen years old, she mourns her past bad behavior, but—as Kendrick suggests of the elegies—in this stanza and the next, she seems determined to evoke a reciprocal response in her reader: a regret for past actions and a desire for reform. The final stanza returns to the retribution awaiting those who dare "the vengeance of the skies" (43) and act without acknowledging the pain memory (in this case "Recollection") will eventually bring: "He howls in anguish, and repents too late" (46). It is also in this final stanza that the melding of the poet and Mneme is complete:

> But O! what peace, what joys are hers t'impart
> To ev'ry holy, ev'ry upright heart!

Thrice blest the man, who in her sacred shrine,
Feels himself shelter'd from the wrath divine!
(47–50)

It is difficult to determine whether the wrath described here will be that of Mneme or God, but the implication seems clear: those who sin will be punished, and that punishment will begin on earth. It will also be a punishment of the mind, not of the body, continuing the emphasis on the intellect with which the poem begins.

This veneration of the mind and its abilities continues in "On Imagination," a poem in which Wheatley also seems to take a more sardonic, but ultimately negative, view of her enslavement. The poem opens with several images of female empowerment: the figure of Imagination as an "imperial queen" (1), as one who one is "potent" (4), followed by a depiction of "the roving *Fancy*" (9) as an almost implike spirit who then proceeds to "With silken fetters all the senses bind" while her "soft captivity involves the mind" (11–12). The power of imagination is such that it can give one the ability to escape the bonds of the earth, permit a view of "the mighty whole" (21), "Or with new worlds amaze th' unbounded soul" (22). Wheatley does imply here that the bound—the enslaved—soul is not open to the workings of imagination. Once freed, however, and open to the influence of Fancy, the inspired soul can turn winter into spring: "The frozen deeps may break their iron bands, / And bid their waters murmur o'er the sands" (25–26). It is clear that for Wheatley the workings of the mind are superior and control the impulses of the body, for it is imagination that is "sov'reign ruler" of the "subject-passions" (38) and at whose working "joy rushes on the heart, / And through the glowing veins the spirits dart" (39–40).

Yet, as opposed to the first stanzas of the poem, in which the influence of imagination seems unimpaired, the final stanza of the poem contains a sense of uncertainty, primarily due to Wheatley's repeated use of the word "might": "*Fancy* might now her silken pinions try / To rise from earth, and sweep th'expanse on high" (41–42); "From *Tithon's* bed now might *Aurora* rise" (43); and "The monarch of the day I might behold" (46). As if her actual state has returned to haunt her, Wheatley ends the poem on a more somber note.

Winter austere forbids me to aspire,
And northern tempests damp the rising fire;

They chill the tides of *Fancy's* flowing sea,
Cease then, my song, cease the unequal lay.
(50–53)

"Fancy" is one aspect of sensibility and refinement, but it is also depicted here as "roving" and even fickle.[13] Returning to the bounds of earth, both literally and figuratively, the poet comes to grips with the limitations of her state. Her gift, and Fancy itself, it turns out, is ultimately unequal to the task of overcoming the reality of her life; she must "reluctant leave the pleasing views" (48).[14]

There is an inherent tension in Wheatley's efforts to use the social discourse of her day to distract the reader's attention from the body that self inhabits, especially since her body is defined by that very discourse as inherently uncivilized and inferior. As a slave, Wheatley cannot lay claim to her actual body, but she can claim ownership of her mind and her soul, which is what she attempts time after time in her poetry, letters, and possibly even in her portrait. The effort does not come without a struggle or moments of doubt. Emphasizing the mind over the body, Wheatley can aspire to the heights of Fancy, and even occasionally achieve them, but she ultimately cannot escape the physical self and the silken ties that bind her.

NOTES

1. See, for example, Helen Burke, "The Rhetoric and Politics of Marginality: The Subject of Phillis Wheatley"; John C. Shields, "Phillis Wheatley's Struggle for Freedom in Her Poetry and Prose"; Henry Louis Gates Jr., "In Her Own Write"; and Hilene Flanzbaum, "Unprecedented Liberties: Re-Reading Phillis Wheatley."

2. See Cynthia Hogue's *Scheming Women: Poetry, Privilege, and the Politics of Subjectivity.*

3. Lori Hope Lefkovitz provides a good general overview of the important studies in this field in *Textual Bodies: Changing Boundaries of Literary Representation.*

4. For an overview of the scientific rationale for black inferiority in the Enlightenment, see "Medicine, Racism, and Anti-Semitism: A Dimension of Enlightenment Culture," by Richard Popkin in *The Languages of Psyche.*

Mary McAleer Balkun

5. For an early discussion of how Wheatley utilizes the rhetoric of revolution and revivalism, see *Revolutionary Women* by Betsy Erkkila.

6. Carretta also describes the David in her poem "Goliath of Gath" as "a relatively feminized hero" (xxi).

7. The poem was written for the Countess of Huntingdon; Whitefield was her chaplain.

8. See Peter Coviello's essay "Agonizing Affection: Affect and Nation in Early America" for a discussion of the capacity for an intense emotional response as "a veritable prerequisite for virtuous citizenship" (443).

9. See also Norbert Elias's classic three-volume study *The Civilizing Process* for more on the development of manners and civility in Western culture.

10. One example is Walt Nott's essay, "From 'Uncultivated Barbarian' to 'Poetical Genius': The Public Presence of Phillis Wheatley."

11. A conduct book of the period includes the following: "'One of the chieftest beauties in a female character . . . is that modest reserve, that retiring delicacy, which avoids the public eye, and is disconcerted even at the gaze of admiration'" (Bushman 81).

12. Frank Shuffleton's essay "On Her Own Footing: Phillis Wheatley in Freedom" is an insightful examination of Wheatley after the publication of her book and her subsequent manumission.

13. Julie Ellison discusses the concept of "fancy" in Wheatley's poetry in "The Politics of Fancy in the Age of Sensibility."

14. Hilene Flanzbaum offers a similar reading of this poem, but one that focuses strictly on Wheatley's ultimate obedience to cultural norms. For example, while she sees Wheatley surrendering to the female muse, I see her establishing an affinity with the models of female empowerment that fill the poem.

WORKS CITED

Burke, Helen M. "The Rhetoric and Politics of Marginality: The Subject of Phillis Wheatley." *Tulsa Studies in Women's Literature* 10.1 (Spring 1991): 31–45.

Bushman, Richard L. *The Refinement of America: Persons, Houses, Cities.* New York: Vintage, 1993.

Carretta, Vincent. "Introduction." *Complete Writings: Phillis Wheatley.*
Ed. Vincent Carretta. New York: Penguin, 2001. xiii–xli.

———, ed. *Complete Writings: Phillis Wheatley.* New York: Penguin,
2001.

Coviello, Peter. "Agonizing Affection: Affect and Nation in Early America." *Early American Literature* 37.3 (2002): 439–68.

Elias, Norbert. *The Civilizing Process.* Oxford: Basic Blackwell, 1978.

Ellison, Julie. "The Politics of Fancy in the Age of Sensibility." *Re-Visioning
Romanticism: British Women Writers, 1776–1837.* Ed. Carol Shiner
Wilson and Joel Haefner. Philadelphia: U of Pennsylvania P, 1994.
228–55.

Erkkila, Betsy. "Revolutionary Women." *Tulsa Studies in Women's Literature* 6.2 (Autumn 1987): 189–223.

Eze, Emmanuel Chukwudi. "Introduction." *Race and the Enlightenment:
A Reader.* Ed. Emmanuel Chukwudi Eze. Cambridge: Blackwell,
1997. 1–9.

Fishburn, Katherine. *The Problem of Embodiment in Early African American Narrative.* Westport: Greenwood, 1997.

Flanzbaum, Hilene. "Unprecedented Liberties: Re-Reading Phillis
Wheatley." MELUS 18.3 (Fall 1993): 71–81.

Foucault, Michel. *Discipline and Punish: The Birth of the Prison.* 1975.
New York: Vintage, 1995.

———. *The History of Sexuality, Vol. 1: An Introduction.* 1978. New York:
Vintage, 1990.

Gates, Henry Louis, Jr. "Foreword: In Her Own Write." *The Collected
Works of Phillis Wheatley.* Ed. John C. Shields. New York: Oxford UP,
1988. vii–xxii.

Hammond, Jeffrey. *The American Puritan Elegy; A Literary and Cultural
Study.* Cambridge: Cambridge UP, 2000.

Hogue, Cynthia. *Scheming Women: Poetry, Privilege, and the Politics of
Subjectivity.* Albany: State U of New York P, 1995.

Johnson, Samuel. "Intelligency." *A Dictionary of the English Language.*
Philadelphia: Moses Thomas, 1818.

Kendrick, Robert. "Other Questions: Phillis Wheatley and the Ethics of
Interpretation." *Cultural Critique* 38 (Winter 1997–98): 39–64.

Kuklick, Bruce. *A History of Philosophy in America, 1720–2000.* Oxford: Clarendon, 2001.

Lacey, Barbara. *"Visual Images of Blacks in Early American Imprints." William and Mary Quarterly* 53.1 (January 1996): 137–80.

Lacquer, Thomas, and Catherine Gallacher. *The Making of the Modern Body: Sexuality and Society in the Nineteenth Century.* Berkeley: U of California P, 1987.

Lefkovitz, Lori Hope. "Introduction: Textual Bodies: Changing Boundaries of Literary Representation." *Textual Bodies: Changing Boundaries of Literary Representation.* Ed. Lori Hope Lefkovitz. Albany: State U of New York P, 1997.

Lindeman, Janet Moore, and Michele Lise Tarter. "The earthly frame, a minute fabrick, a Centre of Wonders." *A Centre of Wonders: The Body in Early America.* Ed. Janet Moore Lindeman and Michele Lise Tarter. Ithaca: Cornell UP, 2001. 1–9.

Nott, Walt. "From 'Uncultivated Barbarian' to 'Poetical Genius': The Public Presence of Phillis Wheatley." *MELUS* 18.3 (Fall 1993): 21–32.

Popkin, Richard H. "Medicine, Racism, and Anti-Semitism: A Dimension of Enlightenment Culture." *The Languages of Psyche: Mind and Body in Enlightenment Thought.* Ed. G. S. Rousseau. Berkeley: U of California P, 1990. 405–42.

Porter, Roy. *Flesh in the Age of Reason.* New York: W. W. Norton, 2003.

Scarry, Elaine. *The Body in Pain: The Making and Unmaking of the World.* Oxford: Oxford UP, 1985.

Scruggs, Charles. "Phillis Wheatley and the Poetical Legacy of Eighteenth-Century England." *Studies in Eighteenth-Century Culture* 10 (1981): 279–95.

Shields, John C. "Phillis Wheatley's Struggle for Freedom in Her Poetry and Prose." *The Collected Works of Phillis Wheatley.* Ed. John C. Shields. New York: Oxford UP, 1988. 229–70.

Shuffleton, Frank. "On Her Own Footing: Phillis Wheatley in Freedom." In *Genius in Bondage: Literature of the Early Black Atlantic.* Ed. Vincent Carretta and Philip Gould. Lexington: UP of Kentucky, 2001. 175–89.

Stafford, Barbara Marie. *Body Criticism: Imaging the Unseen in Enlightenment Art and Medicine.* Cambridge: MIT P, 1993.

Stallybrass, Peter, and Allon White. *The Politics and Poetics of Transgression.* Ithaca: Cornell UP, 1986.

Sweet, John Wood. *Bodies Politic: Negotiating Race in the American North, 1730–1830.* Baltimore: Johns Hopkins UP, 2003.

Wheatley, Phillis. *The Collected Works of Phillis Wheatley.* Ed. John C. Shields. New York: Oxford UP, 1988

Wilcox, Kirstin. "The Body into Print: Marketing Phillis Wheatley." *American Literature: A Journal of Literary History, Criticism, and Bibliography* 71.1 (March 1999): 1–29.

Mary McAleer Balkun

Contributors

MAUREEN ANDERSON is Assistant Professor and Chair of the English Department at the University of South Carolina Salkehatchie. She has published in several journals, including *The African American Review,* and has authored several essays in the award-winning *Greenwood Encyclopedia of American Poets and Poetry.* At the present time, she is completing a book, *Mercy Otis: Women's Use of Classicism,* for the University of Tennessee Press's new Classicism in American Culture series.

MARY BALKUN is Professor and Chair of the Department of English at Seton Hall University. She served as Associate Editor of the five-volume, award-winning *Greenwood Encyclopedia of American Poets and Poetry* and is author of *The American Counterfeit: Authenticity and Identity in American Literature and Culture,* as well as numerous articles on American literary figures.

JENNIFER BILLINGSLEY is Associate Dean of Continuing Education at MacMurray College. She has contributed essays to the award-winning *Greenwood Encyclopedia of American Poets and Poetry* and is completing a book on *The Concept of Wonder in American Poetry before 1900.*

KAREN DOVELL teaches American literature and composition at SUNY Suffolk County Community College. From 2006 to 2008, she was a postdoctoral fellow with the Program in Writing and Rhetoric at Stony Brook University, where she has taught courses on American literature, women's studies, and composition. Her 2004 Ph.D. dissertation was "'When Plato Was a Certainty': Classical Tradition and Difference in Works by Phillis Wheatley, Margaret Fuller, and Emily Dickinson." Her current work in progress includes a study of classical tradition in the American Renaissance.

ERIC ASHLEY HAIRSTON is Assistant Professor of English and of Law and Humanities at Elon University. He holds the Ph.D. in English Language and Literature from the University of Virginia and the J.D. from the University of North Carolina at Chapel Hill. His research interests include classical influences on American Literature, African American intellectual history, law and literature, Southern literature, and Asian-American literature. He is the founding director of the Center for Law in the Humanities at the Elon University Center for the Advancement of Teaching and Learning.

ERIC LAMORE is Assistant Professor of English at the University of Puerto Rico at Mayaguez, where he teaches courses in early American studies, African American studies, and Caribbean studies. He has published several entries in the awad-winning *Greenwood Encyclopedia of American Poets and Poetry*. He is currently editing a volume that outlines concrete pedagogical strategies for teaching Olaudah Equiano's *Narrative*.

BABACAR M'BAYE is Assistant Professor of English and Pan-African Studies at Kent State University. His work has appeared in the *Journal of African Literature and Culture, Journal of Pan-African Studies, New England Journal of History, African American Review*, and other publications. M'Baye's research examines Black Atlantic discourses in early and twentieth-century Black Diaspora and African literatures. He is author of *The Trickster Comes West: Pan-African Influence in Early Black Diasporan Narratives*.

DEVONA MALLORY is currently Assistant Professor of English at Albany State University in Albany, Georgia. Her areas of study include magical realism in literature, multiethnic literature, and women's literature. Mallory's work has been featured previously in such Greenwood publications as *Writing African American Women: An Encyclopedia of Literature by and about Women of Color, The Greenwood Encyclopedia of American Poets And Poetry*, and *The Greenwood Encyclopedia of Multiethnic American Literature*, and in the Oxford University Press's *American National Biography* and *African American Lives*.

TOM C. MCCULLEY is Assistant Professor and Chair of the English Department at Heartland Community College. He studies and teaches classes concerning the American gay lifestyle.

PATRICK MOSELEY is a student of American literary culture. An independent scholar, Moseley has published essays in the award-winning *Greenwood Encyclopedia of American Poets and Poetry*.

ZACH PETREA is Assistant Professor at Heartland Community College. He has published essays in the award-winning *Greenwood Encyclopedia of American Poets and Poetry* and is completing a book on Ann Bleecker.

PHILLIP RICHARDS is Professor in the Department of English at Colgate University. He is author of *Black Heart: The Moral Life of Recent African American Letters* and has published essays in such journals as *Style, The American Quarterly, The American Scholar, The Massachusetts Review* and *Eighteenth-Century Studies.*

JOHN SHIELDS is Distinguished Professor of English, American, and Comparative Literatures at the Illinois State University. He also directs the Center for Classicism in American Culture and serves as General Editor of the series on Classicism in American Culture for the University of Tennessee Press. As well, he has authored or edited many volumes, the latest of which is *Phillis Wheatley and the Romantics.*

JENNIFER R. YOUNG is Associate Professor of English and Women's Studies at Hope College. She earned her Ph.D. in English from Howard University in 2004. Her recent publications have included topics on Phillis Wheatley and the Black Atlantic, twentieth-century Black television characters, and hip hop as lyricism. She is the recipient of several fellowships, including one at the Bridwell Library. Currently she is writing a book about the critical relationships between leaders of African descent in the colonial Atlantic world.

Index

Bruce, Dickson, 248
Bull, Josiah, 320, 327
Bullard, John, 317
Burr, Esther Edwards, xvi, 300–303, 313
Bush, Douglas, 160
Bushman, Richard, 384, 386–88, 393
Butler, Judith, 192, 205
Byles, Mather, xviii, xxiii, 59, 60, 66, 76, 77, 79, 80, 91, 92, 95, 103, 127, 128, 129, 160, 162, 266, 338, 343, 349, 355, 356, 357, 358, 359
Bynum, Caroline, 164–67, 170, 185, 187

Calef, Robert, 101, 147, 172, 187
Calliope, xii, 22, 120, 352
Campbell, Jan, 206
Carretta, Vincent, 113, 146, 223, 237, 242, 250, 377, 386, 393
Carter, Elizabeth, 307, 325
Champagne, Rosaria, 206
Charron, Pierre, 339, 341–45, 348, 349, 354, 357, 359, 360, 361, 363
Chauncy, Charles, 319, 349, 350
Christian, xi–xiii, 3, 4, 5, 7, 8, 11, 14, 15, 39, 42–45, 48, 49, 51, 58, 64, 66, 70, 75, 76, 77, 79, 80, 83, 84, 87–90, 111, 115, 127, 146, 148, 151, 166, 174, 175, 186, 195, 197, 201, 202, 209, 211, 220, 226, 237, 251–57, 260, 261, 271, 280, 281, 284, 285, 306, 319, 340, 369, 380, 382, 383, 386
Cima, Gay Gibson, 311, 315, 322
Clarkson, Thomas, 218, 223, 322, 329
Cohen, Daniel, 253
Coleridge, Samuel Taylor, 322
Collins, Terence, 162
Columbia, 48, 54, 143, 264, 289, 290, 368
Colvin, Lucie, 278
Conant, Sylvanus, 266
Cooper, Samuel, 10, 59, 213, 342, 349–52, 359, 367
Coviello, Peter, 265, 267, 393
Crawford, Richard, 353

D'Elia, Donald, 51, 310, 311
Descartes, xvii, 371, 375
Dido, xi, 3, 5–17, 98, 107, 109
Diop, Samba, 289
Douglass, Frederick, 200, 201, 223, 227, 236, 238, 239, 388
Dowling, William, 116

Dryden, John, xiii, 4, 6, 9, 10, 13, 96, 108, 127, 139, 146, 343, 344
Duff, William, 348, 349
Dunlap, John, 210, 217
Duyckinck, George, 233
Dwight, Timothy, xxii, 115, 116

Eastman, Mary, 221–23, 238
Eaton, Arthur, 60
Eclogue, xx, 69, 115, 118, 128, 130, 148, 149
Eger, Elizabeth, 324
Elegy, xix, xx, 31, 32, 57, 86, 87, 112, 118, 135, 136, 178, 211, 213, 216, 222, 257, 277, 278, 339, 340, 352, 372, 380–84, 388, 390
Elias, Norbert, 393
Engell, James, 337, 338, 343, 348, 349, 350
Ennis, Daniel, 138, 139, 314, 315
Epic, xii, xix, 3, 4, 5, 14, 15, 22, 49, 57, 69, 71, 77, 80, 85, 89–91, 97, 98, 104, 106, 108, 113, 115–18, 120, 128, 146, 149, 182, 287, 320
Equiano, Olaudah, xv, 117, 146, 148, 218, 248, 249, 271
Erkkila, Betsy, 38, 52, 144, 285, 393
Estell, Kenneth, 274, 275
Evans, Nathaniel, xxiii, 313
Eze, Emmanuel, 375

Fanon, Frantz, 206
Felker, Christopher, 237
Ferguson, Elizabeth Graeme, 298, 313, 314
Finch, Annie, 254
Fishburn, Katherine, 373, 374
Flanzbaum, Hilene, 373, 392, 393
Franklin, Benjamin, xviii, 62, 63, 103, 217, 309, 310, 314, 315, 319, 320, 376
Freneau, Philip, xviii, xxii, 38, 218, 233, 337, 349
Frymer-Kensky, Tikva, 21, 23, 32

Gambia, 20, 22, 96, 121–26, 129, 137, 138, 274, 287, 364, 365
Gamble, David, 278
Garrison, William, 228, 230, 231, 240, 241
Gates, Henry Louis, Jr., 36, 57, 90, 105, 160, 194, 273, 275, 375, 392
Geertz, Clifford, 248
Georgic, xiii, xix, 111, 113, 115–19, 121–25, 127–30, 131, 133, 134, 135, 137–43, 145–48, 149, 151, 153, 155

Gilroy, Paul, 51, 273
Goodman, Paul, 240, 241
Gould, Nathaniel, 241, 352
Graces, 12, 13, 14, 352
Graham-White, Anthony, 287
Granger, Mary, 137
Green, Joseph, xx, 313
Greenblatt, Stephen, xiv, 167, 184
Greene, Lorenzo, 51, 266
Grégoire, Henri, 218, 225, 226, 227, 240, 296
Greven, Philip, 251, 253
Griffits, Hannah, 313, 314
Grimsted, David, 103, 296, 300, 304, 306, 307, 321, 327
Griswold, Rufus, 311
Guillory, John, 240
Gura, Philip, 298

Hambrick–Stowe, Charles, 267
Hamilton, Alexander, xviii
Hammon, Jupiter, xv, 200, 210, 216, 218, 225, 239, 247, 248, 249
Hammond, Jeffrey, 381
Harvey, Paul, 285
Hastings, Selina,The Countess of Huntingdon, xvi, 62, 63, 103, 105, 111, 211, 217, 237, 279, 305, 310, 319, 341
Hawley, John, 205
Hayes, Kevin J., xviii–xx, xxii–xxv
Haynes, Lemuel, xv, 247, 251, 254, 266
Heartman, Chas, 317
Herron, Carolivia, 51
Hobbes, Thomas, 173, 174, 175, 176, 177, 179, 180, 187, 338, 343
Hogue, Cynthia, 392
Homer, xiii, 36, 58, 59, 60, 65, 69, 70, 77, 79, 88, 113, 114, 128, 182, 233, 288, 338, 376, 377
Hopkins, Samuel, 180, 254, 255, 265, 267, 268, 315, 319
Horace, xxi, 58, 59, 65–68, 74, 75, 79, 89, 90, 101, 104, 107, 109, 128, 149, 226, 227, 343, 376
Hornstein, Jacqueline, 306, 307
Horton, George Moses, 200, 201, 218, 231, 232, 242
Hume, David, 104, 113, 169, 275
Husain, Shahrukh, 27
Hutchinson, Thomas, 275

"Hymn to Humanity," 3–5, 14–16, 41, 171, 173, 179, 183, 224, 227, 286
"Hymn to the Evening," 19
"Hymn to the Morning," 4, 19, 40, 41, 76, 223, 224, 229, 352

Imagination, xiii, xvi, xxiii, 52, 64, 95, 97, 100, 101, 105, 107, 108, 112, 116, 118, 131–36, 148, 151, 171, 174, 176–78, 180, 181, 187, 202, 203, 204, 227, 237, 276, 285, 329, 337, 338, 339, 355, 357–91
Imlay, Gilbert, 218, 303
Isani, Mukhtar Ali, 297, 306, 315

Jefferson, Thomas, xx, 36, 64, 72, 83, 95, 112, 115–17, 145, 164, 215, 217, 226, 233, 235, 237, 265, 267, 275, 295, 296, 299, 306, 315
Jones, John Paul, 139, 314, 317

Kames, Lord, Henry Home, 170, 175, 177, 180, 181, 182, 183, 345, 347, 351
Kant, Immanuel, 72, 104, 171, 174, 176–78, 275, 345–47, 364, 376
Kaplan, Sidney, 295, 309
Keats, John, xiii, 96, 346, 358, 361, 367
Kendrick, Robert, 15, 146, 372
Kenseth, Joy, 164, 166, 187
Kerber, Linda, 328
Kerenyi, Karl, 44
King, William, 365
Klein, Milton, 321
Klingberg, Frank, 322, 327, 329
Knapp, Isaac, 227, 229, 231
Kristeva, Julia, 36
Kuklick, Bruce, 389
"Kumba the Orphan Girl," 279
Kurtz, Benjamin, 182
Kutchen, Larry, 115
Kyper, Peter, 95, 338

Lacey, Barbara, 377, 388
Larson, Edith, 324, 325
Lefkovitz, Lori, 392
Leonard, Garry, 194–96, 342
Lessing, Gotthold, 159, 160, 186
Levernier, James A., 126, 194, 315
Liberty, 31, 35, 38, 39, 40, 45, 46, 47, 48, 49, 50, 52, 63, 70, 144, 145, 232, 259, 260, 288, 350, 352

Index